inspiring

MEN

OF THE FAITH

D1449689

C. S. LEWIS · DAVID LIVINGSTONE · MARTIN LUTHER · D. L. MOODY

For Shanth,

Happy Birthday and

Gods Best Blessing

Love,

MOM

Member of the
Evangelical Christian
Publishers Association

inspiring MEN OF THE FAITH

C. S. LEWIS · DAVID LIVINGSTONE · MARTIN LUTHER · D. L. MOODY

BARBOUR
PUBLISHING

MARTIN LUTHER

HEART OF THE REFORMATION

Edwin P. Booth

EDITED AND ABRIDGED BY
DAN HARMON

ONE

On the morning of November 11, 1483, Bartholomew Rennebrecher, the parish priest of the Church of St. Peter in Eisleben, baptized the day-old son of Hans and Margaret Luther.

It was St. Martin's Day. True and devout Catholics, the father and mother offered the name Martin for their firstborn. Father Rennebrecher took the baby in his arms, touched his fingertips in the holy water in the fine old font, and laid them gently on the boy's head. The sign of the cross, ancient symbol of glory and humility, he marked on the little forehead to ward off the devil and all his works.

Hans Luther, strong and determined but not ungentle, had come up from the land, son and grandson of peasants. He had courted Margaret in the town of her birth and girlhood, Eisenach.

Her people had been burghers; his had been peasants. The Zieglers were not sure the marriage was a good one for her, preferring a union with an established Eisenach family. But she was not afraid of life with him, for they had talked long and often about the way in which, someday forsaking the land of the mines, they would work their way steadily up in life. They would stay awhile now in Eisleben, until the little fellow was more ready for traveling, and then they would move on to the center of the mining area and set up their home.

Hans Luther worked daily in the mines of Eisleben. He had been reared on the land in Mohra with older and younger members in the family. By the custom of his people, the home and land in Mohra would fall to the youngest son, not the eldest. So Hans had known for a long time that he must cut his own path. In journeys to Eisenach he had met and loved Margaret Ziegler and now knew the fruition of their love in marriage, a home, and a son. Hans was sturdy and fearless. He honored the church, was devout in his religious practices, and believed, as had his people for many generations, in the grand dogmas of an otherworldly Christianity. He must keep his courage stout and fight for sustenance for himself and his family. The devil would do strange and unexpected things; the mines were treacherous; plagues would come but he would make for himself a place of respectability in the world he knew. So in firm spirit, with confidence in his ability to work his way through, Hans was laying the foundation of his family security. Hans and Margaret lived in a common house, small and dark, on a narrow, unpretentious street. It was near the great St. Peter's Church.

Through the winter months of 1483–84 Hans worked, Margaret kept house, and the baby grew. Eisleben did not satisfy the hopes of the family, and in the early summer they moved to Mansfield. Here they were in the center of one of the mining districts, and here Hans could hope to lease a mine of his own.

This was a happier, livelier town. The counts of Mansfield, living in a fine stone castle on a neighboring hill, guarded the town's prosperity and encouraged its workmen. The early months and years in Mansfield were not easy for Hans and Margaret. But Hans's hold on work and reward grew steadily stronger, and the future held some promise as the Luthers daily carried on their routines. The father and mother early instituted a rigorous but fair discipline. Obedience was exacted, and Martin knew, often to his discomfort, that neither parent would let offenses go unpunished. Conflict between the straight-seeing, decisive Hans and the boy was, of course, inevitable. Slight offenses by the boy were punished severely. The home was oriented along thoroughly Christian lines. The vigor of the Thuringian* custom—not the absence of love or the exercise of brutality—was responsible for the parents' severity. Martin certainly feared his father and mother, but the fear was grounded in the knowledge of certain retribution following undesirable activity. The love that lighted the home in Eisleben in November 1483 never was absent from the home in Mansfield as the years went by. The newer children were as well loved as Martin, and the whole atmosphere carried a sense of protection and affection into the lives of the children.

Hans and Margaret were building their lives well in Mansfield. Many a quiet evening must have seen the Luther family in happy companionship. Long winter evenings around the great, decorated porcelain stove and long summer evenings, sitting through the twilight, marked the little hearts gathered around Hans and Margaret with family love.

Taught by his mother, Martin learned the Lord's Prayer, wondering often what it was all about. He waited for the years to give it meaning. The Ten Commandments he slowly mastered, reciting them to a father and mother who taught him that in the breaking of any of them he would earn a terrible, eternal punishment. The Apostles' Creed, too, they taught him—valiant words they understood little themselves, but words upon which their church was built, words as lovely coming from the stumbling memorization of the little boy as from the chant of the cathedral choir. They told him of the God who creates and governs, who watches, rewards, and punishes. They told him of the Christ who came for his salvation, and they sang with him the infinitely tender and empathic Christmas songs of Thuringian tradition. Through song and picture, he learned of the little Christ of love and the supreme Christ of judgment. His parents taught him that Christ sits to judge the living and the dead; He will exact from His people the holy life, and dreadful is His wrath. When they took

---

*Luther was born at Eisleben in Thuringe, Saxony.

Martin to church each week, he looked with strange and ever-growing intelligence upon a sword-holding, thunder-visaged Christ on a rainbow in the great stained-glass window. They told him of the saints who in tender mercy would help him if he would only call upon them, interceding for him with the great Judge.

Slowly, as he grew, these strong teachings became fixed in his mind. He was early apprised of the existence of the spirit world. His otherwise self-sufficient father was sure of the work of the devil and the need for saints.

Martin saw his mother's face when she knelt before the crucifix, and he felt it must be some holy power indeed to bring such strange beauty to her whom he knew so well. He heard both father and mother appeal with fervor and sincerity to St. Anna, protectress of the miners, and in his own way he breathed many a prayer to her, too.

While he grew, his father rose to a place of respect and affection in the town. Hans was friendly with the priest at the church, sang lustily and well at the church festivals, and maintained an ever-increasing connection with all the affairs of the parish. When Martin was eight and in the first year of school, his father was elected to the town council and continued with distinction to serve in this capacity until his death.

The burden of poverty lightened, for Hans now was leasing mines and smelting furnaces to operate for himself. So they prospered, and Martin entered the common school in Mansfield as the son of an independent and respected family.

Latin—not the boys of Mansfield—was the object of the school's existence. The methods were strict and brutal, the teachers ignorant and unsympathetic, the entire atmosphere one to charge any boy's mind with thorough dislike and even hatred. To memorize slowly and without interest the rules of Latin grammar from that thousand-year-old textbook of Donatus, to be beaten by the assistant for faulty memory as well as for breaks in discipline, to be forced to talk in Latin instead of German—this became Martin's lot. There were great days of excitement and interest, of course, when the church festivals came around and the whole town turned out to celebrate. But the burden of the school was always on the boys.

Neither stupid nor rebellious, Martin moved in a fair way through his early schooling. He sang with the sons of rich and poor alike in many a street serenade and many a church choir. His clothes and his food were typical, and he was content. But the Mansfield school was not where his interest lay. His interest was where his brothers and sisters were growing up, where his father would sing to him and tell him stories. Lovely indeed is the picture, drawn long afterward by Martin, of his father laughing. Here is revealed the true Hans Luther with the burden of the day removed and the sternness of discipline relaxed, while friendship, family life, and deep good humor lightened up the evening.

While Martin sat through the school year during his late second and early third class, with his teachers doing their best to hold his mind to the dreadful routine of grammatical rules, events of almost unbelievable importance were happening elsewhere. In 1492, the world into which he had been born was passing away. While he mastered the old declensions, Columbus's sailors looked in mingled terror and hope at endless miles of water. While he ran from school to play, Lorenzo the Magnificent lay dying in Florence; when he died, so did the city-state that had been the glory of the Renaissance. While Martin gathered wood from the forest and set the yard in order, Rodrigo Borgia ascended St. Peter's throne to bring to a climax the deadly secularization of the church these northern peasants loved so well.

While Martin listened to the evening conversation of his home, another home in far-away Spain rejoiced in the coming of a little son named Ignatius. While Martin played at warfare with the boys of Mansfield, the combined armies of Ferdinand and Isabella, in a last charge of knighthood, drove the Moors from Spain and set the Christian flag above Granada. While he watched his mother care for his little brother, another mother was taking care of two little brothers named Arthur and Henry, and her husband, Henry VII, was nationalizing England. Toward the close of the year, Martin might have heard some neighbor tell his father that Maximilian was to be the new emperor of the Holy Roman Empire, to which his people owed allegiance.

The world was fixed and stable for him and his Mansfield elders, but while they taught its flatness and immobility to the little Luther, the eyes of Copernicus were poring over his books in his second year at the University of Cracow. Little ships and great men were moving, thrones were rising, ancient truths were falling—while in Mansfield, nine-year-old Martin learned his Latin, sang his folk songs, loved his family, and dreamed the dreams of boyhood.

ANCESTRAL MUSIC
1497–1501

Through the winter of 1496–97 Hans Luther and his friend Reinicke talked often about their sons. Hans's oldest boy, Martin, was now thirteen, and Reinicke's oldest son, John, was nearly the same. The boys had been together through the work of the Mansfield schools, and it was now time that they should either continue their educations in some larger town or abandon their schooling and go to work. Hans wanted Martin to continue his studies, since he showed promise of being able to work in one of the professions, possibly law.

In the neighboring town of Magdeburg, much larger than Mansfield, were good schools. There, too, was a mutual friend, Paul Mosshauer, who could receive the boys. Their childhood was over. Educational custom called for a change of school every so often, and it was time for the boys to take the open road and test their courage and ability in competition. So the fathers agreed to send their sons off together to the school in Magdeburg.

Martin and John heard the decision gladly. They had been close friends and were to remain so through life. They looked forward eagerly to Magdeburg.

Some money was available, but not much, and it would be the boys' task to help as best they could with begging and street singing. These were normal activities of "wandering students." Special laws exempted students from the regular civil police power and gave them certain freedoms.

Their clothes were arranged in the lightest possible bundle, to be strapped on their backs. Shoes were set in order for the walk to Magdeburg. Food was prepared. Letters to Paul Mosshauer were written. Money was provided, and they were ready.

Martin bade good-bye to his father, mother, brothers, and sisters, settled his pack, picked up his walking stick, joined John Reinicke, and headed away from Mansfield along the narrow, winding road.

He was strong and well grown when he started out that Easter season of 1497. Well disciplined at home, he was usually in control of a quick and powerful temper. Naïve, spontaneous, he laughed heartily. He enjoyed life. Religious in the way of his people, he relied on the word of his parents and priests for the truth of the Christian faith in which he had been reared. Sensitive to beauty, he knew the native flowers of Mansfield, loved its fields and forests, and looked with quiet contentment on its hills.

What we call roughness and coarseness in speech and action were, in him and his companions, normal expressions. Compared with his people and his time, Martin was more sensitive to beauty and the things of the spirit than the average boy of thirteen. There was no brooding, abnormal moroseness, no sullen rebellion against the discipline of home and school. He was not independent of his father's will in major decisions of life, nor did he desire to be. The trip to Magdeburg was his father's will, so Martin moved in honorable fear of his father's judgment, and he lived with firm assurance of his family's support.

The walk was not long, and the boys were strong and enthusiastic. In Magdeburg they found shelter in Mosshauer's home. They sang on the streets for their bread. Martin's voice and his feeling for music were exceptionally good and would bring him enjoyment throughout his life. Yet it was not easy to secure a good living, and there is reason to believe that in Magdeburg he learned from experience, as he had never known at home, what poverty and hunger could mean.

Magdeburg had a fine, large cathedral, built toward the close of the twelfth and opening of the thirteenth centuries. The citizens were proud of its exceptional architecture. It was the seat of the archbishop and was prominent in the affairs of church and state.

Attached to the cathedral, in the custom of the period, was a well-known and popular cathedral school. The normal course of study of the advanced Latin school was pursued. Additional studies included logic, rhetoric, dialectic, doctrine, and theology, subjects Mansfield had not taught.

Martin became a regular scholar of the cathedral. In the cathedral choir he took his place and absorbed the mighty liturgy of his church. More important than all else in this new school was a new emphasis by his teachers. He never quite forgot the harshness of the municipal grammar school teachers in Mansfield, but here the well-loved Brethren of the Common Life taught him.

Founded in Holland, about 1380, on the gentle piety of Gerhard Groote and his first disciple, Florentius Radewijns, the brotherhood had two objectives: education and social service. Groote had begun both in his own lifetime, and the advance had been rapid. In education, the brotherhood almost invariably entered existing schools as teachers rather than setting up new schools of their own. They were more intent on the growth of their pupils in Christian character than learning. The Brethren touched and trained more of the leaders of the Reformation period than any other teaching group. Erasmus, Calvin, Loyola, John Sturm of Strassburg, and a host of others knew the steady pressure of the quiet, learned Brethren. Thomas à Kempis was a brother and set down the order's regular ideals. Thomas wrote the first biography of Groote, in whose footsteps he strove to follow.

Day after day throughout the fall and winter of his fourteenth year, Martin pursued the paths of education under the watch of men devoted to the teaching profession, absorbing from them far more in spirit and intuition than he ever realized. Magdeburg was filled with other church orders, too, and the boy became familiar with the strange, lovely devotion of the ascetics, who scorned the world and sought severe discipline.

The Brethren taught him the pure Catholic faith. They were not among the heretical, and they did not lay in Luther's mind the foundations for any subsequent rebellion against doctrine. But they set in his life, by example and precept, the precious essence of the church's historic piety. To live in sincere simplicity, avoid sin, take duty seriously, serve fearlessly the commands of conscience, refuse wealth and position, scorn sin in high places, and feel the mystic satisfaction available to the Christian in prayer—these marked their daily lives. They were simple and obedient in doctrine. In life, they were quiet, controlled, and sincere.

This quiet goodness and firm peace sank deeply into Luther's nature. He was happy in school here and prospered in study and character. But the bread was hard to earn, there was no relative nearby, and he often longed for the coming of summer and his return to Mansfield.

When he went back home, he had grown, his Latin was better, and his habits were more regular. When Hans and Margaret talked of further schooling, his eyes lit up, and he spoke with great enthusiasm of the studies and of the men who had been his teachers in Magdeburg.

Margaret remembered her own people and her home in Eisenach and suggested he go there for a year. Her people could keep an eye on him, and he could roam the streets she loved so well. There were three fine churches there, many monasteries, and so much religious organizational activity that one in ten persons was in the business of the church. The Luthers were not dissatisfied with the year at Magdeburg, but Eisenach seemed a better place for their son.

John Trebonius was headmaster at the school attached to the Church of St. George. To Trebonius, Martin Luther would owe a lifelong debt of gratitude. Trebonius taught in the late medieval style, with lecture and question, textbook and recitation. But he possessed the great teaching gift to inspire the student. So sensitive was Trebonius to the possibilities in his students that he and his assistants would lift their hats when they entered the older classes, recognizing the future greatness in their scholars.

Under Trebonius, Luther found new life and enthusiasm in the grand old studies of the medieval Latin school. The strange new world of the "humanities" was not opened to him; that was to come in Erfurt. But here the old world of grammar, rhetoric, and dialectic was taught with expert skill, and he was ever grateful.

Eisenach brought him many things outside of school. His relatives were not unkind, and one of them, Conrad Hutter, seems to have won young Martin to affection. Other families also entered his life. As in Magdeburg, he sang on the streets and accepted bread in return. But he did not have to depend on singing and begging for a living.

The Schalbes, wealthy and prominent, took him under wing. They were greatly interested in religious activity and supported a foundation for one of the monastic orders called the Kollegium. Luther was well known to the monks of this Kollegium; he spent a great deal of time with them, and to them he was indebted for many permanent influences. Another family, the Cottas, also captured his heart. Frau Cotta heard him sing in the church choir and, taking a fancy to him, invited him—in proper Eisenach fashion—to her home. In this home he learned the grace of Thuringian custom; before, he had known its rougher aspects. Here he sang the traditional folk songs of his people, folk songs of the free, natural life unrestricted by religious tradition. He laughed and drank and danced, and knew the open freedom of a beloved circle of friends. Frau Cotta had a genius for friendship and for the gentility that makes an evening pass in harmony and happiness.

So the coarser habits of Mansfield and Magdeburg were softened considerably as the three years sped by at Eisenach. There were trips home to visit the family, then the return to school and friends, and Martin's life was happy.

Another friend touched his life deeply in Eisenach. John Braun, vicar of St. Mary's Church, was a man of rich and varied experience. Many years older than Luther, he befriended the students at Eisenach. They would gather at his rooms for long evenings of conversation and singing. He was a fine musician and taught Luther much.

Music had interested Martin since his early youth. He had been in church choirs at Mansfield, Magdeburg, and Eisenach. Now John Braun was giving him systematic and affectionate leadership. They played different instruments and sang far into the night.

Braun was a man of deep religious experience. Luther found himself taking for granted the supreme desirability of the religious calling. Braun must have told him many times of the struggles that preceded and the deep peace that followed his own decision to take Holy Orders. And Luther must have walked home at night through the quiet streets of Eisenach, turning over in his mind the all-important question: Would he, too, be a priest? On occasion when he reached a temporary decision to serve the church and God, he must have walked with light step and singing heart.

But then the morning would come with the old interests all around him, and he would put off the day of decision into the future. His father had his heart set on the law for Luther, and that was enough for the present.

He would walk into the lovely valleys and drink again and again of their powerful earthly beauty. He knew here, as he had at Mansfield, all the flowers and animals that made these valleys their home. And lifting his eyes to the gray, great castle of Wartburg, he would dream of the strength of Teutonic arms against the enemy, dream of the ethereal beauty of St. Elizabeth, dream of the day when they held the contest of the minstrels here. But he did not yet dream that God was to be to him like "ein feste Burg,"* and that these castle walls would hide him from the wrath of a Spanish emperor and Italian pope.

His mind and heart were growing steadily, yet the strange superstitions of the countryside were to him as real as to the humblest peasant. These Thuringian beliefs were set deep into his nature.

Countless religious superstitions were mixed with countless old wives' tales. It was a strange, dark world, and the devil moved through it secretly.

---

*German meaning "strong castle"

One was thought to be secure only by the constant use of the saints and the means of salvation provided in the church and its traditions.

Luther's mind was solid and terrifically honest. Once the beliefs of his boyhood were confirmed in serious study, as they were at Eisenach, the future could not wholly eradicate them. He was to remain a child of the light and darkness of his Eisenach world.

His days there were happy. When they came to an end, it was hard to part with the Schalbes, the Cottas, Conrad Hutter, John Braun, and other friends. But Erfurt lay just ahead, and Martin in his eighteenth year was ready to go.

TWO

Erfurt in the early sixteenth century was Germany's greatest university. The old scholastic interests were well represented on the faculty, but there also had grown up a fine center of the newer humanistic studies, and the combination had brought renown to the school. Attached to the major department of arts were the schools of law and theology.

Martin lived at the student dormitory called the Burse of St. George. Here was where most of the boys from Thuringe lived, and Luther would be among his own. He came in May 1501, procured his room, and went up to the university offices to register. His name appears on the university books as Martinus Ludher ex Mansfield. He paid his tuition in cash and settled down to his new life.

Registering in the faculty of arts, he set himself up for the bachelor's degree. His studies now introduced him to philosophy. Under the guidance of professors Trutvetter and Usingen, he accepted the positions of the followers of William of Occam, a system saturated with Aristotelian thought. To the normal lectures in rhetoric and its kindred arts were added those in arithmetic, the natural sciences, ethics, and metaphysics. It seemed to Luther to be a self-contained and quite intellectually satisfying world.

But he met another world entirely in the poets and humanists who were bringing renown to Erfurt. He never was able to spend the time in these latter studies that he wanted to, for the routine kept him at work. He did, however, become familiar with the mood of the humanists and with the Renaissance-style poetry of the very popular Baptista Mantuan. Among his fellow students, during leisure hours, he heard the exaltation of humanism and enjoyed a philosophy more human and lovely than that of the scholastics. But his training in dialectics had been precise, and he never quite shook it off, remaining through life somewhat of a master in that art.

He was an excellent student. At his promotion to the bachelor's degree in 1502 he held a respectable ranking, and two years later, at his master's graduation, he was second in a class of seventeen.

Life at Erfurt University was what he had known and anticipated. His Catholicity was unquestioned; his philosophy, that of his teachers; his use of Latin and of the processes of dialectic, unaltered.

But now, at eighteen, other and deeper currents were moving in his soul. He had been away from the direct influence of his home since he was fourteen. During these years he found himself struggling with the major problems of life. There had been security in following his father's strong will. That will had held the family safe during hard years of poverty. It had reared Martin through boyhood in a strict discipline. It had directed his work through the Mansfield grammar school and sent him on to Magdeburg. It had chosen Eisenach for his three-year schooling. It had furnished the incentive and money for the great privilege to attend Erfurt University. It had destined him for the law. But now young Luther was seeing things a little differently.

He had lived those earlier years without much thought of conflict. Now, as he matured, he was disturbed by the call of other interests unknown to his father. His native religious sensitivity began to assert itself. He thought again and again of John Braun's devotion to his sacred calling at Eisenach.

There was a great preacher in the Erfurt Cathedral who often left with Luther a divine restlessness. The mighty cathedral organ, the wonder of Thuringe, spoke to him with an unnamed, unknown power. Slowly, through these student days, came the vision of the eternal calling. He was happy, carefree, enjoying student fellowship, and singing as always, but the problem was forming. He was thinking deeply of the horrors of sin and its punishment.

He had good cause to think of it. His father had never minimized this part of life. His mother lived in terror of the unknown punishments of eternity. His people dwelt in continual fear of hell's torment. His church taught him constantly of the anger and wrath of God, of the judgment of Jesus.

And then there came to mind the great salvation in which he had been reared to believe. His father and mother had taught him of this, too. They had taught him of the grace of God and the mercy of Jesus, taught him of the favor of the saints. He could remember all the miners living on the hope of St. Anna, their protectress, and all the good people of Eisenach relying on the intercession of St. Elizabeth. His parents had taught him the value of good works, taught him reliance on the priesthood and deep faith in the church. His father walked uprightly and lived in honor, carrying the doctrines of Catholicism close to his heart.

So Luther fought the great battle. As the months of study drew to a close, he faced the possibility of entering professional school. It seemed to Hans that the climax of long planning was almost at hand, but to Martin the air was charged with uncertain terror. He clearly felt a religious calling, but he had always followed his father's will, and these two things were warring in his mind.

Happiness for a night would help him forget, but the morning found the problem unsolved. Steady work at his books and the routine of university life could not quiet the storm within him. To discuss it at home or write to his parents about these feelings seemed impossible. He did not know how to approach Hans on any issue of disagreement.

The day came for him to be awarded the master's degree. He was elated by the procession in cap and gown through the streets of Erfurt to the convocation. But he could not forget as he walked that some of the boys who had come thus far through school with him were dead or dying from the plague that had ravaged the town in the spring of 1505. Like many another serious student, Luther found that life takes on a new meaning with the approach of death.

Also in his mind were the books of the philosophers on one hand, seemingly at odds with the simplicity of the Bible—which he had come to know at Erfurt—on the other.

Despite his apprehension and native dislike for law, Martin followed the wishes of Hans and entered the faculty in May 1505. He was under obligation, with his master's degree, to teach two years in the faculty of arts, but this did not preclude his own studies.

Hans was proud of his boy and addressed him formally. His commencement gift to his son was a copy of the expensive but necessary *Corpus Juris*.

In June Martin, now nearly twenty-two, left school to visit his home. On the return from this visit, he later wrote, as he came near the village of Stotterheim, he was caught in a thunderstorm and knocked from his horse by lightning. Fearing instant death, he vowed his life to the monastic calling if St. Anna would save him.

Yet the decision undoubtedly had already been made when the lightning bolt surprised him into acknowledging it. Through years of training he had been moving this way. Many a hand had helped guide him. The lightning and the nearness of eternal judgment only broke the power of his father's will. Perhaps it substituted another, greater will than his father's—the will of the church.

Luther evidently was at peace as he continued the journey from Stotterheim to Erfurt. One cannot move forward as rapidly as he did now, defying the pressure of home and friends, unless he has won peace within himself. Luther immediately ended his studies and sought admittance to the monastery.

He chose the Augustinian order. Founded in the mid-thirteenth century, it had been split by a quarrel between lax and strict observers of the order; the monastery in Erfurt was of the stricter branch. The vicar-general of the Saxon Province, in which Erfurt lay, was John von Staupitz, a man known for gentle piety and ordered life. The local congregation was widely known for strictness and honor in its vows and obligations. It had a highly reputed theological school. To Luther, studying theology in the peace of the monastic life was a vision of paradise.

On the evening of July 16, he called some of his friends to his room. They feasted, drank, and sang. Luther was the happy, warm spirit they had long known. Then he told them that the next day he was to enter the Augustinian monastery. In tears, they pleaded against his decision, but his heart was set.

On July 17, with his friends accompanying him, he walked down the familiar streets of Erfurt to the long, high wall that enclosed the buildings of his chosen home, quietly knocked on the wooden gate, bade farewell to his companions, and entered the haven of his dreams.

The act was not so much a conversion as a conclusion. It was sudden, carrying with it a violent break from his past life. But he was ready—even eager—for the experiences of the monastery. Trained since age six in schools of the church, or schools directly under the church's influence, he was accustomed to thinking of the church's calling as the highest on earth. Away from home since age fourteen, he had come unconsciously to think of himself as permanently detached from the obligations he owed his family.

But it was no easy task now to write his father. He knew Hans would be heartbroken over the change of plans his father had nursed for many years. Heartbroken he was—heartbroken in emotion and furious in mind and will.

Hans was not one to let the main line of life be broken this easily. He refused to give his permission. Martin pleaded with him. Hans came to see him and found his son immovable. It seemed for many months that the break between them would be severe and permanent. But the plague intervened.

The disease came again to Erfurt in late fall, and rumor drifted up to Mansfield that it had claimed Martin Luther. Poor Hans could not believe it. Meanwhile, he was fearful for the lives of his two younger sons, for the plague had come to Mansfield, too. In middle life, his heart heavy with the defection of Martin, he stood by their bedsides as they died. Crushed by grief, it brought him some relief to be told the report of Martin's death had been false.

Neighbors pleaded that Hans allow God the service of his oldest son. At last he consented, but inwardly he never approved.

Martin rejoiced, although he knew his father was consenting without delight. In the Erfurt monastery the newcomer to the Augustinians submitted himself willingly to disciplines of the order. Luther's mind and heart were fixed on the holy life. He was taught how to walk, how to sit at table, how to rise, how to understand the sign language of the daily routine, how to wear his clothes, and how to do all the other little things that make the monastic day an ordered existence. There was no undue severity, only the well-known regimen of the monastery.

The discipline endured. His father's permission granted and his mind at ease, Luther was ready for the final vows by September 1506. In accordance with the ritual of the order, he vowed his life to the service of God in the monastic calling. He was tonsured and received the habit of the order.

So his mature years opened with the prospect of vigorous, efficient, satisfying service to the church. His years under his father's control had passed, and he was at the absolute command of his superiors in the "warfare of Christ."

THE WARFARE OF CHRIST
1506–1510

Increasingly, Luther's thoughts turned to the problems of religion. His life in the monastery was moving steadily toward the conquest of fleshly desires. He and his comrades fought persistently against the encroachment of worldly thought. This, his first test in the religious life, called for heroic efforts. He examined his conscience severely and with the relentless honesty that was one of his most outstanding characteristics. Again and again, the desires of the world still found a home in his mind.

The monastic routine was intensified in an effort to bring him the release he so greatly needed. Day after day, in prayer and work, he concentrated on the cleansing of his mind. But the mind does not cleanse easily.

So Luther drove himself still harder. In later years he referred to this experience as his "martyrdom" in the monastery. In fact, he was moving in the accepted paths of the historic church when he bore down upon himself. This was the way the saints trod. He fasted until the hours seemed unreal and strength was so far gone that he could hardly move. In this weakened condition, his thoughts loomed large and intense. In his struggle to understand God, the elements of judgment and fear were uppermost, and there was no one to relieve his terror. He locked himself into his unheated cell and remained there to pray until exhaustion overcame him and his brethren had to break in the door. Before the altar of the monastery church he spent long hours in prayer, to the point of slipping unconscious to the cold floor.

Luther was not abused by the order. He was following to the extreme the counsels of his order and his church, seeking to know that his life was well accepted in the sight of God. One does not find this part of Luther in the remarks taken down around the Wittenburg table after 1530, when the great struggle was over and Luther was idolized. But it is seen in the letters written in the early years to Braun and Staupitz.

Luther was a marked man in the order. His fine record in the university was known; his personality was felt throughout Erfurt; and he showed promise of great usefulness when he entered the monastery. His superiors were attentive to him, kind, and gently concerned. They set him to study and destined him to teach theology. His monastic preceptor,* unknown to us by name, was sympathetic and was always loved by Luther.

This inner strife increased as the day approached for his ordination and the

---

*Tutor

saying of his first mass. Luther approached these events with mingled terror and exaltation. He was to know now the sacred hand of the church placed upon his head, setting him apart for the work of salvation. The superiors had instructed him well in the meaning of ordination. He had moved step by step in the custom of the church, becoming subdeacon and deacon, and now was to be made a priest.

In preparing for the ordination, he read Gabriel Biel's *Canon of the Mass*. Staupitz and John Nathin, his teacher, both had studied under Biel. So Luther read the work with a sense of authority. Here he learned of the supreme worth and necessity of the priest, of the tremendous moment when the priest in prayer at the altar "makes the body of Christ" and calls upon God to consider the needs of the people. When he thought of himself, Martin Luther, standing before the cross and offering—under the divine law of his church—the Crucified One again to God in propitiation for sin, the idea was almost more than his sensitive spirit could stand. His whole heart went out in love and adoration at the thought of the Mass. But when he turned inward and considered how unworthy he was for such a task, the world seemed to fall in blinding light around him, and his strength failed.

In April 1507, when he was twenty-three, Luther knelt at the feet of his superiors to be made one in the long succession of priests in the western Catholic Church. He was deeply conscious of his high calling and fervent in accepting all the church's major doctrines.

He sang his first Mass on May 2, 1507. The date was set for the convenience of Hans Luther and other friends. Conrad Hutter and John Braun, vicar of St. Mary's, were invited from Eisenach.

His Mansfield friends showed no lack of interest. On the appointed day, Hans Luther, now prosperous, rode into Erfurt at the head of twenty horsemen. He presented himself at the monastery, was well received by the monks, and gave them a gift of money large enough to pay for all expenses. They visited and talked until the hour for service, then silently took their places in the church.

Luther had been preparing for this hour for many months, yet it seemed now that his will would fail. The kindly words of a superior just before he entered steadied him some, but hardly enough. At the thought of addressing God personally he was terror stricken: The words almost stopped in his throat, his tongue cleaved to the roof of his mouth, and he felt an almost uncontrollable desire to turn and run from the altar.

Fright mixed with sensitive appreciation took possession of him. The fear arose from the realization of what he was doing. A release from this terror would come later, with a keener sense of the place of the human in the church organization, a maturing attitude toward the observance, a stronger assurance, and a little experience in the technique of priesthood.

But fear was not all. Here was a sincere, devout young man standing for the first time in his life at the height of religious experience. Here was honest, searching appreciation of the act of worship.

Martin Luther stood at the altar of the medieval church, with every nerve trembling while the mightiest words known to man came slowly and with difficulty from his lips. Hans Luther bowed his heart in prayer in the cool, silent church and heard the voice of his boy fill the house with the presence of God.

Later, at the table in the refectory, Hans and Martin, who had not seen each other since July 1505, talked over the affairs of life. Hans described the health and activity of Margaret, the growth of the brothers and sisters, and the general condition of the mines and furnaces. He told of the plague in that terrible summer and fall of 1505 and of the deaths of Martin's brothers.

Life seemed suddenly serious and quiet then, and the talk turned to Martin. Hans was still unhappy over the religious calling. Martin argued that it was the will of God and told again of the divine call that had come to him on the road near Stotterheim.

But Hans was unsure. "God grant that it was not a mere illusion and deception," he said.

This disturbed Martin, but he suggested that his happiness in the cloister was sufficient justification for his action. Hans remained wistful over his broken dreams. He called Martin sharply on his disobedience, saying, while all around the table listened, "Have you not read in scripture that one shall honor one's father and mother?"

So the conversation ended. Martin never forgot his father's appeal to scripture, and he felt himself tempted more than once by Hans's suggestion that the vision at Stotterheim could have come from the devil as well as from God.

Hans rode out from the monastery courtyard at the head of his party and started home. Martin returned contentedly to his study and prayer.

Luther's personal religious development paralleled his theological and biblical study in the Erfurt monastery. Here he studied under very highly regarded teachers. The interplay of theological study and personal experience was very definite. During the years when he was deeply troubled by the lack of inner peace, he was studying the theorists of the church. Inevitably, this meant every theory of theology would be tested in his personal experience. By the intensity of that personal experience, he became a religious pragmatist. And the studies brought to the battleground of his personal faith many a worthy protagonist from the fathers of the church, from the scholastics, or from scripture itself.

The Erfurt monastery took its task of study faithfully, furnishing the teachers for the theological faculty at the university. Under one of them, John

Nathin, Luther studied systematically. Nathin was not a particularly good teacher, but he was teaching in the reigning tradition as interpreted by Gabriel Biel. As Luther was influenced by Biel in preparing for the priesthood, so he was influenced by him as he laid the foundation of his philosophic thought.

The Biel tradition gave Luther a distrust of Aristotle, whose principles of logic underlay the major work of the scholastic movement. It also encouraged the development of the critical faculties—something Occam, founder of this philosophic school, had done so sharply. Occam was a Franciscan who had carried to logical completion the implied distrust of the papacy, which the Franciscan order had always known. He was openly convinced popes and councils could err. Most important of the influences by Nathin and the philosophers was the conviction that man could attain righteousness by his own will and action. They taught Luther he could rely on stern, rigorous thinking and decisive, ordered action to produce a sense of assurance in his life. So Luther went from study to prayer to action, striving to find the peace of God. Yet all the while, he knew the immovable righteousness of God which he, in his humble human life, was utterly unable to gain.

He found a hopeful, happy counterbalance in biblical studies. The rules of the Augustinian order required it, and Luther was given a red-bound Bible for his personal use when he entered the order. This book was precious to him. He read it so steadily and thoroughly that he could quote whole passages by heart. Biblical content became the major unit in his thinking, and he used it as a criterion for all judgments.

Luther immersed himself in the Bible at Erfurt. He read it long and carefully, grounding himself in it with intense, imaginative eagerness. His mind and heart found great refreshment in the exhaustless well. The Christ in the Gospels and the Christ in the letters of Paul began slowly to supplant in Luther's mind the Christ of stern, severe judgment.

But it is no wonder he found his mind in constant upheaval, turning from philosophy to scripture and back to philosophy again. One taught him to counter his sense of insufficiency with more strident efforts of the will and action; the other taught the open acceptance of the free love of God, unearned and undeserved, but real and historic in Christ.

His study broadened now, and in the fathers of the church he began to find the central stream of piety, the source of assurance other men had possessed. He longed for the sense that he was God's. The great insatiable desire of Christianity for the perfect life was upon him. He was not at war with gross temptation and the life of the flesh, in open defiance of God's commands. This struggle was within the mind. The stark reality of Jesus' requirement that the mind be pure terrified him. There were fewer obstacles to God's commandments within the monastic life, but Luther's elemental honesty refused to let the cry of his conscience be stilled.

In the sacrament of penance he hoped to find relief. But the beauty of this sacrament lies in the heart's belief in God's forgiving goodness. Thus the sacrament becomes an expression, not a contributing cause. And Luther did not believe.

He argued it out with his confessor, holding that God necessarily must be angry at him for his sins. The gentler, older man told him to go read his Apostles' Creed again. There he would find the commandment to believe in the "forgiveness of sins." He finally told Luther point-blank, "It is not God Who is angry with you. It is you who are angry with God."

The confessor told Luther to read the works of Bernard of Clairvaux, who found the grace of God to be the source of peace. So Luther sat in his cell in Erfurt, and the centuries disappeared while Bernard spoke to him. He told Luther of the surpassing sweetness of the historic Christ and led Luther into a vision of the crucifixion from which the riches of the love of God could be understood. Luther felt the hold of sin weakening, the dread of death lessening. Bernard, too, had felt the strong sense of sin, and he, too, had fled the world to make in the monastic life the mighty effort for redemption.

The winters passed over Luther's head and the sense of sin remained within him, but in the historic work of Christ he found the proof of God's everlasting affection. Around Christ and the crucifixion, then, he wove his hope. All the operations of the visible, established church, which he loved dearly, became avenues of the grace of God. So Luther, understanding Bernard, found the way a little easier and the nearness of God a little more discernible.

Eager in his studies, Luther turned to Augustine, whose name his order bore. The magic of this name was everywhere, and Luther read his works to learn what he knew of the way to God. The issues that confronted Luther were issues of personal religion, but the solutions were sought in the realms of systematic thought. The combination of these two realms is more apparent in Augustine than in any of the great church fathers, for he was, to a greater degree, the product of his own religious experience. Only grace could have rescued him from the depths of depravity to which he had sunk; thus grace occupied his thoughts. Sin was central in his teachings because he knew it personally. Grace was irresistible because he himself could not resist it. He taught that the human will is impotent, because his was impotent.

When Luther turned to scripture for confirmation of these concepts, he found it. His sinful nature found its cause in Adam. Paul affirmed his doctrine of the enslaved. Supremely important, his Christ of faith and experience became the great liberating agent of the whole scriptural story; metaphysics clothed the humble human experience with dignity.

It was with growing satisfaction that Luther read the pages of St. Augustine. No father of the church could speak more directly and more strongly on the very points where he felt himself lost. The difficulties of his speculative thought began to disappear in the presence of Augustine's piety. A strong and new conception of Christ began slowly to establish itself in his heart.

Luther was greatly troubled by the spectre of eternal damnation involved in the doctrine of predestination. In Augustine, he had the chance to study the master of that doctrine, who was at the same time the master of the doctrine of God's free grace in Christ. So predestination lost its terror and passed into the larger doctrine of human dependence on the will of God. Its solution was offered in Christ simultaneously with its damnation in Adam. Augustine was indeed a rock in a weary land, and Luther temporarily rested.

The ritual of the church also began to yield up to Luther its hidden spirit. In service after service of the appointed monastic round, he heard the historic affirmations of the reliance of the church on Christ's mercies. He chanted the great liturgical praises to Jesus as the hope and salvation of the world.

He did not always transfer the strength and beauty of these forms of worship into his own life. He had difficulty giving the "praises" a living reality. No matter how lovely the liturgy was in theory, Luther received it under the aspect of his own environment. The men around him were more real interpreters of the faith than was the liturgy they chanted. The theoretical position of the church was available for normal purposes only in the personal interpretation and emphasis it received from its local representatives. Luther had to struggle through the interpretations to the essence. Only when he got into the thick of study and personal guidance did his thought begin to clarify; then it outstripped its local time period in its return to the older Augustinian position.

The man most influential in Luther's development was John von Staupitz. He had entered the university at Leipzig in 1485, received his MA at Tubingen, and lectured there in theology. He joined the Augustinian order and was chosen vicar of the Saxon Province in 1503, two years before Luther entered. When the elector Frederick established the University of Wittenberg, Staupitz was made dean of the theological faculty. Staupitz, visiting the Erfurt monastery, became interested in the young monk who had so suddenly left the university for the cloister. He watched Luther's inner spiritual struggle, which was reflected so thoroughly in his external appearance. Luther had come to the monastery a strong, enthusiastic young man of twenty-two, and Staupitz watched him grow thin, tired, and nervous.

Eager to help and conserve this brilliant new member of the order, Staupitz befriended him. As the first two severe years went by, Luther began to feel that in Staupitz he had a sympathetic, understanding superior. Time after time he unburdened his soul to Staupitz. The advice of Staupitz was always gentle and to the point. With keen insight he tried to make Luther see the introspective quality of his meditation and to direct him to historic and actual things.

One day Staupitz said, "Look not on your own imaginary sins, but look at

Christ crucified, where your real sins are forgiven, and hold with deep courage to God." Luther never forgot this. Throughout his life he acknowledged his indebtedness to Staupitz for teaching him to center the conception of forgiveness around the crucifixion of Christ.

They spent many hours together, and the older man grew increasingly fond of the younger. He knew Luther's restless, sensitive spirit needed constant work, and he recognized the fine quality of his mind.

It was not entirely a surprise, then, when in 1508 Staupitz moved Luther from the Erfurt monastery to the one at Wittenberg. Luther was ready for active work. The change came suddenly, and he found himself at Wittenberg with hardly an opportunity to bid good-bye to his old friends.

He was definitely committed now to biblical studies, chafing under the philosophical emphasis. The whole desire of his life focused more and more around the Bible. He could not teach it, however, until he had earned his doctor's degree. He therefore was lecturing on Aristotle's ethics, scholastic philosophy having been his major study at Erfurt.

On March 9, 1509, he took his first degree in theology at the University of Wittenberg. Staupitz now insisted that Luther continue studying for his doctorate in theology so he could become a professor on the theological faculty.

In preparation for lecturing on the Bible, the university required that the candidate teach for three semesters the *Sentences* of Peter Lombard. This standard textbook in theological instruction was written at Paris, where Peter was made bishop in 1159. For this work Luther returned to Erfurt. The text of the *Sentences* from which Luther lectured is known, as are his marginal notes. He was not unfriendly to the author's thinking, but it is interesting to note the deficiency he perceived in Lombard. "He would have been a great man," Luther said years later, "if he had read more in the Bible and incorporated it in his writings."

The notes Luther made that winter indicate vast reading. He continually emphasized faith against reason, tradition against speculation, theology against philosophy. He evidenced a keen consciousness of the power of sin, and tended to bring every problem around the person of Jesus. Luther expressly asserted that Christ, not wisdom, was the first creation. Christ—the son of God and our Redeemer—was the center of Luther's reflection on sin.

It is not clear by any means that Luther took a new position during or before these lectures, but it is clear that some of the elements necessary to a new position found expression. Sin and grace were evidently the centers of thought. Christ was receiving some of the adjectives and descriptive phrases that show Him as the way by which sin is overcome and forgiven, and grace is received.

There were strength and independence of thought in the notes. Luther was growing, was becoming master of his own mind, and was ready for increased responsibilities.

THREE

The experiences of Erfurt in this second residence were broken by the great opportunity to visit Rome.

In October 1510, John von Mecheln and Martin Luther left Erfurt on their long walk to Rome. Insofar as possible, they were to spend the nights in friendly cloisters. It was the custom of the men of the order when journeying to walk silently, one behind the other.

The long discipline of the monastic life had changed Luther considerably. Gone was the quick, elastic, joyous step of his late boyhood. Yet as the days passed, he found the strength of youth returning to him. He carried in his heart and mind the great soul struggles that were his all-absorbing passion, but he also was breathing the open air. With his books and study far behind, he saw the lovely hills of southern Germany. Journeying over the Alps, he felt the awe those majestic mountains always have inspired.

Descending through the rich plains of northern Italy, the brothers came to Florence. A quarter of a century past the height of its Renaissance, it still possessed rich treasures unsurpassed in the world of art. Raphael, Leonardo da Vinci, Michelangelo, and many other creative geniuses worked in Italy.

But Luther's attention was elsewhere. Oblivious to Florence's beauty in stone and on canvas, he visited the hospitals and churches of the city. Long years afterward he described in detail the fine work of the Florentines in their hospitals. He remembered their cleanliness, efficiency, courtesy, and intelligence. He heard with amazement stories of the papal court at Rome and saw at Florence the lives of churchmen of such quality as to shock his quick consciousness of sin. From Florence down toward Rome the brothers journeyed, through the lovely fields and under the quiet skies of Umbria. They passed towns blessed by the presence of Francis of Assisi and churches immortalized by the works of Giotto.

The night before they arrived in sight of the holy city, behind the hills that separated Rome from the north, Luther's religious devotion rose to almost ecstatic heights. He believed thoroughly in the remission of sins that he should win at the holy places in the city of his faith. His mind was fastened on the great traditions of his fathers in Christian history.

The next day, as he came over the top of Mt. Mario, he saw spread out before him the central city of western Christendom. Overcome with joy, he fell on his knees and cried, "Hail, Holy Rome! Thrice blessed in the blood of the martyrs!" With high expectation he followed John von Mecheln through the gate and walked at last within the sacred city.

They lodged in a monastery, where they were treated with kindness. But here they were severely shocked at the indifference and ease with which the monks went through their routine services.

Pope Julius was away from Rome on a campaign against Bologna. The future Pope Leo X, now Cardinal Medici, was at the head of a papal army attacking his native city, Florence. So John von Mecheln carried his papers to the cardinal secretary of state.

Luther was a real pilgrim. He anxiously and joyously sought the great church shrines. He visited the catacombs, recently rediscovered and the object of great interest, and felt the strange influence that comes from the memories of the martyrs buried there. His entire religious quest focused itself on the desire to win release from sin's terror. He visited the shrines not only for the sake of his own soul, but for the souls of his family and friends. He was even tempted to wish his father and mother were dead so that his prayers might release them from purgatory. For his grandfather, long since dead, he could perform this incomparable service.

He went, as was the custom with Roman pilgrims, to the great sacred stairs. Up near the Lateran Church, the real mother church of Roman Catholicism, these stairs were set, leading to a room containing relics of the saints. Roman tradition told Luther the steps were those up which Jesus had walked the night He appeared before Pilate. Pope Leo IV had granted an indulgence of nine years for every step, and there were twenty-eight steps. For centuries the devout in the Catholic faith have climbed these steps, with the proper prayers in their hearts and on their lips, believing in the benefits their church offered for this action. Luther was among them in this belief. He had walked the great pathway of penitence for five years now, and this was a kind of climax.

Yet all the while he had walked the way of penitence, another way had been appearing to him as superior. He had read of it many times in the Bible, in Bernard, in Augustine, and Staupitz had pointed it out to him. Luther had read the great Pauline testimony to faith. Bernard and Augustine had died in the pure faith and told Luther so. Staupitz and others had pointed him that way, and the whole trend of his purest Catholic tradition was to turn to the prayers of faith and away from the superstitious confidence in good works. His mind was keen. He had studied these things intently for years, and he well may have felt the hollowness of this action—especially in view of the impossibility that these steps were true relics.

Preaching in Wittenberg the year before his death, Martin told of some experiences in Rome and related how, as he had reached the top of the stairs, a doubt regarding the power of the practice had come into his mind. "Who knows whether this be true?" he had thought.

Luther did not come down from these steps a rebel against his church.

His mind and soul were forming themselves in tremendous, moving experiences. The Holy Steps were not crucial but were only one more movement in the experience. He was a child of Rome when he came, and he was a child of Rome when he left.

But the Rome of Luther's dreams and ideal was broken and forever shattered. The Renaissance papacy, which had controlled Rome since 1447, with the accession of Nicholas V, had steadily centered its policy around the secularization of the church. Without any leadership from the popes, the moral life of Rome had degenerated steadily. With each of these popes setting an example that defied every one of the Ten Commandments, Rome had become a place of notorious anti-Christian life.

Luther saw and felt a Rome utterly abandoned to money, luxury, and kindred evils. He was stunned and unable to understand it—but he did not stay in Rome long enough to rebel against it. Four or five weeks at most, and he had to start his journey northward again. One cannot hear scandal enough in four or five weeks or see sufficient evil in that length of time to unseat a devotion held since birth.

Yet as the years went by for Luther and as other things in theology and church organization became clear to him, he remembered the Rome of his visit and could see far more clearly how utterly corrupt was the leadership offered to the great church in 1510.

THE RISING TIDE
1511–1516

Luther resumed his work in the Erfurt monastery, teaching there until Staupitz called him again to Wittenberg in the autumn of 1511. Wittenberg was now to be his home until his death.

It was a small, humble town. The 356 houses provided homes for some three thousand people. The Elbe River, upon which Wittenberg is situated, was at this point shallow and slow moving. No commerce of any kind was possible on it. The soil of the countryside was sandy and poor. The entire area was flat and uninviting. The townspeople were uneducated, coarse, and generally uncultured.

The town had two churches. The elector, who filled it with relics, supported the cathedral church attached to the university. A smaller, less conspicuous parish church served the inhabitants of the town. The Augustinian monks owned a cloister there, known as the Black Cloister because of the black robes they always wore. Luther came to this cloister.

His duties the first year of his Wittenberg residence were mainly personal study. He was following the plans laid by himself and Staupitz for his doctor's degree, preparing for the professorship in biblical interpretation. Throughout the first year he prepared himself for his examinations. But his life was varied, and he found himself deeply interested in the affairs of his order.

His mission to Rome the previous year had been only the beginning of a rise to recognition from his brother monks. In May 1512 he and Staupitz journeyed to Cologne to attend the district meeting. Here Luther was elected subprior of the Wittenberg monastery. On his return from Cologne he assumed many administrative functions under the prior.

On October 18, 1512, he received the doctor of theology degree. Elector Frederick, apparently at the request of Staupitz, paid the usual fee for the promotion—fifty gulden. He wrote to invite his friends from Erfurt to come up for his promotion, but relations now were strained between Luther and the Erfurt superiors. The Erfurt men, particularly his teacher Nathin, resented very much his transfer to Wittenberg. They thought he was breaking one of the major obligations of university honor by taking his degree at Wittenberg instead of Erfurt. In the opening sentence of his letter Luther stated the cause of his Wittenberg residence as the command of his superiors. Nevertheless, from this day there was to be an increasing difference between Luther and the Erfurt teaching tradition. He steadily stressed the biblical aspect of theology, in opposition to the philosophical bias at Erfurt. The Erfurt men did not come to Wittenberg.

Six days after receiving his doctor's degree, he was admitted to the university senate, which finally gave him full rights in the teaching profession. He accepted these obligations with his usual intensity and sincerity. He believed the church had set him apart to teach, and to this he was bound. He felt an apostolic authority lay behind his work of exposition.

When Wittenberg—only nine years old as a university—admitted Martin Luther to its staff of professors, it placed itself in line for leadership of all the universities of western Europe. Strong men already on the faculty, such as Nicholas Armsdorf and Andrew Bodenstein (known to history as Carlstadt), soon succumbed to the intellectual leadership and moral vigor of their new colleague. Around Luther there grew a Wittenberg tradition so that within a few years men began to speak of "the Wittenberg theology."

Sometime during this year of 1512–13, Luther for the first time focused his conflicting thoughts and saw them temporarily in such clarity and harmony that he called this experience the birthday of his faith. In the tower of the Black Cloister, where he often studied, he kept his attention on the great text in Romans 1:17: "The just shall live by faith."

The whole problem of his life, since he first felt the call of religion in boyhood, was the problem of sin and the acceptance of his life in the sight of God.

MARTIN LUTHER

He believed so thoroughly in the perfect righteousness and perfect justice of God and felt so thoroughly his own sinfulness that he could not understand how anyone could be justified in the sight of God.

What, then, did Paul mean when he wrote, "The just shall live by faith"? Paul, above all other men, had pointed out the sinfulness of the human race. Paul had cried out, as Luther so often cried out, "O wretched man that I am! who shall deliver me from the body of this death?" Paul had talked of the warfare between flesh and spirit. Paul had believed in the immovable and eternal will of God operating in human life.

Luther's mind marshaled to its task the positions of Bernard and Augustine, and he remembered the constant advice of Staupitz to look upon the crucifixion. He recalled how in countless places Paul had centered his whole thought around the crucifixion. By belief in the crucifixion, could Luther find release from this burden of sinfulness? Was it, then, by faith in the historic work of Christ? Paul must have meant by "faith" the acceptance of the work of Christ! He must have meant that God had, through Christ, wrought a justification of sinful men who would open their lives to the Word!

Could even he, then, Martin Luther, by the sheer act of acceptance of the historic work of Christ, find that mighty gulf between himself and God bridged? Was it true that God's righteousness was not the righteousness of condemnation but the righteousness transferred from Christ to him?

He then could feel the mighty rhythm of Pauline thought, wherein his sinfulness was ever present, yet God's justification, likewise, was ever present. Inwardly he felt the ancient, pure strength so well known to Pauline Christians. It was now no longer a battle with God to force God's recognition of his good deeds, for God was on his side. He saw, as it were, in one great vision, all the tremendous movement in the human race, from its sin in Adam to its redemption in Christ. He, Martin Luther, could stand steadfast by faith in Christ and know that the tremendous pressure of his sin was offset by the endless mercy made possible in Christ.

This was the hour of his freedom, the hour of his great illumination. From this day forth there was a new note in his message. All his teachings began, centered, and ended in the history of redemption.

He came from the tower room not with his whole theology clearly wrought, but with its basis fixed. He faced the first years of his biblical lecturing secure in the conviction that he had found the key to understanding the scriptures. Through all the wars into which his life carried him, he held steadfast to his understanding that "the just shall live by faith." It was not that faith moved without works, but that life came by faith, and works were the result.

He lectured in the university from 1513–1515 on the Psalms. His method was to have a copy of the psalm on his desk before him. The copy he used had been printed a month before he began to lecture. It had wide spaces between the printed lines. Luther wrote his comments and notes between the lines. These notes still can be read.

His heart had been troubled for many years over the mighty problems of religious peace. Now his students heard, as though listening to an autobiography, all the tremendous spiritual depth of the Psalms come to life. He lectured in Latin. If his Latin came to him with too much stereotyped scholastic form, he would break into German. His notes show the language changing in mid-sentence.

When the old forms of university lectures were insufficient to hold the fullness of his message, he created new and striking illustrations. For example, "As the meadow is to the cow, the house to the man, and the nest to the bird, the rock to the chamois, and the stream to the fish, so is the Holy Scripture to the believing soul." When Luther spoke to his students on a particular psalm, they could feel that they were listening to one who spoke with authority, and they flocked to his classroom. "We students heard him gladly, for he spoke to us in our mother-tongue," wrote one of his scholars.

In 1515–16 he lectured on Paul's Epistle to the Romans. This was his own great document, and as he set forth before his students the mind of Paul through chapter after chapter of this book, they saw once again the whole drama of heavenly redemption unveiled before them.

Just before he began his lectures on the ninth chapter of Romans, Erasmus's edition of the Greek New Testament came into his hands, and from that point on it was his lecture book. Erasmus provided fine Greek and Latin helps. Also, though unskilled in its use, Luther kept the Hebrew grammar and lexicon of Reuchlin always on his desk. He strove to bring to Old and New Testament alike the finest aids scholarship could give him.

Here, in the lectures on Psalms and Romans, his conception of theology was formulated systematically. Although his interest was never in the system, as such, but always in practical piety, in these lectures he brought his thoughts into ordered shape. He was jubilant as he found, month after month, all the great problems of his life falling into relation with each other around his acceptance of the historic—not speculative—basis for Christian thought.

As he lectured on Romans, he brought before the judgment bar of this mighty book the society of his day. He bitterly attacked Julius II and the frightful immorality of Rome. He denounced the governing Curia and all the church hierarchy for their widespread corruption and vileness. Luxury and avarice, pride and selfishness were rampant in the pope's city. Romans 13:13, a text that had brought home its terrible lesson to the unconverted Augustine, now gave Luther a vocabulary for describing Rome: "rioting. . .drunkenness. . . chambering. . .wantonness. . .strife. . .envying." And he begged his generation to heed the glorious exhortation of verse 14: "Put ye on the Lord Jesus Christ, and make not provision for the flesh, to fulfil the lusts thereof." In severe language he arraigned the clergy for thinking its task was to defend the church instead of to preach the Gospel.

He had said to Staupitz a few years earlier that he could not survive the duties of the doctorate many months. But he found to his amazement that strength was added to strength as his life organized itself in his new field. Staupitz had known the caliber of Luther and now saw with great joy the steady progress of the teacher.

In 1516, while these lectures were being given, he published his first book. He had discovered the works of Tauler and the great German mystics. He was so enthusiastic over the little book *A German Theology* that he edited it, saying in the preface that there was no better book after the Bible and Augustine where one could learn the nature of "God, Christ, man, and all things."

The influence of this mystic school in German thought softened Luther considerably in his inner piety. He never became a thorough adherent of the mystic school, for his interests were too practical. But the contribution of the quiet, passive acceptance of the will of God—the central thought of the German mystics—brought to him in these days of inner turmoil a blessed peace.

Luther's days at Wittenberg were not confined to the professorship. His elevation to the doctor's degree involved preaching to his brother monks. He had objected steadfastly to this in the early years, looking forward to it with fear and trembling. He argued the case with Staupitz, describing his fear. Staupitz said he, too, had been afraid of preaching in his early days, but the fear had vanished.

So Luther began, at first preaching only to the monks in their little wooden chapel, twenty by thirty feet, attached to the cloister. Here his sermons developed a distinctive quality and attracted such attention that the town council of Wittenberg petitioned him to preach in the parish church. So he took up the duties of parish preacher.

The earliest sermon extant is one he preached, in all probability, in 1514. His text was, "Whatsoever ye would that men should do to you, do you even so to them." The sermon showed what was to be the major quality of his preaching. He talked simply and straightforwardly. He named the areas of life in which his hearers lived, talked about things they knew daily, analyzed them in the light of Christian principles, and exhorted his people to walk in Christian ways.

Added to the burdens of the professorship and preaching came Luther's election in May 1515, at the district meeting of the Order at Gotha, as district vicar of the monasteries in Meissen and Thuringe. There were ten monasteries in the district when he first was elected, with the addition later of Eisleben, the town of his birth. He was required, by the rules of his office, to visit each of these monasteries once a year. Each visit naturally involved time and effort.

His correspondence increased tremendously with this new responsibility. He found all the hours of his day filled with important tasks. He had to preach to monk and villager. He had not only to lecture, but to lecture with intensity and intelligence, for he was already the acknowledged leader in a new movement. He had to exercise discipline in his administration over distant monasteries. He ceased to be the introspective, troubled monk of the Erfurt days, becoming a strong, assured, confident leader, enjoying the respect and confidence of his entire circle.

Yet humility, genuineness, and deep piety remained the root characteristics of his life. He possessed that strangely fascinating characteristic of being so humble in personal thought that he lost himself completely in public action and professional responsibility. He was a tireless worker. He saw the detail of his many tasks clearly and kept a personal understanding of the problems that confronted him.

As though his tasks were not enough, and responsibility that rested upon him insufficient to try his soul, the plague came to Wittenberg in the fall of 1516. Many citizens left immediately, and many of the monks were transferred temporarily to other cloisters. But Luther stayed in Wittenberg. Here his task was set, here his superiors had placed him, and here he would stay. Throughout his life this stalwart courage is discernible. Neither plague nor emperor nor pope was ever able to move him from his chosen course.

In 1516, the year before his public controversy, Luther was a well-recognized, self-controlled, intelligent leader in the affairs of his environment. The strong and steady discipline of the home in Mansfield stood him in good stead. The deep intensity of his religious struggles in Erfurt had been resolved into a quiet strength. His mind, his soul, and his physical strength were at work in the kingdom of the church.

By his position, he was obligated to recite the offices of the church at regular intervals daily, but the pressure of his many duties was so great day after day that he had little time for prayer or sleep. Unfriendly critics called this negligence. To Luther it was necessity. Many evenings he was too tired even to unclothe himself before falling asleep on his narrow cot in the cloister cell. He tried to catch up sometimes on his omitted prayers by reciting them all at once, when he found a break in his week's routine. He was truly in the "warfare of Christ," to which he had vowed himself when he had entered the Erfurt monastery.

The interests aroused inwardly by his personal experiences and teaching were all accentuated by his experience in the parish church. He found himself in a life strangely adapted to bringing him information, almost as though fate were preparing him to be the focus for the problems of his age. In pastoral work, student direction, biblical study, philosophic speculation, private devotional life, and the many cares of administering eleven monasteries, Luther gathered experience that daily formed within him a broad, sensitive, accurate understanding of his environment.

A major disturbance to him was one of the sensitive spots in the old doctrine of good works. This was the veneration of relics—the belief that the relics carried spiritual power. The elector of Saxony, Luther's own civil lord, had assembled hundreds of relics in the Wittenberg cathedral. Many of the claims for the relics were preposterous. Luther had seen several exhibits, in widely scattered places, of the "whole seamless robe of our Lord."

These and other absurdities disturbed the Wittenberg preacher greatly. Throughout 1515 and 1516 and into early 1517, a note of protest was sounded again and again in his sermons and lectures. Luther was in no sense a rebel. A devout son of the church, wholly in the atmosphere of the great historic piety of Catholicism, he labored in his chosen field. But he protested increasingly—not against thought or history, but against abuse.

Rome could not hold the lid on Europe's disaffection much longer. John Colet, Sir Thomas More, and others in England steadfastly had called for a higher, cleaner administration throughout the church. Erasmus had insisted that the church reform itself. Leaders of the church in Italy had banded into a society dedicated to reform. Throughout the length and breadth of western Christendom, the cry of scandal had been heard steadily for fifty years. The oncoming tide of reform was gathering resistless pressure. What it needed and longed for was accurate, consecrated, intelligent leadership.

The root cause was religious. Leadership thus had to come from religious sources. The Brethren of the Common Life, magnificent reformers in limited spheres, had not carried the attack far enough. Erasmus, with the whole school of the humanists, would not move into the field of pure religion. The churchmen in Italy were defeated because they lived too close to the source of the infection.

Here in far-off Wittenberg, so miserable and common that few people paid attention to it, was being formed a religious experience strong enough, intelligent enough, courageous enough to bring leadership. Yet Luther, so busy with his work, was unaware of anything except that he had discovered the source of the early piety of the church and that he could not be silent in the face of abuse. He was thoroughly conservative by nature. He loved his tradition, his church, and his people.

But he was honest. He hated sin in all places, high and low. He would protect his people. He would honor the obligations of his teaching office. He would speak clearly, decisively, directly.

Luther pleaded in lecture and sermon for the commoner, whose blood was his own. The strong claim of the people, rising steadily for half a century, now found a voice. He championed the peasant, challenging the right of the members of the nobility to enact and enforce laws whereby they reserved game for themselves and punished severely—often with death—the poor for shooting one rabbit.

He called the great civil lords "robbers" or "sons of robbers." The oppression of the underclasses by civil and ecclesiastical overlords moved him to fury, and he spoke openly against it. He severely condemned the greed and avarice that lies behind all war. He pronounced Julius II, Duke George of Saxony, Elector Frederick, and other princes guilty of this devastating petty warfare. He was a gloriously eloquent spokesman in the name of religion for all the mighty causes that uplift mankind. He "bore in his hands the banners of a nobler humanity." He fought without timidity. The elemental peasant blood was in him, and the lords and rulers must answer to the written word of scripture for their unchristian exploitation of the sons of God.

Rome, with the abuses it created and lived upon, was the heretic! Martin Luther was the Catholic.

FOUR

Hans Luther was sitting one evening toward the middle of November 1517 by his home in Mansfield. One of his close friends and neighbors came over and handed him a long, closely printed, double-columned, single-sheet tract from Wittenberg. Hans read:

> *Out of love for the truth and from a desire to elucidate it, the Reverend Father Martin Luther, Master of Arts in Sacred Theology, and ordinary lecturer therein at Wittenberg, intends to defend the following statements and dispute on them in that place.*
>
> *Therefore he asks that those who cannot be present to dispute with him orally shall do so in their absence by letter.*
>
> *In the name of our Lord Jesus Christ. Amen.*

1. Our Lord and Master Jesus Christ in saying, "Penitentiam agite," meant that the whole life of the faithful should be repentance....
2. And these words cannot refer to penance—that is confession and satisfaction....
5. The Pope does not wish, nor is he able, to remit any penalty except what he or the Canon Law has imposed....
6. The Pope is not able to remit guilt except by declaring it forgiven by God—or in cases reserved to himself....
11. The erroneous opinion that canonical penance and punishment in purgatory are the same assuredly seems to be a tare sown while the bishops were asleep....
28. It is certain that avarice is fostered by the money clinking in the chest, but to answer the prayers of the Church is in the power of God alone.

The paper shook in his hand, and great excitement possessed him as he realized with stunning force that his son was challenging the mightiest institution on earth. To Hans, Martin was still a boy, only 34. Yet those sentences spoke from the anvils of experience.

His eye returned to the page:

29. Who knows whether all the souls in purgatory want to be freed? ...
50. Christians are taught that if the Pope knew exactions of the

37

preachers of indulgences he would rather have St. Peter's Church in ashes than have it built with the flesh and bones of his sheep. . . .

62. The treasury of the Church is the power of the keys given by Christ's merit. . . .

71. Who speaks against the apostolic truth of indulgences, let him be anathema. . . .

72. But who opposes the lust and license of the preachers of pardons, let him be blessed. . . .

82. Why does not the Pope empty purgatory from charity?

This sharp and incisive reasoning took Hans off guard. Martin was right! If the pope could help those in purgatory, then charity should move him to do so.

Hans closed his eyes a moment and felt intuitively the approaching hour when Martin would be called to answer for this. The church would not brook such exposure. But it was abusive of the church to do these things, Hans thought, and he was thrilled that his flesh and blood was so courageous.

92. Let all those prophets depart who say to the people of Christ, peace, where there is no peace. . . .

93. But all those prophets do well who say to the people of Christ, Cross, cross, and there is no cross.

So Hans read slowly and thoughtfully the ninety-five propositions. He asked his neighbor what information the messenger had brought from Wittenberg along with the tract. He was told Martin had set this statement on the bulletin board of the university at noon on All Saints Day. The original had been in Martin's handwriting, and the Wittenberg printers had rapidly published both Latin and Greek texts for broadcast throughout Germany.

Hans thought over the past few years and remembered how earnest Martin had been, how long and bitter had been his soul's struggle for peace. He had thought, in recent years, that Martin was speaking out rather boldly against well-known practices of the church. He knew that two years ago his son, in the Wittenberg pulpit, had directly denounced the abuse of indulgences. He wondered if, after all the years of struggle and study, Martin was about to step into an immense disaster.

The evening grew dark. Hans went inside and told Margaret of Martin's challenge against indulgences. He did not know the full background of the situation or Martin's ultimate intention. But he knew that for a long time he and his fellow citizens had balked under the financial pressure and abuses of the church. If his boy, now grown to manhood, could defend successfully a more ancient and worthy practice, then the name of Luther would be more highly distinguished than he had ever dreamed when he had envisioned Martin as a lawyer.

Mansfield and the rest of Germany and Europe throughout November and December excitedly discussed the issues raised by the theses on indulgences. In Wittenberg, Martin Luther was sure the whole indulgence practice had come to such abuse that a direct attack was the only hope for it. He had been brought to this public contest by long and careful preparation. In his search for an honest piety, he had come to discount heavily the penitential customs of the church.

In the Wittenberg parish in 1517, his people had come to him with letters of indulgence they had bought. On the basis of these letters, they argued for release from certain consequences of sinning. He could hold his peace no longer.

Unwilling to believe the stories told to him by his parishioners, he procured the letter of instructions given by Albert, Archbishop of Magdeburg, to the commissioner who had sold the indulgences. In these instructions he found confirmation for all the positions maintained by the Wittenberg people.

He knew Archbishop Albert—a prince in the house of Brandenburg, Archbishop of Magdeburg, and acting Bishop of Halberstadt—had secured likewise his election to the archbishopric of Mayence. But he did not know that in order to secure himself in these three bishoprics—which canon law forbade him to hold—Albert had made a financial bargain with the papacy. All Luther knew was that the clear and expressed intention of Christian piety had been brutally and inexcusably broken by this particular indulgence sale.

He sat in his study in the Black Cloister and argued with himself through August, September, and October, while the sale went on. Luther's own prince, the elector of Saxony, was too wise to allow his subjects to be bled for Rome and refused permission for the selling of the indulgences in his territory. Thus Wittenberg did not see the indulgence seller. But Luther's people walked just a few miles to the west and bought their indulgence tickets at the town of Zerbst, or a few miles to the east at Juterbog. The commissioner for the indulgence visited both of these towns, outside the dominion of the elector.

Luther could not believe what his people told him was true. He knew the church believed Christ had stored up great benefits for the human race by means of His passion. He knew the church believed the heroic Christian activity of the saints benefited the common Christian. He knew the church believed the Bishop of Rome held the "power of the Keys." He believed these things, too. But this sale was different.

The prior of the Dominican convent at Leipzig, John Tetzel, was selling these indulgences. When he entered Juterbog where Luther's people went to see and hear him, he had the papal bull, announcing the indulgence, carried on velvet cloth at the head of a procession. With great pomp and ceremony he marched through the streets of the town to the place of preaching. There, in unbelievable boldness, he promised to the Saxons that they could buy release from all punishment imposed by church law; they also could buy release from the penances they must do in purgatory for their sins.

With mock pathos and brutal hypocrisy, he painted for the benefit of his hearers the sufferings of their dead relatives in purgatory and told them point-blank that they could release their loved ones from suffering by paying a little money. Duped by these promises, the unlettered Germans, whom Luther looked upon as his sheep, believed the great reward of character thus could be bought.

The Black Cloister became the scene of a furious battle in Luther's heart and mind. How could the heads of the church act like this? Did they not understand the limits of papal power? Did they not know the mercy of Christ is not for sale—or was everything for sale in Rome? Furious at the way the sacred things of life thus were destroyed, but cool and determined in mind, he quietly wrote out ninety-five distinct sentences, each of which was a debatable point in the whole question of the office of penance—particularly the indulgence phase. These things, he thought, should be cleared up. And he, as a teacher of theology and possessor of the sacred right of clarifying scripture, was in a position to express himself.

So on October 31, 1517, when Wittenberg was crowded for the anniversary of the consecration of the Cathedral Church, he posted his ninety-five sentences with a brief preamble. The wooden doors of the Cathedral Church were used as the bulletin board, since the church was attached to the school. It was not as though Luther took a hammer, symbolic of revolution, and struck at the portals of this church, symbolic of the whole church. Rather, here was a theology professor and village preacher calling his colleagues to dispute, in correct academic fashion, the fundamental questions of the generation.

He was totally unprepared, however, for the torrential way these theses on indulgences swept through Europe. They appeared in every language and every place in Christendom "as though carried by angelic messengers."

The strong, sturdy, quiet teacher in Wittenberg now found himself the rallying leader for the disaffection of half a century. Hans Luther's son was forced to direct a campaign for the clarification of the gospel and the reform of the church.

Luther had no intention of conducting any of this work under cover. With the publication of his theses he wrote a letter to Albert, who had to bear the responsibility for the indulgence sale.

Initiation of a movement opposing Luther came from Albert on receipt of this letter. He brought the matter to the attention of Rome, for the work of Luther had been so successful in diminishing the confidence of the people in the indulgences that the sales had been seriously curtailed. But the head of the church in Rome was in no mood to give serious consideration to a question of piety.

The son of Lorenzo the Magnificent, tonsured at age seven, made a cardinal at fourteen, given voting power in the Curia at seventeen, Giovanni d'Medici was elected to the papacy in February 1513. He was ordained a priest the next month, made a bishop two days later, and installed in the papal office two days after that, taking the name Leo X. He is reported to have said to his brother when informed of his election, "Let us now enjoy the papacy, since God has given it to us." Regardless of whether the quotation is accurate, its central idea of enjoyment is a true description of Leo's intention.

The brilliant heir of the Medicean Renaissance, enthroned in Rome, surrounded by the finest art and poetry in Europe, was matched with the son of Thuringian peasants. In this battle, Leo X—many times the victor in matters of literature, politics, art, and the refinements of living—was unequipped to meet a man whose sole interest was practical religion.

Luther wrote to the pope in May 1518. He told him he had always accepted papal authority and in no way desired to appear heretical, but the recent papal indulgence had spread grave scandal and mockery, driving him to protest the abuse. Luther now desired only that the pope should understand his position and carefully consider the matters at issue.

Careful consideration was not something Leo X was prepared to give. He allowed the situation to develop rather haphazardly.

The attempt to control Luther began—as it should have begun—through his order. Leo thought a drunken monk who would see things clearer when he was sober had composed the theses. He instructed the general of the Augustinian Order to quench these fires of rebellion. Accordingly, the matter was brought up at the meeting of the order at Heidelberg in May 1518.

Luther was present, as was his friend Staupitz. The brothers discussed quietly the position of the accused; Luther explained and defended his theses. Some brothers agreed with him; some disagreed. Luther thought the issue was serious, and he did not want to involve his order, so he resigned as district vicar. Luther's mind obviously was unchanged after the Heidelberg meeting. One young, enthusiastic conservative at the meeting told Luther he dared not teach such doctrines to the peasants, or they would stone him to death. But Luther had read the temper of the peasants more correctly. He was not in danger of his life, and he returned to Wittenberg to await the next move—but Tetzel, who had sold the indulgences, was afraid to move outside his cloister at Leipzig.

At one o'clock in the afternoon of August 25, 1518, twenty-two-year-old Philip Melanchthon entered Wittenberg. He had come to teach Greek. The establishment of chairs of Greek had been slow in the northern universities, and he was the first teacher of Greek to be invited to Wittenberg.

Luther had urged the appointment of another candidate and looked on Melanchthon with considerable anxiety. His anxiety vanished four days later when Melanchthon delivered his installation address to the university faculty. Melanchthon made impassioned pleas for an orientation of the curriculum around the humanities and the New Testament.

At thirty-five, Luther was at his greatest strength; Melanchthon was at the very beginning of his career. A steadfast friendship sprang up between them instantly, never to be broken until death. The ability and devotion of Melanchthon became more important each day to Luther. Now he had at his elbow the finest humanist Germany had yet produced. As Melanchthon argued before the faculty and students at Wittenberg for a union of classical and Pauline studies, Luther's heart rejoiced. The fine, sensitive, accurate, grammatical scholarship of Melanchthon was joined to the powerful, emotional dynamic of Luther.

Rome, meanwhile, did not let the case rest. Luther was forced to defend his action before a representative of the pope in Augsburg. Initially, in August 1518, he had been ordered to appear in person in Rome, but the Augsburg meeting was substituted. Luther was glad for the change, for he knew—as every leader of his age knew—that to step within the control of his enemies now was to meet death.

He journeyed to Augsburg in October and met Cardinal Cajetan, the general of the Dominican Order. The cardinal, true to the Dominican type, was zealous for papal rights. His master, Leo X, in 1516 had reinforced the belief in the supreme authority of the papacy over a church council. Cardinal Cajetan was unwilling even to let Luther talk.

Luther, on the other hand, had come to Augsburg expecting to defend himself. At the first meeting, he fell on his face before the cardinal and accorded him the respect of his rank. But they could get nowhere. Luther tried to interrupt the cardinal's steady flow of contradiction and abuse, and the cardinal shouted louder and louder until Luther himself finally lost his moderation and shouted likewise.

The conference ended in thorough misunderstanding. The cardinal insisted that Luther recant. Luther insisted on discussing the issue. The cardinal claimed heresy. Luther challenged him to prove any statement of the theses to be heretical; the cardinal was unable to do so.

Friends tried to effect a reconciliation. Luther apologized for his conduct at their second meeting, and the cardinal accepted the apology. But at the third and last meeting it was the same story: a call for recantation and a refusal.

Luther withdrew from the audience and waited a few days in Augsburg. He heard rumors that a trap was laid for his arrest. So by night, he quietly left the city, riding steadily to the north. Both horse and rider were thin and haggard.

On his return, he wrote a description of his meeting with Cardinal Cajetan for public reading. He also wrote a letter to Pope Leo, which he called "An appeal from the Pope ill informed to the Pope well informed."

Charles von Miltitz, a papal ambassador to the Elector Frederick, conducted the next attempt at reconciliation. This attempt was colored by political necessities. The Diet* of the Holy Roman Empire was soon to meet for the election of an emperor, and the pope wanted the favor of Elector Frederick so he could control Frederick's vote in the election. The elector was a devout Catholic, never in sympathy with Luther's theology, but he was a staunch defender of the rights of his subjects. He refused to be a party to an intrigue that would surrender Luther without a fair defense.

Miltitz failed in his attempt to conciliate the parties. But in January 1519, he won from Luther a promise to write the pope a letter of apology for the whole business. Luther promised to agree to support indulgences in their proper sense and urge steady reverence for the Holy See. But the mission of Miltitz was disowned by his superiors and came to naught.

The next stage in the controversy was far more dramatic than any before. John Eck was a professor of theology at the University of Ingolstadt, a Dominican monk, and a man of considerable ability in debating. He challenged Luther and his Wittenberg colleague, Andrew Bodenstein, to a public discussion in Leipzig.

The issues were not at all clear. Luther could not be classed with the heretics. Bodenstein was more impetuous and apt to go off half-cocked. If Eck could succeed in wringing from either of them heretical statements, then Rome could silence both men.

Eck was masterful at this. Leipzig was in the unfriendly territory of Duke George of Saxony. The University of Leipzig was jealous of the growing prestige of the University of Wittenberg. Tetzel's home convent was in Leipzig. Everything looked bad for Luther.

He was considerably disturbed as he set forth from Wittenberg. But the faculty and students of his home university would not let him go alone. The professors rode in two country carts, while two hundred students, thoroughly armed, walked beside and behind them. With Luther rode Melanchthon, Justus Jonas, Nicholas Amsdorf, Andrew Bodenstein, and Duke Barnim, the rector of the university.

---

*Formal assembly of princes

When members of the Wittenberg group arrived in Leipzig, there was a constant menace of rioting. They kept guards placed in the inns where they lodged. They went in groups, well armed, from inn to church and to the council chamber where the debate was to be held. Leipzig itself furnished extra police to keep order.

After a preliminary debate between Eck and Bodenstein, Luther entered the lists July 4, 1519. They were assembled in the largest hall of Duke George's own palace, and the duke was present. Eck was the dominant figure.

The debate moved into a field where Luther did not want it. Eck constantly shifted from the present considerations to past records. He wanted to drive Luther into admitting a position similar to that held by heretical groups throughout church history. If that could be done, then he could set the label of heretic on the Wittenberger.

Eck tried the Waldensian history, but to no avail. Then he called forth the activity of Wycliffe, but Luther was not caught. Finally he brought up the work of John Hus. After a particularly vigorous expression of opinion by Eck, Luther interrupted him. "But good Dr. Eck, every Hussite opinion is not wrong."

Eck was jubilant. He countered Luther with the challenge that the church had denounced the Hussite opinions, that the Council of Constance had condemned them, that the pope had declared them heretical. Luther was driven finally with remorseless logic to the damning admission that popes and councils could err.

The Leipzig debates ended. Eck started southward to Rome, triumphant. He had unmasked another heretic. The Wittenberger and his friends journeyed homeward. Luther left Leipzig branded as a "heretic, rebel, a thing to flout."

Luther sensed deeply that dark days were ahead of him. But he felt strength, too. The days of indecision were over. Now he was out in the open. He could move quite clearly now.

The winter of 1519–20 passed uneventfully in Wittenberg while the opposing forces gathered their strength. Luther, Melanchthon, and their colleagues talked steadily, corresponded at length with friends all over Europe, and prepared themselves for the next meeting.

It came in the early summer of 1520. On June 15, Leo signed the bull *Exurge Domine*. This was the work of Eck, not of Leo himself. It called upon Luther to recant within sixty days or be excommunicated. It affirmed the heretical quality of Luther's position in opposing the sale of indulgences, and it did so in open defiance of the finest thought of the historic Catholic Church. Framed by Leo's belligerent advisers, headed by Eck, it caused further disaffection rather than healing of the church. In many of the northern provinces, people now were so thoroughly on Luther's side that they refused to allow the bull to be published. It often was torn into bits and scattered in the streets.

In the summer of 1520, Luther presented his reasoned opinions on the entire question to the Christian public. In three famous pamphlets, he drew up his offensive and defensive positions. In August he published *To the Christian Nobility of the German Nation on the Improvement of the Christian Estate*. Here, with clear, forceful logic and powerful emotion, he attacked the sole, arbitrary authority of the papacy. In the spirit of growing nationalism, he appealed to the German people to free themselves from the tyranny of papal power. He contradicted the famous Roman positions that the clergy are superior to the laity in controlling the church, that only the pope may interpret scripture authoritatively, and that only the pope may call a church council. These, he said, were the three walls behind which the power of Rome had hidden itself. All of them, he maintained, are invalid in light of the great essential doctrine of the priesthood of all believers. There is no essential distinction between priest and people. Each Christian is, in spiritual reality, a priest.

To German ears, this was a glorious appeal for freedom from Italian control. Even his bitter antagonist, Duke George, admitted a thrill of exaltation as he read this call to Germany. On one hand, a nationalistic view prompted its writing. But on the other hand was a deeper, more powerful sense of the immortal doctrine of the priesthood of all believers.

Hardly had Europe caught its breath from this powerful attack on what was considered a centuries-old authority when Luther published in October a work intended to undermine still further the power of the Roman church. *On the Babylonian Captivity of the Church* examined the sacramental system of the Roman church, a system built up during the same few centuries preceding Luther, which had seen the rise of the pope's autocratic power. Luther maintained no sacrament was valid if it could not find justification in the New Testament.

Starting from the New Testament premise, Luther could justify wholly only the Eucharist and baptism. There was partial justification also, he admitted, for the sacrament of penance. Christians were in captivity like the Jews of old in Babylon; the seven sacraments of Rome were the chains by which the captor, Rome, held them in slavery. There was no sacramental quality, in the true sense, to confirmation, marriage, holy orders, or extreme unction. These might be great Christian customs worthy of the church's blessing, but they were not sacraments.

The Roman church held everyone in fear by means of the sacrament. The true Christian church, Luther believed, should be built only upon the three valid sacraments.

In November 1520, Luther followed these aggressive documents with the sensitive, lovely presentation of the center of his own belief, *The Freedom of the*

Christian Man. Here he stated the paradox:

> *A Christian man is the most free lord of all, subject to no one.*
> *A Christian man is the dutiful servant of all, subject to everyone.*

From this he wrung a glorious presentation of the free spiritual life of the Christian believer. The grace of God, accepted by faith, makes the Christian lord of the universe. He may starve in a dungeon or reign from a prince's throne, and still possess inwardly the glorious freedom of the children of God. It is a free gift, made possible by faith in Christ. But because he is thus free, the Christian is bound by the great law of Christian love and by the indwelling spirit of Christ to serve in perfect charity all mankind.

Remembering his pledge to Miltitz, he sent this document to Leo X. He wrote a letter to accompany the little tract, which read in part:

> *Of your person, excellent Leo, I have heard only what is honorable and good. . .but of the Roman See, as you and all men must know, it is more scandalous and shameful than any Sodom or Babylon, and, as far as I can see, its wickedness is beyond all counsel and help, having become desperate and abysmal. It made me sick at heart to see that under your name and that of the Roman Church, the poor people in all the world are cheated and injured, against which thing I have set myself and will set myself as long as I have life, not that I hope to reform that horrible Roman Sodom, but that I know I am the debtor and servant of all Christians, and that it is my duty to counsel and warn them. . . .*
>
> *Finally, that I come not before your Holiness without a gift, I offer you this little treatise, dedicated to you as an augury of peace and good hope; by this book you may see how fruitfully I might employ my time, as I should prefer to, if only those impious flatterers of yours would let me. It is a little book as respects size, but if I mistake not, the whole sum of a Christian life is set down therein, in respect to contents. I am poor and have nothing else to send you, nor do you stand in need of any but my spiritual gifts.*

THE EPIC HOUR
1521

Through the winter of 1520–21, Luther was active in all his regular work. He preached daily—often twice a day. He taught his regular classes in the university. He wrote commentaries on Genesis and the Psalms. He published a sensitive, tender commentary on the Magnificat, in which Mary's canticle became again the song of the lowly and the meek. He answered the criticism of his enemies with insults and biting sarcasm of his own. The division was becoming more severe daily, and men were being called on for decisions.

It saddened Luther tremendously to find his beloved Staupitz unwilling to take to the open rebellion. Staupitz was well along in years now and had retired to Salzburg.

Staupitz wrote in January 1521 to their mutual friend Link: "Martin has undertaken a hard task and acts with great courage illuminated by God; I stammer and am a child needing milk."

Finally the old vicar wrote an open letter in which he tried to be conciliatory, but which bore evidence of his allegiance to Rome. This was not an hour for hesitation, and Luther gently wrote him:

> *At Worms they have as yet done nothing against me, although the papists contrive harm with extraordinary fury. Yet Spalatin writes the Evangelic cause has so much favor there that he does not expect I shall be condemned unheard. . . .*
>
> *I have heard with no great pain that you are attacked by Pope Leo, for thus the cross you have preached to others you may exemplify yourself. I hope that wolf, for you honor him too much to call him a Lion [Leo], will not be satisfied with your declaration, which will be interpreted to mean that you deny me and mine, inasmuch as you submit to the Pope's judgment.*
>
> *If Christ loves you he will make you revoke that declaration, since the Pope's bull must condemn all you have hitherto taught and believed about the mercy of God. As you knew this would be the case, it seems to me that you offend Christ in proposing Leo for a judge, whom you see to be an enemy of Christ running wild [debacchari] against the Word of his grace. You should have stood up for Christ and have contradicted the Pope's impiety. This is not the time to tremble but to cry aloud, while our Lord Jesus Christ is being condemned, burned, and blasphemed. Wherefore as much as you exhort me to humility, I exhort you to pride. You are too yielding. I am too stiff-necked.*
>
> *Indeed it is a solemn matter. We see Christ suffer. Should we keep silence and humble ourselves? Now that our dearest Saviour, who gave Himself for us, is made a mock in the world, should we not fight and offer our lives for Him? Dear father, the present crisis is graver than many think. Now applies the great gospel text, "Whosoever shall confess me before men, him shall the Son of man also confess before the angels of God, for whosoever shall be ashamed of me and of my words, of him shall the Son*

of man be ashamed, when he shall come in his own glory." May I be found guilty of pride, avarice, adultery, murder, opposition to the Pope, and all other sins, rather than be silent when the Lord suffers and says, "I looked on my right hand, and beheld, but there was no man that would know me; refuge failed me: no man cared for my soul." By confessing Him I hope to be absolved from all my sins. Wherefore I have raised my horns with confidence against the Roman idol, and the true Antichrist. The word of Christ is not the word of peace, but the word of the sword. But why should I, a fool, teach a wise man?

Truly your submission has saddened me not a little, and has shown me that you are different from that Staupitz who was the herald of grace and of the cross.

Intimation that he would be called to the Imperial Diet came to Luther throughout the winter. Charles V, newly elected head of the Holy Roman Empire, was holding his first diet at Worms, a German town on the Rhine. It opened January 25, 1521, to consider all the affairs of the empire.

One of the minor questions, technically, was "to take notice of the books and descriptions made by Friar Martin Luther against the Court of Rome." Before the arrival of the imperial party at Worms, Frederick the Elector had met Charles and his retinue at Cologne in October and November 1520. Frederick carried a letter from Luther to the emperor, asking for protection and a fair trial. The two men talked over the possibilities, and the emperor promised Frederick that Luther would be treated lawfully.

Then Frederick had a conference with the papal representatives to the court of Charles, who demanded that all Luther's work be burned and that Luther be delivered up bound. Frederick decided to stand by Luther and see him through at the coming diet.

The bull "Exurge Domine" only had threatened excommunication. But Luther's reception of it had brought an end to the matter, and on January 3, 1521, Leo X signed the final bull demanding complete excommunication. So when the Roman party acted at Worms, they acted on the principle that Luther was already condemned. He should not be heard. He should be executed as a heretic. The civil authority was not bound to keep faith with a heretic. He should either recant or die; even if he recanted, it was not certain he should live.

The representatives of Rome were Jerome Aleander and Marino Caracciola. Aleander was the chief. He was librarian of the Vatican, was later to be a cardinal, knew Greek and the classics, and had lectured at Paris. By temperament he was an inquisitor. It was easy for him to light bonfires for books or men. He could see men die for the glory of God without a troubled conscience. At Worms, he held to one line of reasoning: Luther must die!

On February 13, Aleander spoke to the diet for three hours, demanding that Luther be condemned without a hearing. But to Luther the quarrel was not concluded. The question was open. He was a spokesman for a living, growing movement.

On March 26, Luther, working in Wittenberg, received the summons from Charles V. It addressed him as honored, dear, and pious son and called on him to appear in order "to obtain information about certain doctrines originating with you and certain books written by you."

Luther was no coward, but he knew the game he played now. The sensitive balance could break at any moment, and he would be in the hands of the enemy. But he would not stay away. He had been born for this hour. Now the emperor, the papal representative, and the German people would hear his blessed doctrine. His life was not the issue.

On April 2, he left for Worms. Melanchthon wanted to go, but Luther would not have it, saying, "Dear brother, if I do not come back, if my enemies put me to death, you go on teaching and standing fast in the truth. If you live, my death will matter little."

The magistrates of the city hired a driver and horses for the open country wagon, half-filled with straw, in which they rode. Amsdorf, Peter Swaven—a Danish student who also had gone armed to Leipzig in 1519, and John Petzensteiner, Peter's Augustinian companion, were with Luther. Caspar Sturm, the imperial herald, rode ahead on horseback, carrying the royal coat-of-arms, a square, yellow banner with a black, two-headed eagle. Again and again, friends interceded to stop his approach. Sturm, the herald, pointed out the emperor's March edict to seize all Luther's books, and asked if Luther should proceed to Worms. Luther's reply was yes.

Efforts were made to get him to stop at Ebernburg, a day's journey from Worms. Ebernburg was a fine castle owned by Francis von Sickingen, who was able and willing to give Luther protection. But he would not be stopped. The pressure of destiny was in him.

At Offenheim, he sent a terse, courageous reply to Spalatin, the elector's secretary who had repeatedly warned him of the impending dangers: "I shall go to Worms though there were as many devils there as tiles on the roofs." So the little procession moved onward.

Just before ten in the morning of Tuesday, April 16, the cathedral tower watchman blew his horn loudly to announce the party's arrival. Thousands gathered along the road, and Luther rode triumphantly into Worms in his humble wagon. The papal legate wrote to Rome that Luther stepped from the vehicle saying, "God will be with me," and looking around at the people with "demoniacal" eyes.

He was put up at the house of the Knights of St. John. There the crowd gathered rapidly and kept him busy with visitors until late into the night. Aleander said all the world went to see Luther. Friends and supporters were at the inn, and at "the Swan" nearby.

Wednesday morning he prepared for his appearance, finding time to administer the last sacrament to a dying Saxon noble who sent for him. At four in the afternoon the day after his arrival, the herald and the imperial marshal came to the inn for him.

Luther was dressed in his black Augustinian gown. He was sturdy, large-boned, but not stout. His eyes were set deep and glowed with exceptional brightness. Tonsure newly shaved, he was crowned with a circle of thick, black hair. Cranach's painting of him that year shows clearly the strong, resolute, fiery, and animated features. He was in his thirty-eighth year, his heart still unsoiled by the terrors of public warfare, his mind still vigorous, his spirit undampened by the long stresses of defeat and compromise. Peasant strength, monastic training, personal piety, elemental honesty, and courage were all his.

The crowds were so thick in the main streets that the men went through gardens from house to house to the hallway entrance in the bishop's palace. Luther stood outside about two hours. Finally, at six o'clock, he was ushered into the meeting of the diet.

Charles V was the central figure. Only twenty years old, pale, quiet, he was surrounded by all his counselors. Six electors of the empire were there, including the Elector Frederick, Luther's own civil lord. The papal legates were there, unable to control events completely. Bishops, princes, deputies, and ambassadors filled the hall. Spanish and German soldiers were on guard. Thousands of persons jammed the passageways and doors.

Before Charles V in person and Leo X in representation, the son of Hans Luther stood quietly for a moment. Looking around, he saw Aleander glaring at him. "So the Jews must have looked at Christ," he thought.

His gaze finally came to rest on the youthful emperor. Their eyes met, but not their spirits. Each failed to read the strength in the other. Luther saw Charles surrounded by his court, and he seemed to Luther like "some poor lamb amid swine and hounds."

A movement before him broke his reverie. He watched an official rise and turn to him. He was told that his case was now before the diet and he was to say nothing except in answer to questions. He thought this admonition strange, and waited anxiously.

Dr. Eck—not the debater of Leipzig fame but the representative of the archbishop's court—pointed to a group of books on a central table. He asked Luther if these books were his and if he would recant of the positions set forth in them.

This was too sudden for Luther. He had thought, as Charles's summons had indicated, that this was to be a hearing, not a demand. He seemed powerless to answer. Jerome Schurf, his friend and lawyer, stepped to his rescue, crying out, "Let the titles of the books be read."

They were read. *"To the Christian Nobility of the German Nation! On the Babylonish Captivity of the Church! The Freedom of the Christian Man! . . ."*

By the time the reading was over, Luther had recovered his presence. He was not to be driven too quickly. This was his hour.

He spoke slowly:

> *His Imperial Majesty asks me two things: first, whether these books are mine, and secondly, whether I will stand by them or recant part of what I have published. First, the books are mine; I deny none of them. The second question, whether I will reassert all or recant what is said to have been written without warrant of scripture, concerns faith and the salvation of souls and the Divine Word, than which nothing is greater in heaven or in earth, and which we all ought to reverence. Therefore it would be rash and dangerous to say anything without due consideration, since I might say more than the thing demands or less than the truth, either of which would bring me in danger of the sentence of Christ. "Whosoever shall deny me before men, him will I also deny before my Father which is in heaven." Wherefore, I humbly beg your Imperial Majesty to grant me time for deliberation, that I may answer without injury to the Divine Word, or peril to my soul.*

Confusion followed for a moment. Charles conferred with his counselors and then with Dr. Eck. Finally Eck addressed Luther:

> *Although, Martin, you knew from the imperial mandate why you were summoned and therefore you do not deserve to have a longer time given you, yet his Imperial Majesty of his great clemency, grants you one day more, commanding that you appear tomorrow at this time and deliver your answer orally and not in writing.*

Luther withdrew from the hall and returned to his rooms. The experience was exacting. For a moment it had looked bad for him. His enemies had almost succeeded in forcing too hasty a statement. Now he knew the question and he would be ready.

That night, greatly excited, he wrote to a friend: "This hour I have stood before the Emperor and the Diet, asked whether I would revoke my books. . . . Truly, with Christ's aid I shall not retract one jot or tittle."

He was in prayer much of the night. In the morning, friend after friend came to visit. Luther was in the best of spirits. He was well and strong, laughed heartily, and was in constant good humor. With his intimate associates he planned the work of the afternoon, and he was ready when at four o'clock the herald came. Again through gardens they reached the palace entrance. There they stood in the hot, pressing crowd for an hour and a half.

His mind was fastened rigidly to its one great task. Life was precious to him. His enemies were strong. They might march him easily from the hall of the diet to the stake of Hus. He knew Rome had pleaded with Charles not to keep the promise of safe conduct. But here was his real and valid opportunity to confess his truth before the world. A strange mingling of faith, fear, strength, and exaltation possessed him. And his mind was clear: He would be honest!

At six the emperor and court entered. Aleander and Caracciolo would not come; they said they would not listen to a heretic! Luther entered, cheered by German knights and soldiers.

Dr. Eck again conducted the session. He turned to Luther, both men standing, and said:

> *His Imperial Majesty has assigned this time to you, Martin Luther, to answer for the books which you yesterday openly acknowledged to be yours. You asked time to deliberate on the question whether you would take back part of what you had said or would stand by all of it. You did not deserve this respite, which has now come to an end, for you knew long before why you were summoned. And everyone—especially a professor of theology—ought to be so certain of his faith that whenever questioned about it he can give a sure and positive answer. Now at last reply to the demand of his Majesty, whose clemency you have experienced in obtaining time to deliberate. Do you wish to defend all of your books or to retract part of them?*

Luther was self-possessed. He had gained the hour of his life. He spoke to the greatest assembly of princes Germany could muster. This was no persecuted pleading, but a clear appeal, in ancient prophetic fervor:

> *Most Serene Emperor, Most Illustrious Princes, Most Clement Lords! At the time fixed yesterday I obediently appear, begging for the mercy of God, that your Most Serene Majesty and your illustrious lordships may deign to hear this cause which I hope may be called the cause of justice and truth, with clemency, and if, by my inexperience, I should fail to give anyone the titles due him, or should sin against the etiquette of the court, please forgive me, as a man who has lived not in courts but in monastic nooks, one who can say nothing for himself, but that he has hitherto tried to teach and to write but with a sincere mind and single*

eye to the glory of God and the edification of Christians.

Most Serene Emperor, Most Illustrious Princes! Two questions were asked me yesterday. To the first, whether I would recognize that the books published under my name were mine, I gave plain answer, to which I hold and will hold forever, namely, that the books are mine, as I published them, unless perchance it may have happened that the guile or meddlesome wisdom of my opponents has changed something in them. For I only recognize what has been written by myself alone, and not the interpretation added by another.

In reply to the second question, I beg your Most Sacred Majesty and your lordships to be pleased to consider that all my books are not of the same kind. In some I have treated piety, faith, and morals so simply and evangelically that my adversaries themselves are forced to confess that these books are useful, innocent, and worthy to be read by Christians. Even the bull, though fierce and cruel, states that some things in my books are harmless, although it condemns them by a judgment simply monstrous. If, therefore, I should undertake to recant these, would it not happen that I alone of all men should damn the truth which all—friends and enemies alike—confess?

Luther spoke calmly, in complete command of himself, but his deep intensity stilled every noise in the hall. He was being heard clearly.

The second class of my works inveighs against the papacy as against that which both by precept and example has laid waste all Christendom, body and soul. No one can deny or dissemble this fact, since general complaints witness that the consciences of all believers are snared, harassed, and tormented by the laws of the pope and the doctrines of men, and especially that the goods of this famous German nation have been and are devoured in numerous and ignoble ways. Yet the Canon Law provides that the laws and doctrines of the pope contrary to the Gospel and the fathers are to be held erroneous and rejected. If, therefore, I should withdraw these books, I would add strength to tyranny and open windows and doors to their impiety, which would then flourish and burgeon more freely than it ever dared before. It would come to pass that their wickedness would go unpunished, and therefore, would become more licentious on account of my recantation, and their government of the people, thus confirmed and established, would become intolerable, especially if they could boast that I had recanted with the full authority of your Sacred and Most Serene Majesty and of the whole Roman Empire. Good God! In that case, I would be the tool of iniquity and tyranny.

The sound of his voice uplifted in rebuke to high sin brought a welcome thrill to many a heart. Men forgot the heat and smoke. The defense continued:

> *In a third sort of book I have written against some private individuals who tried to defend the Roman tyranny and tear down my pious doctrine. In these I confess I was more bitter than is becoming to a minister of religion. For I do not pose as a saint, nor do I discuss my life but the doctrine of Christ. Yet neither is it right for me to recant what I have said in these, for then tyranny and impiety would rage and reign against the people of God more violently than ever by reason of my acquiescence.*

Luther paused a moment, then picked up a triumphant strain, moving in prophetic humility from rebuke to proof, and calling on all present to rise and answer him.

> *As I am a man and not God, I wish to claim no other defense for my doctrine than that which the Lord Jesus put forward when He was questioned before Annas and smitten by a servant: He then said, "If I have spoken evil, bear witness of the evil." If the Lord Himself, who knew that He could not err, did not scorn to hear testimony against His doctrine from a miserable servant, how much more should I, the dregs of men, who can do nothing but err, seek and hope that someone should bear witness against my doctrine? I therefore beg by God's mercy that if your Majesty or your illustrious lordships, from the highest to the lowest, can do it, you should bear witness and convict me of error and conquer me by proofs drawn from the Gospels or the prophets, for I am most ready to be instructed and when convinced will be the first to throw my books into the fire.*
>
> *From this I think it is sufficiently clear that I have carefully considered and weighed the discords, perils, emulation, and dissension excited by my teaching, concerning which I was gravely and urgently admonished yesterday. To me the happiest side of the whole affair is that the Word of God is made the object of emulation and dissent. For this is the course, the fate, and the result of the Word of God. As Christ says, "I am come not to send peace, but a sword, to set a man against his father and a daughter against her mother." We must consider that our God is wonderful and terrible in His counsels. If we should begin to heal our dissensions by damning the Word of God, we should only turn loose an intolerable deluge of woes.*

He spoke now to the heads of the empire. From authority born in scripture and conscience, he called on the lords of Germany in terms no underling could use. Spaniards and Germans watched the gestureless monk in the uncertain, hot light and heard, unbelieving:

> *Let us take care that the rule of this excellent youth, Prince Charles (in whom, next to God, there is much hope), does not begin inauspiciously. For I could show by many examples drawn from scripture that when Pharaoh and the King of Babylon and the kings of Israel thought to pacify and strengthen their kingdoms by their own wisdom, they really only ruined themselves. For he taketh the wise in their own craftiness and removeth mountains and they know it not. We must fear God. I do not say this as though your lordships needed either my teaching or my admonition, but because I could not shirk the duty I owed Germany. With these words I commend myself to your Majesty and your lordships, humbly begging that you will not let my enemies make me hateful to you without cause. I have spoken.*

In proper custom, he spoke in Latin. Many of the northerners did not understand it, and there were cries for it in German. The hall was hot, Luther perspiring. He seemed on the point of collapse. Luther repeated it in German. But Charles V, in whose hands was the destiny of Europe, understood neither Latin nor German! And Leo X, master of the church, who alone had power sufficient for this healing, was far away.

Eck rose, amazed that Luther would dare to speak this way, and said:

> *Luther, you have not answered to the point. You ought not to call in question what has been decided and condemned by councils. Therefore I beg you to give a simple, unsophisticated answer without horns. Will you recant or not?*

Luther, realizing the point had been called for sharply, said briefly and exactly:

> *Since your Majesty and your lordships ask for a plain answer, I will give you one without either horns or teeth. Unless I am convinced by scripture or by right reason—for I trust neither in popes nor in councils, since they have often erred and contradicted themselves—unless I am thus convinced, I am bound by the texts of the Bible; my conscience is captive to the Word of God. I neither can nor will recant anything, since it is neither right nor safe to act against conscience. God help me. Amen.*

Eck, furious, called again for recantation. Luther replied, while the tumult increased. Charles V rose abruptly and left the room, signifying an end of the audience. The marshal took Luther quickly from the hall, while the Germans cheered and the Spaniards hissed. Fearing an attempt on his life, friends gathered in a marching circle around him. With hands held high in an old Saxon sign of victory, they escorted him through the crowds who jammed the palace court and streets.

Back in his rooms, Luther clapped his hands and shouted happily, "I am through! I am through!"

But he wasn't.

Friends gathered around Luther in the hotel that night, overjoyed with his strong stand at the diet. The Elector Frederick was greatly pleased and remarked to Spalatin how well his Dr. Martin had spoken at the diet that day.

Affairs in the political realm were so tense that the counselors of Frederick and the emperor tried hard to arrive at a compromise. They called on Luther several times during the succeeding few days, but he was adamant. If any compromise involved the surrender of his position, then it was impossible. He had taken his position in public on his conscience. As he saw it, the authority upon which that conscience based its decision was the written Word of God. In this field, compromise was out of the question.

In despair, the intermediaries gave up.

Feeling no longer needed in Worms and wanting to get far away before the safe conduct would expire, Luther silently slipped out on the morning of April 26, in the company of the same few friends with whom he had come. The imperial herald, Sturm, did not ride with him for fear of attracting too much attention but met the party a few miles to the north.

FIVE

The journey home was more leisurely and not filled with the anxiety the journey southward had known. Coming into Eisenach, Luther visited his relatives in Mohra. His father's brother Heinz Luther entertained him overnight, and Luther preached the next day in the village. Back in the field and forest of his family, Luther relaxed some from the severe experiences of the past few months and visited many friends and relatives in and around Eisenach.

He resumed his journey May 4. Riding with relatives along a narrow road through the forest, he was surprised by a company of armed horsemen. They forced his carriage to stop, assured the companions no harm was meant, and whispered something to Luther. He turned to his friends and told them he had to leave, but all was well and he would write to them soon. Luther mounted, and off they galloped through the forest.

After a hard ride through the day and well into the night, they arrived at the castle of Wartburg, where Luther was turned over to the commandant.

Word spread rapidly that Luther had been kidnapped. The eyewitnesses told the little that was known about the affair, but no one knew who the kidnappers were or why the deed had been done. Rumor said Luther had been killed. Aleander heard the news and reported to Rome, "Some say that I have had him killed, others the Archbishop of Mayence. Would God it were true!"

The secret of his disappearance was guarded rigidly. Suspicions that the Elector Frederick had a hand in it could not be proved, and no one except a few in the intimate circle had any idea what had happened. To reassure some of his most intimate friends, Luther wrote them after a few weeks to tell them of his health and safety, but he did not divulge his hiding place. The Elector Frederick was afraid Luther would be assassinated, as the Romanists wished. In all probability, the plans for this ruse were laid in the emperor's own private chambers, with only Spalatin and a few others aware of them.

Luther himself was taken by surprise, but he was quickly reassured at Wartburg. There he was treated as a guest, with respect and honor. Hidden now from the world of turmoil, he lived as one set apart from that world. He dressed as a knight and was spoken to by everyone as Sir George. Thick black hair appeared over his tonsure, and a full beard covered his chin.

The first few weeks of his hiding passed quickly and quietly. Then the old restlessness repossessed him. He had been born, it seems, for battle, and for ten long years he had been moving steadily in public warfare. The great desire of his mind and heart was to give what he called "evangelical leadership" to the people of Saxony.

And so in his room in the Wartburg, undisturbed by the routine duties of professorship and parish, he set his fine abilities to a task he long had anticipated. He would translate his beloved New Testament into the German language. Many German translations were available, but each was in dialect. He would set forth the blessed stories so they could be understood generally.

Throughout the long summer months and well into the winter he labored at these tasks. Not only did the New Testament translation progress in the Wartburg; there also came from his pen tract after tract on all the major issues of the controversy. He wrote sermons on the Gospels and Epistles to be used in the regular cycle of the church year. He wrote on the Mass and on monastic vows.

As he wrote on monastic vows, with much time for reflection, the old controversy between himself and his father, when he had taken his own vows, came to mind. He could see now, as he could not see then, something intrinsically wrong in the Roman practice with regard to vows. The deep piety of his father was clearer to him. He could understand now how piety and resistance to the organization could be united in one person. When the book was ready for the public, Martin wrote to Hans:

> *This book, dear father, I wish to dedicate to you, not to make your name famous in the world, for fame puffeth up the flesh, according to the doctrine of St. Paul, but that I might have occasion in a short preface as it were between you and me to point out to the Christian reader the argument and contents of the book, together with an illustrative example. . . .*
>
> *It is now sixteen years since I became a monk, having taken the vow without your knowledge and against your will. You were anxious and fearful about my weakness, because I was a young blood of twenty-two; that is, to use St. Augustine's words, it was still hot youth with me, and you had learned from numerous examples that monkery made many unblessed and so were determined to marry me honorably and tie me down. This fear, this anxiety, this nonconsent of yours were for a time simply irreconcilable.*
>
> *And, indeed, my vow was not worth a fig, since it was taken without the consent of the parents God gave me. Moreover it was a godless vow both because taken against your will and without my whole heart. In short, it was simple doctrine of men; that is, of the spiritual state of hypocrites, a doctrine not commanded by God. . . .*
>
> *Dear father, will you still take me out of the cloister? If so, do not boast of it, for God has anticipated you and taken me out himself. What difference does it make whether I retain or lay aside the cowl and the tonsure? Do they make the monk? . . . My conscience is free and redeemed;*

therefore I am still a monk but not a monk, and a new creature not of the Pope, but of Christ, for the Pope also has creatures and is a creator of puppets and idols and masks and straw men, of which I was formerly one, but now have escaped by the Word....

He treated the problem of vows as he did everything else, asking only one question: What does scripture say? From scripture he argued vows were hostile to the good of Christianity. He strongly cut away the basis for the great monastic emphasis on celibacy. The Bible encourages marriage, does not place a greater premium on virginity, and destroys the distinction between clergy and laity.

The book was widely read and very influential. Once again it touched a source of income for Albert, Archbishop of Mayence, for he sold licenses to priests to permit them to keep concubines. Marriage of the clergy assumed an important phase of the struggle after the appearance of this book.

There were many lovely incidents during his Wartburg stay. The hills around the castle, familiar to him since school days in Eisenach, were the scene of many walks. The flowers and the same fields that had delighted the eye of his childhood were now his joy.

His life was centered, however, in the moments in his room when all the strength of his nature was concentrated on religious study. He had been so active during the past five years and now was forced to inaction, concentrating on Greek and Hebrew grammar, wrestling with New Testament phrases to bring them into his beloved German language. No wonder that fury possessed him when he thought of the way Rome had handled the precious gospel and himself, its proclaimer.

As he sat in Wartburg, Archbishop Albert displayed at Halle nine thousand relics, including manna from the wilderness, the burning bush of Moses, and jars from the wedding at Cana, with the promise of indulgence for those who came. Albert also reopened the indulgence sale. Against this abuse Luther wrote a terrible pamphlet titled "The Idol of Halle." He gave it to Spalatin to print, but Spalatin showed it to Frederick, and Luther was urged not to publish it. However, Luther wrote a powerful letter to Albert, demanding once again that Albert cease the abusive practices:

Your Grace doubtless remembers vividly that I have written you twice before, the first time at the beginning of the indulgence fraud protected by your Grace's name.

But as this my true admonition was mocked by your Grace, obtaining ingratitude instead of thanks, I wrote you a second time (Feb. 4, 1520) humbly asking for information. To this I got a hard, improper, unepiscopal, unchristian answer (Feb. 26, 1520), referring me to higher powers for information. As these two letters did no good, I am now sending your Grace a third warning, according to the Gospel, this time in German, hoping that such admonition and prayer, which ought to be superfluous and unnecessary, may help.

Your Grace has again erected at Halle that idol which robs poor simple Christians of their money and their souls. You have thus shown that the criminal blunder for which Tetzel was blamed was not due to him alone, but also to the Archbishop of Mayence, who, not regarding my gentleness to him, insists on taking all the blame on himself. Perhaps your Grace thinks I am no more to be reckoned with, but am looking out for my own safety, and that his Imperial Majesty has extinguished the poor monk. On the contrary, I wish Your Grace to know that I will do what Christian love demands without fearing the gates of hell, much less un-learned popes, bishops, and cardinals. I will not suffer it nor keep silence when the Archbishop of Mayence gives out that it is none of his business to give information to a poor man who asks for it. The truth is that your ignorance is wilful, as long as the thing ignored brings you in money. I am not to blame, but your own conduct.

Luther was in earnest. His mind worked clearly and quickly. His sentences cut through to the issue every time. He heard the roar of the Lion of Amos and could not keep silent.

I humbly pray your Grace, therefore, to leave poor people undeceived and unrobbed, and show yourself a bishop rather than a wolf. It has been made clear enough that indulgences are only knavery and fraud, and that only Christ should be preached to the people, so that your Grace has not the excuse of ignorance.

Luther was certain that in this cause emperors were no match for the Holy Spirit. He took upon himself the prophet's authority and delivered an ultimatum to the cardinal:

Wherefore I write to tell your Grace that if the idol is not taken down, my duty to godly doctrine and Christian salvation will absolutely force me to attack your Grace publicly as I did the Pope, and oppose your undertaking, and lay all the odiums which Tetzel once had, on the Archbishop of Mayence, and show all the world the difference between a bishop and a wolf. . . .

I beg and expect a right speedy answer from your Grace within the next fortnight, for at the expiration of that time my pamphlet against the Idol of Halle will be published unless a proper answer comes.

Luther's letter was dated December 1. Before the end of the month a messenger brought to the Wartburg a letter addressed to "Martin Luther, in care of Spalatin." Luther opened it and read:

Halle, December 21, 1521

> *My dear doctor, I have received your letter and I take it in good part and graciously, and will see to it that the thing that moved you so be done away, and I will act, God willing, as becomes a pious, spiritual, and Christian prince, as far as God gives me grace and strength, for which I earnestly pray and have prayers said for me, for I can do nothing of myself, and know well that without God's grace there is no good in me, but that I am as much foul mud as any other, if not more. I do not wish to conceal this, for I am more than willing to show you grace and favor for Christ's sake, and I can well bear fraternal and Christian punishment. I hope the merciful, kind God will give me herein more grace, strength, and patience to live in this matter and in others by his will.*

> *Albert, with his own hand*

It was not easy for Luther to remain out of leadership in the most crucial days of the new movement. He thought with bitterness and scorn of the tricks to which Aleander and Charles V had resorted at Worms. He read the Edict of Worms, calling on the people of Germany to surrender him for his proper condemnation, with a warning to all who gave him shelter, food, or clothes or who read, bought, sold, or printed any of his books. He paced back and forth through the halls of Wartburg, impatient at Frederick's continued demand for his seclusion.

There were days in the Wartburg when his gifts of clear exposition were at their height and he felt himself working with the highest efficiency. But on other days all the distractions and balked fury of these years of quarreling got the better of him.

Impatient, restless for leadership, Frederick finally permitted Luther to come out of his seclusion by the course of events at Wittenberg. There, in his absence, colleagues like Andrew Bodenstein were moving too rapidly. They wanted to throw over the entire ancient organization and faith. Luther, by nature and training, was thoroughly conservative. He had been driven by life's severest experiences to open up the abuses in his church, but he devoutly loved the church itself, and he would keep all its ancient customs. Not so the more radical men who had welcomed his leadership. Wittenberg needed him badly.

He had corresponded with his friends all winter and knew the situation exactly. Melanchthon pleaded with him to return. Finally, in the spring of 1522, he quietly slipped away from the Wartburg. Still with a beard and full head of hair, dressed as a knight and with a sword by his side, he journeyed incognito through the territory of Duke George of Saxony—who willingly would have turned him over to the authorities, had he caught him. He arrived safely at Wittenberg. He talked with Melanchthon and his other friends and analyzed the situation with them. Then for eight successive days he preached in the village church against the fanatical activities that had resulted in the destruction of pictures and images and in the breakdown of organizational morale.

At the close of the week he was once again the leader of the Wittenberg movement. The radical wing of the Reformation would locate its center elsewhere.

Luther, with Melanchthon's help, now concentrated on the clear formulation of the Wittenberg position. Throughout 1520 and 1521, Melanchthon had worked on an outline of theology constructed from Paul's letter to the Romans. He had sent a copy to Luther at the Wartburg. Now, with Luther's approval, he published it in Wittenberg, calling it *Loci Communes Rerum Theologicarum* ("Theological Commonplaces"). It moved in the evangelic circle of ideas, beginning with the doctrine of the Trinity and then setting forth the idea of Man, Sin, The Law, The Gospel, Grace, Faith, The Sacraments, The Magistracy, Church Government, Condemnation, and Blessedness.

Such a logical, systematic presentation was needed, and Melanchthon's detailed skill was equal to the task. The proofs of argument were all scriptural, and the book marked a tremendous advance for the Luther forces.

Far away in his retreat at Salzburg, Staupitz watched Luther's progress with both sorrow and joy. He had loved the sensitive, enthusiastic boy who had come to the Augustinian monastery at Erfurt in 1505. Augustinian? The old vicar-general meditated on the changes of life that had driven him from the order he loved to take refuge, by papal arrangement, with the Benedictines, while the young monk, now mature, battled for piety in the open world.

The last exchange of letters between the two old friends was in 1523–24, after the great crisis in the battle had passed. Luther wrote in September 1523:

> *Reverend Father in Christ, your silence is most unjust, and you know that we are obliged to think of it. But even if you are no longer pleased with me, it is not fitting that I should forget you, who first made the light of the Gospel to shine in my heart.*

This called forth the last letter, dated April 1, 1524, from Salzburg:

> *My love to you is most constant, passing the love of women, always unbroken. . . . But as I do not grasp all of your ideas, I keep silence with them. . . . But we owe much to you, Martin, for having led us back from the husks which the swine did eat to the pastures of life and the words of salvation.*

Staupitz died in December 1524.

THE WHIRLWIND
1525

The severest test Luther ever had to face came in 1524–25, during the so-called "Peasants' Revolt." The causes of the revolt lay deep in human history, completely disconnected from the Reformation.

For centuries in central Europe both civil and ecclesiastical nobles had ruled the peasant class strictly. The long story of uprisings to gain their birthright is told throughout history.

In the German area where Luther was called upon to face the movement, these uprisings had become increasingly severe and frequent during the 150 years preceding 1525. The leaders of the church were more at fault than those of the laity. For centuries, bishops and other high church officials had kept serfs in severe oppression.

Two sources contributed to the peasant rebellion throughout these years: first, the refusal of the oppressed classes to bear oppression beyond a certain point; and second, the preaching of the New Testament. The same church that reared and owned ecclesiastical princes, preserved in other priests the strange gospel message of equality.

Long before Luther, these two streams of rebellion and the gospel had met in the forests of central Germany. The Bundschuh was a secret society dedicated to social rebellion. Its symbol was the peasant's shoe—tied, in token of servility, instead of buckled, as were the shoes of the nobility. When this symbol was carried through the country on Bundschuh banners, it stirred tremendous feeling and instilled strong allegiance. Great preachers of the social gospel, like Hans Boheim, inspired the peasants' efforts.

In the volatile days of the late fifteenth and early sixteenth centuries, there was a groundswell of rebellion throughout central Europe. The papacy, ancient symbol of autocratic strength, was weakening and fighting for its hold on Europe. The Holy Roman Empire was no longer the source of strength it once had been, and many princes were refusing allegiance to their chief. Feudalism was in its last stages. Francis I in France, Henry VIII in England, Charles V in Spain, Caesar Borgia in Italy, and Julius II in Rome all acted from personal will, in violent disregard of human rights and accepted medieval law. Wealth increasingly was concentrated in the hands of the few, stolen from the many. Luxury and its ever-present companions, immorality and brutality, spread through Europe's armed classes. Hundreds of the finest minds of Christendom attacked from all angles the abuse in recognized authority.

The European peasants moved in perfect rhythm with this transforming and reforming world. This was their hour to strike. The restless movement grew steadily—unfortunately led by men unequipped for the task.

Thomas Munzer, who at Zwickau had organized a fanatical sect dedicated to church and state reform, assumed a precarious leadership throughout these years. He had been driven from Zwickau and Wittenberg. After a hazardous existence in many cities, he had established his leadership in the town of Muhlhausen. There he preached a violent rebellion, claiming this was the hour when the Holy Spirit would lead the peasants to their rightful reward. He himself was unbalanced, hasty, and ignorant, but moved by a fiery spirit. His father had been killed brutally by nobles. He urged the peasants to strike for the biblical "promised land" and assured them legions of angels would fight for them.

As the movement spread violently northward into Saxony, it became increasingly clear Luther had to speak. This was no child's play. It was the opening of the rebellion. During the summer of 1524, the peasants were successful everywhere. When they captured a castle or an estate, they robbed, pillaged, and murdered without restraint. The torch and the sword, with all the accompanying hideousness to which a human mob can descend, rose menacingly above Germany.

Luther's mind was clear. He was thoroughly conservative in civil affairs. Never in his life had he sanctioned force, except by the civil magistrate. He would have died unresisting at Worms, had they led him to the stake. He would never have approved an armed defense by the Elector Frederick and Saxon warriors on his behalf.

On his return from the Wartburg to Wittenberg in 1522, during the memorable week of preaching in which he had stilled the revolution there, he had said:

> *I will preach, speak, write, but I will force no one; for faith must be voluntary. Take me as an example. I stood up against the Pope, indulgences, and all the papists, but without violence or uproar. I only urged, preached, and declared God's Word, nothing else. And yet while I was*

asleep, or with my Philip Melanchthon and Amsdorf, the word inflicted greater injury on popery than prince or emperor ever did. I did nothing; the Word did everything. Had I appealed to force, all Germany might have been deluged with blood. Yes, I might have kindled a conflict at Worms, so that the emperor would not have been safe. But what would have been the result? Ruin and desolation of body and soul. I therefore kept quiet, and gave the Word free course through the world.

His heart was ever a peasant's heart. The blood in his veins, he boasted, was peasant blood. No one in Europe had spoken more directly against the abuses of the ruling class than he, and now he faced the strange, terrible conflict between his native, idealistic sympathy for the peasants and his strong belief in the divine order of civil government. The princes he had known in Saxony, chiefly the Elector Frederick, had been wise and well controlled. But in this hour when the uprising was at its height, Frederick was on his deathbed and could not organize his followers to the defense.

Luther was in hearty sympathy with the peasants' demands. The peasant leaders had stated their position in the famous Twelve Articles, drawn up during the winter of 1524–25 and adopted in a council at Memmingen on March 7. Luther read these carefully:

1. The right to choose their own pastors.
2. They would pay tithe of corn, out of which the pastors should be paid, the rest going to the use of the parish. But small tithes, i.e., of the produce of animals, every tenth calf, or pig, or egg, and so on, they would not pay.
3. They would be free, and no longer serfs and bondmen.
4. Wild game and fish are to be free to all.
5. Woods and forests belong to all for fuel.
6. No services of labor to be more than were required of their forefathers.
7. If more service required, wages must be paid for it.
8. Rent, when above the value of the land, to be properly valued and lowered.
9. Punishments for crimes to be fixed.
10. Common land to be given up again to common use.
11. Death gifts (i.e., the right of the lord to take the best chattel of the deceased tenant) to be done away with.
12. Any of these articles proved to be contrary to the scriptures or God's justice, to be null and void.

This, he thought, was clear and honorable. He left Wittenberg, journeyed down through the insurrection areas, visited the peasant camps, and in Eisleben wrote his *Exhortation to Peace on the Twelve Articles of the Swabian Peasants.* In this, he spoke to the nobles:

> *We need thank no one on earth for this foolish rebellion but you, my lords, and especially you blind bishops, parsons, and monks, for you, even yet hardened, cease not to rage against the holy Gospel, although you know that our cause is right and you cannot controvert it. Besides this, in civil government you do nothing but oppress and tax to maintain your pomp and pride, until the poor common man neither can nor will bear it longer. . . .*
>
> *But the prophets of murder are hostile to you as to me, and they have gone among the people these three years and no one has withstood them but I.*

He also spoke to the peasants:

> *It is my friendly and fraternal prayer, dearest brothers, to be very careful what you do. Believe not all spirits and preachers. . . .*
> *Those who take the sword shall perish by the sword and every soul should be subject to the powers that be, in fear and honor. . . . If the government is bad and intolerable, that is no excuse for riot and insurrection, for to punish evil belongs not to everyone, but to the civil authority which bears the sword. . . . Suffering tyranny is a cross given by God.*

He believed firmly in the peasants' rights. He also believed in the rights of civil government, and he hoped for arbitration. But it was too late for arbitration. Not even Luther's powerful spirit could check the rising fury of the suicidal struggle. He saw with increasing anguish his country broken, its fields destroyed, cloisters and castles burned, all types of violence and anarchy.

His mind dwelt on the progress of his own great cause. He remembered the Diet of Worms and saw the evangelical faith defended by the princes of northern Germany. He knew how terrible and unchecked was the license of Munzer and the radicals. He knew the hopelessness and helplessness of destructive civil war. He preached in town after town and in the camps of peasants, gathered for war, against this violence. He pleaded for peace. He visited the wounded and plague-stricken in the gathering places of the peasant army.

In Nordhauser, Munzer's friends drowned the sound of Luther's voice by ringing church bells. Yet in Eisleben, Stalberg, Erfurt, Wallhausen, Weimar, and many other towns he continued to strive for peace.

Throughout March and April the situation grew worse. Both Frederick and his brother, who was to succeed him as elector of Saxony, were unable to cope with the uprising. The staunch old elector, ever loyal to his subjects, weakened physically while Luther preached against the revolution. Word came to Luther at Weimar that he was wanted at the deathbed, but it was too late; Frederick died, to Luther's deep sorrow. His strong protector was gone, and rioting was everywhere.

In desperation, angered at the continued resistance of the peasants to his counsels of peace, resting on the old Pauline assertion that they must obey the rulers God had set over them, Luther argued for the relief—not for the destruction—of his people. It was a frightful, bitter hour. He was driven to choose between two evils, sensing anarchy in his native land. In May, he wrote the pamphlet *Against the Thievish, Murderous Hordes of Peasants.*

> *In my former book* [Exhortation to Peace], *I dared not judge the peasants, since they asked to be instructed, and Christ says Judge not. But before I could look around they forgot their request and betake themselves to violence—rob, rage, and act like mad dogs, whereby one may see what they had in their false minds, and that their pretense to speak in the name of the Gospel in the Twelve Articles was a simple lie. They do mere devil's work, especially that Satan of Muhlhausen does nothing but rob, murder, and pour out blood.*
>
> *The peasants have deserved death for three reasons: (1) because they have broken their oath of fealty; (2) for rioting and plundering; and (3) for having covered their terrible sins with the name of the Gospel. Wherefore, my lords, free, save, help, and pity the poor people; stab, smite, and slay all ye that can. If you die in battle you could never have a more blessed end, for you die obedient to God's Word in Romans 13, and in the service of love to free your neighbor from the bands of hell and the devil. I implore everyone who can to avoid the peasants as he would the devil himself. I pray God will enlighten them and turn their hearts. But if they do not turn, I wish them no happiness for ever more. . . . Let none think this too hard who considers how intolerable is rebellion.*

His heart was sensitive to peasant and noble alike, but this was an issue of lasting social consequence. He knew the peasant leadership was thoughtless, impractical, without hope of salvation. He was confident in his Saxon princes. He was not deserting the peasant cause; the peasants had never accepted his leadership. His gospel had never undergirded the revolution. The peasants had followed the brutal, insane leadership of men like Munzer— "that Satan of Muhlhausen."

The decisive battle of the revolution was fought near Frankenhausen on May 15. It was terrible. The peasants were equipped with rude weapons—pitchforks, wood axes, scythes, spears, and bows. Across a long, open field they barricaded themselves behind overturned farm wagons and whatever other impediments they could find. Exhorted by Munzer's promises that a miracle would occur, they awaited the attack.

The charge came under the able leadership of the Landgrave Philip of Hesse. Well-armed knights on armored horses, with stout lances and sharp swords, swept all before them. No peasant was alive when the sun went down, except those who had hidden or fled. Thomas Munzer was executed.

Social darkness settled over Germany. A great cause had been miserably led. The peasants felt hurt that the lion of Wittenberg had not fought with them. All over Europe, the conservative class—men who rationalized their own desires—blamed Luther for the rebellion. They could not see that their miserable, selfish actions over the centuries had stirred up the fury. Had the peasants followed Luther's advice, sought their freedom in the inner life and worked it out in heroic civic exertion, they might have achieved great freedom.

Luther was no coward. He stood his ground. He had worked for the peasants. He would be a peasant until his death. But physical violence was not his to command.

Regardless, against his will and by force of circumstance, the church that bears his name moved from that day closer and closer to the princes, with disastrous consequences.

The peasant rebellion brought the last argument necessary to force one other break in the ranks of reform. The humanist group, headed by Erasmus, in the early days had been jubilant over Luther's leadership. Then, as they had seen the movement result in a separation from Rome, one by one they had dropped away, preferring to stay in the atmosphere of the ancient faith.

Erasmus had been so thoroughly connected with the reform movement during its origin that a current proverb quipped: "Erasmus laid the egg and Luther hatched it." Erasmus denied it as historic fact, but he could not deny the close affiliation between his humanism and certain phases of Luther's Reformation.

Refusing to follow Luther away from the Catholic Church, Erasmus felt their paths separating. A man of finesse in the field of criticism and abuse, he resented Luther's coarser method. Erasmus always avoided terrible social upheavals, and he saw the peasant rebellion as being caused partially, at least, by Luther's unbridled attack on pope and emperor.

But their final separation came in the field of thought. The question was the doctrine of free will and predestination. Erasmus published first. He maintained the doctrine of the freedom of the will, at least to the extent that the individual must accept the grace of God by his or her own free will. His pamphlet carried harsh words against Luther, of course.

Luther gave the matter serious consideration, and after a long interval—for him—he published in December 1525 his reply, *On the Slavery of the Will*. Here his mind is shown moving from religious experience into the problems of thought. The history of the church usually shows that the approach from logic leads to the doctrine of free will, and the approach from religious experience, as such, leads to the doctrine of the absolute will of God. So Luther stated in strong, terse sentences that the human will is devoid of all freedom, that in its sinful, normal state, it is ridden by the devil as a human rides a horse. Likewise, in its saved state, the Holy Spirit rides it.

The basis of this belief was a firm conviction in the absolute, total sovereignty of God. To permit free will is to deny the power and glory of the creating mind. This is not a thought in which the humanistic mind can rest content. When it became obvious, after the exchange of several pamphlets between Luther and Erasmus, where Luther stood, most of the humanists left his following.

Poor Philip Melanchthon, overawed both by Luther's affection and by his strength, was unable to protest to the master himself, but all his life he sympathized with the humanist position.

SIX

Luther's boyhood in Mansfield had given him a deep and affectionate appreciation of a Christian home. His friendship with Ursula Cotta in Eisenach had strengthened his belief in the essential piety of family life. But any thoughts of a wife and family had been forced to the background when he had taken the vows in the Erfurt monastery in 1505. There is no authentic record that Luther had loved and courted during his young manhood, although he was happy, free, and often in mixed company throughout his student days.

In the Erfurt monastery his great struggle had not been against sexual desire or indulgence. He tried to purge his mind of thoughts he considered unworthy of his Christian calling. It had been a long, hard fight, but it had not been a fight against action or a fight to control overpowering passion.

During the opening days of the Reformation, he had moved impersonally through the great disputes. At the Wartburg, writing against monastic vows, he was still as a knight on a battlefield, not a criminal in court. His boyhood home was clearly in his mind when he wrote against the vows.

Back in Wittenberg after the Wartburg seclusion, he found that as a result of his attack on monastic vows, men and women were leaving monastery and convent—some probably from nonevangelical motives, but the great majority for honorable reasons. Many fine thinkers before and after him believed the vows were against the commandments of scripture.

Luther defended marriage of the clergy on the grounds that it was the first picture of humanity presented in the opening chapters of Genesis. God had created man and woman and had called for their life together. All through the scriptures, marriage appears as the ideal life. Nowhere in Luther's reading of the Old Testament could he find justification for suspending this relationship. The laws of nature and the laws of God justify the married life.

The Roman Catholic position—a position not shared by the older Greek Catholic Church—based the celibate ideal on the separation of clergy and laity. Luther steadfastly denied this separation, setting forth his famous doctrine of the priesthood of all believers.

So he found only cause for joy when his friends in Wittenberg and other northern German towns, released from their vows by allegiance to the Reformation, began to marry. Philip Melanchthon, Justus Jonas, and other leaders in the movement were established in homes of their own by 1525. Melanchthon, though overawed by the might of Luther, had protested that the cares of married life might inconvenience his studies. But he finally was won over and married the daughter of the chief magistrate of Wittenberg; they lived together for almost half a century in quiet contentment.

The issue took on serious consequences, however, when nuns came to Wittenberg from the convents without economic security, expecting guidance. Among several groups of nuns seeking refuge in Wittenberg came a group of nine in April 1523. Luther wrote to George Spalatin:

> *Nine fugitive nuns, a wretched crowd, have been brought to me by honest citizens of Torgau. I pity them much, but most of all the others who are dying everywhere in such numbers in their cursed and impure celibacy. You ask what I shall do with them? First I shall inform their relatives and ask them to support the girls; if they will not I shall have the girls otherwise provided for. Some of the families have already promised me to take them; for some I shall get husbands if I can. Their names are Magdalene von Staupitz, Elsa von Canitz, Ave Gross, Ave von Schonfeld and her sister Margaret, Laneta von Goltz, Margaret and Catharine Zeschau, and Catharine von Bora. Here are they, who serve Christ, in need of true pity. They have escaped from the cloister in miserable condition. I pray you also do the work of charity and beg some money for me from your rich courtiers, by which I can support the girls for a week or two until their kinsmen or others provide for them. For my Capernaans have no wealth but that of the Word, so that I myself could not find the loan of ten gulden for a poor citizen the other day.*

He must have talked with great interest to Magdalene von Staupitz, thinking of the long affection, now strained, between her brother and himself.

One after another, the nuns in this group were cared for by friends or married to suitors. All except Catharine von Bora.

Catharine had been born in a little village twenty miles south of Leipzig in January 1499. Her mother's early death and her father's remarriage had placed her in a convent school at age five. She had received the veil at sixteen, when Luther was lecturing on Romans in Wittenberg. Two of her aunts were in the same convent.

In the general exodus from the monasteries, some of the young nuns at Nimbschen tried to escape. They were disciplined and guarded. Through a conspiracy with a businessman in Torgau, near Nimbschen, twelve of the nuns, including Catharine, succeeded in making their escape on the night of April 4, 1523. They met in Catharine's room, escaped through the window to the garden, and then climbed the fence to the street. Hidden in empty beer barrels, they rode away from Nimbschen.

Catharine was twenty-four. Arriving in Wittenberg, she settled in the home of a wealthy citizen named Reichenbach, where for two years she helped with the housework. Toward the end of 1523 she fell in love with Jerome Baumgartner, a student guest in Melanchthon's home. They were engaged, and it seemed Catharine's future was secure.

But Baumgartner left Wittenberg and neglected Catharine, neither writing nor visiting. Luther interceded, writing to Baumgartner that he would like to see them married as soon as possible. Baumgartner refused his advice, announcing early the next year his engagement to the daughter of a wealthy family. Catharine understandably was quite hurt.

Not long afterward, a friend of Luther named Dr. Glatz courted Catharine and decided to marry her, but she refused and laughingly said she would marry only Dr. Amsdorf or Dr. Luther. Luther suddenly decided to marry. For a long time his father had been urging him to. Hans, with his strong family feelings, wanted to see Martin established in his own home. Grandchildren would delight the old man.

Luther connected his marriage, as he did everything else, with the gospel. He wrote to a friend that he would marry to "please his father, tease the pope, and spite the devil." This was worded in his normal semihumorous vein, but the justification nevertheless described his state of mind. He loved and honored his father, and marriage would please him. He held the pope as his mortal enemy, and it would further indicate the irreconcilable breach. The devil, he thought, was behind the celibacy law of the Catholic Church, hoping to trick innocent priests into mortal sin; thus marriage would defeat the devil.

So Luther did not marry for youthful, idealistic affection but for the heroic, mature consummation of the evangelical life he now professed. Catharine von Bora held for him no youthful charms; he was forty-two, she twenty-six. His mind and heart, exposed for years to public life, were somewhat toughened. The long years of monastic discipline had given him complete control over himself. This decision was a choice, not an emotion.

Catharine was of a good family. She was capable of the duties that would fall on the wife of Martin Luther. She was strong, rugged, healthy, with vitality and good humor. Luther had seen her many times in Wittenberg, and when he heard she had said she would marry no one but him or Amsdorf, it probably piqued his curiosity just enough to cause him to investigate.

In the spring, he spoke to her of his hopes. It was not easy. They both had known the monastic life. He knew what would be said of them. He reminded her that he was under the death sentence from the pope and emperor.

Luther appreciated her love for Baumgartner, but his heart was gentle and his honor unassailable. They were immediately in harmony, and when once the gentle words were said, the differences in age and temperament dissolved. Catharine held him in high respect. He was the "great doctor," but also her lover.

On the evening of June 13, 1525, they were married in Luther's home by

John Bugenhagen, a faculty colleague. After the quiet wedding, Luther sent invitations for a public announcement and festivities. On June 27, Hans and Margaret Luther and many friends gathered in Wittenberg to celebrate the marriage.

They received a rich silver goblet from the university. Among their other presents were a barrel of Eimbeck beer, good wine, silver, and gold. Archbishop Albert of Mayence sent them twenty gulden in gold; Martin refused it, but Catharine kept it.

They went to live in the rooms Luther had occupied in the Black Cloister. Lucas Cranach came to visit them often, and for his wedding gift he painted their portraits.

Europe went into turmoil with the report of the wedding. The bitter, unscrupulous tongues of Luther's more violent Catholic opponents lashed at him. Rumor was spread that it was a marriage of necessity—but this was too much even for Erasmus, who came to Luther's defense.

Erasmus defended only the rumor of scandal. He thought the wedding itself was a tragedy—or, as he said, the Reformation "started out like a tragedy but ended as all comedies do in a wedding." Rome predicted the Antichrist would result from the union (popular tradition expected the Antichrist to be born from the marriage of a monk and a nun). Erasmus again silenced the enemy with the remark that if such were the case, the Antichrist had had plenty of opportunities before this.

With rumors unchecked and the sources of information so impartial, it was impossible for Luther's marriage to be represented properly throughout Europe. Many a sincere and sensitive Catholic mind Luther had won earlier now were lost by what appeared to be an improper relationship. People could not forget Martin and Catharine each had taken in youth what were supposed to be irrevocable vows. Many did not share the power of the evangelical faith that had been, for Martin and Catharine, sufficient to break obedience to the vows.

Luther married with a clear expectation of the difficulties to follow. He was not prepared for the strange, quiet happiness that slowly came into his life as their home settled into a normal routine. Catharine brought to him a strong and willing service, a loyal and sympathetic heart, and a keen and delightful sense of humor. She was increasingly a source of joy and peace to him for the rest of his life.

The highest tribute he ever paid her was when he spoke one day of St. Paul's Epistle to the Romans: "This is my Catharine von Bora." In the Epistle to the Romans, Luther's heart first had found its religious peace.

THE MILLS OF GOD
1526–1545

In 1526, Luther's life settled into three types of activity. First, he had to carry on the great battle with the papacy and the state. Simultaneously he must construct the Evangelical Church in all its branches. Third, his home began increasingly to call for his attention and strength.

In the first of these fields he was technically an outlaw and had to be constantly on the lookout not to step unwarily into traps set for his capture. The Edict of Worms was supposed to be in force. Under its provisions, any German citizen was obligated to deliver Luther alive or dead to the authorities. His friends were careful not to allow strangers around his home or the university, fearing an assassin deeply loyal to the ancient church would take his life. Luther was unable to appear in person at any of the great meetings held during the fifteen years after Worms to try to heal the schism. The chief leader of the reforming party was forced to remain in seclusion. Attempts at reconciliation must be carried on through his subordinates, chiefly Melanchthon and Bucer.

The emperor was still pressing for clarification of the Lutheran issue. The first important diet after Worms was held in the German town of Speyer in 1526. Charles V was unable to attend because of the constant turmoil in European politics. The diet met at Speyer under the presidency of Charles's brother Ferdinand.

After a long debate, the Catholic party, headed by Ferdinand, insisted on the execution of the Edict of Worms. The Protestant party, headed by the Saxon elector, steadfastly refused to carry it out. They agreed that "each state should so live as it hoped to answer for its conduct to God and the emperor."

This was a victory for the reforming units of the empire. They were permitted to return to their states and continue their evangelical work.

At home in Wittenberg, Martin anxiously watched the work of Catharine, whom he called Katie. Watching her, he knew the beauty of the stirring life that had brought the Magnificat to Mary's lips. Katie sat by Martin's side through many hours of reading and study, asking questions whenever the opportunity arose. Early in June they knew the wait would be over soon. Great was the rejoicing when, on June 6, Martin saw his firstborn son.

Luther preached and taught daily, and his health began to show signs of weakening under the long strain. As early as 1521, in the Wartburg he had experienced severe digestive disturbances. Throughout the month of March 1523, he had been afflicted with constant nausea and vomiting. Nervous headaches began the same month, never to leave him for the rest of his life. On July 6, 1527, rising from the dinner table, he fainted before he could reach his room. For days he was seriously ill.

Before his recovery was complete, the plague came again to Wittenberg. With its arrival the university moved to Jena—but not Luther, who never fled the plague. Catharine was carrying their second child. Little Hans, now more than a year old, fell desperately ill and for eleven days could neither eat nor drink.

Martin, weak and exhausted, summoned the strength to bear the burdens of home and church. One of his closest friends, who had stayed with him during the exodus to Jena, lost his wife to the plague, and Luther feared for Catharine's life.

It was a time of deep misery and uncertainty. Death was all around him. The great authorities of his childhood, church and state, were battling each other. Yet Luther found strength through his faith in God. Poring over the Forty-Sixth Psalm, he knew the strength of the castle walls that crowned his Teutonic hills. He knew how, in the hour of battle, his people were safe behind these majestic fortresses. So he was safe in God, when death and destruction were all around him. He remembered how secure he had been from violence in the castle above Eisenach. The devil was behind these unhappy movements in the world, but God was his protection from the devil.

From this, his hour of deep distress, came his song of triumph:

> *A mighty fortress is our God,*
> *A bulwark never failing;*
> *Our helper he, amid the flood*
> *Of mortal ills prevailing.*
> *For still our ancient foe*
> *Doth seek to work us woe,*
> *His craft and power are great;*
> *And armed with cruel hate*
> *On earth is not his equal.*
>
> *And though this world with devils filled*
> *Should threaten to undo us;*
> *We will not fear, for God hath willed*
> *His truth to triumph through us.*
> *The prince of darkness grim,*
> *We tremble not for him*
> *His rage we can endure,*
> *For lo, his doom is sure,*
> *One little word shall fell him.*

That word above all earthly powers,
No thanks to them abideth;
The spirit and the gift are ours
Through him who with us sideth.
Let goods and kindred go,
This mortal life also;
The body they may kill—
God's truth abideth still,
His kingdom is forever.

He also wrote the cadenced, solemn music for this, his marching song. While he hummed the melody into form, he watched Hans recover and rejoiced to see him strong again. Catharine weathered the plague and entered the last few weeks of her pregnancy in fair health.

A daughter was born December 10. They named the little girl Elizabeth. But she was not strong, and before a year had passed, they buried her.

Luther, writing to a friend just after Elizabeth's death, said, "Little Hans thanks you for the rattle of which he is inordinately proud. . . . My little daughter, Elizabeth, is dead. She has left me wonderfully sick at heart and almost womanish, I am so moved by pity for her. I could never have believed how a father's heart could soften for his child."

As though his work was not enough, he turned his attention to the condition of the parishes in the section of Germany that now was accepting reform. With Melanchthon and others, he journeyed through the Saxon province, visiting town after town, examining each one's educational system and church practices. This was tremendously hard work, with rough travel, uncomfortable lodging, and irregular food. But Luther felt keenly the tremendous need for education if his new church was to support itself.

On his return from the trip he called attention to the miserable state of instruction throughout the province. He insisted that pastors thoroughly reconstruct this phase of their work, and he set himself to writing a catechism. This work was completed two years after his journey through the province. In it is the full, accurate expression of Luther's entire belief.

The Smaller Catechism, which he designed for family and school use, set in gentle, quiet form all the familiar doctrines of historic Christianity. The Ten Commandments were to be memorized to create a sense of sin; the Apostles' Creed was to be memorized for the message of the great redemption from sin; and the Lord's Prayer was to be memorized for the constant spiritual sustenance it could bring to the believer.

When Luther handled this massive theology in catechetical form, his mind and heart sympathized with the little boys and girls who would have to learn it.

His great gift for practical application was never put to better advantage than when he explained the doctrines of the church to little children.

Charles V returned his attention to his rebellious Germany. In 1529 he called for a second diet to meet at Speyer. Controlling this diet in person, the emperor forced the delegates to annul the action of 1526. He succeeded in obtaining a majority vote to prohibit reformed worship.

In response, on April 19 the delegates from the Lutheran areas presented a formal protest to the diet. They stated that by the law of the empire, a majority decision of the present diet could not rescind the unanimous decision of the previous diet, and they would stand on the action of 1526. The representatives of Saxony, Brandenburg, Brunswick, Hesse, Anhalt, and fourteen of the free cities signed this protest.

From this point on, the party of non-Catholic adherents was called Protestant. Some of the signers of the protest were not supporters of Luther, so the term Protestant carried a broad connotation.

The emperor was unable to heal the breach, and the diet closed with the two parties well-defined. Receiving news of the diet at home in Wittenberg, Luther saw a political party grow out of his religious reform and he was unable to control it.

His family life continued normally, despite political tensions. On May 4, almost a year after her little sister had died, Magdalene Luther was born. She was named for Magdalene von Bora, Catharine's aunt, who had been a companion in the Nimbschen convent and who was now a well-loved member of the Wittenberg home.

The best effort Charles V made to reconcile the differences in Germany was at Augsburg in 1530. Thomas Lindsay in his *History of the Reformation* described Charles's entrance into Augsburg:

> The summons to the Diet, commanding the Electors, princes, and all the Estates of the Empire to meet at Augsburg on the 8th of April, 1530, had been issued when Charles was at Bologna. No threats marred the invitation. The Emperor announced that he meant to leave all past errors to the judgment of the Saviour; that he wished to give a charitable hearing to every man's opinions, thoughts, and ideas; and that his only desire was to secure that all might live under the one Christ, in one Commonwealth, one Church, and one Unity. He left Innsbruck on the 6th of June, and, traveling slowly, reached the bridge on the Lech, a little distance from Augsburg, on the evening of the 15th. The procession—one of the most gorgeous Germany had ever seen—was marshaled for the ceremonial entry into the town. The retinues of the Electors

were all in their appropriate colors and arms—Saxony, by ancient prescriptive right, leading the van. Then came the Emperor alone, a baldachino carried over his head. He had wished the nuncio and his brother to ride beside him under the canopy; but the Germans would not suffer it; no Pope's representative was to be permitted to ride shoulder to shoulder with the head of the German Empire entering the most important of his imperial cities.

At the gates of the town, the clergy, singing the "Advenisti desiderabilis," met the procession. All—Emperor, clergy, princes, and their retinues—entered the cathedral. The *Te Deum* was sung, and the Emperor received the benediction. Then the procession reformed, and accompanied Charles to his lodgings in the Bishop's Palace.

In response to this summons the Saxon elector, in company with Luther and Melanchthon, had waited at Coburg, the southernmost town in the province, for word of safe conduct from the emperor. When it arrived, it omitted Luther's name. While the elector, Melanchthon, and the rest of the company journeyed on to Augsburg, Luther took refuge in the great castle overlooking the town of Coburg. He remained there from April 25 through October 4.

These were bitter days for him. He was sick and discouraged, but he kept himself busy. He finished the translation of Jeremiah, began Ezekiel, and completed all the lesser prophets. He published some of Aesop's fables in German and wrote twelve other complete works. There are 123 letters preserved from these months in the Coburg castle.

All the while, he received messages from Augsburg, where the diet was in session. They told how the evangelical princes refused to march in the Corpus Christi procession through the streets of Augsburg. They told how stalwart George of Brandenburg had told the emperor—whom he loved—that rather than deny his God he would kneel then and allow his head to be cut off. They told how steadfastly his friends were maintaining the faith.

But Luther grew anxious when they brought him news that Melanchthon was drawing up the great confession. Melanchthon was a bit too conciliatory for Luther, who always feared the younger man would concede too much to the papists. The fear was well grounded, for Melanchthon was eager, above all else, to heal the break.

Terrific loyalties conflicted in Melanchthon's mind. The nephew of Reuchlin could not understand the necessity of the departure; the friend of Erasmus still honored the mother church. But these loyalties were overpowered by his tremendous affection for and belief in Martin Luther.

Now, in Augsburg, he did his best to phrase a conciliatory statement. Christian Bayer, chancellor of Saxony, read the confession of the Protestant princes written by Melanchthon in the diet on July 25.

It was a clear, concise statement containing two sections. In the first it set forth the religious views of the Lutherans. In the second it listed the abuses that must be corrected. It was theologically conservative. Luther rejoiced when word came that they had been permitted to read their confession before the diet, but his rejoicing was short-lived, for Charles asked a group of papal theologians, headed by Eck of Ingolstadt, to prepare an answer.

Here is seen once again the deadly fault in the imperial policy. Eck was a bitter man. Five times his report was returned to the committee for softening and revision. When it finally was brought forth, it still was too harsh for the Lutherans.

John, the elector of Saxony, called "the Steadfast" by his people, refused to remain at the diet under such conditions and departed after a difficult scene with the emperor. Charles V and John admired each other, and the elector honored his emperor with the ancient civil loyalty of the Germans. But this was a case where his emperor required the surrender of his conscience. He told Charles he must stand by his faith.

Charles's final words to him were: "Uncle, uncle, I did not expect this from you." Tears were in the elector's eyes as he turned his back on his sovereign and started northward.

Meanwhile, Luther waited anxiously. During a week of sickness a messenger arrived from Wittenberg, bringing little gifts from Catharine and the family, including a picture painted by Lucas Cranach of the one-year-old Magdalene. Luther held it lovingly in his hands and remarked to his secretary, "She is so dark. She does not look like Magdalene. She has the mouth of Hans." He hung it on the wall in his study, where it was a constant source of joy.

Luther was unhappy, separated from his family, and he corresponded faithfully. His son Hans was now four. While his heart was entranced and his mind happy with meditations on the life of little Hans, John Reinicke, the friend of his school days, brought him news that old Hans was dead. Luther had left Wittenberg for Coburg, knowing of his father's sickness. He had written that he was unable to come to Mansfield and had gently recalled to Hans, in his last letter, the faith in which they lived. The pastor at Mansfield read the letter to Hans and asked if he believed this faith. Hans replied, "Aye, he would be a knave who didn't."

It had been thirty-three years since the two boys, John and Martin, had left their homes in Mansfield for school in Magdeburg. Luther could picture Hans now as he had been in those days long past. He heard, as if in a dream, Reinicke telling him how old Hans had died.

Gone. Life over. His father's spirit at the last great judgment.

Luther rose, took his psalter, and entered the study, where he stayed for almost two days in unnerved sorrowing. Forty-seven years before Hans had carried his little boy to Bartholomew Rennebecher for baptism, and now the little boy's heart, welded to his father through years of affection, was broken.

But prayer and faith again were his sources of strength. Near the close of the second day he regained control and picked up the routine of life.

A few days later his friend Wenzel Link opened a letter from Luther and read:

> *Now I am sorrowful, for I have received tidings of the death of my father, that dear and gentle old man whose name I bear, and although I am glad for his sake that his journey to Christ was so easy and pious and that, freed from the monsters of this world, he rests in peace, nevertheless my heart is moved to sorrow. For under God, I owe my life and bringing up to him.*

The Diet of Augsburg closed unhappily for the Protestants. Luther returned to Wittenberg in the fall, knowing that imperial pressure would be more severe than ever. From now on it would be a battle of political alliances, with Luther more and more in the background. He watched through the succeeding years the organization of the Schmaldkalden League for the protection of the reformed territory, with Hesse and Saxony at its head. He heard of the riotings in Munster and the murderous overthrow of the Anabaptists gathered there. With the death of Clement VII and the election of Paul III, he knew a strong and able pope now controlled the Catholic Church. He watched with interest the long game of political chess between Henry VIII and the papacy, climaxing in the severance of England's loyalty to Rome.

In 1539 he read a book by the young John Calvin and wrote him a letter of commendation, but he did not sense that under Calvin's control the Swiss city of Geneva would rise to a prominence equal that of Wittenberg. He heard of the formation of the Society of Jesus, but he did not know that behind the society was a spirit as intense and devoted as his own, and superior in organizational ability. He was relieved to learn of the defeat and retreat of the Turks from Vienna; he trembled, with the rest of Europe, at the narrow escape from control by Suliman the Magnificent. He mourned the death of the Elector John but rejoiced that his successor, John Frederick, was a staunch Protestant.

Throughout this troubled time, he was seldom called into actual leadership. He journeyed in 1537 to Schmaldkalden, where he struggled to draw up a confession of faith, emphasizing the differences between Protestants and Catholics more strongly than the "Augsburg Confession." Many other Protestant leaders were there, as was the papal nuncio, Vergerio, trying to institute conciliatory proceedings. Luther's health broke; he suffered the severely painful affliction known as "the stone." He longed again for his wife and children, fearing he would never see them again.

John Frederick ordered him carried home, and sent word ahead for Catharine von Bora to meet him on the way. Luther traveled in John Frederick's own carriage; the jolting caused such agony they could take him only two miles the first day.

Relief came during the night. The messenger who rode back to Schmaldkalden with news of Luther's recovery was so happy he stopped by the papal legate's window and shouted "Luther lives!" before he took the word to John Frederick.

Though returned to health, Luther felt rather uncertain of life. On the way home, at Gotha, he wrote his first will, beginning: "God be praised, I know I did right to attack the papacy which injures the cause of God, Christ, and the Gospel!" It closed: "Now I commend my soul into the hands of my Lord Jesus Christ whom I have preached and confessed on earth."

He returned to Wittenberg to continue his labors, but life was increasingly painful. The severity of his headaches, severe rheumatism, the recurring digestive disturbances, neuritis in his chest, and a dizzying disease in the middle ear all plagued him.

In 1539 Duke George of Saxony, the fairest and staunchest Catholic defender, died. His successor was an admirer of Luther and an adherent to the reformed faith. Luther rode from Wittenberg to Leipzig to attend the installation. Once again he stood in the hall of the ducal palace where, twenty years before, he had debated with John Eck. He had a deep, quiet sense of victory now as he stood to proclaim, in this room, the evangelical faith. His appearance at Leipzig in 1519 had been the prelude to a long, stern warfare. The warfare was not over, but already he could see lasting consequences, and he was glad to add Leipzig to his inheritance.

The inner life of the Lutheran Church developed steadily. A man of deep historic piety, Luther constantly struggled to impart this feeling to his people. The translation of the Bible, begun at the Wartburg and continuing through the disastrous days of 1530, finally was completed in 1534. The last edition to have his personal supervision came in 1545.

In his translation work, Luther struggled to create a version understandable by all Germans. He succeeded far beyond his fondest dreams. So powerful was his work that it practically created a new German language. Since the Bible was being read feverishly by hundreds of thousands of Germans, the imprint of Luther's style and phrasing was permanent.

He also brought into the German language the great Catholic services in which he had been raised. The Mass, the central point in Lutheran worship, was set in German under Luther's personal editorship. He produced a series of noble hymns for public worship.

During the bitter days after the Diet at Worms, prosecution of the edict, in July 1523, had raised the first Lutheran martyrs in the Netherlands. Luther was tremendously disturbed to hear that two young men, affirming their confidence in the new faith, had been put to death. He would have stood in their places. Unable to do so, he celebrated their confession by writing his first hymn, a powerful, militant appeal beginning "Ein neues Lied wir heben an."* They were indeed uplifting a new song. Steadily, Luther added hymn after hymn to his church's worship. They were bold, martial, triumphant expressions, addressing the doctrine of redemption and revolving around the blood and sacrifice of Jesus. Immersed in the ancient psalms and their adaptation in Catholic hymnody, he brought these, too, to the German tongue. The One Hundred Thirtieth Psalm became "Aus tiefer Not schrei ich zu dir," the Twelfth "Ach Gott, vom Himmel sieh darein." The Lutherans sang "Te Deum laudamus" as "Herr Gott, dich loben wir." The "Veni Creator Spiritus" uplifted them in "Kom, Gott, Schöpfer, heiliger Geist."

He sensitively furnished both music and words for the rhythm of his movement. Loveliest of all his hymns, perhaps, are those he wrote for his children. Many were the evenings in the Luther home when father, mother, and children sang their Christian faith. Luther appreciated the gentleness, beauty, and simplicity of a child's understanding. When the family entered the Christmas season together, he told the story of Bethlehem so his sons and daughters could understand it. For them he wrote "Von Himmel kam der Engel Schaar, Vom Himmel hoch da komin ich her"* and our familiar "Away in a Manger, No Crib for His Bed." The student who had sung lustily in the streets of Magdeburg and Eisenach now sang from new experiences the gentle songs of Christian childhood. He who had carried his lute on the all-important journey to the Imperial Diet, singing and playing in the evenings as he rested at the inns along the way, now applied to music the joyous, triumphant strain of his Christian life.

Many a heart unable to fathom the depths of Melanchthon's theology found rich comfort in the songs from Luther's soul. Year after year as he grew older, he could hear his German people marching victoriously to the rhythm of his music. His religious life expressed itself between the cradle songs of Jesus and the strong fortress of God.

Katie von Bora had plenty to do during these hectic years. Managing a household with insufficient finances is hard enough, but she had many other tasks. Luther's salary did not cover his needs, even though he received many

---

*German for "a new song we sing"
*German for "The angels came from heaven, from heaven I came from"

presents, including a pension from the king of Denmark for services rendered to the church. There were always friends and guests to be given lodging and food. Over the years eleven orphaned relatives found support in Luther's home.

Luther was thoroughly unsystematic in the use of money. He never sold a book or manuscript in his life, steadfastly refusing, although printers offered him hundreds of dollars a year for his written works. These, he said, were the gifts of God and were not for sale. Nor did he receive a salary for teaching. He was supported after the break from the monastic order by an annual gift from the elector, which was increased steadily until it reached 400 gulden. But even with this he wrote a pathetic letter one day to a friend who had asked him for money, saying there was no money to be had—they even were pawning their wedding gifts.

Lucas Cranach, ever a friend in need, loaned him money steadily. The family had cattle, a large garden, and a fishpond to support themselves. They owned a farm a few miles from Wittenberg on the road to Zulsdorf, which Katie managed.

They had no privacy. Luther's tremendous reputation and the insatiable curiosity of his followers kept the family constantly in the public eye.

But underneath the stress of this visible life was a very quiet, gentle current. Katie and Martin loved each other more dearly as the years passed. Their conversation around the home and their correspondence reveals a steady banter that revealed a very happy affection. She never lost her high respect for him—but neither did she surrender her independent will. Luther often laughingly told Melanchthon and other friends that he had merely exchanged one authority for another when he married. Katie expressed her opinions, even with guests present. Luther called these expressions "sermons." He often told her he wished she would preface the sermon with a prayer; he knew she would pray so long she would never get to the sermon!

Luther was particularly happy with the smallest children in the house. He constantly held his youngest child in his lap, talking and playing. Having lost one daughter in infancy, Luther watched the growth of his second daughter, Magdalene, with tender, sensitive affection. He knew the heights of a father's love as she grew nearer and dearer to him. When Magdalene became seriously ill in September 1542, he entered the depths of human sorrow. One who was with him through this trial wrote:

> As his daughter lay very ill, Dr. Luther said: "I love her very much, but, dear God, if it be thy will to take her, I submit to thee." Then he said to her as she lay in bed: "Magdalene, my dear little daughter, would you like to stay here with your father, or would you willingly go to your Father yonder?" She answered: "Darling father, as God wills." Then said he:

"Dearest child, the spirit is willing but the flesh is weak." Then he turned away and said: "I love her very much; if my flesh is so strong, what can my spirit do? God has given no bishop so great a gift in a thousand years as he has given me in her. I am angry with myself that I cannot rejoice in heart and be thoughtful as I ought."

Now as Magdalene lay in the agony of death, her father fell down before the bed on his knees and wept bitterly and prayed that God might free her. Then she departed and fell asleep in her father's arms.

As they laid her in the coffin he said: "Darling Lena, you will rise and shine like a star, yea, like the sun. . . . I am happy in spirit, but the flesh is sorrowful and will not be content; the parting grieves me beyond measure. . . . I have sent a saint to heaven."

Justus Jonas, always close to Luther's mind when big events occurred, received the following letter from Luther a few days after Magdalene died:

I believe that you have already heard that my dearest daughter Magdalene has been reborn to the eternal kingdom of Christ; and although my wife and I ought to give thanks and rejoice at such a happy pilgrimage and blessed end, whereby she has escaped the power of the flesh, the world, the Turk, and the devil, yet so strong is natural affection that we must sob and groan in heart under the oppression of killing grief. . . . Would that I and all mine might have such a death, or rather such a life. She was, as you know, of a sweet, gentle, and loving nature.

The constant pressure of twenty-five years of public life was breaking Luther. He grew touchy and sensitive. He felt Wittenberg no longer honored him properly and no one paid any attention to him. The villagers disregarded the stern ethics he preached.

In the late spring of 1545 he traveled to the town of Zeitz, south of Leipzig. His son Hans was with him. Luther decided to stay away forever from the town he thought was repudiating his leadership. He sent this letter to his wife:

Dear Katie:

. . .I should like to arrange not to go back to Wittenberg. My heart has grown cold so that I do not care to live there, but wish you would sell the garden and the farm, house and buildings, except the big house, which I should like to give back to my gracious lord. Your best course would be to go to Zulsdorf; while I am alive you could improve the little estate with my salary, for I hope my gracious lord will let my salary go on at least

during this last year of my life. After my death the four elements will not suffer you to live at Wittenberg, therefore it will be better for you to do during my lifetime what you will have to do after my death. It looks as if Wittenberg and her government would catch—not St. Vitus' dance or St. John's dance, but the beggars' dance and Beelzebub's dance; the women and girls have begun to go bare before and behind and there is no one to punish or correct them and God's word is mocked. Away with this Sodom. . . . Day after tomorrow I am going to Merseburg, for Prince George has pressed me to do so. I will wander around here and eat the bread of charity before I will martyr and soil my poor old last days with the disordered life of Wittenberg, where I lose all my bitter, costly work. You may tell Melanchthon and Bugenhagen this, if you will, and ask the latter to give Wittenberg my blessing, for I can no longer bear its wrath and displeasure. God bless you. Amen.

Martin Luther

Wittenberg was not to let such a tragedy occur and sent Melanchthon, Bugenhagen, the burgomaster, and the elector's physician to bring Luther home. They met him in Merseburg, paid him due honor, and brought him home in triumph.

The evening of life had come.

SEVEN

On November 10, 1545, there was a birthday celebration in the Luther home. Old friends came to honor the man they loved.

Katie, as ever, was efficient and thoughtful. Hans, home from school, was now nineteen. Martin was fourteen, Paul twelve, and Margaret ten. Song and laughter rang through the rooms.

But Luther's heart did not rejoice. The infirmities of age weighed heavily on him. Like a stranger in a foreign land, he longed for the sweetness of death. He wanted peace and quiet, but the world would not permit it. Now, certain of approaching death, he lived in two worlds. In the present world he loved and enjoyed Katie, children, and friends. But in the world of the spirit he could almost commune with his Lord and Master. He felt a strong sense of companionship with the dead—with his father Hans and mother Margaret, Elizabeth, and Magdalene.

He looked at Katie across the room filled with friends. She was older and stouter now. Time had taken a heavy toll from her. He thought of the iron will that had carried her and her family through many hard hours. He saw her hands, roughened by the work of house and farm. In his heart he thanked God for her life and love.

Her eye caught his, and quickly she was at his side to touch his hand and ask his slightest wish. Friends departed and night settled over them.

It had been sixty-two years since the sun had gone down on his parents with their new child. Sixty-two years! He had been an instrument in the hands of God, he believed. He had followed his conscience through all circumstances. His mind had been set staunchly in the written word of God, but his conscience rather than the Word had been his guide.

God had been merciful. Tomorrow he would finish his present lecture series and then be through. Tired and anxious for his homegoing, he slept.

The next day he lectured on the book of Genesis. He closed his notebook, looked up gently, and quietly told his students, "This is dear Genesis. God grant that others do better with it after me. I am weak. Pray God to grant me a good, blessed hour."

He left the lecture hall around which, for one mighty hour, he had held the swinging, whirling universe. Dear Genesis! Yes, dear indeed. In the beginning God created. . . . Let there be light. . .and. . .it was good. . .male and female created he them. . .the serpent. . .the seed of the woman. . .in the sweat of thy brow. . .in travail!

His race was not yet run. In his childhood home of Mansfield, Counts

Albert and Gebhardt were in bitter dispute, and only Luther could solve the difficulty. He left for Mansfield in a cold December storm. He spent Christmas there, but his heart was in Wittenberg with Katie. Then Melanchthon's health broke, and Luther returned home in January with the dispute unsettled.

On January 23 he left home again. Katie begged him not to go because of his health and the bitter weather. But Luther had known only duty for too long. He could not spare himself. In tears wrung from honest love and a presentiment of death, he kissed his "Lord Katie" good-bye.

His sons Hans, Martin, and Paul went with him, as did his friend John Aurifaber. Two days' journey brought them to Halle, where they were delayed by a flooding of the Saale River. He wrote lovingly to Katie, joking that a lady of the Anabaptist persuasion detained them.

Crossing the flood, they reached Eisleben, where he wrote home, describing the journey:

> *I wish you grace and peace in Christ, and send you my poor, old, infirm love. Dear Katie, I was weak on the road to Eisleben, but that was my own fault. . . . As I drove through the village such a cold wind blew from behind through my cap on my head that it was like to turn my brain to ice. This may have helped my vertigo, but now, thank God, I am so well that I am sore tempted by fair women and care not how gallant I am. . . .*
>
> *Your little sons went to Mansfield day before yesterday, after they had humbly begged Jackanapes to take them. I don't know what they are doing; if it were cold they might freeze, but as it is warm they may do or suffer what they like. God bless you with all my household and remember me to my table companions.*

The negotiations continued in Eisleben. Luther hoped to solve the problem through brotherly love and affection, but the lawyers, he said, made it difficult.

His boys were with relatives in Mansfield. His mind was in Wittenberg. On February 14 he wrote again:

> *Dear Katie, we hope to come home this week if God wills. God has shown great grace to the lords, who have been reconciled in all but two or three points. It still remains to make the brothers Count Albert and Count Gebhardt real brothers; this I shall undertake today and shall invite both to visit me, that they may see each other, for hitherto they have not spoken, but have embittered each other by writing. But the young*

lords and the young ladies, too, are happy and make parties for fools' bells and skating, and have masquerades, and are all very jolly, even Count Gebhardt's son. So we see that God hears prayers.

I send you the trout given me by the Countess Albert. She is heartily happy at this union.

Your little sons are still at Mansfield. James Luther will take care of them. We eat and drink like lords here and they wait on us so well—too well, indeed, for they might make us forget you at Wittenberg. Moreover I am no more troubled with the stone. Jonas' leg has become right bad; it is looser on the shin-bone, but God will help it.

You may tell Melanchthon and Bugenhagen and Cruciger everything.

A report has reached here that Dr. Martin Luther has left for Leipzig or Magdeburg. Such tales are invented by those silly wiseacres, your countrymen. Some say the Emperor is thirty miles from here, at Soest in Westphalia; some say that the French and the Landgrave of Hesse are raising troops. Let them say and sing; we will wait on God.

Three days later the counts signed an agreement settling the dispute. Luther's work was done. The boys came from Mansfield, and preparations for the homeward journey were made.

But Luther was sick. Faintness would not leave so easily now. He felt a tightness in the chest. Hot towels and brandy helped, and he tried to sleep. But the ailment kept its grip on him. He could not rest quietly. At two o'clock in the morning of the eighteenth, he roused his friends and lay down on a couch. Jonas, ever faithful, was there. Colius, the Mansfield preacher, had come down. One of the countesses of Mansfield, also staying at the inn, came to the room. Martin and Paul stood by their father's side.

The agony increased. Terrific pain seized him—but he was accustomed to pain. He called on Jonas and Colius to pray for the great battle within the church. Then phrases of scripture were heard from his lips. Three times he repeated, "God so loved the world, that he gave his only begotten Son, that whosoever believeth in him should not perish, but have everlasting life." His boys heard him whisper, "Father, into thy hands I commend my spirit."

The pain would not subside. Jonas asked, "Dear Father, will you stand by Christ and the doctrine you have preached?"

Stand by Christ and the doctrine? In the hour of death? Luther's mighty will held off the coming stroke, and he answered, "Yes."

In the final moment, his halting voice whispered the glorious message, "Who. . .hath. . .my word. . .shall. . . not. . .see. . .death. . . ."

Then darkness.

His body was taken back over the beloved road to Wittenberg. On February

22 they buried him in the cathedral church. Melanchthon preached.

Katie gathered her children around her that night in the Black Cloister. Later, she wrote to Christina von Bora:

> *Grace and peace in God the Father of our Lord Jesus Christ. Kind, dear sister! I can easily believe that you have hearty sympathy with me and my poor children. Who would not be sorrowful and mourn for so noble a man as was my dear lord, who much served not only one city, or a single land, but the whole world? Truly, I am so distressed that I cannot tell my great heart sorrow to anyone, and neither can I sleep. If I had had a principality, or an empire, it would never have cost me so much pain to lose them as I have now that our Lord God has taken from me, and not from me only, but from the whole world, this dear and precious man. . . .*

EIGHT

The world would not let Luther rest. He had set a mighty force in motion, and long before his physical death, that power had transcended his limitations to make its way in the land.

Charles V continued to strive to bring his domains under control. At the head of a victorious army he entered Wittenberg in 1547, one year after Luther's death. Catharine, fleeing the emperor's approach, was thrown from her cart on the rough roads. She never recovered from her injuries and shock.

In the castle church, Charles stood before Luther's grave. It had been twenty-six years since they had seen each other at Worms. Then, Charles had not been much impressed by the strong, intense Augustinian—but now half his empire was enthralled by the monk's high ideal! Medieval practice tempted Charles to dig up and scatter the heretic's dust, as Wycliffe's ashes had been scattered. But Charles placed honor above such an action. He is reported to have said, "I make war on the living, not on the dead."

Luther's spirit was living indeed, and the warfare continued. Men with Luther's vision carried on the battle for freedom. Luther had risen to protest abuse within a system. The defenders, refusing to consider correction, had brought the attack directly against the system itself. Luther understood the abuse to be within the Roman—not the Catholic—aspect of the system. But many had been too long accustomed to Roman authority to follow the new leadership easily.

The rising tide of nationalism was ready for Luther's attack on Rome's power. Yet Luther was not really a nationalist. He would rather have surrendered all of Germany than seen the creation of a German church that was not Catholic and Christian, with an evangelical emphasis. The nationalistic backing furnished Luther with necessary temporal support in his revolt from Rome, but it was in no way integral to the religious issue. A state church—with the implication that the state dictates the thought of corporate or individual Christians—was unthinkable in Luther's doctrine. He would have opposed Hitler as decisively as he would have Lenin.

The differences between the Roman and Lutheran concepts of Catholicism were disputed in political warfare. The battle raged over central Europe for all too long. The pure religious issue was lost early. The long struggle became a confusion of dynastic, national, economic, and religious issues.

A pitiful attempt at peace in Augsburg in 1555 brought only a breathing period. The warring parties agreed that the prince of any given political unit should decide the form of religion his subjects should adopt. If they disapproved the prince's choice, the subjects could move to another province. This freedom to move was an advance over the Roman Catholic policy, where one could move only to the next world—via the stake—if he or she disagreed with Roman dogma.

Events came swiftly following the break up of the medieval world. Luther could claim for his own Scotland, Denmark, Scandinavia, northern Germany, northern Switzerland, the Protestant units in France and the Netherlands (Huguenots), and smaller groups in England. England proper was not his.

Ulrich Zwingli's followers in Switzerland sustained their independence from Wittenberg in thought and practice, but not their freedom from Rome. That victory was Luther's alone.

John Calvin, the leader in France, moved into the evangelical faith under direct Lutheran influence while being taught New Testament Greek by a German of Wittenberg sympathies. Calvin then combined his gifts of clarity, precision, indomitable will, and rich humility with the Lutherans' scriptural authority to construct the powerful Puritan theology.

At the feet of Calvin, the Scottish leader John Knox learned the inner strength of the independent evangelical faith. In Edinburgh he built the foundations of the stern and lovely piety of the Presbyterians.

But all these movements, as well as Lutheranism, soon moved far from the basic strength of Martin Luther. They defined faith and doctrinal standards so strictly that the ancient freedom of Christians again was denied.

Through the years, the spirit of the great Saxon has touched his people. Pietist and Moravian both have held it for a moment. In England, when the common people heard the evangelical message preached by the Wesleys and Whitefield, it was the voice of Luther. His commentaries on Romans and Galatians were the cradles of the Wesleyan life.

And what of his great enemy? The Roman church, whose historic Catholicism was the center and soul of Luther's life, should number him among the saints. In an hour when everything Catholicism holds dear was disappearing from the church's leadership, he stood valiantly for Catholic tradition. Julius II, Leo X, and Clement VII had brought to the verge of ruin the authority of the church in thought and practice. Cardinal Cajetan at Augsburg, John Eck at Leipzig, the cardinal archbishop of Mayence, Aleander at Worms—all were willing to sacrifice God and the human soul to Roman power. Luther fought, against his Catholic will but driven by spiritual honesty, for the Catholic faith. The present Roman church is built in large measure on the results of his magnificent, lifelong campaign.

The power for this rebuilding came from within the older church itself. Ignatius Loyola and the Society of Jesus furnished that leadership. But the superb Loyola would have been burned, excommunicated, outlawed, and gone the way of the dove in the power of serpents, had not Luther brought down the Renaissance papacy.

It is foolish to say Luther was the first "modern" man, or to date the so-called modern world from the Diet of Worms in 1521. It is equally foolish to claim for Luther the consummation of Christian thought. He cannot furnish us with leadership in all things. Gone forever is the world in which he was born and worked. He was studying Paul's epistles while the Americas were being mapped. The Americas are mapped now—but Paul's letters still call for study.

Devils, witches, and the world of superstition were his native environment; he is not to be followed as a critic of folklore. But the devils in character were his chief antagonists, and these remain with us. In the Wartburg he may have thrown an inkwell at an imagined devil, but in the Wartburg he also translated the New Testament—an epoch-making, language-creating service.

He was never a fundamentalist, in the word's modern connotation. The Bible was to him the glorious and eternally true Word of God, but he exercised a sovereign freedom in interpreting it. Neither was he a humanist; the all-creating, all-sustaining, all-merciful grace of God excludes a humanistic basis for theology.

Luther was a man of his own day. Rough, strong, boisterous, he knew he and his Germans were unlettered and uncultured. But he knew also the sweet gentleness of friendship and affection, the strong attachment to hill and valley, the haunting comfort of music. He knew the hatreds, prejudices, sciences, philosophies, habits, and pleasures of Saxony in the year 1500.

But in terms of the external, Luther was free, transcending all things constricted by time and custom. He knew the Hebrew prophets, the church's first evangelists, the martyrs, bishops, and saints of Christian history. He wrestled with the moral law and came to understand the first great principle of all ethics: that humankind, not law, is the objective. He tuned his inner life to the rhythm of the psalms and knew their midnight cry for aid. He centered his life and thoughts in the Lord of Christian hope. The humanity of Jesus was the foundation of his faith, the key to all his theology.

Were Martin Luther to speak to us again, we would hear the old, old plea of the believing heart to hold by faith to the truth of the historic life of Jesus, to move by faith from this to its high implications for the character of God, and to live by faith in the eternal, blessed communion of the timeless City of God.

To see him grow into the beauty of the church; to watch him win the personal faith of Christian experience; to be present while he feeds his sheep in lecture hall, confessional, and pulpit; to see him battle for the honor and purity of the faith; to know him standing in quiet, stubborn peace, as the martyrs of old, before the rulers, affirming the sufficiency of his faith; to walk with him through the long, difficult years after the glamour and shouting; to hear his cradle songs of Christian beauty; and then to see him die, his heart unshaken—is this not enough?

In a world of swift changes, Luther sought and held steadfast the ancient truth.

DAVID LIVINGSTONE

FROM AFRICA TO ETERNITY

Sam Wellman

ONE

On a hillside above the village of Blantyre in Scotland, three boys sat in the brown winter-dead grass. It was the afternoon of March 19, 1826, the Lord's Day.

One boy had tousled brown hair and hazel eyes so lively they seemed restless even reading a book, which was exactly what he was doing. He held a tuft of grass in his free hand. "Yes, here it is," he murmured to himself as he glanced from the book to the tuft of grass and back again.

"Here is what, David?" asked a small boy squirming beside him.

"It shows a picture of this very grass and gives its scientific name, Charles."

"Father doesn't like you to read science," grumbled an older boy, who ripped up blades of grass and flipped them into the air listlessly.

"I don't see the harm, John," said the boy named David. "The book seems very truthful to me."

John just grunted. David saw John glance down toward their home in Shuttle Row. John said, "Let's go home. It's almost time for cake."

David disliked being told what to do. Oh, he didn't mind obeying his parents. At the cotton mill, boys were always scoffing at the books he read during the lunch break: "Why are you so high and mighty? You'll never be anything but a cotton piecer like the rest of us!" He used to scream at them: "I can think and act for myself!" But it didn't stop them from needling him.

"Are you coming or not?" grumbled John.

"Of course," answered David. "Come on, Charles."

They ambled down the hill toward the village of Blantyre. John walked ahead, intent on cake. David held Charles's hand. They walked under the ashes and immense oaks on the grand Bothwell Estate. They descended a bank to reach a three-story brick tenement building that was on another bank above the great cotton factory, which was really a monotonous group of long five-story buildings on the banks of the Clyde.

On any other day after the boys entered a turret on the tenement building they would have clomped up spiral stairs to the top floor. But today they entered a door to the first floor. By the time David and Charles looked down the hallway, John was darting inside an open door. When they reached the open door, John had vanished within the people milling around inside the small room. There seemed barely room to stand.

"Happy birthday, laddie!" roared Grandpa Hunter as he shook David's hand. "Thirteen years old."

"Thank you, sir," said David, humbled by Grandpa Hunter's eighty years.

"I'll not be outdone by a Lowlander!" bellowed Grandpa Livingstone. "Happy birthday to you, David."

"Thank you," said David, slightly embarrassed by Grandpa Livingstone's pride in being a Highlander. Grandpa Hunter was probably just as proud of being a Lowlander. But David took after his father, Neil, who confessed to feeling like a Highlander in his heart yet dreamed of other lands beyond either Highland or Lowland. Of course his father, Neil, was in the room, too. His father didn't actually go to other lands like a missionary. He was only a wanderer, compared to the men who worked in the factory, because he traveled the shire to sell tea. David's mother was here, too. And Grandma Livingstone. After all, the celebration was being held in her apartment so the old folks wouldn't have to struggle up the stairs to the top floor. And, of course, now that David had reached his teens, he would soon join brother John in sleeping in this very room. There was a trundle bed under the grandparents' bed.

David's two sisters were also here. David liked being the big brother to Janet, an affectionate seven-year-old. But Agnes was only a bawling infant. There were nine gathered together this afternoon to honor David on his thirteenth birthday.

"I'll spin you a good yarn, laddie," said Grandpa Hunter.

Both grandpas could tell wonderful stories. David's mother could tell a good story, too. And David's father, Neil, could, as well. Hours around the fireplace inspired storytelling. But they all deferred to the two old men on this day. It wasn't often that all the grandparents were there at the same time.

After the cake the two old men were telling their stories again. Grandpa Livingstone continued, "I can tell you the name of every Livingstone back for six generations, every one a true Highlander. A long time ago we were called the Mac an Leighs in the Gaelic tongue. We were in the clan of the MacQuaires on the island of Ulva. And it was one of our own grandfathers, boys and girls, who said on his deathbed to his family, 'I have diligently searched through the annals of our family. Never has there been a dishonest man or woman. So if one of you finds himself or herself doing a dishonest deed, you can not say it runs in your blood!'"

"Honest, yes," muttered Grandpa Hunter, "but not always agreeable. I never had a more unwilling apprentice tailor in the cotton factory than a Master Neil Livingstone you sent me." He stopped as the children glanced at their father, Neil, to see if he was laughing. He was grinning. Grandpa Hunter went ahead, "If he hadn't stopped to talk to my bonny daughter, the lass you children know as your mother, he would have completely sewed his thumbs together, the poor boy."

Neil Livingstone laughed. "And what a blessing she was. And still is."

David's mother lowered her eyes. "Neil is a blessing, too. He provides for us by selling tea all over the shire and beyond. Our whole family is blessed by God. I just know it."

And the grandpas sat in two chairs by the fireplace and traded story after story until it was dark outside.

TWO

Home was almost sacred to David. He fell asleep that night, remembering warm verses from "The Cotter's Saturday Night." To David the poem was the best of Bobby Burns, because it so perfectly described his family.

The Livingstone children did swap stories among themselves. Yes, David's mother made old clothes look almost as good as new. And father, Neil, certainly had advice to give. David believed with all his heart that duties must be done—respectfully, too. He couldn't accept the joking and playing of other boys when they were supposed to be working. And, of course, he feared the Lord. In fact, this was a great worry to him. Because he knew Christ in his head, but not in his heart. Where was the love? The joy? What choice did he have but to continue to seek God? But was he destined to be undeserving of joy?

The poem described the simple supper the family ate. But David didn't think living on a diet of milk, porridge, and cheese was peculiar at all. Meat? Bread? What luxuries. Would he ever know them?

> The cheerful supper done, wi' serious face,
> They, round the ingle, form a circle wide;
> The sire turns o'er, wi' patriarchal grace,
> The big ha'-Bible, ance his father's pride. . . .

That was indeed David's father, Neil, opening the Bible beside the fire, reading the Old Testament, then the New. The readings done, Father Neil would bow his head and pray, just as the father in the poem. David saw this scene every night in the home of his father and mother, even after he began sleeping at Grandpa Livingstone's apartment. How wonderful home was. And home gave him relief from the factory.

Hundreds of spinners and three times that many piecers made yarn where David worked. David was one of three piecers who worked for his spinner. The piecers had to spot broken threads coming off the reels of the machines called jennies and tie them before the flaws were incorporated into the yarn. A piecer clambered over and under machinery to mend threads hour after hour. When the piecer was not mending, he had to watch for flaws like a hawk watched for mice. After many hours, the best of piecers was exhausted. But any flaw in yarn was held against the spinner. So it was not uncommon to see a spinner whip a groggy piecer with a leather strap to wake him up. And if the spinner got careless, he was whipped by a foreman.

In spite of stinging leather straps, factory work was boring. That was one reason why David sneaked books into the factory, whether the other piecers liked it or not.

One day a man screamed at him angrily, "Hey, you there!"

David slipped his books under the machinery. The vast interior of the factory now seemed very small. He looked up into a red face. "Y-y-yes, sir?"

"What do you have under there, you scamp?" yelled the man.

David couldn't lie to the man. "Books, sir."

"Let me see them," growled the man. "What? A Bible?" The man's anger evaporated. He began speaking so softly, his voice disappeared into the clatter of machinery. David had to read his lips. The man asked, "And what is this other book, laddie?"

"It's a Latin book I'm studying," mouthed David, so the man could read his lips. He hated yelling.

"Studying? Come with me," snapped the man.

David followed him into a room where the workers were forbidden to go. It was a room full of dials and gauges. Only the foreman was supposed to go there. So David knew this angry man must be the new foreman.

"All right," said the man in an almost normal tone of voice, "What's this about studying books out there with all that racket?"

"I was coming back from my lunch break, sir."

"Is that so? Did you get here on time this morning? I can check, you know."

"Yes, sir. Right at six o'clock."

"How long have you worked here, laddie?"

"Since I was ten, sir. Six years."

"Where did a sixteen-year-old like you get such a nice Bible?"

"I won it in a contest. I memorized Psalm 119." There was no point telling the man he won the Bible when he was nine. The man didn't believe him anyway.

"The psalm that's so very, very long?" asked the man skeptically.

"Yes, sir."

"Prove it. . . ."

So David began to recite Psalm 119, all 176 verses, all 2,337 words! Before he could finish the psalm, the foreman held up his hands in surrender.

"That's enough," said the foreman. "I can't be off the floor that long. I believe you. What's your name?"

"David Livingstone."

"Well, David Livingstone," sighed the man, "you go right ahead and bring your books. You might even leave your book open on a jenny so you can lap up a drop or two of knowledge on your way past the blasted machine. I'll not stop such a determined lad from learning his way out of such an infernal place as this. Now when the whistle blows at eight o'clock tonight, you get yourself home to your mother, laddie."

"That's good advice, sir. But I must go to my Latin lesson at Mr. Mc-Skimming's."

"A Latin lesson with the schoolmaster?"

"Yes, sir. Until ten."

"You must have the energy of a dozen boys. No wonder you're so thin." The man smiled. "I can see real grit in your face, laddie. It's nigh the time you stepped up to something more responsible. I'll be thinking on it."

David went back to work. He didn't tell the man his Grandma Livingstone often had to take the book out of his hands at midnight with a mild "Don't you ever know when to quit?" and blow out the candle to force him to go to sleep. His brother John would already be long asleep.

Was it wrong to pursue knowledge so hard? Was he testing his grandparents too much? And his parents, too? His father sold tea all over the shire and beyond. He never came closer to the factory than the tenement they lived in. That's why it was perfectly safe for David to bring to the factory a book on the plants of the local shire, although his father had urged David not to read science. This advice troubled David, because when he took the book into the hills south of Blantyre and opened it to a map of the shire of Lanark, the book seemed perfectly true. There below him flowed the river Clyde that powered the great cotton factory of Monteith & Company where he worked. Married to the factory was his own village of Blantyre. Three miles upstream on the Clyde was the village of Hamilton. Eight miles downstream on the Clyde glistened the great city of Glasgow. And when David pulled a tuft of grass and studied it, he soon found a drawing of the same grass in the book. It seemed to him that this book must be written by a man of truth and righteousness. David had never yet found anything untrue in the book.

Yet he knew his Bible well enough to be cautious. "Forgive me, Lord. I am a sinner," he prayed. And he quoted First Corinthians, "Knowledge puffeth up, but charity edifieth. And if any man think that he knoweth any thing, he knoweth nothing yet as he ought to know. But if any man love God, the same is known of him." For a long time David had been afraid he knew God in his head but not in his heart. Did reading science make him unworthy of God's love?

How David loved to pursue knowledge! And yet, on the other hand, he had defied his father over knowledge only last week. His father insisted he read *Practical Christianity* by a man named William Wilberforce. David refused. And his father had given him the switch across the back of his legs. What had come over David to rebel like that? He didn't get home until ten o'clock anyway. He didn't even sleep in the same apartment with his father. It was just that he craved books on travel and science, and, of course, he had to read his Bible and Latin, too. He couldn't bring himself to even pretend to be reading the dry religious dogma of a man named Wilberforce.

"In the meantime," he said into the roar of the machinery, "I'll obey my foreman." He propped his Latin book open on the side of the jenny. "It won't hurt to translate a word or two of Virgil as I run past."

THREE

Would he ever see the world? How would he do it? He had no money. What was he going to do?

As if to reinforce his nagging doubt about getting anywhere in the world, it was three years before the foreman promoted David to spinner in the factory. He still propped his books up on the jennies and grabbed a sentence or two as he rushed past. Was this his destiny? What was the use? And besides, he was still torn by guilt over loving to read science.

Then he read *The Philosophy of the Future State* by a Scotsman named Thomas Dick. Dick, a clergyman who was also an astronomer, convinced David in his book that God and science were completely compatible. After all, what was science but the study of God's laws of nature? And yet David still had lingering doubt because of his father's opposition to science.

One evening he confided to his father, "I can't find all the answers to my questions in this book by Dr. Thomas Dick."

"Philosophy?" His father frowned. "Perhaps you could talk to the learned man. Isn't he a Scotsman?"

"Do you think I should go see him?"

"Yes. Start early. It's a good walk to Glasgow." His father assumed all the learned Scots lived in Glasgow.

The next morning David packed some food and announced as he left, "I'll be going now to ask a question or two of Dr. Thomas Dick."

"Do you have his address?" asked his father.

"Broughty Ferry near Dundee." David hurried off before the news sunk in. He was going to walk east across the Lowlands the entire breadth of Scotland to the town of Dundee on the east coast!

David had walked everywhere he wanted to go his entire life. And he fell into a steady pace of four miles an hour. At dusk of the first night, he crawled into the warmth of a haystack. Before noon the next day, he was knocking on the door of a house on a hill in Broughty Ferry.

"What is it, young man?" asked a man of about sixty who opened the door.

"I'm David Livingstone from Blantyre. I have some questions for Dr. Dick."

"I'm Thomas Dick. Come in."

As David walked by the man's welcoming gesture, he said bluntly, "This hill your house is built on doesn't seem natural in this setting, sir."

Thomas Dick laughed. "You are observant, young man. And direct. Qualities the Savior approves of. And you are correct, too. There is nothing natural about my hill. I hauled load after load of dirt with my wheelbarrow to build this mound."

"Load after load?"

"Eight thousand loads, young man." Doctor Dick saw his blank expression. "We are in the Lowlands. I needed the extra height for my telescope. I am an astronomer."

"You built your own hill?"

"Oh, everyone around here thinks I'm crazy as a tick." He shook his finger at David. "Don't wait for the approval of everyone around you, young man. Do what you have to do. And do it now." He laughed. "But I needn't tell you that. I know of no other man, young or old, who ever walked across Scotland to talk to me."

David asked his questions about the Bible and science. Some people said the two were incompatible. Which was wrong then? Science? Or the Bible?

Dr. Dick smiled. "Such a common error. Some scientific observations are false because men are imperfect. But some science is true, too. On the other hand, every word in the Bible is true, but the truth takes several forms."

"How so?"

He inquired of David, "When our Savior asked 'And why beholdest thou the mote that is in thy brother's eye, but considerest not the beam that is in thine own eye?' did our Savior actually mean there was a plank in the eye of the man He was talking to?

"Of course not. He was using hyperbole."

"And did Saint John in the book of Revelation intend to represent reality with symbols?"

"Yes, sir. I believe he did."

"The Bible is the Word of God, the wisest book we have or ever will have. But you must not be a fool with its wisdom."

David floated back to Blantyre. He felt as light as a dove. The resolution of science with God's Word freed David of the awful contradiction with which he had struggled. How could two truths be opposed? In that false issue, he was certain now his father was wrong. Now, if only he could resolve his doubts about deserving salvation.

As if to match David's unorthodox behavior, his father left the Church of Scotland. This was not as abrupt as it seemed to those outside the family. Neil had agonized many years over the autocratic attitude of the ministers who were appointed by authorities completely unknown to the local congregation. Many of their edicts were based on traditions of the church and not found in the Bible at all, which David's father read constantly. He began walking the entire family three miles to Hamilton to an independent church. It was run by local elders. The minister was selected by the local elders. They preached that there were no elect, no predestined few who were to be saved. Salvation was by God's grace alone!

So at this same time, David found the greatest truth of all: Salvation was his. He embraced Christ. Christ was no longer just in his head. Suddenly, he felt deep love for Christ. At long last he felt the profound love for God that St. Augustine wrote about so movingly. David felt a deep obligation for Christ's suffering. His inner spiritual life was born. The Holy Spirit had reached David Livingstone through God's grace. At last he was free. And his world seemed to explode with possibilities.

It was not long after his meeting with Dr. Dick that David, too, became a full member of the independent church in Hamilton. Membership was earned. For five months he had to be instructed by one of the elders. And soon after David became a member, he heard the minister read an appeal for medical missionaries to go to China. To combine healing with the gospel was really living as Christ Himself. Yet medical missions in China were revolutionary for the Scots of 1834. David's heart was completely won by the idea of going to China as a medical missionary. How much more could one man do than save souls for eternity and save lives here on earth? But for many weeks, David ruminated on how to accomplish this lofty goal before he told his parents.

"David, how can such an impossibility be conquered?" gasped his father. What was the point of expanding on how poor they were?

David said, "I've told no one but you two and the Reverend Moir. My plan is to save every extra penny I can for several years, then continue to work at the factory in the summers and go to Glasgow during the winter session to study medicine. It costs twelve pounds a session at Anderson College."

"Twelve pounds!" His father looked faint. "And you make five shillings a week? That's one pound a month. That's exactly one year's wages. And that's if you could save every penny. Impossible!"

His mother smiled. "I always knew David was special. There are so few factory boys who can even read."

"Not one in ten," muttered Neil, still numb.

Mother added, "There are so few factory boys who study Latin."

Neil grunted. "What factory boy can work fourteen hours a day, sweating like a dray horse, then run into the cold Scottish night to study Latin? Only one in a thousand and we're looking at him."

Mother smiled. "Yes. A boy who studied books until they were taken out of his hands at midnight. . ."

"And still got to work every morning on time," added Neil proudly. "He's no boy now, but a man."

Mother said, "John will have to help David."

"But how can John help?" asked David. "He has a family."

"It's tradition," snapped Neil. "The oldest son must."

"Do you mean you approve, Father?" interrupted David.

Neil laughed. "I guess I do. You've got all us skeptics scheming and planning the impossible already. There's not another man in Scotland like you, David."

David was twenty-three in the fall of 1836 when his father Neil walked the snowy road into Glasgow with him, helping carry clothes and books. David rented a room for two shillings and sixpence. So he added living expenses during each session of six pounds. But he had planned long and well and remembered the Lord's sermon on the mount in Matthew: "Take no thought for your life, what ye shall eat, or what ye shall drink; nor yet for your body, what ye shall put on."

Being a student was ecstasy. "What joy!" he cried to God. "For thirteen years I worked fourteen hours a day so I could study for a few hours a day. Now I can study every waking hour of the day. This is truly paradise on earth. Praise the Lord for this joy."

He milked every minute out of every day. He walked to Glasgow University for Greek classes and to Congregational College for lectures on religion. But medicine and chemistry at Anderson College occupied most of his time. He had to learn anatomy and surgery by dissecting corpses. He learned to diagnose chest diseases with a new instrument that every physician was talking about: the stethoscope. Now the doctor could hear air rushing through the lungs or hear gurgling blood pulsing from the heart.

After his first session, he returned to Blantyre to work in the factory once again as a spinner. Also that summer, he applied to the London Missionary Society. It had missions in the South Seas, West Indies, India, Africa, and, best of all, China. And the society had no religious dogma. It pushed no religion but the gospel.

Early in his second session at Glasgow, the society sent him a list of questions to answer. Two answers David worked especially hard to articulate. On what he thought were the duties of a missionary, he answered:

> His duties chiefly are, I apprehend, to endeavor by every means in his power to make known the gospel by preaching, exhortation, conversation, instruction of the young; improving, so far as in his power, the temporal condition of those among whom he labors, by introducing the arts and sciences of civilization, and doing everything in his power to commend Christianity to their hearts and consciences.

Another answer, to a question about his attitude toward marriage, was no less definite:

> Unmarried; under no engagement relating to marriage, never

made proposals of marriage, nor conducted myself to any woman as to cause her to suspect that I intended anything related to marriage; and, so far as my present wishes are concerned, I should prefer going out unmarried, that I might be without that care which the concerns of a family necessarily induce and give myself wholly to the work.

Young ladies were not attracted to him, either. He knew that well enough. At five feet eight inches, he was tall for his time. He had a manly build: large in the chest and shoulders, otherwise trim. He had thick brown hair and intelligent soulful eyes. In one of her more tactless moments, his sister Janet had told him why young ladies were not drawn to him. It was his earnestness, his resolve, his fortitude, his tenacity that drew in and dimpled his chin and made him seem humorless. David Livingstone was not a bonny lad. In the meantime, David was conscious of no loss at all. He continued his studies, no small benefit of which were the friendships he developed with students and faculty. The assistant to the chemistry professor was a young man named James Young. David and he became good friends, Young even showing him how to operate a lathe and do simple carpentry. James and William Thomson, two young sons of the mathematics professor, frequented the chemistry lab, too.

One day David overheard Young telling the boys, "He has more true trust in God, more of the true spirit of Christ, more true honesty, more purity of character, more unselfish love for others than any other man I've ever known."

"That sounds a bit thick," objected one of the boys.

"I've seen a good many men. I'm not saying it lightly," answered Young.

David shook his head. "Are you speaking of Professor Thomson, the boys' father?"

He was puzzled by their embarrassed silence. Later he began to suspect Young had been talking about him. What praise! Was it possible? Was he held in such high regard? All his life he had been scorned and ridiculed and teased by his peers in the factory. Was it only the complacent and fearful who scorned him? Was it only his fellow risk-takers who appreciated him? But he decided then and there he must not hate those who scorned him. After all, the Lord's own family and friends thought He was insane when they first heard about His ministry in Galilee.

By the fall of 1838, David was north of London, lodging with other students in the small market town of Chipping Ongar. He had been accepted by the London Missionary Society. It seemed a dream to be walking the environs of London. With another student, Joseph Moore, he visited the buried heroes at Westminster Abbey, watched the changing of the guard at Buckingham Palace, and admired the Gothic spires of the Houses of Parliament. Was it really true that he, the poor Scots boy from the aging factories of Blantyre, would become an extension of this grandeur?

But it would take determination. After all, he was no missionary yet. He was only beginning three months of probation. Rev. Richard Cecil was to make sure David was proficient in Latin, Greek, and theology before he began more formal training. Some students would continue in theology at nearby Cheshunt College. Some students, like David, were to go to London for more medical training. But there was the constant threat of failure. Only the very best students were allowed to go on with formal training. Of course, someone who failed could still be sent to the missions after acquiring skills in carpentry and bricklaying to work for the real missionaries. Or one could simply drop out of sight.

David didn't make any excuses for himself. But he was worried. Rev. Cecil didn't seem to recognize his better qualities, as others had. The reverend worked hard with him to get his Latin and Greek up to snuff, frowning all the while. He only grudgingly admitted David's theology was simple but sound. He even questioned David's motivation, even though every time David was called upon to lead a prayer, he concluded, "Let us imitate Christ in all His inimitable perfections."

There was another qualification to be a missionary. It was too critical to ignore. Every missionary had to preach the gospel. Each student had to write his sermon, then subject it to Rev. Cecil's persnickety review. After the reverend's inevitable revisions the student memorized the approved sermon and delivered it passionately to a local congregation. David's opportunity came when the minister at a church in Stanford Rivers became ill. David was told to deliver the evening sermon. He read through his approved sermon one last time and mounted the podium.

"Good evening, friends. . . ," he began.

His mind immediately went as black as midnight.

FOUR

David's mind buzzed with horror: He mustn't fail his sermon!

His logic was impeccable. Even his memory was impenetrable. How could this happen to someone who memorized the One Hundred Nineteenth Psalm? If only he could remember the first sentence. That would be the spark to set him ablaze. He had to remember it. His faltering way of speaking was one of Rev. Cecil's main criticisms of him. What was the first sentence? Suddenly he noticed Rev. Cecil in the front pew. His eyes were lowered in disappointment, but it seemed a disappointment he had expected.

David stammered, "Friends, I have forgotten all I had to say." He rushed out of the chapel, smothered by the silence of the congregation.

What humiliation. He had failed. And he had failed Rev. Cecil. How could David have suffered such a setback?

"Has God abandoned me?" he cried.

He went back to his room and opened his Bible. He remembered well a saint in the Bible who seemed to have a similar problem, but David always felt insignificant, even a little sacrilegious, when he was bold enough to apply what happened to saints to himself. But there it was in the fourth chapter of Exodus:

> And Moses said unto the LORD, O my LORD, I am. . .slow of speech, and of a slow tongue. And the LORD said unto him, Who hath made man's mouth? or who maketh the dumb, or deaf, or the seeing, or the blind? have not I the LORD? Now therefore go, and I will be with thy mouth, and teach thee what thou shalt say.

David closed his Bible. "I must trust God," he told himself. "For some reason He did not want me to speak today. I must be too proud."

It was no surprise when Rev. Cecil solemnly came to him later. "Three months of probation is over, Livingstone. I am required to make my recommendation. In view of your inability to deliver a sermon and your generally halting manner of speaking, I will not be able to recommend you."

David felt like God had kicked him in the teeth. He left his room in a daze. He wandered the grounds. He made excuses for himself. It was his cursed uvula, the fleshy lobe hanging down from the back of his palate. It was too large. He hadn't realized it until he started studying medicine. It made his speech thick and indistinct. It worried him. The worry threw him off his stride. That was it. It was not God. It was a medical problem. . . .

A voice trailed him, "Livingstone?"

"Huh?" He turned to see Joseph Moore. "I've failed, Moore."

"Me, too."

"You, too!" Why was it he felt better when a friend joined his misery? God forgive him. "What are we going to do, Moore?"

"Keep trying."

"What do you mean?"

"Rev. Cecil said I was getting a second chance. Didn't he tell you that?"

"No." David's last hopes crumbled into dust.

"He must have forgot. Surely you'll get a second chance. You're so highly regarded here."

"What an inflated assessment." David laughed bitterly. "Your friendship has blinded you."

"I heard Rev. Isaac Taylor and his son talking about you the other day. One of them said 'When Livingstone walks he has a very particular stride, solid and determined, not fast, not slow—his stride simply guarantees he is going to get there!'"

David raised an eyebrow. "I guess that could be considered a compliment—if I were to become a postman delivering mail. But thanks anyway, Moore."

"I heard another fellow say you have charm, which despite your ungainly ways, attracts almost everyone."

"Thanks again. . .I think." David stifled a chuckle at the flawed compliments.

"I heard another fellow say you are kind and gentle, both in word and deed. Always ready with a comforting word. Or an act of sympathy."

"Stop, Moore. Your words are appreciated. But it doesn't change the fact that I must leave."

He walked in the countryside that afternoon, feeling very foolish. He had dreamed how he could convince the Missionary Society that he should go to China and not some other country. What a presumptuous fool he had been. He was not even going to become a missionary. The enormity of his failure grew on him. What about all his friends back in Scotland who had helped him? And now to top it off, he was wallowing in self-pity. What was happening to him?

The Reverend Cecil was waiting in his room when he returned. "I must speak with you, Livingstone."

"Of course," replied David curtly. Was he going to be lectured on his multitude of shortcomings? Was he going to be told which paths were left for him to follow now? Was it to be bricklaying or carpentry? "Oh, Jesus," he prayed, "relieve me of this bitterness."

"They tell me you worked in a cotton factory fourteen hours a day, six days a week, for thirteen years."

"I was very lucky to have that honest job," answered David defensively. What was the reverend getting at? Was he going to ask David to apply his spinning skills in some backward country?

"I've judged you as if you came to me from a school for the well-to-do, like Eton. I must admit I have been severe with you. For that I am sorry. See me tomorrow morning, and we will discuss your next sermon."

David was stunned. A second chance! Praise the Lord. And praise whoever might have spoken in his behalf. "Could you tell me who spoke in my behalf, sir?"

"It would take too long."

David worked very hard over the next several months, hard enough to realize he was finally going to pass muster with Rev. Cecil—despite his halting, barely adequate sermons. David's faith kept him afloat. That was fortunate because he was more fit to handle his next disappointment: England was having trouble with China over opium. The situation in China was explosive. The London Missionary Society was not going to send any more missionaries to China until the problem was resolved!

"God will surely provide the answer," said David, but he was shaken. He was often shaken, but to show it meant showing others a lack of trust in God.

A missionary named Robert Moffat was in London after years in South Africa. Moffat said that from his mission he could see in the distant north the smoke from a thousand villages! David was shocked. That was the exact opposite of what he had been told: The interior of Africa was a wasteland. David began following Moffat on his lecture tour around the London area. Soon Moffat knew him well. David would approach him after each talk, always with more questions. David knew virtually nothing about Africa. How could any European know anything? After three hundred years Europeans had only poked around the shorelines. The southern half of Africa, in particular, had few good harbors. Its rivers were not navigable by any vessel larger than a canoe. The interior was a mystery.

David soon heard Rev. Cecil's thoughts on where he should go. "China is closed to you indefinitely, Livingstone. We presently have missions in the South Seas, West Indies, India, and Africa. I will recommend you for the West Indies."

"I have given it much thought myself, sir. I wish to continue with my medical studies, under the auspices of the society, of course. And I wish a more primitive land. I wish very much to go to South Africa."

Rev. Cecil was peeved when he left. He undoubtedly regarded David as an ingrate. But surely the reverend had forgotten the medical aspect. So David weighed the reverend's feelings against what David knew was right. He wished he was as sure of the rightness of South Africa as he was of the wrongness of the West Indies. Europeans called the continent of Africa the white man's grave.

The board approved his request for more medical training. By the beginning of 1840, he moved into London proper and wasted no time rushing to the Aldersgate Street Dispensary. In the office of Dr. Bennett, he said, "I'm David Livingstone, sir. I'm here from the society."

"Sit down, Livingstone. Forgive me for being abrupt. You'll soon discover in the actual practice of medicine there's little time for normal courtesies. Save them for your patients, who need much reassurance."

"Of course, sir."

The doctor brusquely asked him a number of questions about medicine. Finally, the doctor said, "You have a very sound background in academic medicine. Now you must see real diseases in real people, Livingstone. I'll clear you for Charing Cross Hospital."

For weeks, David spent every working moment with Dr. Bennett. He saw pneumonia, tuberculosis, cancer, and every other disease under the English sun. He began to feel very confident about examining and diagnosing patients. His only regret was the limited resources doctors had to cure patients. There were never enough hours in the day for everything David wanted to do. He began attending lectures of Richard Owen on comparative anatomy. As shy as he was, he forced himself to meet Owen, just as he had forced himself to meet Moffat, and even Mrs. Moffat. Once, he attended a lecture sponsored by the African Civilization Society. Thomas Buxton explained to the audience how only Christianity and commerce would change the evil practice of slavery in Africa. If slavery was to be abolished, the powerful African chiefs had to have not only Christianity but a means of providing goods for their people.

It was an unforgettable evening. David was struck by the logic of Buxton's message. When someone told him Buxton was advancing the same message as Wilberforce, David felt a pang of guilt as he remembered how he disobeyed his father so many years ago and refused to read the book by Wilberforce.

As the months passed, it became clear where various students were going. Joseph Moore was headed to Tahiti in the South Seas. David's close friend in London, D. G. Watt, was going to India. And now it seemed definite that David would be headed for South Africa—to the very mission run by Robert Moffat.

Before he left for Africa, David returned to Scotland. There he passed the examination for his physician's license. Most important of all, he had to say good-bye to his family. Father Neil was now fifty-two, apparently in good health in the physician's eyes of David. Mother was a concern; she seemed worn out and declining. Brother John was a man of twenty-nine, a merchant like his father. The others seemed to be following David into professions. Brother Charles had immigrated to the United States, where he studied for the ministry at Oberlin College in the state of Ohio. Sister Agnes, sixteen, was preparing for a career in teaching. Sister Janet was already a schoolteacher who loved to write and read poetry. The visit home to Shuttle Row was spent in discussions by the fire. The Livingstones were optimists. Every new invention and every new discovery would advance the welfare of mankind. Even though they were products of the working class, they did not despise the upper class. Many of the upper class were generous. The Livingstones prayed the rich could be enlisted in the missionary effort, too.

At five o'clock on the morning of November 17, 1840, they rose to coffee and prayer. Tears flowed freely as David parted. Sailing to another continent in 1840 was very risky in itself. And who knew what waited for him in Africa—the "white man's grave"? Once again, Father Neil walked with him into Glasgow—this time to catch the packet steamer to England. All through his youth, his father and mother had guided him on the path of righteousness, encouraging him to study the Bible, encouraging him to go to college, encouraging him in his missionary work, encouraging him to despise slavery. They sent every child to school even though it meant they had to live in poverty. How could David ever thank them? Only by showing them that the effort produced results a hundredfold could he do it. He must do it—for them.

In London, three days later he was ordained Rev. Livingstone along with fellow student William Ross. On December 8, David sailed with Ross and his wife toward Africa on the *George*. Always restless, always eager for opportunity, Livingstone asked Captain Donaldsen to explain the art of navigation to him. The captain was obliging, to the point of showing him how to take lunar observations at midnight with a quadrant. Services on the ship were conducted on Sundays, not by the captain, who was not a Christian, but by David.

Sailing was arduous. Space was limited. Often during rough weather, the passengers huddled below in the hold, sick and scared. In midvoyage a mast broke in a storm. Caught in the easterly trade winds and the prevailing easterly currents, the captain navigated the crippled ship across the Atlantic to Rio de Janeiro! David was stunned. Never had he expected to visit the continent of South America. But always ready for opportunity, while the ship was being repaired, he went ashore.

The fact that the Rosses refused to go ashore reinforced his low opinion of them. They had been seasick the entire voyage. David had not been seasick at all, and he doctored them. He knew seasickness was a fickle thing that attacked one person and not another. He felt no superiority at all. But Ross acted as if his manhood was threatened. And Ross had made it clear Livingstone was not to doctor his wife anymore.

Ashore, David threw himself headlong into an active mission society, passing out tracts and Bibles to seamen in sleazy waterfront bars. He even visited hospitals to talk to seamen, some debilitated by alcohol, some stabbed, some beaten.

Only when the *George* was ready to sail again did he return to the ship. On board, his relationship with the Rosses worsened from mutual dislike to mutual scorn. In March 1841, the *George* anchored at Simon's Bay off of Cape Town. The new missionaries were to stay one month at Cape Town before continuing on to their final destination of Port Elizabeth. This time they were all guests of the local station of the London Missionary Society, run by Dr. John Phillips.

From what David had heard about Dr. Phillips from Moffat, he expected Phillips to be an ogre. But Phillips was calm and rational, even forgiving. It was obvious to David now that the differences of opinion among missionaries were based on factors more complicated than he yet understood. But he could not sympathize with a missionary who remained in what was already a strong Christian enclave, unless it was because he was campaigning against slavery, like Phillips. Some missionaries he met in Cape Town were ministering only to white Christians along the coast, more or less living the soft life of colonists.

Yet, deep in his heart, he hoped William Ross and his wife would stay with Dr. Phillips in Cape Town. Phillips had said he needed help. He walked to the pier that morning in April of 1841 when the *George* was to embark, praying it was God's will that the Rosses would not be sailing with him.

FIVE

The Rosses were at the pier, their eyes glacially preoccupied as he approached. David contented himself with the fact that during the voyage he would have pleasant conversations with Captain Donaldsen of the *George*.

Several days later, they sailed into Algoa Bay and left the *George*. Livingstone and Ross began procuring supplies. A covered wagon cost fifty pounds. Twelve oxen, each costing three pounds, were required to pull it. Tea, bacon, coffee, cheese, beans, and flour—enough food for three months of travel—would be stowed on the wagon. Cots could be stretched inside the wagon itself at night for sheltered sleeping. Three natives were hired to guide them and drive the oxen. The acquisition process was slow. David began to realize that a task that took a few days in Scotland might take several weeks in Africa.

One morning in the hotel where he stayed, he woke William Ross to say, "While we are waiting for our guides to show up I'm going to visit the mission at Hankey."

Hankey was thirty miles west along the coastline. He was going to accompany the missionary from Hankey, who had just arrived in Port Elizabeth and was returning to Hankey. He felt slightly guilty at first, leaving the Rosses behind, but he soon put it out of his mind. He had long been used to weighing the merits of different alternatives, then plunging ahead. He was sure he was living in Christ. The New Testament was full of stories of how Jesus moved ahead, while everyone around Him worried and dallied.

"I want to meet the Hottentots," he told the missionary.

"They are not Hottentots, old boy. That's a white man's name for them. They are the Khoikhoi."

"Do you speak their language?" asked David.

"Hardly." The missionary laughed.

As they cantered toward Hankey on a sandy wagon trail, sun-bleached Africa dazzled David. To his left stretched beaches of white sand, spattered by azure waves of Jeffrey's Bay. To his right climbed green hills, dotted with mimosa shrubs and runtish acacia trees. Elephants were up there in hidden valleys, he was told. What would he do if he saw such a behemoth? It seemed like a dream to be in Africa. It was pleasing beyond anything he imagined.

The Khoikhoi fired welcome shots as they approached. People swarmed around them and shook their hands. Faces lit with sunny smiles. What a happy mission. David forgave the missionary's comments about the native language when he heard the Khoikhoi speaking. He felt like he was surrounded by crickets. Their speech was punctuated with clicks.

"Can you ever learn it?" asked David, with much more respect.

"They do." The missionary pointed at children playing. "I do understand quite a bit of it myself. But speaking it is very difficult."

"Yes." David was depressed. He wasn't the most distinct speaker anyway. "And I thought I was going to learn African."

"Oh, but you can if you want to, old boy. The natives speak Bantu where you are going. I'm not saying it is easy to learn, but it is not as difficult as Nama, the language of the Khoikhoi. You'll probably meet Bushmen north of Kuruman if you ever venture out into the Kalihari wilderness. They also speak Nama."

David sat down in the sun and began writing in a notebook. First of all, the Khoikhoi were not at all like he imagined African natives. Their skin was almost yellow in color. They had high cheekbones and small foreheads. Their black hair coiled tight and flat on their head. It struck him again how limited his imagination had been. Africa was a treasure. And he had only arrived.

When he returned to Port Elizabeth, the Rosses were cool. They acted as if they had supervised the entire preparation for the trip in his absence. But David learned they had spent their time strolling past the Regency houses on Cora Terrace, idly wandering through the park created by Sir Rufane Donkin in memory of his wife, and gazing at the walls of Fort Frederick. They had talked of visiting the deserted home of Peter Retief but it was a good two miles away.

Peter Retief had led the Dutch Boers off to the northeast just a few years ago to escape domination by the British. They called themselves *voortrekkers* or pioneers; many were still migrating northeast. The first ones to reach their destination had claimed land held by the Zulus. Now many Zulus were pushed south and west, clashing with the African tribes that held those lands. So two mighty forces were at unrest in the north and east: the Boers and the Zulus. Only a fool would think the English were rid of the problem.

They began their own trek in the middle of May. It was late fall in southern Africa. Temperatures dropped below 40 degrees at night and peaked at 70 degrees in the afternoon. Of course, to a Scotsman like David it seemed balmy. The twelve oxen pulled the wagon onto a terrace in the midst of peaks. They were doing well to travel ten miles a day. The Rosses rode in the wagon. David rode the back of an ox. The oxen had horns that swept back behind their heads. He soon learned a bad-tempered ox could knock a man breathless with one quick twist of its neck. But David would risk that, rather than ride with the Rosses. The Rosses slept in the wagon. David pitched a tent and slept on the ground. He made up his mind to keep peace with the Rosses. If he had to avoid them to accomplish that, he would. The three were together only when they gathered around a fire every morning and every night to cook a meal.

After one week, they saw in the distance one of their own missions. "Somerset East!" yelled David, from the back of the ox.

A week after Somerset East, they stopped at a mission in Graaf Reinet. It was a small warm town of bright pastels, in spite of being in the shadow of somber pillars eroded from limestone. The town's name seemed to symbolize South Africa to David: Have no fear. They climbed onto yet another terrace among peaks to continue on to a mission at Colesburg. Then they crossed the boulder-bedded Orange River and reached their mission at Phillipolis. The travelers continually rose onto new terraces, reaching new missions. The air grew warmer and drier, the countryside scrubbier. They followed the north bank of the Orange River to a mission at Douglas, then crossed the Vaal River to arrive at Griqua Town.

The land became distinctly flat and arid, occasionally cut by a dry riverbed. Trees seemed never at hand, although a few could be seen on the horizon. Yet the land teemed with life, even now in the cool dry season. A traveler had to watch his feet. The ground crawled with snakes, scorpions, spiders, ants, and lizards. Had any white man ever described them before? He had read everything about Africa he could get his hands on. Only one real naturalist had ever worked in South Africa: William Burchell. Burchell had never ventured this far inland. What treasure. Wildebeests, springbucks, and other antelope flourished in the distance. David suspected a lot of life crept and slithered around his tent after the sun went down, too.

They arrived at Kuruman on July 31, 1841.

Robert Moffat was not there. He was still in England. David and the Rosses were to wait for him to come back to Kuruman. Robert Hamilton was there. And so was Roger Edwards and his wife. Hamilton was in his fifties, Edwards in his late forties, and Ross in his late thirties. David was twenty-eight.

Moffat had built a high-vaulted airy church of adobe. The residences of the missionaries were low buildings with wide eaves and long verandas. Arranged in a pattern were neat native huts of thatch, circular with cone-shaped roofs. Several hundred natives lived there. Fruit trees and flowering shrubs lent blazes of greenery and color. Vegetables abounded in gardens, fed through irrigation ditches from a magnificent spring called the Eye of Kuruman. There were a blacksmith shop, a carpentry shed, and several workshops. Nearby was a large corral for cattle. It really was a showcase. David soon learned why other missionaries had criticized Moffat. There were over three hundred natives who regularly participated in church. But only forty were communicants. Moffat was not going to allow anyone to water down Christianity. How could David argue with that rigor? Moffat had converted forty natives in twenty years—or two per year! And yet he still was adding manpower. For what?

In no time at all, David resolved to push on to the north. There were far too many missionaries at Kuruman. And hadn't Moffat claimed thousands of natives lived to the north? Within days after his arrival, he confided in a letter to Henry Drummond of Blantyre that he was determined to push on to the north until he found villages of these natives and furthermore, he intended to be "excluded from all European society." It was not a rash decision. He thought about it all the way from Griqua Town to Kuruman. And he had given no little thought to being hidden in the shadow of Moffat after meeting Robert Hamilton and Roger Edwards.

Oh, they were kind souls. But how they must have chaffed at the bit over the years. Moffat had used them as artisans, building his showcase. Hamilton was plainly worn out. But Edwards was not.

On September 24, 1841, David left with Roger Edwards and two native Africans who were Christians. David even talked of leaving one of the natives in the north to preach. As they journeyed northeast by ox wagon, he learned from Edwards even more reasons to establish a mission in the north. In the vicinity of Kuruman was a peculiar tribe called Griquas. They were a mix of Khoikhoi and Dutch. They spoke Dutch and used rifles. Many years ago, they had driven the various Bechuana tribes out of the vicinity of Kuruman to the north. Now Griqua hunters were venturing north among the Bechuana tribes. The Griquas were not only spreading venereal diseases but lies about the missionaries. It was important for missionaries to get north before the minds of the Bechuana chiefs were permanently poisoned against them.

"How do you know so much about the tribes to the north if no missionary has been there?" asked David.

"Don't underestimate Moffat. He is fluent in the Sechuana dialect of Bantu. That is the language the Bechuanas speak. He talks to Bechuanas who wander into Kuruman from the north. Don't forget something else: He opened up Namaqualand to the west by bringing the notorious outlaw Afrikaner to Christ. And in the old days before the Boers took over the east, Moffat used to travel to the east, too. He is even a friend of the vicious Zulu chief, Mosilikatze!"

David was heartened by Edward's respect for Moffat. So Moffat was quite shrewd after all. And Moffat knew over twenty years of African history that David was only now learning. He had so much to learn. And he knew he would never reach the hearts of the Africans unless he learned to speak Bantu dialects like Moffat had done.

The country was grassland, flat and scrabbly, scraped by an occasional dry riverbed. Locally, the grassland swelled into low brushy hills. Every night, they heard lions and hyenas, sometimes in a frenzy as if they were devouring something. Once in a while at night, the ground thumped from heavy legs. Rhinoceros, speculated David. Too hurried, too confused for elephant. For two weeks, as they traveled during the day they saw only distant antelope in the scrabble and thorn bushes.

David was having doubts. "Where are the Bechuanas, Edwards?"

"Our guides tell me we are very close."

Their two Bechuana guides did not look like the Khoikhoi David had seen at Port Elizabeth. They were darker skinned, taller, and more heavily built. Their features were more like what David expected African natives to look like. The black hair was not coiled as tight and flat as the Khoikhois's. Their cheekbones were more rounded.

His eye caught something on the horizon. "Look, Edwards!"

"I can't see anything."

"It's haze, perhaps smoke from a village."

One of the Bechuana guides named Pomare turned and grinned. "*Ewe!*"

He said "yes," marveled Edwards as he strained to see ahead.

Soon the scrubby grassland was dotted with rangy, big-boned cattle. And then they saw a herd boy, dressed in a leather robe, carrying a spear. Suddenly, the herd boy darted through the cattle toward what must have been the village. After a few minutes David saw the conical roofs. Dozens. Then hundreds.

Now as the ox wagon rumbled past a field of corn, David heard women screaming, "*Luliloo! Luliloo!*"

Men with spears ran from the village to surround their wagon. There seemed to be no animosity. All concerned were overwhelmed with curiosity. David examined their leather robes decorated with beads and some kind of paint, which were worn over leather aprons of the same kind. He puzzled over the strange appearance of their skin. He was sure they were of the same race as their guides but these villagers had apparently smeared grease over their skin. And it had the sheen of metal.

The natives led them to a man who must have been the chief. From his robe of leopard skin dangled tails of lions. His headdress was of some kind of dark fur. Warriors, carrying long spears and gray shields of what must have been rhinoceros or elephant hide, guarded the chief.

After a few words between the guides and the chief, which David didn't understand, Edwards gave the chief a string of beads and said in an extremely loud voice, "*Igama lam ngu* Rev. Edwards!" He turned to gesture toward David. "Rev. Livingstone!"

"*Igama lam ngu* Moseealele," bellowed the chief, even louder than Edwards.

"They are the Bakhatlas," said Edwards to David, never forgetting to smile.

A woman stepped boldly forward and touched David's hair. She tugged it gently and shook her head. Yes, she concluded, David's drab brown thatch must be real hair. She gently pushed the end of his nose. Yes, it was real, too, although it was so much larger than a decent nose should be. In spite of his unease, David could hardly keep from laughing. But that could be fatal. This spoiled woman surely must be a favorite wife of the chief's. Suddenly he felt elated. This was exactly why he came to Africa. These Africans were friendly. They could be reached for Christ. He was sure of it. He felt a smile spread over his face.

"Let me show something," he said. A few murmurs were heard around him. They enjoyed hearing his strange brogue. They, too, were curious. David pointed to his wrist and hand, which were very tan for a Scotsman. He held his hand next to the woman's dark brown arm. "See? My skin is tan. Now see this." He rolled up his sleeve to expose his arm—as pale white as an ostrich egg.

"Hay!" gasped the woman.

The chief was surprised, too, but he motioned the woman to step back. He had indulged her enough. He began talking to the guides. And the guides talked to Edwards. The blood seemed to drain from Edwards's face.

Finally, Edwards spoke with David. "Moseealele wishes to see what we have in the wagon. He is particularly interested in our fire stick."

"Our rifle?"

"Yes, our rifle," said Edwards, forgetting to smile.

SIX

Edwards was pale. His voice trembled. "The chief obviously has heard of firearms. There are Griqua hunters shooting rifles out in the grasslands. The government is very strict about keeping firearms away from natives. I don't believe we should show him. I'll have Pomare tell him we don't have one."

David kept smiling. "But if he finds out later we have a rifle, we'll be forever branded as liars to the Bakhatlas."

"But we know nothing about this chief. Maybe he wants to disarm us before he overpowers us."

"I see." David turned and walked through the throng of natives toward the wagon.

"What are you doing, Livingstone?" yelled Edwards.

David reached up under the front seat of the wagon. He turned and two barrels of a very large rifle gaped toward the natives.

"You are going to get us killed!" yelled Edwards.

"It's not loaded." David pointed the barrels at the ground anyway. "I'm just going to show it to the chief."

Edwards's smile was sick. "For goodness' sake, you might have told me what you were going to do before you did it."

"I was too busy praying. We must trust God, Edwards."

David walked up close to Moseealele to show him the rifle. Moseealele examined the weapon very closely. He pulled back the hammers and pulled the triggers. He peered keenly at the rifle. The chief knew far too much about rifles.

"He already has a rifle," said David, smiling vacantly.

"I think you're right," agreed Edwards. But why such interest? Our rifle is not exactly the latest model.

"I think maybe his rifle is broken. Judging from the fact he's pulled the triggers a dozen times I'll bet it's the trigger mechanism. Ask Pomare to tell him I will fix his rifle for him after we return from visiting the tribes farther north."

"But what if you can't fix it?"

"Well, they will probably eat us, Edwards."

"For God's sake, Livingstone."

"Don't forget to smile."

The chief sent one of the warriors to his hut to fetch something. It was his own rifle, a muzzle-loader, even older than David's. David examined it. The trigger mechanism was broken. "Yes. I'll fix it," he told the chief in a very loud voice. And with gestures he showed the chief he knew it was broken, and he could repair it. David noticed Edwards close his eyes as if in prayer.

The missionaries showed other possessions, things that might be used to encourage cooperation from the Bakhatlas later. First they showed them a large mirror. The Bakhatlas went wild over it, passing it around to a constant chorus of laughter. But the missionaries could not make it a gift. They had no more mirrors, and they hoped to visit other villages. The Bakhatlas were respectful of the watch, enjoying the sight of the tiny hand moving, but plainly saw little use for it. Did white men not look at the sun? It was in the sky every day. The chief liked the compass very much, but again why did one need such a thing when the stars in the sky told a man just exactly where to go.

David would not show them the contents of his black doctor's bag. The chief seemed to understand his reticence perfectly. What Bakhatla shaman would show the unknowing his magic wares? And as the word spread that David was a shaman of the whites, there was a groundswell of complaints. Bakhatlas lined up. David insisted on a hut for privacy. He toiled the rest of the afternoon. Most complaints were rheumatism, indigestion, and eye infections. That evening, a cow was slaughtered in honor of the missionaries. Fires were already roaring. The missionaries watched. One of the warriors speared the animal deftly in the heart. There was hardly a visible wound. The animal barely stopped kicking when warriors leaped in to butcher it. Apparently, the butchers were entitled to the blood and the heart. Chunks of meat were sliced up and distributed. Their recipients immediately threw them on the fire.

Things could hardly have been better. David estimated there were two thousand of these Bakhatlas. But he had more appreciation for what Moffat had done. He could see a missionary could not hope to reach the Bakhatlas with the message of Christ without knowing their dialect of Bantu. Learning their language would have to become a top priority for him.

Later, they burned an area of the ground away from the huts and covered it with a tarpaulin. Then they pitched their tent, where they intended to sleep for the duration. David explained to the chief that his medicine worked better there. And it certainly did for him. Dozens of Bakhatlas gathered around their tent all day, waiting to see the white shaman.

Over the next few days, David and Edwards learned much about the customs of the Bakhatlas through hand gestures and help from their two guides. Someday, the chief would pass his authority on to the oldest son of his favorite wife. The chief had many wives. Often a chief was a chief simply because he had many wives who had many children.

The Bakhatlas made iron but they were not yet going to show these outsiders how they did it. Both men and women wore leathers and furs, which were hunted, tanned, and even sewn by the men. The women tended the corn, built huts, prepared food, gathered firewood, and hauled water.

"How I hate to leave these wonderful people," said David as he and Edwards climbed into the wagon.

But leave they did. Pomare and the other guide now directed them to the northwest. This time, David was aware of where they were going. To the Bakwains.

Only four days from the Bakhatlas they saw cattle, then another village. Once again a herd boy sounded the alarm. Their greeting was just like the previous meeting: alarm, suspicion, curiosity, appreciation for their gifts of trinkets, then fascination with their possessions—especially the mirror. The chief of these Bakwains was Sechele, a man of about thirty-five. He struck David as being particularly friendly and quick-witted.

The missionaries stayed several days, explaining ahead of time that David could work his medicine only out of his own tent. The Bakwains seemed very much like the Bakhatlas, but David cautioned himself not to jump to conclusions just because they dressed alike and lived in similar huts.

Every step of the journey David seemed to be studying his compass, then scribbling observations and small maps in his notebook.

They returned by the same route. Moseealele greeted them like old friends. And much to Edwards's relief, David managed to repair the trigger mechanism on Moseealele's old musket. Once again, dozens of Bakhatlas lined up to see the white shaman. But David had to be firm. He and Edwards would be there indefinitely if he stayed to doctor all of them. He promised Moseealele he would return. The chief was pleased. After all, David had kept his promise to return before. Here was a man who could be trusted.

"Always make them a promise you can keep," said David their first night away from the Bakhatlas.

"Good grief, Livingstone, you're as cunning a fox as Robert Moffat himself."

They were back in Kuruman by Christmas. Moffat was still not there. That made Edwards feel better about their rash trip north. Not much had happened at the mission. It was now the hottest and wettest time of the year. The natives inundated David for medical treatment at the mission, too. He excised tumors, cured eye infections, and gave tablets for indigestion. He was very skilled at diagnosing ailments. And even if he could not cure every patient, many found comfort in knowing their disease was not going to be fatal. His treatments were limited. But the natives thought he was a wizard.

David had a burning desire to go north again. He was convinced beyond all doubt that the Bechuana tribes would never receive the gospel from a missionary unless the missionary spoke their tongue. This time, Edwards was not willing to go with him. So in February of 1842, David went north again with Pomare and another guide. Never one to miss an opportunity, he took a different route to the Bakwains, making observations and maps all the way. Before he arrived at the location where he was certain to find Sechele and his Bakwains, he found another village!

"What is this place?" he asked his guides in his limited Bantu.

"The village of Chief Bubi of the Bakwains."

Over the next few days, David discerned that Sechele and Bubi were bitter enemies. Years ago when Sechele was a child and the tribe was still whole, Bubi and another man named Molese had murdered the chief, who was Sechele's father. The child Sechele was secreted away far to the north to live with a very great Makalolo chief named Sebitoane. The two murderers split the tribe. Years later, Sechele returned to defeat Molese. But the tribe was still split. And now David was in the village of Sechele's enemy, Bubi.

David picked up Bantu very fast. He was not doctoring all the time. After he learned that every chief also had the responsibility of making rain, he told the Bakwains he, too, could make rain. The natives were astonished to see the white shaman digging earth like an anteater tearing into an anthill. What was he doing?

David believed the other missionaries were too polite, always asking permission to do things. Too often the chief would show his authority by refusing. If David just went ahead and did it, the natives could judge for themselves if it would benefit them. As soon as they realized he was a making a canal from the river to their field of corn, they, too, were digging like anteaters. What a celebration they had when precious water rushed through the canal to their thirsty corn!

David was soon preaching in the native dialect. "Praise the Lord! He has given His blood for your sins. God so loved the world that He gave His one and only Son."

As David sermonized more and more, he uncovered more and more difficulties. The word he was using for "love" was used by the Bakwains for sexual love. The word he was using for "sin" meant cow dung if he said it in the wrong pitch. Bantu was a tonal language. The same word could mean several radically different things, depending on the pitch. But still he had to start his gospel. He had to let them know the real reason he was there. He had to save their souls. Now he was realizing how difficult that would be. Every day he appreciated Robert Moffat's accomplishments more.

After a few weeks David pushed on, accompanied by Bakwain warriors. If larger villages were to the north, he had to know. But the hill-dotted plain became too sandy for his ox wagon. The oxen were taken out of harness and loaded with supplies. The trekkers proceeded on foot. Often David would ride an ox.

Two weeks later, he entered the village of the Bamangwatos. Chief Sekomi informed him that three thousand Bamangwatos lived in the village. When the natives began calling David "God" after he doctored them, he realized again what a task awaited him in explaining the gospel. Their god was far too small.

"Be careful. We have many lions here," warned Sekomi.

David suspected the chief did not want him poking around the village too much. David still did not fear lions. On the trail, he had seen lions approach his oxen at night. As long as the oxen held their ground, the lion would not attack. But if an ox panicked and ran, the lion would attack it immediately. David learned something about the nature of men, too. One night, Sekomi came to his tent privately and said, "I wish I could change my heart. It is always proud and restless. I am always very angry with my people. Give me medicine to change my heart."

David held up the Bible. "This is the only medicine that can change your heart."

"No! I want my heart changed at once. Give me some medicine to drink."

When David would produce no magic elixir, Sekomi left his tent. After a few weeks of working with the Bamangwatos, David told Sekomi that he was going to venture farther north. Sekomi warned David about the Bakaas to the north. They were treacherous. They murdered travelers. He should not go. There were tales that the Bakaas had seen white men before, traders from the east. The Bakaas did not fear white men; neither did they like them.

When David insisted on going, Sekomi sent four warriors with him. They were to accompany him all the way north, then all the way south on his return trip to Kuruman. Of course, David realized their presence was more than protection. The chief wanted information about what all his neighbors were doing. David now had a contingent of Bakwains and Bamangwatos.

Many days farther north, he encountered the Bakaa village. This time there was no welcome, no happy sharing of mirrors and beads. All the village seemed deserted except the chief and his attendants, who simply stood and stared belligerently.

"The chief refuses to offer you food," whispered Pomare. "That is a very bad sign."

SEVEN

For the benefit of those in his own party, David said, "My God will keep us safe. You'll see."

David said a silent prayer. He really did put his trust in God. If God wanted him to bring the gospel to Africa, God would protect him. David coolly prepared his own cornmeal mush, ate it, and then stretched out to nap right in front of the Bakaa chief. What were these Bakaas to make of such trust in this white man?

Finally, with a great sigh of relief, Pomare said, "They are preparing food. They are going to welcome us."

Later, David talked the Bakaas into assembling for a sermon. He climbed a rocky hillside and spoke to them below. He was becoming more skilled at avoiding linguistic pitfalls. But he never knew for sure how the natives interpreted his sermon until they asked him questions afterward. That was very important in his own growth.

He didn't stay with the Bakaas long. He had already been away from Kuruman several months. And when he left the village to venture farther north, the Bakaa chief sent yet more warriors to escort him.

As they left the village, David overheard the Bakaa warriors speaking in Bantu. One said, "This white man is not strong. He is skinny. He only appears to be stout because he puts on baggy clothes. He will soon break down like an old woman."

From that moment, David needed no prodding to maintain a murderous pace. By the time they reached the next village to the north, the village of the Makalakas, his detractors were too exhausted to insult him. The Makalakas were a small tribe. And they were the first tribe he encountered that wasn't like the others farther south. They were darker skinned, spoke a different dialect, and planted their corn on ridges. Pomare told David they were on the fringe of another realm, that of the great Makalolo chief Sebitoane. David had gone far enough this time. He and his escorts headed back to Kuruman.

On the journey back, David had a lot of time to think. Over the weeks he had heard more and more, not only about the Makalolo chief to the north, Sebitoane, but a Zulu chief to the east, that dreaded Mosilikatze. Only the great Sebitoane to the north could stand up to Mosilikatze. Every other tribe was helpless against his onslaught. On his way back David reflected that the desire of all the chiefs to have him come and live with them might not be because they desired the gospel but because they hoped Mosilikatze would not attack a village with a white shaman.

David arrived at Kuruman at the end of June 1843. In five months, he had changed. He was lean and battered, but very confident. He spoke a reasonable amount of Bantu. The missionaries at Kuruman had never seen anyone like him. He was fearless in the wilderness. David assured them that if one was careful with dangerous animals like the lion, rhinoceros, elephant, crocodile, and leopard, one would just have to be very unlucky to get hurt.

"I don't intend to find out," muttered William Ross.

Only Edwards seemed to understand him.

Moffat was still not back from England. So what choice did David have? He doctored the natives at Kuruman through one more hot summer and then left in February of 1843 on another trip. He couldn't waste the valuable cold dry season, the only season really suitable for traveling. Again, he and his guides were alone. David had already heard that Sechele was very angry with him for visiting his rival Bubi. Messengers from Sechele made it clear that the missionary David was no longer welcome.

So naturally David told Pomare, "We shall proceed immediately to the village of Sechele."

When David's wagon arrived at the Bakwain village, Sechele was very agitated. But his agitation had nothing to do with David. Sechele's son was very sick. And the son of one of his best warriors was even sicker, emaciated from dysentery. David began doctoring the boys immediately. Any sickness, especially with fever, was feared with dread. Anyone in the wilderness could appear completely healthy one week and be stone dead from a fever the next week.

He doctored the two boys back to health. Sechele was now a great friend. And Sechele was a fountain of information about Africa. David had already heard of the legendary place west of the realm of Sebitoane called Lake Ngami. It was supposedly paradise right in the middle of the wilderness. One could not reach it by skirting the arid Kalahari wilderness to the east because of Mosilikatze. And, warned Sechele, one could not cross the Kalahari itself unless the previous season had been exceptionally rainy so that one could find plenty of the small striped melons for water.

"And even then one must avoid the dreaded tsetse fly," added Sechele, who proceeded to tell David everything he knew about the pest.

The tsetse fly was a small fly that looked like a bee. It lived north of the Bakaas in wooded areas. It was harmless to all wild game and humans. And yet, no domestic animals except donkeys were safe from it. Oxen, cattle, goats, hogs, horses, and dogs were not safe. Death could be within days or months. But the animal was almost certain to weaken and die. The distribution of the flies was very uneven. One could cross open grassland between wooded areas and be in or out of tsetse country. One might leave a wooded area infested with tsetse flies by crossing a river and enter a wooded area free of the flies. Tsetse flies had contributed heavily to the white man's dread of Africa. After all, how could a white man survive without his livestock?

When David returned to Kuruman, Edwards greeted him. "I have permission to start a new mission station in the north," said Edwards. And he added dryly, "With you, of course."

"Praise the Lord," said David.

Moffat was still not back from England. And that night David thanked God he had not waited. He had been in South Africa for over two years already. He and Edwards proceeded immediately to a location near the Bakhatlas. They signed a formal agreement with Moseealele and his Bakhatlas in August of 1843. They would call the mission Mabotsa. A mission building of fifty feet by eighteen feet was begun, under the skilled hands of Edwards. For all his lack of imagination, Edwards was now the driving force of the mission. He was the artisan. He knew how to set up the physical part of a mission.

Mabotsa was next to wooded hills. The Bakhatlas mined iron ore out of the hills and smelted it. The area had one drawback. The hills were a refuge for countless lions, which preyed on their cattle so boldly they attacked even in daylight. The Bakhatlas had suffered so much from lions, they had become submissive, as if it were their destiny to suffer lions. David encouraged them to confront lions as other tribes did. Warriors of other tribes circled their quarry, always tightening the circle. When close, the warriors would hurl dozens of spears into the beast.

But lions continued to prey on their cattle. David himself had no fear of lions. Yet he was not foolish enough to volunteer his services. His whole experience had been in avoiding fights with lions. Hunting lions was far different. Lions would fight to the death if attacked. And when one man stood alone with one double-barreled rifle that took far too long to reload, the lion had a very good chance of bringing the man down if he missed or the gun misfired. No, he could only encourage the Bakhatla warriors to have the gumption to take care of the lions themselves.

In December, David learned Robert Moffat had finally disembarked at Port Elizabeth and was on his way up the trail to Kuruman. In January, David impulsively jumped on a horse to ride from Mabotsa to meet the Moffats as they crossed the Vaal River 150 miles away.

Moffat showed David a copy of his freshly printed New Testament in the Sechuana dialect. And David saw Moffat's daughters for the first time. Bessie was a teenager, far too young to interest thirty-year-old David, now a weathered outdoorsman. Ann was older but still too young. But Mary was twenty-two. She was not plump but stout. Dark brown hair parted in the middle and pulled severely behind into a bun framed a triangular face as tan as David's. Her nose was long and sharp. By any standard, she was not beautiful. But how alive her face was! David was startled at the warmth coming from her dark eyes. She was no coquette but full of life. And she plainly saw no reason not to let David know she found him very agreeable.

By the time David had accompanied the Moffats to Kuruman, he knew Mary quite well. She, too, was forward, a bit wild in her thinking. Her parents' disapproval of David's impulsiveness had only sharpened her interest in him. Mary even spoke Bantu—with no accent at all. After all, she had been born in Griqua Town and raised in South Africa. When they saw a giraffe, she called it a *tootlooa* as naturally as breathing. An anteater was *takaru*; a rabbit, *tlolo*. Was David wrong in his resolution never to have a wife? He had only considered an English wife, a woman alien to Africa, a woman constantly wistful and unhappy in Africa. How narrow his thinking had been.

While David rode back to Mabotsa in confusion, he became sure of one thing. "I'll write dear Mary!" he cried, startling gemsbok antelopes into springing across the plain.

After he returned to Mabotsa, he did write her. He was very busy now. Edwards and his wife were cooler to him. David's trip had not set well. He was sure Edwards felt he was once again being treated only as an artisan. Edwards wanted to be treated as an equal. He did not want to be dominated again like Robert Moffat had dominated him. David tried to assure him he was an equal. But Edwards was put off by his aggressiveness. And David understood whereas Edwards once bowed to David's domineering ways, he could not bow to David in the presence of his wife.

"Perhaps you can help the Bakhatlas," said Edwards dryly. "They are having more trouble than ever with the lions."

So one day, David rallied them into doing something about it. Spears in hands, the warriors trudged toward a wooded hill they knew was a favorite with the marauders. To encourage them, David promised to back them up. He took the double-barreled rifle. And Mebalwe, a native teacher he was training, also carried a rifle. Together, they stayed on the plain and watched the spectacle, rifles ready.

Sure enough, the warriors trudged up the hill, catching a huge black-maned male in their tightening circle. But the lion broke through. That shouldn't have been possible if the warriors had stood their ground. But their hearts were not in it. David shook his head and walked back to the mission.

Suddenly Mebalwe pointed. *Tau.*

"Lion?" whispered David. "Where?"

Then he saw the huge black-maned lion. It crouched behind a bush, tail rigid; those signs were a prelude to certain attack. A lion could hit top speed almost immediately. A victim would be hit by five hundred pounds of lion going forty miles an hour. This lion crouched no more than two seconds away.

David cocked both hammers of the rifle and fired both barrels into the bush. The bullets were half-ounce slugs. The lion didn't flinch.

Bakhatlas were dancing all around now, screaming in Sechuana, "He's shot! He's shot!"

"Don't anyone approach him!" yelled David. "I want to reload."

He put a packet of powder in the gun and began to ram the bullets down the muzzle of the barrel. He heard screams. It was the lion! The great jaws snapped on his left arm. He was bowled to the ground. The lion shook him. He watched the lion gnashing on the sleeve of his jacket. He felt no fear, no alarm, no regret. The dreamy stupor was surely God's mercy to any poor unfortunate in such circumstances, man and animal alike. He moved his head from under a huge hot paw. The teeth were no longer grinding. The large yellow eyes were intent on something else. David heard an explosion. The lion bolted away from him!

He rolled over to see the lion mauling a native. A rifle went flying. "Oh no!" cried David. "Not faithful Mebalwe!"

One of the Bakhatlas jammed a spear into the lion. The lion abandoned Mebalwe to assail his new attacker. The lion seized his shoulder, then spun and fell dead. David watched Mebalwe trying to rise. His leg was covered with blood. The other Bakhatla was bloody but alive, too. Praise the Lord.

David could barely feel the Bakhatlas carrying him in a litter to the mission. He tried to regain his senses as he was placed on a mat in his hut. He realized Edwards and his wife were standing over him.

"We killed a lion," explained David. "We botched it badly."

"Livingstone," gasped Edwards. His wife's face was white as snow. David knew he must look a bloody mess.

"Wash out the wound first," David instructed Edwards. "Lion bites give terrible infections."

Mrs. Edwards stumbled out of the hut.

"You'll have to feel my arm to see how badly fractured the humerus is," said David as Edwards washed the blood away. "But first, what is the damage to the muscle?"

Edwards winced as he examined the wounds. "I count eleven punctures."

"Could have been worse. Pray I don't get infection."

"Now I'm going to feel the bone, Livingstone. Hang on." Edwards kneaded the arm like bread. "It's completely broken. It's as if you have another joint."

"You're going to have to set it in a splint."

Soon David had a very rigid splint on his arm. Edwards did a good job. Mrs. Edwards returned to say, "Mebalwe's thigh is cut badly, but the bone is not broken. The other man's injuries are even lighter."

At last David could relax. But in his physician's head, he knew relaxation was an illusion. The body's natural painkillers would wear off. And excruciating pain would begin to throb. *Oh God, if this is Your will,* he prayed, *I accept it. Give me the strength I know You can give.*

David fought the pain day after day, always reminding himself to be grateful to God. Yes, he was alive. God had other things for him to do yet. This pain was nothing. This pain was not permanent. It would go away. He didn't even get a bad infection like Mebalwe and the other man got. His jacket must have wiped the filth off the fangs as they penetrated his arm.

David was an invalid for two months. He knew the mending humerus was fragile. Any activity might give him a permanently useless arm. He had a lot of time to think. It was not time wasted. He thought of how terribly difficult it was to convert the Bakhatlas to Christ, even with native teachers. He thought of the most intelligent, most pliable native he had met so far: Sechele. If one could convert a chief like Sechele, wouldn't the rest of the Bakwains quickly follow? He realized now that he and Edwards had picked the right location—but the wrong tribe. They should have connected their mission to Sechele's Bakwains. It was not too late. In fact, it was a solution. Edwards was not happy with David's impulsive acts. So why couldn't David move on to open up yet another mission farther north?

That would be a primary objective. But first, he had something else equally important to do.

EIGHT

"Mary Moffat and I are engaged. We are to be married in Kuruman this coming January."

"Really?" said Edwards unenthusiastically.

When David returned to Mabotsa with his bride Mary in January of 1845, Edwards regarded her as an extension of Robert Moffat. Edwards could not speak his mind; he felt once again under Moffat's thumb. So David's relationship with Edwards worsened. Edwards was now threatening to write letters about David's overbearing behavior. So fiery David wrote a long letter to the London Missionary Society, defending himself. Then Edwards did not send his letter, making David look very thin-skinned.

Yet David felt he had no special influence with Moffat. The missionaries at Kuruman, who now made all decisions by committee, roundly scorned his suggestion for a seminary for natives. And David was more and more disillusioned with the Bakwains, who trudged halfheartedly to sermons but steadfastly rejected the gospel. The only lights in his life were God and his marriage to Mary. She was as bold as David.

Early in 1846, the Livingstones had an infant: Robert. And David had left Mabotsa for a new location farther north: Chonuane. He had to dip into his own meager salary of one hundred pounds a year to finance the buildings, but both he and Mary thought it was worth every penny to get away from Edwards. And the Bakwains seemed intractable in their heathen beliefs.

Sechele was a true prodigy. David started him on Robert Moffat's translation of the Old Testament into the Sechuana dialect. Within two days, Sechele had mastered the alphabet. Within weeks he was reading; Isaiah was his favorite book. David was startled by Sechele's new thirst for anything English. The chief began buying and wearing English clothes. On a particular day, he wore whatever caught his fancy. It was not unusual to see Sechele wearing a red hunting cap and a red blazer over his leather apron.

David's success with Sechele, who now began truly to understand the meaning of Christ, offset the disappointment in Chonuane as a location. Selected in haste, it appeared lush but actually suffered from lack of water. And despite knowing what the missionaries at Kuruman would say, David abandoned it and the investment of his meager salary to move forty miles farther into the wilderness by the river Kolobeng. The new mission, called Kolobeng, was started August 1847. When Mary arrived with Robert and a second infant, Agnes, she saw herds of buffaloes and zebras. Kolobeng seemed an oasis along a river that drained wooded hills all around.

One of David's next goals was to convince Sechele his five wives were four wives too many. Sechele was anxious to cooperate, but the wife problem was very difficult. A chief simply didn't shed his wives. It disgraced them and their families. It seemed inhuman even to David. But Sechele nevertheless tried, even though it undermined his authority as chief.

Another of David's goals was to place native teachers into the lands far to the east of Kolobeng. Always eager to travel he made several trips east. The eastern lands were now settled and controlled by the Dutch Boers. It had been less than fifty years since the English had landed troops in the Cape region. It had been less than fifteen years since the English banned slavery in South Africa. And it had been less than ten years since most of the Boers settled in the lands east of Kolobeng. They despised the British.

When David returned from his last eastern trip, Mary asked, "Were the Boers receptive to a mission this time?"

If only he could spare Mary. But she would want no secrets. And besides, she was far too shrewd about African ways. "Quite the opposite," he answered.

"Quite quite?"

"Yes. Hostile would be the appropriate word."

"They don't fear your missions in the east, David. They fear that you will push north, afraid you will open it up to traders, then merchants, then farmers, and then the English."

"If only I could introduce trade into the north."

"Perhaps that is the answer."

"To spreading the gospel? Yes, I agree with that view more and more. Christianity must be spread in Africa by opening the heathen areas to commerce, too."

"It might also be the answer to preventing the Boers from moving into that area."

"Yes." He frowned. "If Boers ever control the north country, I would never be able to push north."

"You are making wonderful progress with Sechele," she said.

"But the other Bakwains are not earnest in their interest in the gospel. Even Sechele is amazed by their indifference. For seventeen years, they have imitated their chief's every whim. But in loving the gospel, Sechele is an anathema to them. I should be doing so much more."

"What happened to your desire to push north"?

"No funds. Sound familiar?"

"What would excite the interest of the outside world?"

"Why, the legendary Lake Ngami, of course. Yes, that would certainly raise interest in the area if such a place could be found. . ."

"By you?"

"Perhaps one of the recreational hunters would finance a trip. Not for my reasons, of course. But what hunter can resist an area that has never been hunted before?"

"They have resisted the temptation up until now."

David laughed. "You keep pulling me back and forth, Mary. Are you two steps or three steps ahead of me?"

"Well, why haven't the hunters gone north?"

"The natives are too dangerous. Mosilikatze is in the northeast. And Sebitoane is in the north. Not to mention the Bakaas in between."

"But you know the chiefs, don't you?"

"Oh, Mary, all right. But how can I leave you and the children all the time?"

"I know why you are doing it. Do you think my wish to spread the gospel of Jesus Christ is any less than yours? I'm a child of missionaries."

So David, who was a prodigious writer of letters, added Captain Thomas Steele to his long list of correspondents. He first met Steele in the early days of Mabotsa. Steele was exemplary in dealing with natives. He seemed more like a philosopher than a hunter. It was clearly the lure of the exotic countryside that made him hunt.

By the time David's trip north firmed up, Mary had given birth to their third child: Thomas Steele Livingstone. But Steele was not to go with David. He had recommended as his replacement an equally civil hunter named Cotton Oswell. David had met Oswell several years earlier. Oswell was wealthy, classically educated, and totally devoid of personal ambition. Oswell invited his friend Mungo. And yes, the two recreational hunters would finance the entire trip.

When the two hunters arrived in Kolobeng, Oswell informed David, "We have twenty horses, eighty oxen, and two wagons loaded with enough food for a year. Do you think that will suffice, old boy?"

David added himself and thirty Bakwains to the expedition. And much to the distress of every Boer and every missionary in Africa except himself, once again David was off on a trip to the north. This time he had no less a goal than crossing the Kalahari wilderness to reach the legendary Lake Ngami!

The trip was a familiar one to David, as far as the realm of the Bamangwatos. There, Chief Sekomi insisted the white men would die in the Kalahari wilderness. When David persisted, Sekomi insisted on sending two warriors with the expedition.

By June 5, 1849, the caravan passed Serotl, which David considered the gateway to the great Kalahari wilderness, and veered northwest into the wilderness. The next days were tense. The two Bamangwatos moved ahead of the caravan. After awhile, David began to suspect they were scaring off native Bushmen who might have guided the caravan to water. Sekomi had not objected to

David going north to the Bakaas, but for some reason he didn't want David to encroach upon the Kalahari.

They pushed farther and farther. The pace was even slower than usual. The oxen could be driven no more than a few hours after dawn and a few hours before dusk. They were moving a paltry six miles a day. Natives knew of locations where water pooled four or five feet underground on natural pans of sand hardened by lime. Holes had to be dug to the limey pans to water the stock. A careless shovel would puncture the pan and the water would drain right through into the depths. Even with care they were finding only enough water for the horses but not enough for the oxen. Game in the area was the kind that lived far from water: gemsboks, duikers, and springbucks. If only they could see the tracks of zebra, buffalo, or rhino. Those animals were never far from water.

Finally, the travelers were in dire straits. They could not backtrack the oxen to their last water. It was too far. And no water was in sight. They found the juicy striped melons but not nearly enough of them to satisfy their huge contingent of men and animals. Not only did it seem the expedition would fail, there was increasing doubt they would get back at all.

Then both David and Cotton Oswell spotted a figure running through the brush in the distance. "Lion?" asked Oswell.

"It's human. It must be a Bushman!" cried David, who could now distinguish one life form from another, not by actually seeing it but by the way it moved.

Oswell spurred his horse after the fleeing form. His horse easily ran down the fugitive. He escorted the small figure back. "It's a woman of the Bushmen!" yelled Oswell.

David calmed her fears by giving her meat and beads. *Where is water?* he gestured. Of course she knew where water was located. Every Bushman knew where to find water. She led them eight miles to a spring. And better than that, not far beyond the spring stretched a gleaming ribbon across the wilderness.

The next day they inched toward the gleaming ribbon with its green borders. The horses and oxen became very agitated. The oxen sped up. It could only mean one thing. "The animals smell water!" cried David.

The caravan soon reached a village of natives called Bakuratsi on the Zouga River. The river was thirty yards wide and no more than chest deep. But it was precious treasure of clear cold water in the wilderness. And trees towered on its banks. David measured the circumference of one giant tree at seventy feet! Africa was such a wonder. One day a traveler despaired in arid wilderness, the next day he rejoiced in Eden. . . .

David managed to find out that many miles upstream was a lake so large a

Bakuratsi once traveled along its banks all day and it still stretched to the western horizon. This very same Zouga River flowed out of the lake! David and the others felt there was little to risk now. Maybe they were being tricked into heading in the wrong direction but water was plentiful. Supplies of food they had in plenty. Fruit, game, and fish seemed in abundance all along the river. They left one wagon behind and pushed west. The natives along the river lived their lives in huts and canoes. They spoke a language that had almost no words in common with the Sechuana dialect of Bantu. Yet when David saw a major river empty into the Zouga from the north, he managed to figure out that the lands the local natives claimed were lush forests and great wide rivers. That astonished him! Great rivers in the center of Africa? Perhaps river commerce could open up Africa and spread the gospel. It so overwhelmed him that when they found Lake Ngami, a vast lake seventy miles long but only chest deep, he was only mildly interested.

Upon his return to Kolobeng, David sent the London Missionary Society a detailed manuscript of his journey, apprehensive, even defensive, because he had never asked permission of anyone for such a venture. But he had to tell the society about the great rivers in central Africa. The more he thought about their potential, the more obsessed he became. Yes, they might very well be the conduits of the gospel for Africa. And he didn't doubt for a moment that great rivers abounding with fish and game had to have huge populations of Africans.

That summer Moffat brought to Kolobeng the Reverend John Freeman, one of the London Directors of the London Missionary Society. The utter disappointment in Freeman's eyes stung David's heart. He remembered his own amazement that Moffat had only forty converts in twenty years. Now here was David at Kolobeng, after eight years of contact with the Bakwains, with one true convert, a few pretenders, and thousands of unrepentant heathens.

Disillusioned with his accomplishments at Kolobeng, David went north again in 1850. He had many things yet to do. He wanted to go beyond the Zouga River to find Sebitoane, the great chief of the Makalolos.

Enduring the second trip with David and Mary had been four-year-old Robert, three-year-old Agnes, and Thomas, a babe in arms. The second trip accomplished little more than the first. David still was not able to find Sebitoane. Back at Kolobeng, Mary gave birth to daughter Elizabeth within one month. The infant died a month later.

"The trip north had nothing to do with our sweet little blue-eyed Elizabeth's death," insisted David to Robert Moffat at Kuruman, where he took Mary to convalesce. "The sweet little thing died from a respiratory sickness rampant among the Bakwains at Kolobeng. In fact, the poor little dear would have had a better chance of surviving had we still been in the wilderness."

"What do you plan to do next?" asked Moffat, confused by David's logic.

"I am planning another trip north to the Zouga River this next winter season. I must find Sebitoane."

David could tell Robert Moffat was biting his tongue. Surely, Moffat hoped, David would not take Mary and the children again. "I suppose you know best, Livingstone. We can't all stay in one place and try to convert the natives. Of course, I don't mean that as a criticism. Have you received word from the Royal Geographic Society in London?"

"No. Has something happened?"

"Yes, Livingstone. They've awarded you their annual Gold Medal for finding Lake Ngami. You also have a medal from a society in Paris. The London Missionary Society is ecstatic with you, Livingstone. Apparently your exploits have caused donations to pour in." But David's frowning father-in-law did not sound like a man offering praise.

David was not anxious to talk about personal awards. Taking Mary and the children had earned him the scorn of every missionary in Africa. When it became known Mary had been pregnant, few remained silent. When it became known the baby had died and Mary had suffered some kind of stroke after the baby was born, their protests were vehement. They were fully prepared for David's next trip north, but they were unprepared for David's fellow travelers.

Even Cotton Oswell was disturbed. "Are you sure you want to take your family again, old boy?"

"Of course. Do you think they will be safer here at Kolobeng? There are sicknesses here, too. And the Boers are a bigger threat to Mary here than the natives on the trail. Besides, Sechele has been talking of moving his village. The soil is not good for corn at Kolobeng. What would Mary do if the whole village of Bakwains pulled out?"

"But couldn't you have Mary and the children stay at Kuruman?"

"My wife does not wish that. She has left the nest. Besides, if there is a problem, she will be with the only medical doctor north of Cape Town and Port Elizabeth. Me."

Mrs. Moffat had written him a blunt angry letter. She knew Mary was pregnant once again. But nothing hurt David more than Oswell's mild disapproval. Oswell himself was fearless, having narrowly escaped death a dozen times. He was intelligent, mild-mannered, yet fully as fearless as David himself. And it was only in the most casual way that Oswell even mentioned his brushes with death. David valued his friendship very much.

They left Kolobeng on April 24, 1851. Oswell rode ahead to dig out the pans to water the stock.

NINE

On May 8th, the caravan reached the scheming Sekomi and his Bamangwatos. But this time Sekomi had an infected sore on his stomach and he was not about to offend David, the white shaman. So David doctored him. On his way out of the village, David estimated 932 huts and recorded that fact in his notes. He had made up his mind to take better notes, motivated by the enthusiasm for his trip to Lake Ngami. A few people actually seemed interested in what he was doing. So he began to record his exact longitude and latitude every few nights. He always recorded data on water pans, springs, rivers, and wildlife.

One night, they camped by a spring that fed water to a surface pool. Upon hearing the constant chirp of frogs David told the children, "That is the sweetest symphony in all of Africa. It means water, precious water."

Stretches without water, a stomach-churning worry on previous trips, no longer bothered David. He and Oswell now knew where the pans were located, and Oswell continued to ride ahead on horseback to dig them out. For the third time, they entered the village of the Bakuratsi on the Zouga.

Mary sighed. "David, hasn't this chief refused to let you cross the river each time you've been here?"

David answered, "Pray to God that this is our time for justice."

And this time the chief let David cross.

"It was like a miracle," said Mary.

"Disguised in the drab wrappings of man," commented David. "Apparently the chief of the Bakuratsi knows a group of traders are also looking for Sebitoane. This chief of the Bakuratsi fears Sebitoane very much. He is afraid the traders will sell Sebitoane many rifles for ivory. So he wants us to get up there, too, and convert Sebitoane into a man of peace as quickly as possible. Which is exactly what I intend to do."

Perseverance was one of David's greatest gifts. He never gave up easily. He was not inflexible. He had proved that he was flexible by moving his mission twice. But usually he patiently tried again and again. Always polite, as a man of God should be.

On June 7, they entered Goosimjarrah, a village of Bushmen. The Bushmen appeared well fed. Of all the natives David encountered, Bushmen were always the merriest. They seemed constantly joshing each other and laughing. And he had never known a Bushman to lie. If only missionaries could master Nama, their very difficult language of clicks.

The Livingstone children got an extra day to enjoy the village. The next day was Sunday.

On Monday, they left with Shobe, a guide from the village. Shobe was the most unusual guide David ever had. If Shobe felt like sleeping during the day, he would simply lie down under a bush and go to sleep. One day the caravan weaved erratically back and forth. David discovered Shobe was following elephant tracks! One day Shobe disappeared. The next day, he reappeared. Finally, the caravan seemed surrounded by endless thorny scrub in all directions. David began to doubt Shobe—not his honesty but his understanding of where David wanted to go. David had his caravan begin to travel at night, keying on stars of the Northern Bear.

"Thank God, I've found rhino tracks," said Oswell one morning, grinning from ear to ear. He always rode ahead. "We are near water."

Brushy grassland yielded to marsh. Soon they found the Mababe River, which flowed north. Natives along the river were not Bushmen, but Kalakas of Chief Chombo. They lived in two-storied huts. At times, the mosquitoes were so bad these Kalakas lit a fire on the first floor and slept in the smoky upper floor. But when frost was on the ground, as it was now, the mosquitoes were dormant.

That was not true of the tsetse fly. The caravan had reached the realm of the notorious insect. Chombo told them it was safe to travel through infestations of the tsetse at night. They rested another Sunday with the villagers and continued on, traveling at night. During the day they rested, with someone always watching their stock for the beelike tsetse flies.

Finally, the travelers saw the wide Chobe River. The Makalolos, who spoke a dialect of Bantu, expected them. Several of Sebitoane's subchiefs escorted them down the Chobe in canoes. The river was so wide and deep it harbored hippos as well as crocodiles. The canoes stopped at an island that belonged to Maunko, one of Sebitoane's wives. Natives were singing. The song was very pleasant, not jarring like the sharp yiping of vowels in the songs of the southern tribes. And yet, the Makalolos were much more savage in their appearance and demeanor.

There stood the great chief himself. He was a tall, wiry man of about forty-five.

"We come in peace," said David in Sechuana and extended his hand.

This gesture caught Sebitoane completely by surprise. But after the slightest pause, he was quick-witted enough to grasp David's hand. He was smiling but demanded bluntly, "Tell me why you are here."

In Sechuana David told the chief his objectives: to bring the message of the gospel, to encourage Sebitoane not to deal in slaves, and to encourage the end of wars.

The chief smiled but his words were harsh. "I thought you were here to teach me how to use guns. That is how we Makalolos will make peace."

David explained, "We do not sell guns."

"You are not what I expected. We have much to tell each other." And as they ate porridge and beef, Sebitoane began telling his visitors the story of his life. It was not brief. He talked into the night, allowing David to take notes. Many years before he was only a minor subchief. In 1823, he actually took part in an attack on Kuruman. Robert Moffat was there! The Griquas came with rifles and drove Sebitoane and his natives back to the north. Over the years, he fought the Zulus, the Bamangwatos, the Bakhatlas, the Bakuratsi, and every other tribe. He lost some battles and won others. Sebitoane eventually worked his way north, settling into the area round the Sesheke River. This Chobe River, so wide and deep, was a mere tributary to the mighty Sesheke. Along the Sesheke lived Sebitoane's Makalolos on islands and in marshes. Even the Zulus could not defeat them in their realm. Just the previous year Sebitoane himself had fought Zulus hand to hand on the Sesheke River. His people prospered in spite of river fever.

David learned Sebitoane was friendly with all visitors—at first. But with the slightest treachery, a visitor was dead. His stories revealed that he was extraordinarily shrewd. He might have lost a battle or two when he was younger, but he was never outwitted. Now he never lost battles.

After Sebitoane finished talking the next morning, he wished to see their caravan to see if it could be ferried to the north side of the Chobe. The south bank was vulnerable to attacks from Zulus. So they canoed back up the Chobe, David clutching his precious detailed history of one of the greatest chiefs of Africa.

When Sebitoane saw their wagons he said, "We cannot ferry such large things." Then he examined their oxen. "They have all been bitten by the tsetse fly. That's too bad."

"But we watched them so carefully during the day," protested David, "and we traveled only at night."

"Someone lied to you. Tsetses bite at night." Sebitoane pointed. "See the swelling over the eyes?" He felt under the jaws of each ox. "This, too, is swollen. Soon water will run from their eyes and mouth."

David's joy in finding a great chief with such wisdom was cut short. Sebitoane himself became ill. He smoked hashish and coughed, but now he had a fever, too.

"Don't you have some medicine for Sebitoane?" Oswell asked David later in private.

"I don't dare start doctoring him now. I think he has chronic bronchitis from smoking that devilish hashish year after year. Do you see how emaciated he is? His fever may be the onset of pneumonia, which I can't cure. I have no choice but to let his own shamans doctor him."

"I understand perfectly, old boy. If he were to die under your care, we would all be killed."

"Precisely, Oswell."

And when Sebitoane began to cough green phlegm, David knew the great chief not only had pneumonia but was likely to die. Sebitoane's three shamans cut his skin in fifty places to bleed him. They thought that treatment was what cured him the year before.

On July 7, a Sunday, David visited Sebitoane, who was lying inside a hut, almost too weak to lift his arm in greeting. The chief saw little Robert and said, "Take Robert to Maunko's house and get some milk for him."

Later that day Sebitoane died.

David mourned the great chief. Another soul lost! It was heartbreaking. If only he could have met Sebitoane sooner. The chief had great intellect like Sechele. Surely he would have accepted the truth of the gospel. Now it was too late. It was this sense of tragic urgency that hung over David's head all the time. Africans were dying everywhere, souls lost to eternity. What could be more heartbreaking than that? Yet other white men wondered why he took such chances. If only they saw the tragedy the way he saw it!

And why did Sebitoane have to die? For thirty years, Sebitoane dodged death almost daily. For many years David had wanted to seek him. And for several years David did seek him. Now, after finding him, death claimed him in just sixteen days! What did it mean?

David and the caravan stayed on with the Makalolos. Every day, David took notes. His oxen began dying just as Sebitoane had predicted. And David saw sights that would haunt him forever: slaves in chains. He soon learned the exchange rate. One boy was worth about nine yards of good cotton cloth from the slave traders. But a musket was so precious it might cost as much as ten boys.

"Oswell," said David, "to think that cotton cloth I once manufactured is used for such a purpose. If only honest traders could get to the interior of Africa this slave traffic would stop." David could not get that idea out of his mind. It seemed Africa had to be opened to traders with goods that the natives craved. Trade was the key to spreading the gospel and stopping war and slavery. But few traders would travel the harsh way David traveled. How would trade ever reach Africa?

A jaunt to the east with Oswell and their Makalolo companions brought the answer home forcefully. There they saw the Sesheke River. Right there in the center of Africa was a colossal river five hundred yards wide!

The answer to all of Africa's problems hit David like a bull elephant: This great river—if it flowed all the way into the Indian Ocean—would bring traders. And why wouldn't it reach all the way east? It was a mighty river here among the Makalolos, and it would only get larger as it picked up more tributaries.

In August, five weeks after Sebitoane died, the caravan headed south again. The days would get hotter and finally by November, the summer rain would begin. The travelers could not delay any longer. Knowing where water was located and knowing which areas to avoid made a great difference in crossing wilderness. In just two weeks, they reached the Zouga River.

On September 15, still along the banks of the Zouga, Mary gave birth to a boy. They named him William Oswell after their good friend, but David nicknamed the boy "Zouga."

A few days later, Thomas got "river fever." The temperatures along the river during that day were above 100 degrees. David moved the caravan to hills above the river where it was cooler. He wrapped Thomas in damp sheets and made sure he drank plenty of water. Then he gave him doses of quinine. They stayed there nearly a month. Finally, Thomas and the baby Zouga were both healthy enough to travel.

When they reached Kolobeng, David's fears about Sechele's moving his village were justified. Sechele had moved twelve miles from Kolobeng. David's mission at Kolobeng was now isolated. All the way back from Sebitoane's country, David had thought about finding rivers to open the interior of Africa. His lack of converts after ten years made his decision to continue exploring the north country easy. But there was the very grave decision as to where Mary and the children should live. Isolated Kolobeng was no longer an option. Bringing the children on further trips was not an option, either. Next time, he might not get back south again for a very long time.

David broke the news to Mary. "Mary, you must take the children and go live with my parents in Scotland."

David was glad Mary so readily agreed. The children would now get a real education. No Livingstone he ever knew, no matter how poor, ever neglected the education of his children. Even his grandfather, poor as any wretch could be fresh off a failed farm in Ulva, found the pennies to educate seven children. And his father, Neil, had done the very same thing. No Livingstone child— boy or girl—would face life without the power of literacy.

He didn't have to explain to Mary he would rarely be at Kolobeng any more, either. Mary knew exactly what he had in mind. "I know you intend to explore central Africa. And I approve. But it is still very difficult. Yet, I am a missionary's daughter. I know a great deal about separations."

Mary didn't have to reveal all her thoughts to David. By now he knew what she was thinking. She had lived six active years with him; she had four healthy children. She and David would resume their life after he explored awhile. And like every young married woman of her day, she knew togetherness meant constant pregnancies followed by ever-increasing toil. Being separated had its blessings, too. David knew she was thinking of that, as well.

They stayed in Kuruman for three weeks. Mary's brother Robert was there now, newly married. In January of 1852, the Livingstones went southwest. Traveling that civilized route by ox wagon was always pleasant, like a succession of picnics. They reached Cape Town on March 16. But David could not get his family on a ship that sailed any sooner than the middle of April.

He was not one to be idle. His throat was so bad now he could not speak in public. So he had his uvula removed. Then to make sure information gathered on his trip was not in vain, he wrote a paper about the region north of Lake Ngami and sent it to the Royal Geographic Society. He was sorely tempted to call the Sesheke River the Zambesi River but resisted. Cape Town astronomer Thomas Maclear taught him how to make very sophisticated measurements of latitude and longitude in the field with a chronometer and sextant.

He soon discovered it was a good thing he could not speak in public. He was well known enough to be hated by whites in Cape Town, especially Dutch Boers. He was known as the troublemaking missionary who opposed slavery and treated black Africans like equals. He was said to be an exceedingly dangerous man, poking about in the wilds, probably wanting to sell guns to the heathen next. The entire London Missionary Society was hated. But David was by far the most aggressive, by far the most dangerous, and by far the worst.

The atmosphere of hatred made watching his family sail away from Cape Town easier. Through Oswell's generosity, Mary and the children had embarked in brand-new wardrobes.

David had many delays while at Cape Town, often due to deliberate mischief by Boers. That and the prevailing hatred made him sour and anxious to get back to Kolobeng. He didn't reach Kuruman until September. It had been one year since Zouga's birth. He felt he had accomplished almost nothing in one whole year toward opening Africa to the gospel.

But at Kuruman a letter Robert Moffat had received changed his mind completely.

TEN

The letter from Sechele read:

> *My friend of my heart's love. . . .I am undone by the Boers, who have attacked me, though I have no guilt with them. They required that I should be in their kingdom but I refused. They demanded that I should prevent the English and southern tribes from passing through to the north. . . . They began on Monday morning at twilight and fired with all their might and burned the village with fire and scattered us. They killed 60 of my people and captured women and children and men. . .and they took all the cattle and all the goods of the Bakwains. . .the house of Livingstone, they also plundered, taking all his goods. . . .*

How little David had suffered compared to faithful Sechele. But if David had not been delayed at Cape Town and had been at Kolobeng, isolated as it now was from Sechele's warriors, he surely would have been killed. Was that why God delayed him at Cape Town? Yes, he was sure of it. Another brush with death. Yet spared by Providence. He couldn't even return to Kolobeng to visit his daughter Elizabeth's grave. Boers were still in the vicinity. They had gone to Kolobeng first. With four wagons they methodically stole all David's furniture, medical supplies, tools, and food. Then they maliciously ripped apart all his journals and papers and burned them. Then the Boers went after Sechele and his Bakwains.

"These stories about the Boers aren't making it easy to find natives to accompany me back to Sebitoane's country, "David complained to Robert Moffat." The Boers want to cut us off from the north, but they will not succeed."

Moffat was subdued. "Our own government has given up on doing anything with the wilderness. The Boers know that."

Over the days, David collected a retinue of natives. His main companion was a West Indies mulatto named George Fleming. Fleming was a solid man, but the six natives seemed a poor lot. Who else would venture into the teeth of the Boers?

In December, he left Kuruman with two ox wagons. Leaving in the height of summer betrayed his overpowering desire to push north. He skirted Kolobeng and farther on he stayed with the Bakwains for two weeks. He was delighted to see Bakwains were reading the Bible. Good Sechele. But Sechele was not there. Encouraged by Moffat, Sechele had gone to Cape Town to demand justice. David, who had just been in Cape Town, knew scant justice waited for a black African in Cape Town.

The trip through the Kalahari was severe in the heat of summer. In the first weeks he shot steinbucks, impalas, an eland, and even giraffes to feed his men. Some of these animals came to the pans they had dug out to water the oxen. The poor animals were willing to risk death for the water they smelled. David never killed an animal without regretting it. And these particular animals, so desperate to drink, hurt most of all.

David loved the creatures of nature. They revealed God's miraculous creativity. At one spot north of the Zouga River, a nest David found enthralled him. The bird had taken green leaves and woven them together with threads from a spider's web. The bird actually punctured the leaves with its beak, inserted thread through the holes, and somehow thickened the ends into knots! God's unseen hand was everywhere.

By May of 1853, he saw a wonderful sight. "It's the Chobe River!" he called to George Fleming.

Over six thousand natives welcomed him in the main village of Linyanti. The Makalolos had planted a special garden for him, which was now choked with corn. Women immediately began shelling it and grinding cornmeal for him. Yet the atmosphere was thick with worry, too. The new chief of the Makalolos was Sebitoane's son Sekeletu, a youth of eighteen. Sekeletu had inherited a title to a realm he might never merit. It was rumored some warriors were plotting against him.

In that aura of treachery, David came down with the river fever for the first time. He almost welcomed it. He would see if the Makalolo shamans had some marvelous native remedy. But he soon wrote:

> *After being stewed in their vapor bathes, smoked like a red herring over green twigs, and charmed. . .I concluded that I could cure the fever more quickly than they can.*

David resolved that he would act as if he were not sick at all. He had much to do. By canoe—fever or no fever—he ventured north up the wide Sesheke River into the Barotse Valley to find a location for a mission away from the deadly fever-breeding marshes. He knew that much about the cause of the fever. Its outbreaks were concentrated around stagnant waters of the marshes.

Sekeletu went with him. The intrigue continued. One night Sekeletu confided to David, "My half brother Mpepe intends to kill me." David had met Mpepe before. He was a braggart and so disrespectful that Sebitoane himself had told David, "If he ever treats my son Sekeletu with such disrespect, he will be killed." David knew Sebitoane was rarely wrong about anything.

Suddenly, by the side of the fire right in front of David, Sekeletu's warriors seized Mpepe, dragged him to the outskirts of camp, and speared him to death. David was shocked. He had not even had a chance to rise and protest. The execution was so precipitous. Had Sekeletu taken advantage of David's presence? Perhaps David had triggered it. Maybe rivals were saying the white shaman's approval of Sekeletu would strengthen his hold on power, so Sekeletu must be brought down as soon as possible. David convinced himself Mpepe had been conspiring to kill Sekeletu. Still, he would watch the young chief carefully.

The lack of a suitable site for a mission and David's recurring fever tested his resolve. The fever began like a common cold but soon its victim had racking pain in the neck and back, often with a throbbing headache. The pained areas grew hot with fever, yet the victim felt chills. Vomiting was frequent. Ulcers formed around the mouth. Then the victim burned with fever but could not sweat. Finally, profuse sweating broke the fever but left its victim debilitated. About when the poor soul felt healthy, the disease flared up again to run the same painful course. Each morning David greeted the dawn with a reminder from Proverbs 17:22: "A merry heart doeth good like a medicine." It served him well through seven attacks of river fever in nine weeks!

David was never idle no matter how bad he felt. If he was too weak to leave his tent, he worked on his journal. He synthesized observations of twelve years. Although some Europeans had speculated many species of rhinoceros, David clearly saw two species, each with two varieties. He not only described each variety in physical detail, but he recorded their habits.

There was no large mammal that he did not describe succinctly. Yet he saw the small creatures, too. He knew if termites were rushing out of their mounds to retrieve straw, it meant rain was imminent. He recognized fifteen varieties of ants and termites, noting that they occurred in great abundance. Of course, David recorded even more observations about the Africans. Many of their customs weighed heavily on him. The killing of babies by the Bakaas because they cut their upper teeth before they cut their lower teeth was almost too barbarous to record. There were many heartbreaking realities every day with the Makalolos that made the spread of the gospel urgent. David's frequent sermons were well attended by the Makalolos. He read small passages from the Bible, then illustrated what the passages meant with stories. He had a new slide projector that awed the natives even more than his mirror. David called it his "magic lantern." After the sun went down he thrilled the natives with slide shows of scenes from the Bible.

"But the show has become the object of their whole desire," he admitted to himself one evening.

His dissatisfaction with his efforts deepened. Sekeletu not only showed no interest in the gospel, but an aversion. He seemed to already know about the teaching in the Bible that Jesus said a man could have only one wife. Sekeletu had many wives. He enjoyed them very much. When David offered to teach him God's own words out of his Bible in the Sechuana dialect, Sekeletu sent his father-in-law and stepfather in his place.

By November, David was anxious to explore. Once again, he felt he had failed to convert Africans. The painful truth was that they clung fiercely to their native beliefs, protecting their habits of many wives, even the terrible custom of offering a wife to a guest for the night, and worse yet, selling fellow Africans into slavery.

He met slave traders, including the Portuguese Silva Porto. David's stay in Rio de Janeiro had given him enough Portuguese to converse with the aid of much arm waving. Porto was amused when David upbraided him for trading slaves. After all, shrugged Silva Porto, what could one expect a man of the cloth to say? David had more in common with the shrewd Portuguese than he liked to admit. Whereas David was as daring as he was righteous, Porto was as daring as he was evil. He, too, had penetrated where few white men had ever been. He, too, had story after story of rivers and natives but all to the west, all toward the Portuguese haven of Luanda on the Atlantic Ocean. David had always assumed he would first follow the Sesheke downstream to the Indian Ocean. Now he wanted to try the western passage first.

Sekeletu protested David's plans to leave. "Why depart? I hear there are Makalolos who can give your sermons by heart."

"I'll find a great river. Then I will follow it west. To the Atlantic Ocean. Perhaps honest traders—not traders in slaves—will come to you on that river to gladden your heart."

"The slave traders have a well-worn route to that great water to the west."

"I can't follow the slave route. The slave traders know I am against slavery. That route is too dangerous for me now. And the people along the route are probably corrupted. I will go west but I must go north first."

"It is death to go north!"

"I can't use my ox wagons. I need men and canoes."

"I will honor your wish to go north to your death."

Sekeletu's feeling of doom affected David, too. He wrote a few last letters, which Sekeletu promised to send south to Kuruman whenever a traveler was available. To his brother-in-law, David wrote, *I shall open a path into the interior or perish.* George Fleming was not going with him. He would stay behind to try to establish an ivory trade for the Makalolos with the south. If David could not find a great river route to open commerce, perhaps the lure of ivory could bring honest traders from the south to the Makalolos. They must give the Makalolos incentive to give up trading slaves.

David Livingstone

A feeling of impending doom hung over the twenty-seven Makalolos Sekeletu supplied David as porters. For firearms, the escort carried three muskets, one pistol, and a rifle. One man stayed near David, carrying his huge double-barrel. Their supplies included ammunition, tea, sugar, and coffee. It was in packing for the journey that David discovered much of his supply of medicine had been stolen and traded—by some of the very men he brought with him from Kuruman. He immediately dismissed them, resisting the strong temptation to have Sekeletu mete out Makalolo justice.

Large tin canisters protected his best clothing, his magic lantern, and what little medicine remained. His precious instruments were wrapped in water proof oilskin. The sextant was a fine one made by Troughton and Sims of Fleet Street in London. His chronometer watch was made by Dent of the Strand for the Royal Geographic Society. His telescope was small but could be steadied by screwing the base onto a tree. He also had a Dolland thermometer and two compasses, one which he carried in his pocket.

For his own comfort he took a small tent, a rug for a mattress, a sheepskin blanket, and another canister with his books. His books were the Sechuana Testaments, his own Bible in English, several books for astronomical calculations, and a lined ledger that he used for his journal. The ledger was revealing. On previous trips his lock-clasped ledgers had about 350 pages. But the lock-clasped ledger for this trip had well over eight hundred pages.

To show confidence in the expedition, Sekeletu gave him ivory tusks. "Exchange them for European goods," said Sekeletu. "Buy me a horse, too." But his eyes showed he never expected to see David again.

Once more David found himself traveling in the heat of the summer. But he spent too much time waiting anyway. The flotilla of canoes started up the steamy Sesheke River into the Barotse Valley. The first sixty miles were familiar. But soon he was passing out of the influence of the Makalolos into the realm of the Balondas. The expedition left the river for a while to bypass Gonye Falls.

ELEVEN

The country was lush. Seas of grass were interspersed with thick woodlands, even patches of dense forest. Members of the caravan had a routine now. They would rise each morning at five o'clock. In the weak light of dawn, they dressed and made coffee. Then they loaded the canoes and departed. The cool morning was the best part of the day. The men rowed strongly. Yet the speed of the canoes was governed by the speed of oxen being herded along the shore. Not only did the herders have to cut through brush but the Shesheke River was crawling with fat crocodiles. The great reptiles could launch their one thousand pounds completely clear of the water to snap razored jaws on an unsuspecting animal.

By noon, the travelers stopped to drink water, eat leftovers, and rest an hour. Then the heat of the afternoon gradually wore them and their stock down to an indifferent plod. In the evening, the men secured the canoes and cut grass to cushion David's rug. His various canisters and special supplies were arranged around his bed. They pitched the tent over all of that. The main fire crackled only a man's length from the tent. The Makalolos prepared all meals, which were the food the natives normally ate. David indulged only in coffee or tea. At night, the two fiercest Makalolos slept flanking the tent. Mashauana, the head boatman, slept in front of the flap of the tent. The oxen were placed near the fire, encircled by lean-tos of the sleeping porters.

As they approached a village now, they sent an emissary ahead. David knew it was not wise to surprise a village. They had to wait for a welcome, often several days. The river was full of fish. The nearby grasslands teemed with meat on the hoof. So the travelers ate well while waiting. Fever still attacked David. For twelve years, he had suffered only broken bones. His wounds had often been excruciating but they healed. Now suffering seemed constant, alternating from bouts of fever to spells of weakness and dizziness. His quinine, the one thing that seemed to alleviate river fever, had been stolen.

The new year of 1854 brought David completely into the domain of the Balondas. The main chief in the area was called Shinte. David's friendship with Sekeletu was of no value here. Shinte did not like the Makalolos. Balondas were already doing him mischief. David stopped and sent word ahead to their nearest chief, Manenko. She was the niece of Shinte. She sent an envoy to tell him to wait; then, after letting him wait several days, sent another envoy, ordering him to come to her village.

"We will bypass her," David told his men, in a rare show of temper.

The next village had another female chief, Nyamoana, who was the sister

148

of Shinte and the mother of Manenko. And soon Manenko herself appeared. She was a tall, robust woman of twenty. Her husband was her spokesman, constantly rubbing sand on his chest and arms as he greeted them. Other men were thumping their elbows against their ribs.

Once again the travelers were delayed in a whimsical, half-threatening way. When they ran out of food, the Balondas offered them only tasteless tubers for nourishment. David decided to call their bluff and leave. He prided himself on being able to see inside the hearts of Africans. He rarely misjudged them. Being alive was proof of that.

But as he ordered his Makalolos to pack up and launch the canoes, Manenko unloaded such a tirade of abuse on his men, they stopped working. David shrugged and started to load a canoe himself. His example would surely spur them on. Suddenly, he felt a firm hand on his shoulder. It was Manenko, looking at him with pity in her eyes.

She said, "Now, my little man, just do as the rest have done."

David sensed he must not challenge Manenko's authority. She had handled the situation perfectly. So the travelers waited. After an interval of several days, Nyamoana presented him with a necklace as if she was atoning for their delays. It had a seashell that was as highly prized by the Balondas as gold was to an Englishman.

A few days later, they thrashed into thick forest behind Manenko herself to visit the village of Shinte, the head chief of the Balondas. The country could hardly have been more different from the Kalahari wilderness. Vine-draped trees were so dense, the travelers had to hack their way through. And rain, so precious in the south, seemed to fall in buckets.

Manenko set a fast pace. David was sure she had to prove herself constantly to men in the tribe. David had done that once to disbelieving Bakaas. She succeeded, too. Many of the travelers were exhausted. David was spared the exertion by riding his ox Sinbad. Sinbad had a back as soft as a mattress but a nasty disposition. Every time David attempted to use an umbrella in the downpour, Sinbad's great curved horn knocked him flying.

After the travelers arrived at the outskirts of Shinte's village, Manenko awaited her uncle's approval to enter. He kept her waiting in what seemed a whimsical fashion. So David now knew it was the custom of Balondas to behave like that with visitors.

Already in Shinte's village were two half-breeds who spoke Portuguese. They were accompanied by native henchmen, the notorious Mambaris, known throughout the interior for their gaudy European prints. Anywhere a member of this tribe was seen in lands where David had visited, slaves were being bought or captured.

"Look!" said David's head boatman, Mashauana, pointing toward the tents of the Portuguese.

"Slaves," groaned David. In front of the tents were women, chained together in dejection. David approached them. "Where are you from?"

"Lobale," answered one woman fearfully.

"That is the hill country to the west," said Mashauana.

The slave traders maintained military discipline, as if this behavior would intimidate the Balondas. A drummer and a bugler performed at regular intervals. When Shinte finally received David, the Portuguese, too, were seeing him for the first time, and they entered drumming, bugling, and firing their rifles in salute.

The kotla was a square one hundred yards on each side. On one end under banyon trees sat Shinte on a throne covered by leopard skins. He was a man, neither small nor large, in his fifties. He wore a checked jacket over a scarlet kilt of coarse, napped cotton. Around his neck hung many strings of beads. Iron and copper bracelets jangled on his arms. Goose feathers plumed over his pillbox cap of fine beads.

David sat down about forty yards away as the Balondas presented themselves to Shinte. They rubbed ashes over their chests and arms. Suddenly, Shinte's warriors ran toward David, screaming, making faces, and brandishing swords. David knew this display served much the same purpose as the lion's bluff. After he sat expressionless through the display, the warriors turned to Shinte, politely bowed, and moved aside.

Nyamoana then gave a speech, spiced with exaggerated gestures, telling Shinte everything she knew about David. She began by complimenting David on returning prisoners taken by Mpololo of the Makalolos. She praised him for preaching that tribes should live in peace. She said he had a book that he claimed was the word of God. But then she presented David's flaws. He had preached first to their enemies, the Makalolos.

"So maybe," she finished, "he is telling lies to the Balondas."

The entire time that Nyamoana spoke, a hundred women in the same red fabric sat behind Chief Shinte, often interrupting with laughter or chanting in unison. David had been in councils among African tribes for twelve years. Never before had he seen women even allowed in a council. But he had never seen women as chiefs before, either. The Balondas gave their women many rights.

Also while Nyamoana spoke, three men drummed and four men played a marimba, an instrument with fifteen wooden keys. The faster they played, the more excited the gathering became. And Nyamoana was only the first speaker. She was followed by eight others. It was a large council, with over a thousand people gathered around, of which several hundred were warriors.

At long last, Shinte, who had remained as immobile and expressionless as David throughout the speeches, stood up. But he said nothing. The council was over!

The next morning, Shinte summoned David. Shinte said, "During the council yesterday I expected a man who claims he is from God to approach me."

David replied, "When I saw your own warriors keep their distance from you, I thought I should do the same. Have you seen a white man before?"

"Never. Some of the slave traders have brown skin. But your skin is white. And your hair is straight like grass. And I have never seen clothes like yours before."

"I wish you to have one of my oxen," David said.

"Yes. I like that kind of meat very much."

"You could have that kind of meat all the time if you kept oxen yourself. This grassy country is very good for cattle."

"But how would I get cattle?"

"Trade with the Makalolos."

"My enemies?"

"Yes."

Suddenly Manenko appeared. She had been invisible ever since David arrived, making him think perhaps she was not in good standing with her uncle Shinte. But she said sharply to Shinte, "This white man belongs to me. Therefore I want the ox." She had her men slaughter the ox right in front of Shinte and left him only one leg.

Shinte seemed amused by her audacity. The wisdom of David's decision weeks ago to yield to Manenko was borne out. She was a favorite of Chief Shinte. She was very powerful among the Balondas.

When David saw Shinte again later, river fever was racking him. The hot rainy weather seemed to aggravate the fever. Shinte said, "I can send men to guide you toward the great water to the west. But if you have the river fever, you won't make it."

"What do you Balondas do for this fever?"

"Drink lots of beer." Shinte offered him a beer they made from corn.

David politely sipped some beer but he did not believe it was a remedy. It only made a man so drunk he forgot the fever for a while. Shinte, now eating beef, spoke again. "This is very good. I will get cattle from Sekeletu. He is like a son to me. I knew Sebitoane very well."

David was surprised to hear Shinte speak favorably of Sebitoane. And his son Sekeletu. Was the belligerence the Balondas expressed toward the Makalolos mere talk and posturing? Or was Shinte not telling the truth? Some chiefs were as deceptive as any white man.

Later, David showed Shinte and his court his slide show. The first image, that of Abraham holding the knife over Isaac, was life-sized. The women of the court began screaming and fled. They thought they, too, would be knifed. They could not be persuaded to return.

Shinte was pleased with the images. "Those look much more like gods than our own gods of clay and wood."

David let Shinte examine the slide projector so he would know it was only a machine. He did not like to deal in "magic." Shinte also came into his tent in the middle of the night. There he examined David's instruments, the mirror, and everything he considered exotic. To show his gratitude Shinte gave David a very rare seashell.

After being with Shinte for ten days, he left with Shinte's guide, Intemese. The new guide was not honest, often delaying them for false reasons. But he was useful anyway. Without Intemese to smooth things over, villagers went wild with worry as they saw the caravan approach, more frightened by the Makalolos than by David.

The reddish soil was rich in organic matter. The Balondas raised manioc in ridges. It required little care. When they harvested the roots, which were several times larger than a carrot, they started a new plant by simply breaking off a fragment of the stalk and planting it in the freshly created hole. Among the manioc plants, the Balondas planted beans.

Soon the caravan crossed the Leeba River to enter a vast plain of shallow water with occasional small islands. The travelers needed Intemese more than ever. There seemed no landmarks to go by. At night, when they slept on one of the small islands, they had to build mounds for their beds and ridges around their sleeping areas. If they did not make those tedious preparations they spent a wet night.

They left the saturated plain to reach the realm of the Balonda chief Katema. David already knew the Balondas had recently lost their greatest chief, Matiamvo, much like the Makalolos lost Sebitoane. His death made traveling more dangerous, because the lesser chiefs were suspicious of any new development. Some Balonda chief would try to take the throne, and use of outsiders was always suspected. And Makalolos were regarded as the fiercest kind of savage.

Although the Bolandas spoke a dialect of Bantu, David still had to speak through an interpreter to explain the gospel. Only the slide show had held the interest of Shinte's Bolandas. But Katema would not even permit the slide show. From the outset, Katema seemed very different from Shinte. Further proof was in the fields. He had a herd of splendid white brahma cattle. But he had not domesticated them. They were hunted down like wild game. David explained that they could be tamed, even milked.

"I wish to go on to the great waters to the west," said David finally.

"The plains of Lobale are flooded now. You will have to go north where traders have never gone before. I will give you a guide, Shakatwala."

David preferred to be off the slave route anyway. To show his gratitude to

Katema, David had an ox butchered. But Katema would not eat with him. He would accept the meat to be cooked later by his own people, but he would not eat anything prepared by visitors.

The travelers descended into a watery plain again. Africa was so flat that there were few barriers to travel other than hostile animals or natives. David was used to seeing footpaths everywhere. But on these watery plains the paths disappeared or were in water too deep to follow. So they thrashed through tall grass, which was not only tiring but painful.

When they left the watery plain, David recognized a startling change. Rivers now ran north or west instead of south or east. Cool breezes blew from the north. In all his years in Africa, he had never felt a cool breeze from the north. And the topography changed. He saw the first deep canyon since Kolobeng. By traveling west across north-flowing rivers, the travelers wearily passed in and out of valley after valley.

The natives were different, too. The travelers had entered the realm of Katende. Contrary to Katema's belief that traders never came this way, traders had been here. Katende's people were the most corrupt natives David had seen yet. They would not offer food but only sell it. They knew nothing of money, not even gold. But food was not cheap. For payment they wanted gunpowder or cotton cloth or slaves or tusks or beads or copper rings or seashells.

They continued on their travels, encountering one demand for payment after another. Soon David's Makalolos were giving their own possessions, even their clothing, out of fear of being stranded in such a hostile place. If the caravan ever reached the west coast, they might not be wearing anything!

They entered the realm of the Chiboque tribe, still crossing north-flowing rivers. David had an ox slaughtered near the village of a chief named Njambi. The meat was for David's own men, who seemed more and more despondent. But David sent the hump and ribs to the chief with the message that it was payment for passing through.

The next day a messenger came from the village to say, "Njambi will not let you pass for anything less than one man, or one ox, or one gun, or plenty of gunpowder, or a seashell."

TWELVE

David was very angry, but he would let no man die for one ox. So he agreed. After they left the Chiboques, David stopped in the hills to talk with his Makalolos.

He said, "We must continue west without the aid of villagers. Soon we will have nothing left."

"And then you will have to give them one of us," complained one of the Makalolos.

"We will never give up men," insisted David. "We won't fight to save an ox, but we will fight to save a man."

So they continued on to the west. David suffered from river fever again. And ornery Sinbad took advantage of his weakness, often ducking under a low branch to scrape him off, then trying to kick him. The only thing that kept Sinbad from being the first ox butchered long ago was the fact that his back was spongy soft.

David was in the clutches of burning fever now. Finally he was unable to travel. They camped. Once on awakening he overheard mutiny among his men. Some said it was time to go back, before it was too late.

David rushed out, brandishing a pistol. "There will be no more talk like that," he growled, trying not to show how dizzy he was.

He forced himself to travel farther. It was when they were camped, making no progress at all, that the men lost heart. But again he collapsed. They camped on the banks of the Loajima River. David fell into fitful sleep. He awoke to total silence.

"The men have abandoned me," he moaned. "God help me now." He stumbled out of his tent. "You are here!" he exclaimed in gratitude. His men had built a stockade. "What is happening?" asked David.

Mashauana answered, "We are surrounded by Chiboques."

David parleyed with the Chiboques. Once again, they wanted a man, an ox, a tusk, or a gun. David offered copper rings. The Chiboques would settle for nothing less than an ox.

"Tell them I agree. But don't give them Sinbad."

Once again, they pushed on. David was so sick now he no longer cared if he was attacked or not. But he knew he could not collapse in his tent and wait for the fever to break. It wasn't fair to his men. He had to get them out of the country of the Chiboques. Once more Sinbad scraped David off his back, but this time his kick battered David's thigh. And constant wetness had chaffed David's skin to a bloody abrasion. He was nearly an invalid, but he forced himself to continue.

And then they found themselves stopped again. "We won't let you pass!" yelled Chiboques. "You must come to our village!"

David labored to walk to the front of his Makalolos. He turned to them. "We are going ahead, men. Don't fight unless they fight first." He walked forward, and leveled his rifle on a man who seemed to be the leader. He yelled, "I could kill you easily!" He pointed to the sky. "But I fear God!"

The man stepped forward. "I am Ionga Panza. I, too, fear to kill. We only want you to come to our village."

David couldn't resist the man's appeal. And they all proceeded to the village where Ionga Panza presented the travelers with a goat, then demanded an ox and a tusk for payment. To make matters worse, slave traders showed up with firearms and took the side of the Chiboques. So David surrendered one ox and one tusk. Ionga Panza refused the first ox because its tail had been severed in an accident; to the Chiboques that meant the ox was bewitched.

When David parleyed with his Makalolos in the forest after they left the village, they were more discouraged than they had ever been. Several wanted to start back immediately.

"You can't go," pleaded David. "The Portuguese settlements are only a few days away! We're almost there."

One of the Makalolos spoke for the others. "We want to go back now before we lose everything."

"Today is the twenty-fourth of March, men. Give me one more week. And cut off the tails of our last four oxen immediately," said David, amazed he had not thought of it sooner.

Mashauana laughed. "Yes, cut their tails off. We'll surely lose no more oxen.

The Makalolos agreed to continue. They seemed to find relief in the trick to save their oxen. And David tried not to feel too much pleasure in seeing the solution applied to Sinbad. Six days later the caravan reached a ledge and looked one thousand feet down into a colossal valley.

The other side of the valley could not be seen. A blanket of dark green forest stretched north to the horizon. In meander bends of the river were light green meadows of grass. The valley of the Quango seemed paradise.

The descent was so steep that many slopes were bare red soil. David could not ride Sinbad on such slopes. David was so weak Makalolos had to hold him up as he stumbled down the slope on foot or he would have toppled into space. His doctor's mind knew he was almost dead from river fever. He was a bag of bones. Surely God wouldn't let him die just before victory.

When they reached the valley floor, David saw the Quango was very muddy, a circumstance not seen by him in any African river before. The river itself was one hundred fifty yards wide and very deep. The men would need canoes. They worked their way toward a village situated far back from the river.

A local chief met the travelers. "I am Sansawe of the Bashinjes." Sansawe was young. He wore a conical cap that pointed straight back from his head. His beard was forked.

"Why is your village so far off the river?" asked David.

"Because the river swarms with poisonous snakes. You must get our help to cross. I see you have tusks. I want them."

David had never liked to create the impression with natives that he was supernatural. But today when he saw the fear grow in Sansawe's eyes, he fed that fear. Soon Sansawe was sure David was bewitched. He couldn't escape to his village fast enough.

"We'll go farther down the river to find canoes," David told his Makalolos.

The chief from the next village also met them, demanding tribute. Would this evil never end? Somehow they had to get themselves across the Quango.

Mystically, a man approached them. He wore a military uniform! "I am Cypriano di Abreu," the man said in Portuguese. With gestures the soldier explained he was on this side of the Quango to buy beeswax.

David knew enough Portuguese to tell the soldier he wanted to cross the Quango. Soon Cypriano, who was a sergeant, arranged their crossing. On the opposite shore, Cypriano said, "You are now in the domain of the Portuguese. The natives on this side of the Quango are Bangalas, our subjects."

After they reached a small outpost of adobe buildings, David produced a letter of recommendation he had carried with him ever since he left Cape Town in 1852. The letter was written by a powerful Portuguese official. After that, Cypriano treated him like royalty. David learned they were still three hundred miles from the Atlantic Ocean, but the trip was only tedious, not dangerous.

Six days later they departed, rested and well fed, up the west slope of the valley. In three days, they reached Cassange, a Portuguese station with several dozen houses. Every Portuguese soldier stationed there was also a trader, an inducement to live in such a remote area. Again David produced his letter. On April 16, 1854, David celebrated Easter Sunday with the locals. Bangalas participated. There were no priests in Cassange. This reinforced David's opinion that the mere presence of Europeans practicing Christianity was enough to make Africans want to live in Christ.

If only the Portuguese did not practice slavery. In many ways, they were more enlightened than the English. Many Portuguese soldiers had Bangala wives and could not have loved their offspring more. David had seen this wonderful attitude of the Portuguese about race before—in Rio de Janeiro.

The commander, Captain Neva, entertained David. To one who had lived on manioc and scraps of beef for weeks on end, the feast was fit for a king. Captain Neva had cookies from America, beer from England, and wines and preserved fruits from Portugal.

One morning Mashauana came to David, breathless. "We want to trade Sekeletu's tusks here."

"Why not wait? We can probably get more goods for them at Luanda on the seashore."

"Maybe not." Mashauana took David to a trader. "Tell Doctor Livingstone, he said in Bantu to the trader, "what he can get for one tusk."

"Two muskets, three barrels of gunpowder, and sixty yards of English cotton." David was astonished. "One tusk is worth so much here?"

No wonder trade flourished in western Africa. He hadn't known. He thought the main commerce was in slaves. This was very heartening. The Makalolos had almost been giving away their ivory. He had seen a chief trade two tusks for one musket. If the Africans in the interior could trade their tusks near the oceans, they not only could buy abundant goods but there would be less incentive to deal in slaves.

Soon he was trading. Before he knew it he had traded all three of Sekeletu's remaining tusks for that trader's goods and one horse for Sekeletu. His men were very pleased. But David had a problem: His Makalolos wanted to go back now.

"But I can't get to the coast without your help," said David.

"We will be captured. The Portuguese allow slavery."

"I will fight for you, just as I promised you back among the Chiboques." Reluctantly, his men came with him.

As they proceeded, David was disturbed. He was having difficulty making geographical measurements. The procedure itself was extremely complicated, so much so that some men could not learn it at all. But David had had no difficulty before. He also noticed he could not remember some names now. He was a doctor. The conclusion was unmistakable. His illness was grave. He was so anemic his mind was failing.

After a succession of military posts, they reached Luanda on the coast. Civilization staggered his Makalolos. Luandans made buildings that deserved to be called mountains with caves in them. The inhabitants burned black stones for heat. Ships in the harbor held entire villages and carried so much cargo it took weeks to unload. The Atlantic Ocean defied description because it stretched to the horizon, even if one climbed high into the foothills. And there were thousands of black slaves inhabiting Luanda!

David Livingstone was a source of wonder to these Luandans. He had trekked from where? From Cape Town through central Africa? Impossible. He looked as if he was at death's door. The English consul, Edmund Gabriel, hurriedly took him into his own home. David was confined to bed. Doctors visited to diagnose his illness. He received the governor, the Catholic bishop, and every person of influence in Luanda. English officers left their warships to visit him.

David's Makalolos began to relax. David seemed powerful enough to protect them, even after he suffered a severe relapse. Soon he learned in his stupor that his Makalolos were remarkable. They went into the foothills to cut firewood and lug it back to sell in Luanda. They hired out to unload coal ships from England. Praise the Lord for his men's industry. This would benefit them greatly because now they had their own money to buy goods to take back to their homeland.

David fought to recover. There was not one European who did not advise him to return to England as soon as possible. And his answer was always the same: "I must get my Makalolos back to their home."

This loyalty struck a chord among all men. He heard unguarded whispers about his courage. *If only they all knew*, he prayed, *that true courage comes from Christ*. What did they think of him deep in their hearts? Did they think he was a fool?

The bishop came again. To David's men, he presented smart red and blue suits, caps, and blankets. He gave David a very decorous officer's uniform for Sekeletu. He also gave Sekeletu a horse, complete with bridle and saddle! The bishop said David was doing something very special with the Africans in the interior. His work should be encouraged in every way.

David began to recover. He had deteriorated to the absolute limit—and lived, thanks to God. He realized no letters from anyone had found him at Luanda. Who had believed he would be there anyway? He felt well enough to fret over Mary's condition. If only he knew how she and the children were doing. He wrote long letters to her. He wrote letters to all his correspondents, as well. After four months he was ready to travel again.

The bishop continued to astound him. "I've secured twenty porters to help you and your Makalolos on the journey," he told David.

He needed the extra porters. When his departure became known, they were inundated by gifts from the Portuguese: donkeys, beads, cotton goods, ammunition, and muskets. Every one of his men would return armed.

On September 20, 1854, David departed for the country of Sekeletu. The return trip was riddled with bouts of fever. David recorded his own bouts of fever as rigorously as his geographical measurement of longitude and latitude. He suffered well over two dozen attacks since his first attack on the Sesheke almost one year ago. Many Makalolos were also laid low by river fever. Often the caravan had to stop for several days.

After David crossed the Quango and left the hospitable Portuguese, he tried to skirt the troublesome Chiboque chiefs by traveling forty miles farther north. But he encountered many of the same chiefs anyway, with the same haggling over tribute. Several times a battle seemed unavoidable, but at the last second the crisis evaporated.

In June of 1855 near the village of Katema, he passed Dilolo, a triangular lake about eight miles long and two miles wide. One river drained the lake to the north into the river systems of the Kasai. When he reached the south end of the lake, he was shocked to find a river emptying the lake south into the river systems of the Sesheke. The lake was like a fountain welling up on a ridge and spewing water into lowlands on both sides. Water from this one small lake actually flowed both to the Atlantic Ocean and the Indian Ocean. He wanted to study the remarkable phenomenon but began vomiting blood. As he did so often, he surged onward as if that would defeat his sickness.

The African wilderness was not a land that indulged relaxation. Death came unexpectedly: from drowning, from fever, from war, or from animals. Men and women David had met during the trip from the Barotse Valley to Luanda were dead by the time he returned on the same route: Cypriano's mother, Nyamoana's husband, Mpololo's wife and daughter, and several others. Even the ox Sinbad died from tsetse bites near Manenko's village after plodding three thousand cantankerous miles. Yet David lost not one Makalolo from his own party!

Praise the Lord. Surely God was looking over them.

THIRTEEN

By August of 1855, they were cruising down the Sesheke River in canoes again. David was lost in thought. His faculties were almost back to normal. He pondered the geology of southern Africa. It was an ancient landmass, almost flat everywhere, with very minor mountain building. That's why it had such peculiar features as lakes draining into rivers, whereas everywhere else in the world the opposite was true. He had talked to very old men in the villages. They maintained long oral histories. No African between the latitudes of 7 degrees and 27 degrees south of the equator had ever felt an earthquake. That just confirmed what he knew about the flat stable landmass of Africa.

At Linyanti, a massive celebration erupted. "You're alive!" exclaimed Sekeletu.

David and his party had been considered long dead by Sekeletu and his counselors. Now they held a colossal kotla with hours of speeches. Sekeletu was astounded that not one of his twenty-seven Makalolos was lost. How was it possible on such a dangerous journey? It cemented the perception of David as being blessed. Gifts from the west abounded: horses, donkeys, clothing, ammunition, and guns. Sekeletu quickly donned his officer's uniform.

The kotla was thrown into turmoil, too. Ivory could buy so much in the west! And Makalolos had much ivory. So many opportunities! Some wanted to relocate up the Barotse Valley right away to be nearer to the western markets. Others argued they must remain here in the feverish swamps to discourage the Zulus from attacking. David did not discourage their speculation. After all, he wanted trade. No one was talking about trading with slave traders anymore. It was wonderful.

At last, Sekeletu spoke, "I would like to go up the Barotse Valley to live. This new trade route is very good for us. Livingstone is going east now, but he will return and open a mission here."

A complication had jumped out of David's past. He had never found a satisfactory location for a mission. He had forgotten that goal. Trade had become so much more important to him. Even now he could think of little else but exploring the Sesheke River downstream, hopefully east to the Indian Ocean. But he forced himself to think about Sekeletu's wish. Yes, he could start a mission up the Barotse Valley. Perhaps near Shinte. The location was not ideal. River fever was still prevalent. But he could survive there. And Mary was up to it. But not the children.

He told Sekeletu, "I will write the London Missionary Society with suggestions. But next, I must go east. I want to leave in a few days. I am very anxious to see my family."

"The winter is just ending," protested Sekeletu. "Surely you can't travel in the hot season."

"We will travel on a great river. It's not like crossing the Kalahari wilderness."

But it was very hot already. It was over 100 degrees in the shade. The night cooled only to a steamy ninety degrees. David stayed with Sekeletu until the first rain broke the heat. In spite of the hot season, he was going to leave. It was his old problem. He couldn't lose years waiting around for the seasons to mesh with his plans.

In November, Sekeletu and two hundred men escorted him down the Sesheke River. Sekeletu supplied David with twelve oxen and food. Many tusks were in the caravan's cargo for sale downriver. The young chief picked Sekwebu for David's guide down the Sesheke. Sekwebu had been captured by Zulus as a small boy. He escaped but had grown up far down the Sesheke River by the Portuguese settlement of Tete. He knew both banks of the Sesheke for hundreds of miles between Tete and the kingdom of Sekeletu.

As they neared a place called Mosioatunya, David began to understand why Sekeletu was so excited. The phrase *mosi oa tunya* meant "smoke makes sound there." In the distance five columns of white vapor billowed off the river into the clouds. As the travelers got closer to the clouds, a pervasive whisper grew into a roar. They canoed to an island and walked to the end. Then they crawled onto an overhang.

"It's stupendous," said David, his words smothered by the roar. The Sesheke River, two thousand yards wide from bank to bank, cascaded over a ledge into what seemed a boiling cauldron. The water fell three hundred feet. "I shall name it Victoria Falls, after the young queen."

Later he wrote:

> *The whole body of water rolls clear over, quite unbroken; but after a descent of ten or more feet the entire mass becomes like a huge sheet of driven snow. Pieces of water leap off it in the form of comets with tails streaming behind, till the whole snowy sheet becomes myriads of rushing, leaping, aqueous comets.*

Sekeletu left him with 114 Makalolos, most of whom were carrying ivory for trade. South of the river lurked the notorious Zulus; so David and his caravan ascended a plateau north of the river. Cooler drier air soothed them. Game abounded. The soil appeared suitable for crops like coffee and corn.

"This is the best location I've seen for a mission since I came to Sekeletu," he mused. Then he was startled as he realized that was two and a half years ago! He had had no contact whatever with Mary and the children for even longer than that. *God forgive me,* he prayed.

They were in the land of the Batoka. David was not fond of Batokas. Batokas were in the realm of Sekeletu's Makalolos, but they were the most recalcitrant of his subjects. Even the great Sebitoane had failed to stop their disgusting habit of men and women alike knocking out their upper front teeth. As a consequence, the lower teeth seemed to project grotesquely. And their greeting repulsed David. They would lie on their backs, rolling from side to side while slapping their thighs, and yelling *kina bomba*! But he began to wonder if his constant illness from river fever was not making him intolerant of native ways.

Some of his own party of Makalolos were Batokas. They had no grasp of tact. Otherwise, native Batokas were friendly, supplying the party with corn and ground nuts. No tribute was demanded because of the presence of Sekeletu's men.

Hunting in the plateau north of the Sesheke River was unsurpassed. Buffalo and elephants were killed to provide royal quantities of meat for the men. At one spot where they descended into a green valley, David saw so many zebras, buffalo, and elephants and the animals were so tame that the image overwhelmed him. This was paradise. It pained him deeply to think such glimpses into paradise would pass from the earth. In his heart, he knew the arrival of guns into the interior plus the value of ivory would destroy paradise.

The trip was a succession of tribes and friendly villages until early in 1856 when the caravan encountered Chief Mburuma along the great river. The source of the trouble was another white man, an Italian, who, with the help of fifty slaves, tried to establish himself as some kind of chief in the area. The man was killed and now all white men were suspect to Chief Mburuma. David smoothed things over, but he sensed once again he was in territory like that of the Chiboques, beyond the influence of Sekeletu. Every day was filled with danger now.

They passed Zumbo, the site of a former Portuguese outpost. Houses and walls of sandstone had crumbled. It was the best site yet for a mission. Sekwebu told David the Portuguese men in Zumbo had disintegrated long before the sandstone. Instead of trying to grow coffee, wheat, or corn, the Portuguese colonists traded in slaves. And the natives drove them away.

From the village of Chief Mpende, war parties approached, dancing and threatening with spears. But David had dealt with many difficult chiefs. Always he displayed power in firearms while acting very calm and reasonable. Soon Mpende calmed, too, even recommending that David cross to the south side of the river because the journey to Tete was easier that way. David's party was very suspicious. River crossings were notorious for double crosses. Many a party had been split up during a crossing and slaughtered.

"It was a favorite trick of Sebitoane's," Sekwebu told David nervously.

This crossing was uneventful. David bypassed the river to find easier traveling in uplands. They were on constant alert for Zulus. One Makalolo died of fever; one vanished in an area notorious for lions. And the closer the party got to Tete in the colony of Mozambique, the sicker David and the other Makalolos became from fever. Mozambique was known for its unhealthy outposts on the fever-ridden Zambesi River.

On March 2, 1856, David collapsed in his tent, brought down by fever. His mind was muddled again. Only days before he could not remember a simple method of measuring the width of the river with his sextant. Now from his tent, he sent Sekwebu ahead to Tete with letters of recommendation he carried from the bishop in Luanda.

Within hours, soldiers arrived to escort David to Tete. Just the sight of help revived him. He walked the remaining eight miles to Tete to be met by Major Sicard. Then he collapsed, an invalid again among the Portuguese.

David's hope was realized. Sekeletu's Sesheke River that went all the way up into the Barotse Valley to Lake Dilolo really did go all the way to the Indian Ocean as the Zambesi River. He questioned the major about the one hundred miles of Zambesi he had bypassed by using Mpende's shortcut south of the river. The major had heard old-timers say there were some rapids called Kebrabasa in that stretch. They were rapids though, not cataracts.

Of the four thousand inhabitants of Tete, only a few hundred were free. In David's mind slavery was the reason the Portuguese had lost their opportunity to open up Africa. They sat here on a great river highway that reached into the very heart of Africa and did nothing but trade in slaves. Their obsession with slavery worried him now. The Portuguese might not be so friendly to English merchants trying to ply their honest trade on the Zambesi.

David was well enough to travel in April. All but sixteen of Sekeletu's Makalolos were to remain in Tete, free men under the protection of the Portuguese. The sixteen Makalolos and several Portuguese soldiers accompanied him down the Zambesi in canoes. Halfway to the port of Quilimane, David released all the Makalolos. Sekwebu begged to come with him to the Indian Ocean. He relented. In May of 1856, they arrived in Quilimane.

Colonel Nunes was his host. David could tell from the pity in the colonel's eyes, he must have looked pathetic. David felt closer to death than he ever had felt in his life. "You have letters from England here, Dr. Livingstone," said Colonel Nunes to cheer his guest.

"At last! A letter from Mary," cried David as he pawed through the letters. But not one was from Mary. It was crushing. He looked at Colonel Nunes. "I'll read the others later. Before I do, I must make a request. In case of my death, please sell the ivory we brought and give the proceeds to Sekwebu."

"But you will recover," protested his host unconvincingly. "The reason I have letters for you, Dr. Livingstone, is because English warships have been stopping here off and on, asking for you." His face was sour. "Some of the Englishmen from the brigantine *Dart* were drowned on a sandbar off the river's mouth last year trying to reach our port in a rowboat.

"No!"

"Unfortunately, it's true. Two officers and five seamen. Englishmen from the *Frolic* left this for you as well as the letters." David was too numb to see what he had in a box. He stumbled off to bed. Seven men had died because of him.

After a fitful sleep, he opened the box to find medical supplies. He wasted no time taking quinine. Then he opened a letter from Roderick Murchison, a well-known English geologist. Murchison raved that David's trip to Luanda was "the greatest triumph in geographical research. . .in our times." David's only use for praise was the hope that it advanced his missionary work to save souls. Otherwise, praise was nothing but fodder for pride. And the deaths of the seven seamen weighed on his mind.

The next letter he opened was from the London publisher John Murray. Murray wrote that he was interested in publishing a book about David's adventures in Africa. He would pay all expenses involved and give David part of the profits. It sounded much too good to be true.

"Can there really be any interest in such a book?" David asked himself. "No. Probably the enthusiastic Roderick Murchison pressured Murray into writing a letter of interest."

The last letter was from the London Missionary Society. He opened the letter, determined to resist their praise, and read:

> *The Directors, while yielding to none in their appreciation of the objects upon which, for some years past, your energies have been concentrated, or in admiration of the zeal, intrepidity, and success with which they have been carried out, are nevertheless restricted in their power of aiding plans connected only remotely with the spread of the gospel. . . .*

"Connected only remotely with the spread of the gospel?"

David slammed the letter down. They were condemning his activity. They understood nothing of what he was doing. They were pleading lack of funds, when in fact he had spent his own salary for several years. Only the Lord knew what poor Mary and the children were living on. Even years ago he spent his own salary to build the missions at Chonuane and Kolobeng. And the Missionary Society had spent almost nothing on his exploration in the last few years. He closed his eyes and prayed to the Lord to quash his bitterness. But when he opened his eyes, the world looked very sour. So this was a preview of what awaited him in England.

At the bottom of the letter was the news that Mary and the children were doing fine. Praise God for that. By the time the *Frolic* returned in July to anchor offshore, David had conquered his depression. At least his family was all right. As always he had written a flood of letters to his correspondents, even the directors of the London Missionary Society, calmly explaining how his exploration had to precede the spread of the gospel.

As David prepared to leave Quilimane with men from the *Frolic*, Sekwebu begged to go with him. "Let me die at your feet," he cried.

David liked Sekwebu very much. He was intelligent, tactful, and resourceful. He had been the essential man along the Zambesi. "Come along then."

The boat ride down the Zambesi and over the sandbars to the *Frolic* was savage. Waves battered the small boat and swept over the passengers. Veteran crewmen bailed water furiously, making no pretense of hiding their fear. Seven had died on this trip previously.

Sekwebu was terrified. "Is this the way you go in this boat?" he kept repeating.

The *Frolic*, a brig so large she carried sixteen cannon and 130 seamen, was rolling in a violent sea. The men in the boat barely made it aboard. David felt alien to the Englishmen. They gaped when he spoke. His halting English was so rusty he must have spoken with a very peculiar accent. But Sekwebu suffered far more. His eyes were glazed with terror. The ship was a death trap.

For one month, Sekwebu tried to adjust as they sailed the open ocean. When the *Frolic* stopped at an island, Sekwebu tried to abandon ship. David reasoned with him. The captain said Sekwebu was going mad from the sea; he had seen the signs before. Sekwebu must be shackled and confined. David insisted that would be too harsh and prevailed. But Sekwebu did go mad that night. He leaped into the sea, never to be seen again.

"Oh, why did I yield to my own better judgment and bring him? And why did I not listen to the captain?" David lamented to God. "Sekwebu's precious life is on my hands now. What else can go wrong?"

He left the *Frolic* and steamed through the Red Sea on the *Candida*. At Cairo, David finally had a letter from home. His father, Neil, was dead! He died just months before David was to return to England. The mounting heartbreaks were almost too much for David. He felt like Job. Would the suffering ever end? Surely his first meeting with Mary would make up for all the pain. Surely she and the children were all right.

FOURTEEN

David was very anxious to get back to England now. His steamship was delayed at Marseilles due to a broken engine shaft, so he left it and crossed France on the train. In December of 1856 he crossed the channel to England.

"Mary is not here!" he cried in alarm as he docked at Dover. No one was there!

Had Mary not heard of his change of plans? Or had something happened to her? Perhaps she waited for him at Southampton where his steamship from Egypt was supposed to dock. *Please God, let my family be all right,* he prayed as the coach hurtled him toward Southampton.

Mary was waiting where his steamship was supposed to have docked. David was overcome with joy. As he hugged Mary, the children withdrew from him. They had not seen him in four years. David hugged the children. Robert and Mary were ten and nine, quite proper young English children. Thomas and Zouga, seven and five, were not yet molded, still unruly and outspoken. What a joy to see them all healthy.

It was only later that David realized the depths of misery Mary had truly suffered. From the children he was shocked to learn that Mary had not adjusted to living with his father and mother in Hamilton. They had not even been on speaking terms after the first six months.

He learned from Mary that after she had left the children in Hamilton, she drifted from one cheap apartment to another, in Hackney, in Manchester, in Kendal, in Epsom. Occasionally, she stayed with friends of her father, Robert Moffat. She subsisted on tiny handouts from the Missionary Society.

David was shocked. "How can I ever make it up to you?"

His mother-in-law's letters from Kuruman were small comfort. She hid nothing from David. Some missionaries in South Africa ridiculed him as a wandering fool.

He wrote back angrily to denounce "those so-called missionaries to the heathen, who never march into real heathen territory, and quiet their consciences by opposing their do-nothingism to my blundering do-somethingism!"

What was David going to do? Anger did not soothe his guilt and his sense of failure. Sixteen hard years in Africa and what did his own family have to show for it?

When David was asked to take Mary to a meeting of the Royal Geographic Society three days later, he began to get nervous. Yes, he heard it whispered, it was in his honor. Once again he was the recipient of its Gold Medal. The monetary reward was a token amount. When he arrived, he was surprised to see the meeting overflowing with dukes and earls and the haughtiest members of London society. He was cheered to see his old friends Cotton Oswell and Captain Thomas Steele.

"They seem to have gone to quite a lot of bother, Mary," he murmured. He wore blue trousers and a black coat with long tails over a white shirt and black bow tie. "Good thing I dressed for it."

Roderick Murchison stood and spoke on and on about the accomplishments of the great missionary David Livingstone. The renowned biologist Richard Owen had tears in his eyes as he told how David, almost dead from fever, brought him a rare coiled tusk from Africa.

David became more and more uncomfortable. What were they making of him? If they only knew all the days he had squirmed and groaned and vomited with river fever. If they only knew how his bad judgment had killed Sekwebu. David was no hero. The only important thing was finding a route for the gospel.

Finally, David himself stood, self-conscious of his rough appearance: dark-skinned, emaciated, face deeply furrowed from worry. His English words of thanks were halting, unsure, and thickly accented. "I am only doing my duty as a missionary in opening up a part of Africa to the sympathy of Christ. Captain Steele or Mr. Cotton Oswell could have done as well as I did. And besides, I am only just now buckling on my armor for the good fight. I have no right to boast of anything. I will not boast until the last slave in Africa is free, and Africa is open to honest trade and the light of Christianity."

After the meeting Murchison took him aside. "When I first saw you, Livingstone, I thought you were as broken down as an old cart horse. 'No more Africa for him,' I thought. But how your eyes burned just then as you talked! You are too modest. I have no doubt whatever that you are the only one in England who could have done what you did in Africa."

"Not so, sir," replied David with complete conviction.

"Naturally," said Murchison, "I would never wish you to fall away from your Missionary Society. But societies are more limited than governments when it comes to funding exploration."

"I'm meeting with the Missionary Society tomorrow," said David, not sure how to reply.

"Good," said Murchison. "I hope you are pleased with the meeting. After all, you know exactly what must be done to serve Christ. However, if you are not pleased with the meeting, perhaps there is another agency that would allow you to do exactly what you know must be done to open up Africa. I urge you to contact me immediately. I know the Earl of Clarendon intimately. He is the foreign secretary under Lord Palmerston, the prime minister."

David was stunned. What was Murchison doing? First, some talk of a book. Now was he hinting of some kind of commission for the government?

The next day, much to David's satisfaction, Mary was also feted with him by the London Missionary Society. Its members praised her for her patient endurance. But as David sat and listened, he could not escape a feeling of bitterness. While he spent his own meager salary on Africa, Mary had suffered for lack of funds. Now they heaped praise on David, thick and gooey. Again he found himself sour. Yes, he had accomplished much, but it seemed only because he leaped ahead and then told the society later what he had done. Sincerely, he thanked them for sixteen years of patience with a missionary who strained the limits. He knew he was very trying to such conservative men. But as he studied their pasty well-fed faces that rarely saw the sun and remembered the unrelenting woes of Africa, anger crept into his heart. He finished with a petulant regret that his ventures were seen as only a tempting of Providence by the weaker brethren.

Afterward Mary said, "David, such a remark is expected in salty letters between friends. Even my mother writes such things. But do you think it is wise to talk that way with the directors?"

"I feel guided by an Unseen Hand. Perhaps the society is not the best way to bring Christ to Africa."

A few days later, the publisher John Murray visited him. "When do we start, Dr. Livingstone?"

David asked bluntly, "Do you mean there may be interest in such a technical book?"

"Didn't you hear what they said about you at the Royal Geographic Society?"

"Yes. But geographers are only human, Mr. Murray. They, too, need to create enthusiasm to generate funds for their society. I realize there is some interest among the gentry."

"You are so down-to-earth, Doctor. Trust me, sir. I am so sure your book will repay me a hundredfold I will give you two-thirds of the profits rather than the customary one-third. When can you start?"

"I must visit my mother and sisters in Scotland first."

Both Janet and Agnes still lived with his mother. They both taught school. John had immigrated to Canada. And Charles was a pastor in America. David had never been in their new home in Hamilton where his father died so recently.

"Tell me about Father," he asked.

Janet told him, "He knew he was dying. He wanted very much to see you again but said the will of the Lord must be done. His last words were 'But I think I'll know in heaven whatever is worth knowing about David. When you see him, tell him that.'"

"Praise the Lord for such a father," said David. And he knew there were those in Scotland and England who praised David not at all. He had neglected his own children to spread the gospel to God's black children. Remarks made by his sisters only reinforced his suspicions that Mary and the children had spent a wretched four years. Couldn't the Missionary Society have been responsive to their needs?

Days later on January 12, 1857, at a board meeting of the London Missionary Society in London, David challenged the directors. In his own mind, it was an ultimatum. He proposed two new missions: one in the land of the Zulus, administered by Robert Moffat and one in the land of Sekeletu's Makalolos, administered by him.

"Of course, you and Mary will reside in the mission among the Makalolos, won't you?" asked a director.

"Perhaps," said David evasively. Six months ago his answer would have been an enthusiastic yes, but Mary's suffering still bothered him. How could the society take so much for granted? Were the wives of these directors suffering from tropical fevers? Were any of their children buried in Africa?

The directors convened the meeting with no decision. David resented that. It meant they would discuss it among themselves privately. Hadn't he earned the right to argue his case right up to the verdict? Would his proposals be defeated in secret? Their elite and undemocratic procedures bothered him more and more. He reminded himself they were only men after all.

He had been staying at Dr. Bennett's house, but now he moved his family to a house in Chelsea. Mary liked her new home. She no longer felt she was living on charity. And David had severed one more tie with the society.

He was told in late January that the society had approved his proposal for the two missions, but first they had to write Robert Moffat. It might take awhile to draft the letter into precise language. Not to mention, thought David, the time it will take for the letter to reach Moffat in Kuruman, the time it will take Moffat to travel to the Zulus to get their permission, or the time it will take Moffat to write back to the society, with his suggested revisions. What year might the proposals be finally approved? 1859? 1860? 1861?

The next day, he wrote a letter to Lord Clarendon. Would the Foreign Office, he asked, be at all interested in funding an expedition to explore the Zambesi River in the very near future?

About the same time, he received a newspaper from Cape Town. He could scarcely believe his eyes. A banquet honored him in Cape Town in November of 1856. On the occasion the governor said:

> *I think no man of the present day is more deserving than David Livingstone—a man whom we, indeed, can hardly regard as belonging to any particular age or time, but who belongs to the whole Christian*

epoch, possessing all those great qualities of mind and that resolute desire at all risks to spread the gospel. . . . Indeed, that man must be regarded as almost of apostolic character.

He read the remarks of the Colonial Secretary:

I am convinced that Livingstone's name will live amongst the first heroes and the first benefactors of our race.

Such praise was so undeserved. Were other men so little? The man representing the London Missionary Society said:

If ever there was a man who, by realizing the obligations of his sacred calling as a Christian missionary, and intelligently comprehending its object, sought to pursue it to a successful issue, such a man is Dr. Livingstone.

David almost believed that flattery, except he had not brought it to a successful issue. What had he accomplished? He was proud, however, when he read the words of Maclear, the Royal Astronomer of Cape Town:

What this man has done is unprecedented. You could go to any point across the entire continent, along Livingstone's track, and feel certain of your position.

Oh, the pain David had endured on some feverish days to take those laborious measurements. And he reflected on Cape Town. Could this be the same city that had stalled him back in 1852? Could this be the same city that balked at selling him supplies? How quickly men were swayed one way or the other. Doubt grew in his heart. All this praise could so quickly turn to scorn. And how could he be a failure one day and be a hero the next? He felt guilty making plans with the British government. But the Missionary Society was so slow. David had only one life to live. And a man must strike for Christ when the time is right. Could the time ever be more right than now?

At Chelsea, he plunged into his book, keeping his antennae up for developments from the Missionary Society or the Foreign Office. He pored over his thick journals and condensed parts of them and expanded other parts of them. Roderick Murchison took him to meet Lord Clarendon. The foreign secretary was effusive. What did David need? What title did he want for his commission? David seemed reluctant to accept such gratuities. Lord Clarendon snapped, "Good heavens, Doctor, I'm not doing you a favor. You are doing England a favor. You are a man who gets things done. Now if you want to save all those African souls as speedily as possible, please send me a detailed proposal so I can show it to the prime minister."

What an opportunity! It seemed David could ask for anything. But could he leave the Mission Society? What would people think? He immediately inquired as to the progress of the letter to Robert Moffat. He was told the society was working on it.

By March 19, the Mission Society still had not drafted the letter. So David sent his official proposal to Lord Clarendon. Later Murchison told him it was well received. "The foreign secretary is off and running," he added.

"To whom?" joked David.

"Prince Albert."

"The prince?" David was surprised.

"To attend to the sensitive relationship with Portugal. You are the one who told us no expedition could ever start up the Zambesi River without their approval. The first thing the prime minister must do is ask Prince Albert to talk to his cousin, who just happens to be the king of Portugal!"

David laughed. Prince Albert was the husband of Queen Victoria. The queen had clashed with Lord Palmerston in the past. How would their Royal Highnesses receive this proposal? How far above David's head all this maneuvering was now. It seemed to be at the very pinnacle of the British Empire!

The Missionary Society did not send the letter to Moffat until April. This constant delay seemed to confirm David's decision to break away. He waited to do it though. Who could know if the government might run afoul of something?

In May, he was notified that the prime minister was considering a consulship for him, but it could not be effective until 1858.

If approved, his title would be "Her Majesty's Consul at Quilimane for the Eastern Coast and independent districts of the interior"—more or less. The salary of 500 pounds—five times his missionary salary—did not catapult him into wealth. His much younger brother Charles was receiving the equivalent of 750 pounds a year, preaching in America. In fact, Charles was back in Scotland, visiting. David urged him to stay awhile longer. He might be able to use him on his expedition.

The secret negotiations began to haunt David. The society was proceeding on the notion he would be instrumental in establishing the mission with the Makalolos. Didn't David trust God? Why was he being so secretive? And with nothing final—neither his book nor his consulship—he suddenly resigned from the society. By the end of July, he finished the manuscript of the book and began a tour of public speaking. He felt very independent now. A woman's criticism of his concern with trade, as if that had nothing to do with

Christ—drew this fiery response:

> *Nowhere have I appeared as anything else but a servant of God, who has simply followed the leading of His hand. My views of what is missionary duty are not so contracted as those whose ideal is a dumpy sort of man with a Bible under his arm. I have labored in bricks and mortar, at the forge and carpenter's bench, as well as preaching.*

He spoke to scientific societies, physicians, and factory workers in towns and cities as far apart as London and Glasgow and Dublin. To his own cotton-spinners in Blantyre, many who remembered him from twenty years before, he said:

> *My great object was to be like Him—to imitate Him as far as He could be imitated. We have not the power of working miracles, but we can do a little in the way of healing the sick, and I sought a medical education in order that I might be like Him.*

At Cambridge University at the end of his plodding factual speech, he suddenly shouted, "Do you carry on the work which I have begun? I leave it with you!"

Murchison told him later that the students and faculty at Cambridge were electrified by his speech. They were talking about establishing a joint missionary effort with Oxford University, just for Africa. By November, he had finished "spouting off," as he called it, and his fat 687-page book, crammed with maps and drawings, was in print. It was titled *Missionary Travels and Researches in South Africa*. He had to laugh. He showed a copy of the tome to Mary. "Do you think anyone will read such a monstrosity? But at least a goodly portion of my sixteen years of work is preserved in print."

FIFTEEN

The first printing of twelve thousand books sold out in a few hours to advance orders. After that the English were buying the book as fast as it could be printed.

"God's work pays well," said Mary, as though it were preposterous.

"Suddenly our assets have grown from nothing but the clothes on our backs to several thousand pounds," agreed David. "Now I can support Mother. The children are assured of decent educations. And it's worth everything to me to know you will never suffer again from want, Mary."

Mary smiled. "And knowing you, a good bit will go to Africa."

"Perhaps we can help your father start his mission among the Zulus."

David soon learned that John Moffat was appointed to the Zulu mission. He wrote to him, offering him not only money, but his own wagon and ox team. Characteristically, he urged John to proceed at once and not wait on a decision for every step of the process. A few days later he learned his advice had been too strong. John resigned from the Missionary Society, expecting to be funded by David. What choice did David have now but to do it?

David regretted every minute now he had to spend in England. His need for Africa burned in his heart like a fire. He had one last task; he appealed to his old friend from Glasgow, James Young, to administer the royalties from his book. Young, who now lived in London, agreed to see that his mother and the three older children had sufficient funds.

In March of 1858, David sailed on the *Pearl* for Cape Town with Mary and their only child not in school, Zouga. The elaborate plan to explore the Zambesi River was well under way. The British government had built a special low-draft paddle wheeler for the Zambesi and loaded it in three sections aboard the *Pearl*. Also aboard were David's handpicked men, not the least of which was his brother Charles as his assistant. Norman Bedingfeld had been selected as the ship's captain. The geologist Richard Thornton was recommended by Murchison, the botanist John Kirk by Sir William Hooker. An artist, an engineer, and a crew of ten were to be added later.

Robert Moffat met the *Pearl* in Cape Town in April. Mary would return with him to Kuruman. In 1860, Mary would go north to Kolobeng to visit the grave of daughter Elizabeth, then continue north to join David on the upper Zambesi in the realm of Sekeletu and the Makalolos. The lower Zambesi was too unhealthy for Mary. David would not tolerate such a risk.

"Back at long last!" greeted Robert Moffat. And he hugged Mary, his daughter he had not seen in six years.

As David speculated earlier, after Robert Moffat received the much-delayed letter from the society in July, he had rushed to the Zulus to get their approval. He had only been back in Kuruman a few days when he left for Cape Town. Moffat was a phenomenon himself. Now sixty-three, he still traveled the wilderness fearlessly. He still was the only white man respected by the notorious Zulu chief Mosilakatse. Like David, he was so earnest and so honest he could win the confidence of anyone.

Ten days later, the *Pearl* sailed around the tip of Africa for the Zambesi. Once again David was without Mary, but he could not take her into the fever country of the lower Zambesi. When he arrived at Quilimane, he learned he had been voted a Fellow in the Royal Society. The honors mounted. But he had no time to bathe in their warmth.

By June, the low-draft paddle wheeler was assembled and named: *Ma-Robert*, the natives' name for Mary, the mother of Robert. Charles and the artist Baines got river fever almost immediately. Captain Bedingfeld turned out to be a complainer. And as they worked their way up the Zambesi, they found themselves in the middle of a war between the Portuguese authorities and rebel natives. David walked a tightrope, trying to stay on good terms with both sides. On one occasion, David helped the sick Portuguese governor to safety as bullets whistled around him.

Captain Bedingfeld's hostility became so corrosive to the crew that David dismissed him. David could navigate the ship. And their Scottish engineer, George Rae, knew more than the captain about the workings of the vessel anyway. The *Ma-Robert* soon proved to be a poor ship at best. Only the hardest wood, acquired with backbreaking labor, fired the furnace hot enough to power the steam engine.

In September when they reached Tete, David's loyal Makalolos almost sank the *Ma-Robert* with their welcome. To his sorrow, thirty of them had died of smallpox and six had been murdered. Yet the rest, numbering over seventy, were not anxious to return to Linyanti. They held steady jobs in Tete and lived in stone barracks generously supplied by Major Nunes.

Relieved from any urgency to return the Makalolos to Sekeletu, David decided to push on to the Kebrabasa Rapids. Their presence had haunted him for two years. Impassable rapids were the one thing that could destroy his dreams of a watery highway into central Africa. So the paddle wheeler *Ma-Robert* built up steam for four hours and wheezed up the Zambesi at full speed, not fast enough to keep pace with a canoe.

Within two days, David saw the Kebrabasa Gorge. "Dr. Kirk," he said to the most helpful man on his staff, "the Kebrabasa Rapids do not look promising."

John Kirk was speechless. It was a period of low water. There was such a jumble of granitic boulders a twig couldn't negotiate the rapids without striking a thousand of them. David anchored the ship and they proceeded up the gorge on foot. Each step added to David's misery.

Kirk finally found his voice. During the rainy season in March, the roiling water would tumble a boat into kindling. In the dry season, the boulders would smash a boat into toothpicks.

David sighed. "I'll take four Makalolos and go on up the gorge. Perhaps the rapids don't stretch very far. One can ford the rapids for a short way, just as one can at Victoria Falls."

"Doctor, it's an insult to leave able-bodied men behind," protested Kirk.

"Able-bodied, are you? Well, come on then." David could hardly keep from smiling. Years ago he had walked Bakaa warriors into the ground. But how broken down by river fever was he at forty-five?

They proceeded into the jumble of boulders. Progress was exhausting. The gorge was very hot and the men had to jump from boulder to boulder. The boulders were so large there was no grip. And the surface was scorching. Soon even the four Makalolos were complaining. Kirk pointed out to David that their feet were blistered. David did not stop. Soon only Kirk and one Makalolo were still stumbling along behind him through the boulders. They climbed into masses of boulders that made even David wonder if he could ever get out. At one point they reached a cascade so bad the only way to continue on was to scale a 300-foot wall of slippery rock. They continued. The rapids went on and on.

Finally, at one rest stop Kirk said, "The bottoms of my boots are worn out. They were brand-new when we started."

David groaned. "I believe now these rapids continue for thirty miles!"

They started back, consoled only by the fact they were starting back. Fifty years before, the Portuguese could have warned David of the extent of these terrible rapids. But now they rarely ventured far from Tete. David returned to Tete. He would go downriver to Sena and follow the very large tributary Shire to the north. Perhaps the Shire River went north, then swung west to eventually bypass the rapids and join the Zambesi. David had seen stranger behavior in African rivers. He and Kirk would leave the others in the party at Tete. Most were sick with river fever. His prissy brother Charles was an embarrassment, requiring a dozen rest stops a day to do anything.

By January 1, 1859, when the *Ma-Robert* steamed up the duckweed-choked Shire against the advice of the Portuguese, David had regained his optimism. "You know, Kirk, I think we can make it up the Kebrabasa Rapids during high water. Of course, we will need a more powerful ship. I wrote Murchison about it."

Kirk's silence betrayed what he thought.

They took the *Ma-Robert* as far north on the Shire River as the village of

Chief Chibisa of the Manganjis. They were above the low-lying fever country. This area David now optimistically dubbed the Highlands of the Shire. The residents, the Manganjis, spoke a different dialect of Bantu, which he immediately resolved to master. From Chibisa's village, he and Kirk trudged north on foot. They found an unwelcome but splendid cataract in the Shire, which David named Murchison Falls after his loyal friend.

Exploration of the Shire River would take almost all of 1859 and three separate trips north to satisfy David. As always, he seemed to know how to calm villagers, whether the villagers were threatening him with spears or not. By September he and Kirk had found two inland lakes hidden in precipitous mountains. The smaller one was Lake Shirwa, which appeared to be over fifty miles long.

At the south end of the larger Lake Nyassa, David asked a native, "How far north is the other end of this lake?"

The native was astounded. "Who ever heard of such a question? If a small boy started walking north he would be an old gray-haired man before he reached the other end."

"Balderdash," muttered Kirk. But when they climbed a considerable mountain to peer north, the lake stretched beyond the horizon.

Of the original crew only Kirk and the engineer Rae were productive. The geologist Thornton and the artist Baines were crippled by fever from the beginning. They could not function. David dismissed them. He had little sympathy for victims of river fever because he had suffered dozens of attacks himself. He believed a cheerful attitude and activity defeated illness, at least enough to continue working. As to medication during the awful bouts of fever, he wrote:

> [Mix]. . .resin of jalap and calomel of each eight grains, quinine and rhubarb of each four grains. . . [and take a] dose of ten to twenty grains. . . . If the violent symptoms are not relieved in four to six hours a desert spoonful of epsom salts may be taken. . . . Quinine in four to six grain doses. . .is generally given till. . .deafness is produced.

That was how drastic his treatment was. Deafness was welcomed by David as the last symptom before recovery. He was then on the go immediately. He drove himself that way constantly, and he had no sympathy for malingerers. Yet he could not bring himself to dismiss his lazy brother Charles. The morale of the other travelers was not helped by David's special treatment of his brother. The grumbling never stopped. How David wished he could work alone again, or perhaps with a common spirit like his sweet Mary, or John Kirk, who never seemed to tire, either.

David began to have problems with hemorrhoids. This kind of bleeding was not a problem one talked about. So he bore the pain and hid his problem from the others. He revealed his problem only to his diary. At times, he bled all night. The *Ma-Robert* was disintegrating, too. And he learned the London Missionary Society was sending missionaries to Sekeletu. It was too soon. He needed to be there to make sure Sekeletu moved into a higher, healthier climate for Europeans, like the area around Zumbo.

But not all the news was bad. In November, he got a letter from Kuruman. "Mary gave birth to Anna Mary! Praise the Lord!" he yelled. "It was one year ago: November sixteenth," he added in surprise.

He redoubled his appeals for a new ship, now touting commerce on giant Lake Nyassa. He also had to get back to Sekeletu. The status of the new missionaries worried him. He soon learned his lectures at Cambridge and Oxford had caused such enthusiasm the two universities started a "Universities Mission to Central Africa." Missionaries were coming to the land around Lake Nyassa he called the Highlands of the Shire. David was really worried now. His appeals had triggered too much activity too soon. These new missions had to be tended with utmost care. How could he possibly attend to missions separated by a thousand miles of rough wilderness—and still explore for his river highway into central Africa?

Only twenty-five Makalolos wanted to return to Sekeletu in May of 1860. David didn't get back up the Zambesi to Sekeletu until August. He and Kirk were none too early. The young chief was a complete invalid with a severe form of eczema. Sekeletu was a sea of scabs. David and Kirk cleaned the sores with zinc sulfate, then daubed them with silver nitrate. Every day they gave him a powder of rhubarb, soda, and quinine to drink with water. He improved markedly but remained in the grips of the disease. The outlook was grim. When his white shaman left, Sekeletu would deteriorate.

Sekeletu's realm was in a shambles. He had refused to move out of the feverish swamps because the Zulus would not attack him there. The only reason he ever agreed to move to a higher, healthier area was because he thought David would be with him. He reasoned shrewdly that if David lived with him the Zulus would not attack him because David was the son-in-law of Robert Moffat, the great friend of the Zulus.

Kirk found the missionaries at Linyanti. "Come with me, Dr. Livingstone. I've found the missionaries."

There was nothing there but a cemetery. Two families, including five children, had arrived among the Makalolos in 1859. By March of 1860, fever had annihilated all but one man and two children, who managed to straggle back to Kuruman. David was soon to learn the Makalolos, falling apart under Sekeletu, were indifferent to the plight of the missionaries. The natives refused to believe they were connected with David.

After only one month, David returned to Tete with a heavy heart. Mary could not join him at Linyanti now. The land of the Makalolos was no longer a prospect for a mission at all. He must explore the Shire and make sure the new missionaries there would be safe. On the way back he impulsively tried to shoot the Kebrabasa Rapids in canoes. It was a disaster. No lives were lost, but Kirk lost eight volumes of botanical notes and everything he owned but the clothes on his back. How he regretted his words of many months before. He had learned only too well it was no insult to be left behind by Livingstone. It was mercy.

By July of the next year, 1861, the *Pioneer*, David's new ship, had arrived. And so had new missionaries for the Highlands of the Shire. They settled at Magomero with Chief Chigunda of the Manganjis.

David explored north, compiling observations on every aspect of Africa. Once in the bush, he was charged by a rhino, which mysteriously stopped just before it reached him, as if it had encountered a stone wall. Then it sauntered away as if nothing had happened. To David, it was God's Unseen Hand again, and he noted the incident in his diary. Once he and Kirk would have been jumped by a crouching lion if one of the Makalolos had not warned them in time. David never recorded the incident in his diary. That sort of close call just happened too often.

Some observations were tantalizing. He noted that where river fever was prevalent, mosquitoes were abundant. But how would he ever find time to conduct an experiment? And when David found Lake Nyassa was not only thirty miles wide but went north for three hundred miles, he postulated a chain of lakes that went all the way to the Dead Sea!

On their way back from the upper reaches of Lake Nyassa, David was alarmed by the changes he had seen along the shores of the lake in just two years. The natives had thinned out. They were not disappearing from disease or famine. They were being shuttled away in chains. He was seeing the diabolical activity of the slave trade.

When he returned to Magomero in November, he had news from the missionaries that shocked him. Mary was on her way to the Zambesi from Cape Town.

SIXTEEN

On January 31, 1862, David held his wife in his arms again. "Mary, at last!" "It's been four long years," she gasped.

David was only too aware he had to get her out of this low-lying fever country. She could go with the other ladies to the mission at Magomero in the Highlands of the Shire. Later, she could stay there while he explored Lake Nyassa—or even go with him to the upper Zambesi realm of Sekeletu. Perhaps it wasn't too late to help the Makalolos after all. With Mary at his side he could do wonders. He liked to explore, but somehow the lower Zambesi had turned into a burden. Supervising other Englishmen was not his cup of tea but more like a cup of bitter gall.

"I must get you up to the Highlands with the other ladies," he said.

"After four years apart? Not on your life."

"But I have to stay here to get the new steamer ready." In the same ocean vessel with the ladies was the steamer David had ordered with his own money. He was going to call it *Lady Nyassa*. He had great plans for the lake.

"It won't take that long to assemble, will it?"

"In Africa? One never knows."

But Mary won the argument. The other ladies were quickly taken to Magomero in the Highlands. And the assembling of *Lady Nyassa* and unloading of their supplies from the ocean vessel dragged on and on. Unloading ships off the mouth of the Zambesi was very difficult and dangerous because of the shallow sandbars. David remembered only too well those very same sandbars had drowned seven men of the *Dart* in 1855.

Shocking news came from Magomero. The wives of the missionaries came upon a tragedy. Coming to meet them, Mackenzie and another missionary had been waylaid by a torrential rain. Both men had sickened and died from exposure and hunger. Was the young mission in danger of collapsing?

Mary shook her head. "My father once told you that no mission should be started unless one of the two of you could personally attend to it."

"At the time, I thought your father was immodest. But how right the wily old veteran has always proved to be."

By April, David and Mary were still in the lower reaches of the Zambesi. Mary could not be sent to Magomero. The mission there seemed to be disintegrating. The missionary Scudamore was down, crippled by river fever. Nothing was going right. And on April 21, Mary became sick at the village of Shupanga. Within hours she showed an extremely virulent form of river fever. Vomiting prevented the restorative powers of quinine. She faded so fast, David

179

gave up on his medical care and prayed. Mary was a mere forty-one years old. But she was very worn down.

In six short days Mary Moffat Livingstone was dead. She was buried beneath a massive baobab tree in Shupanga on the Zambesi River. David wrote in his journal:

> *It is the first heavy stroke I have suffered, and quite takes away my strength. I wept over her who well deserved many tears. I loved her when I married her, and the longer I lived with her I loved her the more. God pity the poor children. . . . For the first time in my life I feel willing to die.*

The next two years were profoundly depressing. The Portuguese were now openly hostile to David as they realized how ardently he opposed slavery. They also suspected correctly he had suggested to the British government a British colony around Lake Nyassa. To make matters worse, David learned that Sekeletu had died and the disheartened Makalolos were scattered by the Balondas. To make the times overwhelmingly tragic, the natives from the Zambesi River to Lake Nyassa were being annihilated by slavery, war, and famine. Bodies bobbed in the Shire River as human flotsam. The Universities' Mission at Magomero was hanging on by a thread.

On March 19, 1863, David's fiftieth birthday, he and Kirk were rushing up the Shire River to the mission. Scudamore had died. Dickinson was gravely ill, and Clark was hysterical. Only Horace Waller was healthy. David and Kirk arrived too late to help Dickinson. Clark was doctored back to sanity, but the mission now seemed doomed. David's work on the Zambesi was not faring much better. Kirk and David's brother Charles were giving up on the work. What a drastic change in fortune for David from ten years earlier. And how his own health had suffered, almost from that fortieth birthday. David had endured ten years of river fever and now had a new thorn in his side: bleeding. Yet he could write to one of his fellow missionaries:

> *Thanks for your kind sympathy* [about the death of Mary]. *In return I say, cherish exalted thoughts of the great* [missionary] *work you have undertaken. It is a work which, if faithful, you will look back on with satisfaction while the eternal ages roll on their everlasting course. The devil will do all he can to hinder you by efforts from without and from within; but remember Him who is with you, and will be with you always.*

Yet, occasionally, he began to suspect that not only was his support from

England and South Africa vanishing, but his time on earth was running out, too. In one letter he wrote, *I don't know whether I am going on the shelf or not. If so, I make the shelf Africa.* David's only tangible accomplishment in the two years after Mary's death was exploring the Rovuma River six hundred miles up the coast from Quilimane. He suspected it might be an easier access to Lake Nyassa. And he could skirt the Portuguese. He was wrong. The river was far too shallow.

I must go back to England, he told himself. *I'll stay with the children for a while.*

But what would he do with *Lady Nyassa*? He couldn't bear to scuttle it. But if he left it, slave traders would surely get their hands on it. In typical fashion David solved the problem with a radical solution. He would sail the *Lady Nyassa* 2,500 miles across the Indian Ocean to India! The engineer Rae, a good hand for so many years and the only man with real experience at sea, refused to go on such a suicide mission. "Dr. Livingstone! If you don't get there in time, the monsoons will blow you right to the bottom of the ocean."

Yet off sailed David with a totally inexperienced crew of three white men and nine African natives in the *Lady Nyassa*. During the voyage he recorded his gloomy thoughts:

> *Often wish that I may be permitted to do something for the benighted of Africa. I shall have nothing to do at home; by the failure of the Universities' mission my work seems in vain. . . . Have I not labored in vain? Am I to be cut off before I can do anything to effect permanent improvement in Africa?. . . God grant that I may be more faithful than I have been, and may He open the way for me.*

Just as the monsoons struck forty-five days later, David anchored the *Lady Nyassa* in India. He found people in Bombay to care for the Africans, left his steamer in the care of a British Naval officer, and embarked on a ship for England. He arrived in London on July 23, 1864. He was publicly criticized for his roles in the failure of the Universities' mission at Magomero and in the tragedy of the London Missionary Society's mission at Linyanti. But his main supporters, Roderick Murchison and Prime Minister Palmerston, staunchly defended him. After all, they had financed his Zambesi exploration, which was the prime reason he was not free to shepherd the new missions.

He went on to Scotland to see his children, his sisters, and his mother. His arrival was no more timely than it had been with his father years before. His mother was senile, thinking he was a grandson. The visit was not all gloom. He saw his daughter Anna Mary for the first time. She was almost six years old. She took more to her uncle Charles, who was back, too, because he was more affable than David. *If only people knew,* thought David, *how miserably Charles acted in trying circumstances.* Charles had actually kicked Makalolos in his temper tantrums.

In Glasgow, David consulted the best physicians in Scotland about his recurrent bleeding. He did not like their diagnosis. His hemorrhoids were so severe he needed an operation. It was not a difficult operation, but recovery was very slow. Time was so precious. David refused to have the operation. He was a doctor himself.

"I'll keep the bleeding under control," he assured himself.

In Bath, he spoke to the British Association about the evil role Portugal played in slavery. Thousands of natives were dying in wars triggered by slave traders. Thousands of natives were disappearing in the ships of the slave traders. England should establish a colony around Lake Nyassa and stop the evil practice. His public denunciation of Portugal was very dangerous. He had to go back to that region of Africa where the Portuguese ruled.

He returned with daughter Agnes to London to write a second book. David was especially fond of Agnes, who was seventeen and no longer in school. They were guests in Newstead Abbey, the home of William Webb, whom he had met in South Africa. David worried about his oldest son Robert, who had tried to join David in Africa. After Robert could not find him, he had impulsively sailed to America, only to find himself fighting for the Union in their Civil War.

In the meantime Murchison urged him, "Return to Africa as a geographer only. You spread yourself too thin. Projects are failing because you try to do too much."

David refused. "I evangelize while I explore. I would give up exploring before I would give up evangelizing."

The new year of 1865 was sad. The Livingstones learned that Robert had died of battle wounds in America. If only Robert could have found David in Africa. But at least Robert died in a cause that David loved himself: ending slavery. Later that year, David's mother died. To add to his misery, the sales of his second book, *Narrative of an Expedition to the Zambesi and its Tributaries,* were puny compared to the first book—not that he cared much for money, but money fueled his exploration. And there wouldn't be any more books. He didn't think he would ever come back to England.

But old friends rallied around him. Murchison raised funds for his next expedition from the Royal Geographic Society. The British government matched that amount. And James Young matched the total of those two donations. David jokingly called his old friend Sir Paraffin Young because he had patented a method to extract paraffin from coal. Clean-burning paraffin was now the major constituent of all candles. James Young was very wealthy.

DAVID LIVINGSTONE

In September 1865, David returned to India to sell *Lady Nyassa* and recruit porters for Africa. Then he sailed to the mouth of the Rovuma River and pushed west. Even if the river was not navigable, he had to establish a new route to Lake Nyassa around the hostile Portuguese on the Zambesi. He had sixty porters, a mix of Indians and Africans of various tribes. After Lake Nyassa they pushed on to the west. How he loved finding a new village in the high country, waiting, parleying, preaching the gospel, then pushing on to the next village.

He enthused in his diary:

> *The mere animal pleasure of travelling in a wild unexplored country is very great. . .brisk exercise imparts elasticity to the muscles, fresh and healthy blood circulates through the brain, the mind works well, the eye is clear, the step is firm, and a day's exertion always makes the evening's repose thoroughly enjoyable. . . . The effect of travel on a man whose heart is in the right place is that the mind is made more self-reliant: It becomes more confident of its own resources—there is a greater presence of mind. The body is soon well-knit; the muscles of the limbs grow as hard as a board and seem to have no fat; the countenance is bronzed and there is no indigestion. . .the sweat of one's brow is no longer a curse when one works for God [but]. . .actually a blessing.*

But this trip was very different from any other. The porters were insolent, with no common bond. Some of them were inexplicably cruel to their animals, actually beating donkeys and oxen to death. They began to desert David. Within six months only eleven men remained. And David found he had passed from one slave-trading realm into another. No longer were the Portuguese the instigators. These new slave traders were Arabs.

In spite of his problems, he was over a hundred miles west of Lake Nyassa by the end of 1866. Losing most of his porters was an improvement. His remaining eleven men were tried-and-true. Two of the most loyal were Susi, a native from Shupanga, and Chuma, a young Ajawa who had gone all the way to India and back with David.

The next years were spent roaming hundreds of miles west of Lake Nyassa. It was not aimless. David discovered two more lakes: Moero and Bangwelo. He took his careful geographic measurements, described animals, recorded each village and its events, preached the gospel, then pushed on. He had some interest in finding the source of the Nile, since it was now widely known it had to be somewhere deep in central Africa. What a stroke of good fortune it would be if he could establish trade in central Africa by a Nile River route. In 1869, after recovering from his first bout with pneumonia, he trekked to Ujiji on Lake Tanganyika north of Lake Nyassa to find mail and send mail. Then he pushed on to the west. His lungs were weak now. Fever struck off and on. Bleeding dogged him. He lost his front teeth, loosened by eating rock-hard corn on the cob. His men dwindled to six. Soon he heard he was very close to a mighty river thousands of feet wide and very deep, flowing north. The Manyuema natives called it the Lualaba. He could not know for sure if it flowed north into the Nile or the Congo. The Congo was an anathema worse than the Zambesi. The Congo River was already known to become unnavigable only eighty miles from the Atlantic Ocean. Raging cataracts stretched upstream as far as English explorers had cared to follow them—for at least one hundred miles. But David would follow this Lualaba downstream by canoe.

Then he was crippled by ulcers on his feet, which refused to heal. Only Susi, Chuma, and another man remained. Although David could almost smell the great Lualaba, he had no choice but to recuperate. At the village of Bambarre, during months of forced rest, he read the Bible four times. But he read Psalm 46 so often the ink was disappearing. Other favorite psalms were numbers 23, 40 through 43, 90, 95 through 113, and 121. He could not bring himself to read the book of Job. He felt as if he were living the life of Job. He was white-bearded now, more and more toothless, weak-lunged, lame, and very emaciated. He had long ago forgotten about his maimed left arm. His objectives had never changed. He would expose the slave trade in every way he could, and he would tell Africans about Jesus. And there was the never-ending hope that he would find some great navigable river in the interior that flowed all the way to the ocean. If honest trade could reach the natives, it would mean the end of slavery and the beginning of Christianity.

In January of 1871, Chuma heard a rumor in the marketplace. "There is a party of white men searching for Dr. Livingstone."

David laughed. "The marketplace is full of rumors. I'm in better health now. We must move on to the great river we've heard about. If it's not a rumor, too."

Then they found it. The Lualaba was truly thousands of feet wide. Soon David was resting in Nyangwe, a very large Manyuema village on the river, negotiating for canoes to take them downstream to explore the river. Nyangwe was the most corrupt village he had ever seen, frequented by Arab slave traders and cannibals. One man wore a necklace of ten human jawbones. He brandished a knife and boasted how he sliced up his victims and ate them. When David blistered him with condemnation, the man laughed and laughed.

But David relished most natives and their marketplaces. This one had about three thousand buyers and sellers in it most days. While staying at any village, he made it a point to stroll through the market often, reassuring the natives of his kindness and good intentions.

SEVENTEEN

By October of 1871, David was camped in Ujiji. Ujiji was also under the fist of the Arabs, but their atrocities here were more subtle. David was reduced to making notes on the backs of scraps of newspaper. He made crude red ink out of the seeds of a plant. To the people in the village, this strange old white man's prospects were dismal. But David trusted God with all his heart and soul.

Then one morning Susi came running. "An Englishman! I see him!"

"An Englishman," replied David. "Is it possible?"

He rose to stare ahead. A caravan of porters heaped with supplies came toiling into the dirt streets of Ujiji. Flying above was the American flag. A young man of about thirty-five strutted ahead of the caravan. Guided by Chuma, he headed toward David's hut.

The young man stopped in front of David and asked, "Dr. Livingstone, I presume?"

"Yes." David tipped the gold-banded blue cap he always wore.

"Thank God I have been permitted to see you, Doctor."

David smiled. "Thank God I am here to welcome you." There was a sad note in his voice. "Come under the veranda. Have a seat." David waved at a straw mat covered with goatskin.

The young man sat. "I'm Henry Stanley, Doctor. I've talked with your old friend John Kirk, the British Consul of Zanzibar."

"Kirk! How is he?"

"Fine. I have something for you. Mail." And Henry Stanley had one of his men bring a bag of mail to David. David placed it on his knee and waited politely. "Please, Doctor, read your mail," insisted Stanley.

"I've waited years for mail. I can wait awhile longer."

But Stanley persisted until David read mail from his children. Agnes was going to be married. Tom was very sick. Then Stanley told him the news of the day: The Suez Canal opened; the Americans had tied their distant coasts with a railroad. As he talked, David's suspicions of the young man dwindled. Stanley knew all about David. He knew all about David's friends and had talked to them. Stanley had managed a very rough journey from the port of Bagamoyo near Zanzibar. David could see he handled himself very well with natives. David learned Stanley had been with the British Army when it moved against the king of Ethiopia. Stanley had fought in the American Civil War. David warmed to him. Perhaps Robert would have been like this young man, had he not been killed in the same war, fighting slavery.

David read the rest of his mail that night. Robert Moffat and his wife were back in England. At seventy-six, Robert was still active. David's strongest convert, Sechele, still ruled the Bakwains. In London, Lord Clarendon had died. William Thomson, the young son of the mathematics professor at the University of Glasgow when David was there so many years ago, was knighted. He was now Lord Kelvin, one of the most famous physicists in the world.

"Quite a little group in that chemistry laboratory back in Glasgow so many years ago: Sir "Paraffin" Young, little Willie Thomson, now Lord Kelvin and, of course myself, the old wheezer of Africa." He chuckled. Mail was such a wonderful tonic.

His old friend Murchison still supported him, garnering yet more funds for supplies. The Royal Geographic Society had even transported parts of a new river boat for him to Lake Nyassa and assembled it there on the lake. But when would David ever get back to Lake Nyassa?

The next morning the young man said, "I represent the *New York Herald*."

"So that's what you do. What is a newspaper correspondent doing here?

"I was sent here to look for you."

"Do Americans care that much about me? How very odd. Well, I'm thankful you came. My supplies are gone. I am almost reduced to begging."

David began to feel so much better that he and Stanley explored the northernmost end of Lake Tanganyika together. Stanley bought him a donkey to ride because of David's horribly ulcerated feet. But help from the donkey was limited. Hemorrhoids prevented David from riding most of the time. On one excursion away from camp as he walked beside his donkey, they were attacked by fierce African bees. The poor beast dropped down and rolled in panic. David plunged into thick brush. Bees were in his hair and his clothes. Finally, the bees he hadn't crushed left him. He emerged from the brush. The donkey was stung to death.

Stanley's donkey had bolted ahead. Stanley had suffered only a few stings on his face. He was horrified when he saw David. "It's many miles back to camp, Doctor. Let me ride ahead and send the litter back for you."

"Too much of a bother," said David. "I can walk to camp by the time you send the litter back." His face and arms weltered with stings, he walked eighteen miles to camp.

That evening as David sipped tea, Stanley said, "Now I know why you've outlasted everybody in Africa."

"Oh poppycock."

"I have seen only one face as grave as yours, Doctor," said Stanley. "It was Abraham Lincoln's."

"Poor Lincoln," muttered David ambiguously.

DAVID LIVINGSTONE

David did not like criticism or compliments. But he liked Stanley. Stanley was a trooper like Kirk. Only one aspect of Stanley's visit irritated him: Stanley's repeated appeals for him to leave Africa. In most disputes David politely refused and went about doing what he wanted to do anyway—with no explanation whatever.

But this time he confided in the younger man, "I feel sometimes as if I am only the first evangelist to attack central Africa, crying in the wilderness, and that other evangelists will shortly follow. And after those, there will come a thousand evangelists. My way is very dark and dreary, but the promise in Psalm 37 is: 'Commit thy way unto the Lord; trust also in him; and he shall bring it to pass. And he shall bring forth thy righteousness as the light, and thy judgment as the noonday.'"

"I may fall by the wayside, being unworthy to see the dawn. I thought I had seen it when the Universities' mission started above the Zambesi, but the darkness settled again. The dawn will come, though. It must come. I do not despair of that day one bit. The whole earth will be covered with the knowledge of the Lord. And as far as the slave trade, my business is to publicize what I see and to rouse up those who have the power to stop it. The evangelists of the gospel will follow."

"But why not return to England, Doctor, and fully recover? Then you can come back and finish your work."

"Oh, I only look worn out. Many years ago I almost died in Luanda. Years ago I almost died in Tete. I've been sick every other day since about 1853."

"But that's eighteen years of hard use."

"I'm so close to my goal. I must go back and follow the Lualaba. Don't you see, Stanley? If I can only get the English traders into the interior, slavery will stop and Christ will triumph. I can't bear to think of all the souls being lost every day. I am so close. Why sail to England? I'm healthy again, thanks to you. Who knows but God? I could go down in a ship returning to England."

In March of 1872 Stanley left, carrying an enormous amount of correspondence from David, including his journals. David knew he could never find a more able or more trustworthy person than Stanley to get his mail to the outside world—which David had not seen for six years!

He waited stoically in Ujiji for supplies he knew would be sent now that Kirk knew where he was. In his condition, he no longer felt days of rest in camp were wasted. Only a certain number of days in the field were left to David. Only God knew how many.

He relaxed in his faith while he waited. He was ecstatic when a letter arrived to tell him that Henry Stanley arrived safely in Zanzibar. Another letter griped that Stanley was going to gain his fame and fortune off David's reputation. David remembered how Stanley had shared everything he had with David right down the middle. He wrote a fellow missionary:

> [Stanley] *behaved as a son to a father—truly overflowing in kindness. The good Lord remember and be gracious unto him in life and in death.* . . . [As to the suggestion Stanley will make a fortune out of me] *he is heartily welcome, for it is a great deal more than I could ever make out of myself.*

David was saddened by a letter that told him Roderick Murchison had died. In his heart, he considered Murchison his staunchest friend. Proof of that soon arrived in the form of supplies. In August 1872, David left to go south to the end of Lake Tanganyika, then strike west to the upper reaches of the Lualaba considerably upstream of the Arab slave traders. Never before did David tire so easily. Never before did he have dysentery so often. Never had he been so constantly wracked by pain. It was in his very bowels now. And most grave of all, never had he bled so often. Yet he continued his long-standing ritual: Approach a village, send word, wait, parley, tell of Christ, move on. Around the south end of the lake, he and his loyal three headed west into a marshy nightmare. For several months, they slogged through muck. It rained daily and progress was very slow. March 19, 1873, was his sixtieth birthday. Ten years before he had been rundown and depressed on his fiftieth. But that fiftieth birthday seemed festive compared to this birthday. His poor health began to frighten him. He knew he should have plenty of years left. His father had enjoyed sixty-eight years, his mother and both grandfathers well over eighty years. And the last time he had letters from the outside world, his older brother John was still alive and in good health. But the bleeding worried David. Still, as long as he rested occasionally for a few days and rebuilt his strength, he should be all right. After all, he was a doctor. So on his sixtieth birthday he wrote hopefully:

> *19 March—Thanks to the Almighty Preserver of men for sparing me thus far on the journey of life. Can I hope for ultimate success? So many obstacles have arisen. Let not Satan prevail over me, Oh my good Lord Jesus!*

By April 1873, however, entries in his diary were unrelentingly grim:

> *10 April—I am pale, bloodless, and weak from bleeding profusely ever since the 31st of March last; an artery gives off a copious stream, and takes away my strength.* . . .

Entries in his diary became ever briefer:

> *21 April—tried to ride, but was forced to lie down and they carried me back to the village exhausted.*
> *22 April—carried in* kitanda [stretcher]. . .*S.W.* [southwest] *2 1/2* [hours of travel].
> *23 April—ditto. 1 1/2* [hours].
> *24 April—ditto. 1.*
> *25 April—ditto. 1.*
> *26 April—ditto. 2 1/2. To Kalunganjofu's, total* [for week]. . .*= 8 1/2* [hours of travel]

On April 27, near the south shore of Lake Bangwelo and the village of Chief Chitambo, he was too sick to travel at all. His hut was hastily built in drizzling rain. Boxes of supplies supported his sleeping mat above the muck and slime. Chitambo came the morning of April 30 to pay his respects. David was too weak to talk to him but implored him to come back the next day. Surely with rest and goat's milk, he would recover his strength. He had been flat on his back before a hundred times.

Later he heard much shouting and called Susi, "Are our men making that noise?"

"No, Doctor, the villagers are driving a buffalo out of their fields."

Pain was agonizing now. He had Susi bring his medical box. With Susi's help, he took a dose of calomel. Perhaps that would help. When he was alone again, he crawled off his bed, and on his knees leaned forward, resting his elbows on the mat. He was bleeding profusely.

He prayed, "Let God's will be done."

The pain subsided. Yes, surely it was God's mercy for the doomed, just as he had felt the pain subside so many years ago in the jaws of the lion. Now he was in the grip of Paradise. Glory must be minutes away.

He ended his prayer, "For to me, to live is Christ, and to die is gain."

The great moment approached. He had not failed. He felt the presence of his dear wife, Mary. Glory, at last.

AFTERWORD

Susi and Chuma buried David Livingstone's heart and internal organs under a *mvula* tree. They preserved his body with salt and sun-dried it for two weeks. They wrapped it in calico, then tree bark, then sail cloth. They lashed that bundle to a pole and tarred it airtight. They and other natives then carried the bundle for eight months—all the way to Zanzibar—over one thousand miles.

On the way, a stranger encouraged them to abandon the bundle. Chuma explained, "No. This is very, very big man!"

The HMS *Vulture* was sent to carry his body to England. On April 18, 1874, Livingstone was buried in Westminster Abbey among the other legends of Britain. Over a period of thirty-two years in Africa he had walked, crawled, climbed, waded, canoed, boated, ridden, and been carried over forty thousand miles of the "white man's grave." He took notes and made maps every step of the way. He told every African he saw the good news about Jesus Christ.

His father-in-law Robert Moffat said, "He sacrificed everything—home, Christian intercourse, lucrative prospects, and earthly honors—for one grand object, to carry the gospel of the Son of God to the heart of Africa."

Livingstone had such power from the Holy Spirit that in the remotest areas Africans, who cared nothing for anyone's honors in the white world, spoke of him decades later.

In 1990, the ten modern African countries where Livingstone trod the old native trails had a population of over 140 million. Of the 125 million non-whites in that number, a staggering total of 75 million are Christians. There are today millions upon millions of nonwhite Christians in the part of Africa that got its first taste of the gospel from David Livingstone.

D. L. MOODY

BONNIE HARVEY

ONE

Dwight Lyman Ryther Moody, born February 5, 1837, grew up in the gentle hill country of Northfield, Massachusetts. From birth, Dwight possessed a rugged constitution and determination to match. His happy-go-lucky father, Edwin, celebrated his son's birth with friends at the local pub.

A stonemason by trade, Edwin enjoyed drinking as well as the social life at the pub. He invited everyone to celebrate Dwight's birth with him. Of course, the pub patrons were only too happy to oblige. The people of Northfield liked Edwin: He was pleasant, hardworking, and easy to get along with. The Ryther part of Dwight's name was dropped when the village doctor, Gideon Ryther, for whom he was named, failed to give the Moodys the expected sheep—the acceptable offering for being someone's namesake. The little boy became known simply as Dwight Lyman Moody.

The small town of Northfield, Massachusetts, was located on both sides of the Connecticut River near the New Hampshire and Vermont borders and had a population of nearly seventeen hundred. During its early years, Northfield was known as Squakeag, an Indian name meaning "salmon." The settlement's strategic location provided a primitive outpost to ward off French and Indian attacks.

The Moodys and Holtons, Dwight's ancestors, appear in Northfield's records nearly from the beginning. The Holtons settled in Northfield by 1672. Isaiah Moody, Dwight's grandfather, moved to Northfield in 1796 in order to practice his brick masonry trade; and Edwin, his first son, was born in 1800.

The two families were united when Dwight's parents were married on January 3, 1828; Betsey Holton was twenty-three, Edwin Moody, twenty-eight. The wedding had been scheduled for New Year's Day, but the Connecticut River unexpectedly thawed and overflowed its banks, so Edwin could not get to the wedding that day. But Edwin, despite this turn of events, detoured many miles, and two days later, married Betsey.

The young couple moved into an unpainted colonial house built by Edwin's cousin, Simeon Moody. Built at the northern edge of town, the house lay at the base of a small, bald knoll in a treeless pasture and looked out over the Connecticut River.

The Moodys shared with their Northfield neighbors a quiet trust in God. After all, Northfield Unitarian Church, even though cold and austere, was considered the center of the community, and membership was assumed for all proper citizens.

But Dwight's mother, Betsey, tall and stately, was really the strong spiritual force in the family's life. As her family began to grow, she taught her children a little Bible lesson every day, and on Sundays she accompanied them to the Unitarian Sunday school. Betsey made all her boys swear vengeance on whiskey and everything that was an enemy to the family.

Like many other newlyweds of the time, the Moodys started married life fairly well-off. Their relative prosperity continued during the early 1830s, but by 1836, the country found itself in a financial depression. Northfield's local economy suffered, and Betsey and Edwin were forced to mortgage their home. They were unable to pay even the small annual $11.70 rent on pew thirteen in the Northfield Church. However, they did not despair. Betsey, an expert weaver, reassured Edwin, "We will manage somehow. The children can help out at some neighboring farms, and perhaps I can weave more items to sell."

"That's good," Edwin responded, "and my work looks promising. The Smiths told me they need a foundation for a new house they want to build. And there's some other projects coming along. Thank God we have such good health—and our children, too."

That winter, finances still tight, Dwight was born. With four brothers and one sister, he had plenty of playmates. But he also learned from an early age to work hard on his parents' small farm. Sturdy and headstrong, dark-haired, brown-eyed Dwight always managed to be the person who took control of most situations. In fact, from the time he was little, Dwight had a bad temper when he didn't get his own way. He even used a good bit of profanity in his early years, although his mother tried to cure him of it.

The Moodys' financial situation continued to be precarious during the first four years of Dwight's life, and it seemed things couldn't get much worse. But when Dwight was just four years old, tragedy struck the family. Edwin had gone to work as usual and was laying brick when he was suddenly seized with an intense pain in his side. Staggering home, he groaned, "Oh, oh, my side hurts so much! Oh, Betsey, get the doctor, quick!" By one o'clock, Edwin's pain was much worse.

He stumbled toward his bed, fell on his knees, and died. Betsey, unaware of the seriousness of his illness, discovered his body, and as the realization of her terrible situation broke in upon her, she also became ill.

Everything changed for the Moody family following Edwin's death, and little Dwight sobbed as he thought, "What a pretty, sunshiny day for my father to fall suddenly dead!"

TWO

From the time of Edwin Moody's death, his family struggled to cope with the loss of its breadwinner. Astonished to see his mother's hair turn white almost overnight, Dwight knew the family barely had enough food to eat. Not only that, but they had little wood to burn in the fireplace, and it was nearly as chilly inside as out. He didn't understand that because of the heavy mortgage on the property, creditors tried to take just about everything in the household.

A month after his father's death, Dwight's mother gave birth to twins, a girl, Lizzie, and a boy, Samuel. Still in bed following their birth, Betsey Moody was surprised to see another creditor, rich Ezra Purple, come into her bedroom to collect the mortgage due on the house. Worse, he wanted her to sign the house over to him! Betsey told Mr. Purple that she would get the money as soon as she could, but he didn't want to wait. Fortunately, two of Betsey's brothers, Charles and Cyrus Holton, were able to raise the needed mortgage funds for the rest of that year.

Dwight's four older brothers, Isaiah, George, Edwin, and Luther, soon found employment on nearby farms and helped support the family. But then fifteen-year-old Isaiah ran away from home. No one knew where Isaiah went or why. Probably the responsibilities that dropped on his shoulders following his father's premature death were simply too much for him.

Because of Mrs. Moody's difficult circumstances, many of the townspeople thought she should send all her children except the twins to live elsewhere. But Dwight's mother wouldn't hear of it. She had already lost one son and was determined that with God's help and hard work, the family would manage. And manage they did, although as the boys got older, some of them began working at farms that were far enough away they had to board with the farmer and only came home occasionally.

Little Dwight loved the members of his family, and despite their hardships, he enjoyed the many good times they had together. Even though his mother spent considerable energy and time milking cows, weaving cloth, spinning yarn, and making children's clothes, she still found time to be with each of her children.

Dwight knew, too, that if he disobeyed his mother—or the schoolmaster or any of his elders—his mother would have him pick out a strong, green switch from the backyard birch. That was one thing he could always count on—getting a good whipping for playing pranks on people or for being disobedient. Dwight rarely suffered any guilt from his impish ways. Even though he and his family went to church regularly, it never occurred to him to call on God in his daily life. But once when he was six and herding cows to pasture, he got pinned under some fence rails. As he struggled unsuccessfully to lift the heavy rails, he began to panic and cry out: "Help me, somebody! Help!"

Nobody came. He began to think he might die. Then Dwight thought about God helping him and he said, "God, help me lift these heavy rails." Right after his prayer, he found he could easily lift the rails.

When Dwight turned ten, his opportunity came to board and help with farmwork in Greenfield, Massachusetts. An older brother already worked in Greenfield, doing chores for a farmer. This brother, who was constantly homesick, wrote frequent letters, wanting Dwight to join him. And one cold day in November, he came home and announced that he had found a good place for Dwight in Greenfield.

Dwight later wrote:

> *Oh, how upset I was! I didn't want to leave the comfort of my home, my mother, my brothers and sisters. I said I wouldn't go. But as mother and I sat by the fire, she said, "Dwight, I think you will have to go. I don't think I shall be able to keep the family together this winter.*
>
> *Mother's wish was enough. I didn't sleep much that night. I cried a great deal. The next morning after breakfast, I took my little bundle and started. About a mile from the house, my brother and I both sat down and cried. I thought I would never get back as long as I lived. We walked over the frozen ground about thirteen miles.*

After the boys arrived in Greenfield and Dwight had been introduced to the old farmer he was to work for, he felt even stranger.

> *I was to milk the cows, go on errands, and go to school. But there were no children anywhere around! That afternoon, as I looked the old man over, I realized he didn't care for boys. Even though he was kinder than I first thought, he could not sympathize with a child. Later when I met his wife and looked her over, I thought she was more cross than he was. Oh, how homesick I was!*

After awhile, Dwight was able to come back home. How happy he was to be back with those he loved, especially his mother. Although the family waged a constant struggle against poverty and sometimes lived for weeks on a diet of cornmeal and milk, they were thankful. Dwight knew, too, that his mother would always find food for any poor person who stopped at their door. She taught each of her children to be generous with what they had.

Dwight's thankfulness extended to two other people who befriended his family. One was the minister, the Reverend Edward Everett, who watched out for the family, supplying what was needed, whether food, encouragement, prayer, or perhaps money. The church people, by and large, seemed indifferent to the Moody family's plight, so Dwight and his family were especially grateful to Pastor Everett for his concern.

Dwight's uncle, Cyrus Holton, proved to be a great help to the Moody family, as well. Dwight knew that when the wood bin was low, his mother would tell the children to stay in bed to keep warm until schooltime. But then, "I would hear the sound of chips flying, and I knew someone was chopping wood in our woodshed, and that we would soon have a fire. I shall never forget Uncle Cyrus coming with what seemed the biggest pile of wood I ever saw in my life."

Despite numerous hardships, Dwight managed to enjoy many things. Shoes and stockings were luxuries reserved for Sundays, and Dwight carried them to within sight of the church before slipping them on. He reveled in sliding barefoot on the winter ice or racing along the dusty summer road. He was too busy having fun to mind the poverty that much.

With the first snowfall, the children brought their sleds out and delighted in sliding down the many hills surrounding Northfield. Dwight possessed a competitive and sometimes mischievous spirit. He loved practical jokes. One time, a farmer for whom he worked was seated in his wagon. He asked Dwight for a jug of cider. Dwight happily obliged, but when the farmer put the jug to his lips, Dwight threw an apple at the horses. They bolted, the farmer flipped up in the air, the jug fell, and Dwight had to look for another job.

Mrs. Moody sent her children to school, but Dwight's time in the classroom was limited because of his need to earn money in the fields and his impatience with book learning. In the schoolroom, the children sat in twos at their little desks, and while some baked by the nearby woodstove, others were chilled by the frigid drafts that shook the windowpanes and doorframe before blowing across the room.

When Dwight did attend school, his prankishness cut into his learning even more, and he received more than his share of whippings from the schoolmaster's rattan or rod. The basic skills that Dwight absorbed from school were minimal. His penmanship, nearly indecipherable, became legible by its size rather than by its neatness. From *McGuffey's Rhetorical Guide Number Five* he learned the principles of elocution, which proved useful later in his life. However, two areas he failed to master were spelling and grammar. A sample letter he wrote at seventeen illustrates his lack in these skills:

I was happy to here from home every weak, but you need not think that I am homesick. . .the time goes by lik a whirl wind how do the things look have you any pears yet Where I bord there is over 50 now and lots of them about my age.

Once, incredibly, Dwight even won a spelling bee! But having little time to study to master basic skills, he became increasingly impatient with school. By the sixth grade, he decided he had had enough of it and left school for good.

Of course, churchgoing tried energetic Dwight perhaps more than school did. His mother insisted that all her children be regular in church attendance. But Dwight showed his reluctance: "I used to look upon Sunday with a certain amount of dread. I don't know that the minister even noticed me, unless it was when I was asleep in the gallery and she woke me up." Then he adds, "It was hard to have to work in the field all the week, and then be obliged to go to church and hear a sermon I didn't understand."

Between his frustration with church, school, and having to work so hard, the time was ripe for Dwight to do something different and see new sights. Since the railroad had come to Northfield when he was eleven, he began to wonder about the world that lay beyond his hometown at the end of the railroad tracks. It was just a matter of time before the desire to find out got the best of him, and he made up his mind to leave Northfield for good.

THREE

On a blustery February day in 1854, seventeen-year-old Dwight Lyman Moody sat in a train car en route to the big city of Boston. His jaw was set firmly, his homespun clothes patched and fairly wrinkle-free as he gazed out the window at the passing landscape.

"I will make a new life for myself in Boston where I don't have to do all those dirty, old farm chores like putting up hay and milking cows all the time. I'll buy some new clothes, see some new things, and. . .and I'll meet some new people. And I'll be successful!" he murmured to himself as the train clacked and jerked along on the sometimes bumpy rails.

Dwight reveled in the journey as the speeding train carried him farther and farther from the small village of Northfield. But a gnawing sensation in the pit of his stomach reminded him that he faced an unfamiliar and uncertain life ahead. He remembered his mother's words uttered with choked emotion: "Please, Dwight, don't leave Northfield just yet. Maybe you can find some work besides those farm chores you hate so much. We don't want you to go far away! Besides, I need you to stay close by and help with the rest of the family." She had sobbed, clinging tightly to him.

But he had made up his mind. He kept to himself whatever misgivings he had about leaving Northfield and going to Boston. The previous Thanksgiving, he had even asked his uncle Samuel Socrates Holton about a position in his shoe store: "Uncle," he faltered at the dinner table, "I want to come to Boston, and have a place in your shoe store. Will you take me?"

Every eye at the table had been fastened on young Dwight. Squirming uncomfortably, he'd looked from face to face.

Uncle Samuel cleared his throat and looked across the table at Dwight's mother. "Shall I take him?"

Twenty-one-year-old brother George blurted out, "No! He'll soon want to run your store!" As Dwight's brown eyes continued to scrutinize each face and glimpsed amusement, consternation, or contempt on each one, they rested finally on Aunt Typhenia, Uncle Samuel's young, second wife. Her eyes offered sympathy and understanding, traits the young Dwight would always hold dear. But nothing was settled for him at that time. He would have to wait until he finally got to Boston.

His thoughts returning to the present, Dwight nervously fingered the five-dollar bill his brother Ed had pressed in his hand. Ed wasn't so hard-hearted after all, he mused. Dwight had regretted all the tearful good-byes, though. But they couldn't be helped. He was going to Boston to make his fortune, and that was that.

Shortly after the Central Vermont train chugged into the station, a confident Dwight marched down to Court Street and Uncle Samuel's shoe store. Uncle Samuel, both surprised and alarmed to see him, found himself at a complete loss of words when confronted with young Dwight's request for employment. After inquiring about the family's health and other matters, he gave no other response. But Uncle Lemuel, his partner in the shoe business, suggested that Dwight stay with him in suburban Winchester while looking for work.

Dwight left the store with a smug look on his face and a swagger in his step. He knew that Uncle Samuel would soon feel chagrin at having missed out on such a good assistant!

But as Dwight stopped at store after store and shop after shop, he realized that there were more people available for jobs than there were jobs to be had.

Many Irish immigrants had come to Boston following the potato famine in Ireland. All of these people were looking for work. Dwight's confidence in finding a job began to lag. By the afternoon of the second day he was miserable and said later, "The feeling. . .that no one wanted you. I shall never forget those two dark days. Oh, the sadness, the loneliness."

He drifted to the docks and pondered signing on as a sailor. He also haunted the post office, hoping for a letter from Northfield. His little twelve-year-old sister Lizzie wrote him, warning him about pickpockets, but Dwight's pockets were as empty as his stomach.

Trudging back to his uncle Lemuel, he made a vow, promising God that "if He would give me work, I would love and serve Him." But when he saw Uncle Lemuel, he was defiant. "I'm going to walk to New York!" he exclaimed.

Wise Uncle Lemuel realized that Dwight's pride had nearly broken and advised him to "ask your uncle Samuel for a job, but be direct about it."

Dwight hesitated. "He knows perfectly well what I want.

Again, Uncle Lemuel urged, "Go on, ask him!"

His uncle won out, and a humbled Dwight sought out Uncle Samuel. Uncle Samuel responded with a long, thoughtful stare.

At last he said, "Dwight, I'm afraid that if you come to work here you will soon want to run the store yourself. Now my men do the work as I want it done." Then he decreed some regulations, laid down certain conditions, and suggested that Dwight think them over during the weekend.

Dwight blurted out, "I don't want to wait till Monday. I promise now!"

Dwight soon entered into Boston's community life. His gregarious, although blunt and sometimes downright tactless, ways soon gained him many friends along with a few enemies.

In summer he delighted in running free across Boston Common—a pastime enjoyed by numerous other newcomers. And in winter, tobogganing captured some of his scant leisure time, but he also watched rich boys race on their highly polished sleds.

Not only did Dwight join in more acceptable kinds of sports, but he relished a good fistfight as well. He remarked later about his many scraps: I used to have a terrible habit of swearing. Whenever I would get mad, out would come oaths and up would come his fists, ready to slug it out with any and all comers.

Most of all, playing practical jokes ranked number one with Dwight: "I was full of animal life, and shut up in the store through the day and sleeping there at night I had to have some outlet, and used to lie awake at nights to think of some new joke to play upon somebody."

Life as a salesman greatly pleased Dwight. Instead of performing unsavory farm chores, he charmed and persuaded people to buy more and costlier shoes. He competed subtly with the other clerks to be the top salesman and reveled in the continual challenges.

For the first time in his life, he had money, although not all that much. He sent a portion home to his mother, informing her, "I would not go back again to live for nothing." Then he added triumphantly, "I never enjoyed myself so well be for in my life the time goes like a whirl wind."

Despite new opportunities, Dwight missed his family and at times experienced considerable loneliness.

Scolding his brother George, he wrote, "What in thunder the reason was I did not get a letter this morning I could not make out. . .I should like to go home this year if I could git away but it is all in vain."

When Uncle Samuel laid down his rules and regulations for Dwight, he included his attendance at Mount Vernon Street Orthodox Church. Coming from his more liberal Unitarian background, Dwight was now confronted, probably for the first time, with the claims of Jesus Christ as his personal Savior.

Uncle Samuel had also insisted that Dwight enroll in Sunday school, and he was assigned to Edward Kimball's class. Attending the first time, Dwight was handed a Bible and told to find the Gospel of John. As he thumbed anxiously through Genesis, the other boys began to snicker at his ignorance. Wisely, Kimball reproved the boys with a glance and quietly exchanged Bibles with Dwight, giving him one marked at the correct place. Dwight's gratefulness became apparent when he told a close friend later that he would "stick by the fellow who had stood by him and had done him a turn like that."

Uncle Samuel suggested to the deacons that Dwight's lack of Bible knowledge was his mother's fault. But that wasn't true. He simply daydreamed through most Bible readings at home, and since grimy youngsters' hands were forbidden to touch the Bible, he failed to glean much Bible knowledge.

Over the next eleven months, Dwight listened to sermon after sermon from Dr. Edward Norris Kirk. The church itself had been formed twelve years earlier by Bostonians unhappy with the rigid doctrinal exclusiveness of another large city church. Pastor Kirk emphasized the sinfulness of man and man's inability to save himself. He spoke of Christ's death on the cross for all mankind, of Christ's resurrection from the dead, and of Christ's desire to be the friend of each one who trusted Him. On the other hand, the minister issued dire warnings to all who refused so great a salvation, and he verbally assaulted those who failed to do so.

Over the next eleven months, as Pastor Kirk's messages and Edward Kimball's teaching combined in Dwight's mind, he found himself caught up in a spiritual struggle: "I thought I would wait till I died and then become a Christian. I thought if I had the consumption or some lingering disease, I would have plenty of time to become one, and in the meantime I would enjoy the best of the pleasures of the world."

Repeatedly stressing that the spiritual issue was one of choice and of yielding one's will to Another, Kirk emphasized that the choice led to a life of faith. Young Dwight sensed the minister was right, yet he seemed unable to yield his will to God.

Then in April, Mount Vernon Church held a revival. And on Saturday, April 21, 1855, Edward Kimball resolutely decided to speak to his recalcitrant Sunday school pupil about his soul.

Arriving at the store, he found Dwight was in the back, wrapping shoes. He didn't want to embarrass him, however, and almost had decided to come back at a more convenient time. "I began to wonder whether I ought to go just then during business hours," he later reported. "And I thought maybe my mission might embarrass the boy, that when I went away the other clerks might ask who I was, and when they learned might taunt Moody and ask if I was trying to make a good boy out of him. Then I decided to make a dash for it and have it over at once."

Going over to Dwight in the back of the shoe store, "I placed my hand on his shoulder, leaned over, and placed my foot on a shoe box."

Kimball looked into Dwight's eyes and "asked him to come to Christ, who loved him and who wanted his love and should have it."

Dwight's struggle came to a head, and he surrendered his will to God's will and came to Christ through Kimball's invitation.

"My plea was a very weak one," Kimball observed later, "but I was sincere." He also realized, "The young man was just ready for the light that broke upon him. For there, at once, in the back of that shoe store in Boston, Dwight gave himself and his life to Christ."

The following morning as he left his room, Dwight's happiness and peace knew no bounds. The wide grin on his face and the fresh sparkle in his big brown eyes reflected his newfound joy, about which he observed, "[I sensed] the old sun shone a good deal brighter than it ever had before I felt that it was just smiling upon me; and as I walked out upon Boston Common and heard the birds singing in the trees, I thought they were all singing a song to me."

As he marched along, it seemed all creation cheered him on his way, and he sensed, "I had not a bitter feeling against any man, and I was ready to take all men to heart."

Then Dwight's thoughts turned to his family, his mother, brothers, and sisters, and he began then and there to pray for them, realizing with sadness that he had never prayed for them before.

He had tried to help his family in different ways, sending not only money but also shoes that he purchased at trade prices. Along with his gifts, Dwight generally offered his sage opinions about everything. Now, he thought, "I could tell them what God has done for me. I thought I would only have to explain it to have them all see the light."

Visiting home a short time later to help bring in the potato and watermelon crops, Dwight attempted to tell his family about his newfound faith. They looked at him blankly, and his mother declared fervently, "I will remain a Unitarian the rest of my life!" They thought Dwight had gotten into some strange doctrine in Boston.

Heavyhearted, Dwight returned to Boston and soon appeared before the Mount Vernon Church board for membership. Not until the applicant answered the board's questions satisfactorily would he be admitted to membership.

Sitting in front of the austere board, Dwight suffered from extreme nervousness: His dry mouth felt as though it was stuffed with cotton. His palms were sweating, and his knees would have knocked together had he been standing. His normal joviality had deserted him in the presence of this august company.

"Ah, Mr. Moody," began Deacon Higginbottom, "have you been awakened? Did you see yourself as a sinner? Do you feel dependent on Christ for forgiveness?"

Dwight found himself at a complete loss for words. His inadequate guttural response consisted of "Yes," "No," and "Sure," which the clerk quickly remedied into correct doctrinal statements.

In exasperation, the chairman rose from his seat and, glowering down on poor Dwight, fairly shouted, "Mr. Moody, what has Christ done for us all—for you—which entitles Him to our love?"

"Hesitatingly, his head hung low, Dwight stammered, I—I don't know. I think Christ has done a good deal for us. But I don't think of anything particular as I know of."

Admission was denied, and the church assigned two pious deacons to teach Dwight the principles of the faith. Dwight would have none of it, avoiding the two well-intentioned men like the plague. As he remarked to a friend, "You might as well try to get a man to go before a justice of the peace."

The next March, the church finally granted Dwight admission, although as Kimball conceded, "Little more light had appeared."

The main proofs that Dwight had become a Christian were slim: He no longer swore, and he said the Bible had changed from being dull and dry to being his favorite book.

Nineteen years old and managing another shoe store for his uncle, Dwight suddenly found Boston stifling. The set ways, the tradition, the old established business houses, the rigid manners and proper social mores discouraged him at every turn. Everything he had been thrilled over when he first came to Boston lay in ashes at his feet.

He was ready for a change, and after he and his uncle Samuel had a falling out over Dwight's request for a raise, he struck out in September 1856 for the booming prairie city of Chicago.

FOUR

Dwight left Boston with mixed emotions. Once more, he had little money but high hopes.

His mother didn't know of his new plans to leave Boston, so he wrote her a letter, telling her of his decision. Evidently Uncle Samuel had not approved of his nephew's plans to go farther west but also refused to increase his salary.

Arriving in Chicago, Dwight's spirits lifted. Another uncle, jovial Uncle Calvin Holton, soon arranged a position for him with Wiswall's shoe store on Lake Street.

He quickly got involved in various activities. The first week after his arrival, he met a Mr. King, a lawyer, at prayer meeting. Mr. King's impression of Dwight provides an interesting observation: "Mr. Moody is one of the happiest looking people I ever saw. His cheeks are full, so red and rosy, and he possesses such a pleasant smile and look, he attracted much attention."

Chicago and Dwight formed an almost immediate bond. He relished nearly every aspect of this sprawling, raucous city. Its stockyards, slaughterhouses, and tanneries filled the air with foul odors; factories and foundries saturated the atmosphere with pungent, thick smoke; and Lake Michigan coated Chicago with mud. But none of Chicago's citizens cared. Like Dwight, they appeared to thrive on all their city's seemingly offensive elements.

Writing home, Dwight exclaimed: "The streets are all lade out strate and broad. You can stand and look as far as the eye can reach and try to walk out of the city." Neither were the buildings as close together as Boston's. Even so, fires were frequent and devastating. Hungry flames would leap from building to building, devouring entire city blocks before being brought under control.

It wasn't long before Dwight found himself caught up in one of Chicagoans' main goals: making money. Tops in selling shoes, he also benefited from personal habits of thrift and exactness. Soon these traits combined with an intense ambition to possess large sums of money.

Because of Dwight's energy and enthusiasm, Wiswall's shoe store appointed him to meet immigrant trains and sell boots to the newcomers. His plain speech and friendly grin worked like a charm to make sales. So intent was he on making money, Dwight prayed that "God would give [him] one hundred thousand dollars."

Some of Dwight's moneymaking strategies included putting savings into land, then selling it at a profit. He also made loans at high rates. He was well on his way to becoming a millionaire.

The city of Chicago also experienced a spiritual revival early in 1857.

Dwight's natural enthusiasm now turned to taking part in the revival. Renting four pews at Plymouth Church, he filled them with young men from Wiswall's shoe store and other nearby stores, and sometimes with people simply walking by the church. On Sunday afternoons, Dwight and a friend often passed out religious literature to sailors and in saloons, boardinghouses, and the shacks of many poor people.

Dwight wanted so much to share his faith! But his efforts in church always seemed to be thwarted. His downfall always came when he opened his mouth and his poor speech came tumbling out. He noticed how people "squirmed their shoulders when [he would] get up to pray at prayer meeting." The church board even notified Uncle Calvin, forbidding Dwight to speak at church because his grammar was too poor!

A new position opened for Dwight near the end of 1857. He became a traveling salesman and debt collector for the wholesale boot and shoe house of C. H. Henderson. With that, Dwight was off and running, soon covering the six states of Missouri, Iowa, Wisconsin, Indiana, Michigan, and Illinois.

He loved his new job, calling it better than anything he had ever done—"it is nothing but excitement all the time!" This job made him even more prosperous, and when back in Chicago, he boarded at an excellent boardinghouse run by Mrs. Hubert Phillips. Many of Chicago's fashionable young bachelors roomed there as well; Dwight's social status had greatly improved.

In his spare time, Dwight sought for a Christian activity in Chicago. Someone suggested he go to Wells Street Mission and ask the people there if he could help with something. When he told the man in charge that he couldn't teach, the man said offhandedly, "Why don't you go out into the alleys and streets and see what boys you can bring in?"

With that directive, Dwight set out to see what boys he could find. Rounding up eighteen ragged, barefoot boys on his first trip to Chicago's seamier side, Dwight joyfully delivered them to the Wells Street Mission. Dressed in a checkered gray suit that covered his stocky frame, Dwight no doubt impressed the boys. He asked them: "Don't you want to go with me to Sunday school?" One of the boys replied, "Are you going to have a picnic?"

Dwight responded, "Come along with me and we will find out." Later Dwight confessed, "That was the happiest Sunday I have ever known! After searching for two years trying to find out what my work was before I succeeded, I finally had found out what my mission was."

Like everything he did, Dwight threw himself wholeheartedly into this new venture of "finding boys."

"Notwithstanding his crude and somewhat uncouth appearance, we became close friends at once," one of the boys remembered about Moody in his later years. "And we found him to be a most agreeable companion—good humored, ready and witty in speech, simple, unaffected and kind, with a charm of manner and a personality so winning and interesting that we all immediately swore allegiance to our new found stranger friend."

Calling his new occupation "drumming up scholars," Dwight often appeared late for the Methodist Episcopal young men's class on Sunday mornings. He had joined the class much to the consternation of his fellow Congregationalists and Plymouth Church.

As Dwight came with his boys to the Wells Street Mission one Sunday, he glimpsed a new teacher for the girls, a good-looking young woman who possessed grace and elegance. He had noticed her a few years earlier at another church.

Although only fifteen, Emma Revell seemed mature beyond her years, and almost before he realized it, Dwight found himself calling at the Washington Street home of Fleming H. Revell, a recent English immigrant. Emma's open acceptance of Dwight, in spite of his uncouth, awkward ways, won his heart early on.

In spite of his new romantic interest, Dwight soon faced a new dilemma.

FIVE

Some of the first boys Dwight brought to the mission had dropped out a short time later due to lack of interest. Dwight's traveling schedule always affected the boys' attendance, and after he was gone a few weeks, they simply stopped coming.

Of course, Dwight also realized that the boys didn't care for the formality and rote learning of the Wells Street Mission. He could hardly blame them—he never cared much for it either.

Back in Chicago in 1858, Dwight had an idea! He and an architect friend obtained an abandoned freight car on North State Street. After rounding up several boys, Dwight asked them, "How'd you boys like to help us start a mission Sunday school?"

The following Sunday, the new mission got underway amid shouts and cheers from numerous boys. A young businessman with a fine voice was brought in to lead the music, but the boys needed to be taught most of the hymns.

Before long, as the boys brought other friends to the new mission, the car became so jam-packed, it nearly burst at the seams. When some of Dwight's friends learned of the crowded conditions, they wanted to help, so they obtained a one-and-a-half-story house on Michigan Street for the mission. The house was a former saloon that was now in disuse; Dwight used the large front room and a store in the back.

The number of boys continued to increase. Sometimes when Dwight was in town during the week, he would have extra meetings, which he conducted himself. To Dwight, these children were precious jewels, and they made up the mission to which God had called him.

Increasingly, Dwight found his traveling job hindered him from the work he loved. He would be gone for nearly a month and missed three out of every four Sundays in Chicago, but he felt loyal to his employer, Mr. Henderson, for he treated Dwight as he would his own son.

Another reason Dwight wished to remain in Chicago was Emma. He visited the Revell house frequently, and Emma's little nine-year-old brother, Fleming, would hide behind the stove and listen to their conversation. He was usually disappointed because Dwight generally brought at least two other young men with him since Emma had two sisters, Anna and Sarah.

If it is true that opposites attract, the love between Emma and Dwight can be easily explained. Emma earned her living as a teacher, and though her father never made much money, their Washington Street home displayed culture and hospitality and reflected their English roots.

While Dwight seemed charged with health and vigor, Emma suffered from asthma and headaches. Shy and retiring, Emma enjoyed being around the extroverted Dwight. He was impulsive, outspoken, domineering, and had little education. Emma was intensely conventional, conservative, far better educated, fond of reading, possessed with discriminating taste, and was self-effacing. Yet they seemed made for each other, and Dwight fell head over heels in love with her.

Dwight's life took another turn when his employer died suddenly in late 1858. Because of a difference of opinion with the new management, Dwight left the firm, going with Buell, Hill, and Granger. Once more, the Sunday school mission outgrew its facilities, and Dwight's friends helped him obtain larger quarters. The lawyer, Mr. King, told another friend, "I became so greatly impressed with the great work, and Moody's earnestness and devotion to it convinced me that I in my humble way should do something similar." So King took Moody to the former mayor of Chicago, Long John Wentworth. Through Wentworth's influence, Dwight secured another building for the mission, a hall built on the site of the old North Market.

The meeting room upstairs had a huge grimy hall with blackened walls and ceiling. It was bare and uninviting. The area underneath was occupied with the local fire truck, and periodically the school session would be interrupted by firemen harnessing their horses, a puffing engine boiler being stoked to get up steam and pump the hose, and the noise of clanging bells as the horses galloped away with the fire engine.

On Saturday nights the German society held dances in the North Market hall. They would pile up the school chairs and other materials in a heap, and they left the floor a mess of cigar stubs, ashes, beer puddles, and papers. Since Dwight refused to employ labor on Sunday, he would do the cleaning himself no matter how late he returned from traveling Saturday night. Following cleanup, Dwight would rush outside to drum up the pupils along with new boys and the girls who were also coming. If he needed to, Dwight would reason with children's parents to permit them to come, and he would even wash and dress the youngsters if necessary.

Given the large numbers, it was imperative that the children be divided into classes. Again, Dwight pressed his friends into teaching the classes, telling them they would be teaching "lambs."

The school grew to six hundred students. Dwight appointed a banker friend, Isaac Burch, as superintendent, and later gave the position to his friend John Farwell. But he himself was the one in charge. Each of the children thought of Dwight as his or her personal friend.

After being gone on a lengthy trip, he wrote one of his brothers, "I shall expect to have a good time next Sunday when I get home, for I have been away some time now and the children are so glad to see me when I return. I think I have got the best school there is in the west; anyway, it is the largest school there is this side of N. York. Only John Wanamaker had a bigger one; it was in Philadelphia."

"Full speed ahead" seemed to be the motto of Dwight's life. The school and his scholars had brought a new impetus to his life. He had so much to do now that he knew what his mission was! But his heart filled with praise to God as he thought to himself: "How good You are, Lord; I just praise You for all You have done for me!" Now he wanted to return his gratitude to God by doing the one thing he knew to do. He had reached a few youngsters through the mission, but there were so many more to be reached! Dwight sensed there was scarcely time enough to do all that needed to be done.

Dwight didn't consider himself able to speak or to teach. He believed his part was simply to round up as many youngsters as he could and let someone else do the speaking and teaching. But sometimes if no speaker came, he had to fill in. At first, the polish and length of contemporary sermons intimidated him; if a minister was present, Dwight became extremely nervous. Eventually he found himself able to talk to an audience of children.

Doing something he enjoyed doing, such as simply telling boys and girls Bible stories or talking about Bible characters as though they were someone living down the street, became easier and easier for Dwight. Before long, he desired to speak and to share. It was as though the love of God had welled up and begun to overflow, and the dam inside him had burst.

Everywhere Dwight went, he would begin to teach and preach about God's love in Christ. Whether he was on a train and had a short layover where he could gather a small crowd, or in larger groups, he relished the opportunity to tell others what Christ had done in his life.

He had shared with many people by this time, but he yearned to go home and tell his family about Christ. Arriving in Northfield two months later, Dwight had issued fair warning to its Unitarian inhabitants that "there is nothing like the religion of Jesus Christ."

Even Uncle Zebulon Allen expressed concern following Dwight's trip home: "My nephew Dwight is crazy, crazy as a March hare. Came on from Chicago last week for a flying visit. I had not seen him, but he drove into my yard this morning. You know how cold it was, and his face was as red as red flannel. Before I could say good morning, he shouted 'Good morning, Uncle Zebulon, what are you going to do for Christ today?' Of course, I was startled and finally managed to say, 'Come in, Dwight, and we will talk it over.' 'No, I can't stop, but I want you to think about it,' and he turned the sleigh around and went up the hill like a streak of lightning. I tell you he is crazy." Dwight left a mark on Northfield after that visit!

D. L. MOODY

Not only Northfield felt the fire of this young evangelist. Everywhere Dwight went, he touched people for Christ. On one occasion, he spoke to a banker on the train about his need for salvation: "Did you ever think what a good heavenly Father we have to give us such a pleasant world to live in?" Dwight asked the stranger. The response, "Yes, indeed."

Dwight: "Are you a Christian?"

The banker: "No."

Dwight: "You are not a Christian? But you ought to be one at once. I get off at the next station. If you will kneel down right here, I will pray to the Lord to make you a Christian."

So they knelt, and Dwight prayed, and the banker prayed. At the train stop, Dwight called back to the banker, "Remember, my friend, now is the time to accept."

In a daze, the banker shouted after him, "Tell me who you are!"

"My name is Moody."

In Chicago sometime later, the banker, Mr. Reynolds, found out where Dwight held his meetings. As he entered the building, "the first thing [he] saw was a man standing up, with a few tallow candles around him, holding a [black] boy, and trying to read to him the story of the prodigal son."

Mr. Reynolds became one of Dwight's staunch supporters, and he delighted in telling friends who were puzzled by his sudden conversion about the meeting on the train with Dwight Moody. He also invited Dwight to come to the country to speak to some people there.

Since Dwight now worked on a part-time commission basis and earned nearly as much as he had before, he had more time to accept opportunities such as that of Reynolds's. He would have been content to continue to finance his Christian endeavors with his own money had God not intervened through one of his mission teachers.

On a beautiful June day in 1860, Dwight was working in his office at Buell, Hill, and Granger when the door suddenly swung open and a pale young man staggered in. Without saying a word, he threw himself down on some nearby boxes.

SIX

A mazed, Dwight gasped, "What's wrong?"

His friend's response: "I have been bleeding at the lungs, and the doctor says that living on Lake Michigan is bad for me. I need to return to New York State—probably to die."

The teacher's ghastly white face and shaken demeanor startled Dwight even more. "What is the matter? Are you afraid to die?"

Again, the teacher shook his head. "Oh, no, sir. But I'm concerned for my class."

Dwight knew the class was made up of frivolous girls from twelve to sixteen. On one occasion, he had had to take the class, and their silly prattling and marching around the room nearly caused him to say, "Leave, and don't come back!"

Now the teacher's real concern came out: "I'm burdened for my class. I have failed them—not one of them has been led to Jesus. Now my strength is gone. I have done the girls more harm than good. How can I face God? Not one of my girls has been converted!"

Dwight listened attentively but with perplexity. He had never heard anyone talk in this manner. His entire effort had concentrated on the numbers of students in the mission. His heart thrilled each time he looked at overflowing crowds, at hundreds of noisy children, and he would be downcast when the numbers dropped even the slightest. He hadn't considered that his wild, young charges could experience conversion like adults; he hadn't thought of them as individuals.

Then Dwight suggested to the teacher, "Why don't you go around and tell them how you feel? If you want, I will go with you in a carriage."

After assisting the man to the street and hiring a carriage, Dwight accompanied his friend to the shabby part of Chicago. As they reached the tenement home of the first girl, the teacher rasped weakly, "I have come just to ask you to come to the Savior." The girl listened with rapt attention as he shared that he must leave Chicago and would die. He urged her to put her trust in Christ. Then, as the teacher prayed, the girl tearfully agreed to settle the question of salvation then and there.

Following this encounter, the men climbed back into the carriage and rode to another girl's home. The teacher again pressed the claims of Christ on this girl, telling her he would be leaving Chicago to die. After making a few calls, he was exhausted, so Dwight drove him home.

Ten days later, Dwight was at work when the teacher came to the store with his face literally shining. He told Dwight, "The last one of my class has yielded herself to Christ. The great vital question of their lives was settled. They have accepted my Savior. My work is done, and I am going home."

But Dwight urged him to wait for a day. Then he suggested getting the entire class together and bringing them over for tea.

That evening, each of the girls and the teacher came to Dwight's place. Then the teacher read some scripture and spoke with them, after which the girls sang a parting hymn. As they knelt to pray, the teacher pleaded with God to deepen the girls' newfound faith. Dwight prayed next and was just rising from his knees when one of the girls began to pray for her dying teacher.

Amazed, Dwight listened to the faltering, spontaneous prayer of a slum girl whom he had known to be an empty-headed scoffer. Another girl prayed, asking God for power to win others to Himself. One after another, the girls haltingly prayed. As Dwight listened incredulously to these genuine, fervent thanksgivings, these earnest petitions, the hundred thousand gold dollars of his dreams turned to tinsel. His ambition to build a commercial empire appeared tawdry and fleeting. All at once, he found himself weighing the desire of the world for wealth and power against the things of eternity. He would rather spend the rest of his years as this dying teacher had spent the past ten days.

The following evening, Dwight hurried to the railway station to see his friend off. Incredibly, without any prearranged plans, each of the girls came to the station to say good-bye to their teacher. They sang a hymn, and as the train rolled out of the depot, Dwight remarked later, "We could see the teacher's pale hand pointing toward the heaven where he wished to meet them."

The impact of this entire episode on Dwight was tremendous. It proved to be God's way of drawing on his heartstrings to leave the business world, but he struggled for over three months before he arrived at a decision. He did not want to leave business! He relished the give-and-take and challenges of business, especially the competitiveness involved in salesmanship. He faced losing the prestige of wealth in a city that only recognized wealth. Then, too, he would have to postpone marriage and be able to offer Emma only a small income when they did marry. His main struggle, however, was over leaving the business world. Emma would understand, but to lose face in the business world simply by bowing out. . .it was nearly unthinkable. At last, Dwight decided to leave Buell, Hill, and Granger. He realized he couldn't serve God and mammon; one had to have first place in his life.

Dwight hadn't shared his long, difficult struggle with anyone, but in the fall of 1860, his friend J. V. Farwell discovered that Dwight had left both his place of employment and Mrs. Phillips's exclusive boardinghouse. Dwight slept on a settee in one of the rooms used by the Young Men's Christian Association

(YMCA) in the Methodist Church block. Instead of nourishing his quite hefty frame in fine restaurants, he either ate in cheap diners or managed on cheese and crackers. Dwight determined to stretch his savings. He told himself, "I'll live on what I've saved. When that is gone and there is no means of support, I'll take it as a call to return to business."

The next year, Dwight received an appointment as an official of the YMCA. The clerk who inserted the Resolution of the Board of Managers put down for Dwight: *For the coming year at a salary of $_____.* The blank was never filled in because Dwight thought receiving a salary would hamper his newfound freedom from monetary restraint. He never again accepted a salary. In a year's time, his income went from roughly $5,000 to $150. He did it gladly in the name of Christ.

Having left the business world, Dwight poured himself with abandon into his mission Sunday school. He still had some financial resources from savings, but he spent freely on his "scholars" and on the school. He would fill his pockets with candy and other confections to entice the children to come to the school. He would also offer prizes, such as a squirrel in a cage, to the scholar who brought the most recruits in a given time. Nor did he ever fail to keep his promises to the children, and they knew they could trust him.

On the other hand, Dwight expected the children to keep their promises to him. One girl recalled: "If for some reason I broke my promise, I would sneak along the streets, in the hope of avoiding Mr. Moody and a reprimand. When I had almost reached home, he would stand before me with his hand outstretched and a sad look, and he would greet me with, 'Why, Jennie, where have you been? I missed you at Sabbath school. I hope you were not ill? Your folks are well? You will not disappoint me this coming Sabbath, will you? It will make me very sad indeed if you fail me.'"

Dwight intensified his efforts to strengthen the school. He pressed his friends into a systematic slum-visitation project. One of them, J. B. Stillson, reported, "We used to carry with us bread tickets, and a little money to relieve the sick, widows, and orphans, and had an arrangement with several physicians to visit the poor and sick without charge, and also to furnish the night watches."

Now that Dwight concentrated all his energy on the school, he became a whirlwind. People found it difficult if not impossible to refuse the persistent Mr. Moody.

Dwight also exhibited a great deal of patience in waiting for his young students. He wasn't easily deterred. A small girl promised she would take Dwight home to get her mother's consent to come to the Sunday school. But she told him she had an errand to run first and asked him to wait on the street corner.

D. L. Moody

Dwight waited and waited at least three hours but still no sign of the girl. A few days later, he caught sight of her and she saw him. She ran. He chased her as she ran over the raised plank sidewalks, clattering down and up the steps where the levels varied, dodging horsedrawn trams, and scattering dogs and old ladies, until finally she dashed through an alley. But Dwight pursued her even as she ran into a saloon and up the stairs to a bedroom and under the bed. Dwight followed her, perspiring and breathless, and at last coaxed the young girl to come out from under the bed. Through his doggedness in pursuing the girl, the entire family came to the Lord.

John Farwell observed the dark circles that had developed under Dwight's eyes and decided to give him a pony to ride so that at least he wouldn't have to walk the considerable distances within the city. People often referred to Dwight at this time as Crazy Moody, because of his stamina and single-mindedness in sharing Christ. He became a familiar figure as a young, twenty-five-year-old man, riding a small pony through the Chicago streets, his trousers in bootlegs and a cap on his head.

Dwight's reputation in and around Chicago grew quickly. People considered him a children's missionary. When some Irish Catholic boys broke some windows in the Mission Hall and beat up the scholars in the streets, Dwight decided it was time to take action. So he went to see the Roman Catholic bishop, the well-known James Duggan. Dwight persuaded the bishop to pray with him, and soon the trouble over the windows was resolved.

Another time, Dwight worked to get a young saloon keeper's son involved in the school. As he recalled: "I had never been in a saloon in my life. I walked by the door about a dozen times. I said, 'I can't go in there. People will think that I have come to get a drink.' Then, as he looked in every direction and didn't see anyone from the church, he dashed in. The old father was behind the bar, and Dwight told him what he had come for. Later Dwight recalled that the father replied: 'We won't have any canting hypocrites here,' so I went back out quickly. But I tried a second time, and again he drove me out. On the third try, the old man wasn't quite so drunk or quite so cross but he said he would rather have his sons drunkards and his daughters harlots than Christians."

But when Dwight discovered that the man edited a small rationalist newsletter, he promised to read Thomas Paine's *The Age of Reason* in return for the man's promise to read the New Testament.

One Sunday morning, Dwight saw an opportunity, so he said to the man, "I wish you would come to church with me."

The man retorted: "I haven't been to church in eighteen years. No, I won't go. But you may have a church here if you want to."

Appalled, Dwight thought, *A church in a saloon?* However, it seemed the only way to reach the man. Afraid of the church officers' disapproval, Dwight scheduled the service for a time when the regular church services were being held.

Then the man said, "I want you to understand, young man, that you are not going to do all the preaching."

"What do you mean?"

The man clarified his remark by saying, "I may want to say something, and my friends may want to say a word. We won't let you preach all the time. We may want to answer back."

So it happened that the atheists would speak forty-five minutes, and Dwight only fifteen. Actually, Dwight wasn't sure he could preach more than fifteen minutes! Word got around about the meeting, and soon the place had to be moved because of the large number of skeptics attending. Dwight simply brought one small boy with him. But as he said, "He was one of my best boys."

Describing the meeting, Dwight said, "They began to poke questions at me, but I said, 'No sir. You have got to preach forty-five minutes.'" Which they did, until Dwight was sick and tired of infidelity. Then he quietly invited them to join him as he said, "Let us pray."

All the while Dwight prayed, they protested, jeered, and sneered. Then he introduced his secret weapon, the small boy who had come with him. The boy prayed with a pleading voice and asked God to forgive these men for talking so against His dear Son. Each of the men began to steal away. Finally, the old saloon keeper said, "If that is what you teach your children, you may have mine."

Dwight rejoiced in the steady growth of the school. Now that he no longer got the children for one hour in the week while the devil had them for the rest, he sensed God's peace about the situation. Seated on the platform, his eyes looking out over the crowd of dirty, ragged scholars, Dwight had no doubt that he had found his life's work and that he would be consumed within the city of Chicago, serving the children of the slums for the rest of his life.

SEVEN

On Sunday, November 25, 1860, President-elect Abraham Lincoln visited Chicago. Through Farwell's invitation, he agreed to come to Moody's school, provided they expected no speech. After attending church in the morning, he got to the mission at noon.

Mr. Lincoln sat through the opening prayers and hymns, then rose to leave. But Dwight boldly put Lincoln on the spot as he announced, "Mr. Lincoln has come to see the school on condition that he not be asked to speak. But if he wishes to say a word before leaving, we all have our ears open."

Lincoln made his way to the platform, then stopped, looked around, and said, "I was once as poor as any boy in the school, but I am now President of the United States, and if you attend to what is taught you here, some one of you may yet be President of the United States. "Following some brief remarks, Mr. Lincoln marched out of the school.

Lincoln's short stay reminded Dwight of two strong opinions he held: He was an advocate for both the Union and abolition. Knowing little about the South, he considered most Southerners slaveholders and felt that was wrong. He viewed the Civil War as a conflict between good and evil and would have been surprised to learn of the spiritual revival that swept through the Southern army.

After the firing on Fort Sumter, at least twenty-five members of Moody's school joined the army. Moody himself held a pacifist view similar to the Quakers; he stated: "I felt that I could not take a gun and shoot down a fellow human being. In this respect I am a Quaker." He also had the school to tend, so dismissed any idea of going into the military.

Chicago, too, found itself much embroiled in the war, primarily through the erection of Camp Douglas, a military city of tents, barrack huts, parade grounds, and guard rooms designed to mobilize and train the citizen army arriving in droves. The camp, located a few miles south of Chicago, soon exerted a certain amount of influence on Chicago. Dwight and his friend Benjamin Franklin Jacobs, a young real estate agent, were appointed by the fledgling YMCA to provide Christian ministry to the new troops.

So Dwight and Benjamin began regular services at Camp Douglas. The men from farms and small towns pouring into the camp seemed ripe for a spiritual harvest. After leading sheltered lives, they found themselves suddenly thrust into the midst of excitement, temptation, and uncertainty of going into combat.

From the beginning, servicemen showed interest in the meetings, and the

YMCA met the growing demand for hymnbooks and other religious material. Dwight and Benjamin were thrilled from the outset with the meetings and the response when hundreds were led to seek Christ. Each night, Dwight returned to his room with several packs of surrendered playing cards, which he carefully stored in a corner of the YMCA rooms.

He still had the responsibilities of Sunday school conventions and his own school, as well, and seemed to be in perpetual motion.

As the war continued, however, and the casualties began to come back to Camp Douglas, Dwight realized more than ever the sacredness of each individual life. Each life mattered to God, and each person needed the gift and assurance of eternal life.

Another dilemma faced him. He could no longer rely completely on Jacobs or others who knew how to preach. Dwight had a burning desire himself each time he met a soldier to tell him the power of Christ to save. He must conquer his shyness and fear of speaking to others! Desiring to talk with the soldiers about his Savior who seemed so near to Dwight, he wondered, "Oh, what would life be without Christ?"

At every turn, he felt his lack, his inadequacy. When Dwight's banker friend, Mr. Reynolds, hosted a dinner for ministers and laymen in the summer of 1861, one of the guests saw clearly Dwight's earnestness in seeking to lead persons to the Savior, and his intense thirst for the knowledge of the Bible; for the entire dinner time was taken by Mr. Moody in quoting verses and in asking the ministers to tell him, "What does this verse mean?" His wasted student life had come back to haunt him.

Farwell called Camp Douglas Dwight's "kindergarten of training." His promotion was rapid, and in the autumn, he considered becoming chaplain, but declined after friends in Chicago begged him not to join the army.

He shared with his brother in a rather sad tone, "I do not get 5 minutes a day to study so I have to talk just as it happens. I do not answer one letter out of ten that I get—I cannot get time—it is eleven to twelve every night when I retire and am up in the morning at light."

Letters such as this one reveal the nonstop dynamo Dwight had become. He tended to measure godliness in terms of ceaseless activity, not according to the time spent with God alone. Still in his mid-twenties, he advocated going to church as much as possible and attending prayer meetings frequently. His motto, a good one, sums up his philosophy: "Do all you can to make the world better than you found it. Do all you can for Christ and then you will make others happy."

In the spring of 1862 following the battle of Shiloh in Tennessee, the YMCA organized a trainload of doctors, nurses, medical students, and supplies to be sent to the front. Dwight accompanied the personnel and supplies.

How his heart broke as he observed the casualties of war! Dwight's urgency to share Christ accelerated, especially in the light of war's catastrophes.

In the midst of wounded and dying men, Dwight witnessed the shattered limbs, the gangrene, the amputations often performed without chloroform, the deaths, and his heart ached. But he knew the urgent message he had to give these men who faced constant death was that of receiving Christ. Repeatedly, he asked them, "Are you a Christian?" When they answered affirmatively, Dwight knew he was in the Lord's will.

Dwight and his companions accompanied over 450 wounded men on a Tennessee River boat. About this experience, Dwight said, "[We] made up our minds we would not let a man die on the boat without telling him of Christ and Heaven—we would tell them of Christ as we gave them a cup of cold water."

The war deeply affected Dwight, but he had some unfinished business with Emma Revell. The man she had originally fallen in love with was a prosperous shoe salesman; now that same man had become a children's missionary and a preacher-at-large. Although Emma wondered where it would all end, she and Dwight were married in Chicago on Thursday, August 28, 1862. She was nineteen, and Dwight was twenty-five. He and Emma moved into a tiny house on Chicago's North Side.

Emma, ever the virtuous wife, set about most subtly to "tame" Dwight. She saw the potential in Dwight—what he could become given some slight adjustments! One of the first things she did was to throw away Dwight's favorite patent shirts. He had boasted that he didn't need to wash them for weeks on end! For the time being, she failed in making him eat regular or adequate meals. One of Emma's greatest assets, however, was that she remained unflustered by the constantly changing events that whirled around Dwight. Dwight praised her in later years as the perfect companion: "She was the only one who never tried to hold me back from anything I wanted to do and was always in sympathy with every new venture."

Even married life failed to slow Dwight down. When brother Samuel came for a brief stay in hopes of finding work, he noted, "Dwight is run from morning to night. He hardly gets time to eat. He holds meetings down at Camp Douglas most every night—it is a treat to go down there and hear the soldiers sing, which is about three hundred or four hundred gathered from most every state." Samuel merely smiled when Dwight talked about religion, but Dwight kept praying for his entire family to come to the Savior.

Going to the war front at least nine times, Dwight ministered to multitudes of soldiers. He was under fire in January 1863 and among the wounded in the battle of Murfreesboro, Tennessee, as Rosecrans pushed toward Nashville. As he ministered, Dwight watched the dying find peace, until the certainty drilled into his consciousness that a person can know immediate, assured salvation.

Spending much of his time moving in and around the wounded men, Dwight had a firsthand opportunity to minister and share his faith with them. Primarily, Dwight seemed to be acutely tuned to the heart needs of the sick and wounded men. More and more he would be invited to speak at gatherings, as well.

His experiences in the war vastly changed Dwight. Gone was the diffident, self-conscious amateur; by the fourth year, he had become a practiced, if homespun, preacher. In the spring of 1864, Major General Oliver Otis Howard, one of the Union generals, wrote of Dwight's effectiveness: "I was bringing together my Fourth Army Corps. Two divisions had already arrived and were encamped in and near Cleveland [Tennessee]. Our soldiers were just about to set out on what we all felt promised to be a hard and bloody campaign, and I think we were especially desirous of strong preaching. Crowds and crowds turned out to hear Moody. He showed them how a soldier could give his heart to God." Howard then gives his estimate of Dwight's preaching; "His preaching was direct and effective, and multitudes responded with a promise to follow Christ."

As this company of soldiers left to fight in the Atlanta campaign and the March to the Sea, Dwight Moody returned to Chicago to some campaigns of another kind. However, he returned a much different individual than the haphazard minister who had left. He had acquired some poise and polish, but more than that, he understood what God required of him: to reach the souls of men.

EIGHT

Returning to Chicago, Dwight found his work cut out for him. The war had brought disruption to his Sunday school mission work, and part of the North Market Hall where they met had burned in the fall of 1862.

When Dwight transferred his Sunday school to the dilapidated Kinzie Hall, enrollment went down. So once more, he set out to bring students in.

He never tired of thinking up new gimmicks and ways to lure boys and girls to the mission. This time, he picked a dozen or so of the most ragged-looking boys he could find, their names reflecting their individuality: Smikes, Madden the Butcher, Darby the Cobbler, Jackey Candles, and Black Stove Pipe. Dwight promised a new suit to each one who attended every Sunday until Christmas.

Dwight organized them into a class under John Farwell, and he deemed the boys "Moody's Bodyguard." He had the boys' picture taken before and after the issue of their new outfits. He captioned the before photo "Does It Pay?" The after photo stated: "It Does Pay." All except one of the boys earned his new suit of clothes—a fact that made Dwight proud.

The succor of the sick and destitute continued to have priority with Dwight in his work. He had little patience with those who preached bliss in heaven while doing little to alleviate misery on earth.

Another way Dwight used to interest students in Sunday school was his picnics, and he became well known for those alone. He himself loved contests and games of skill. Farwell only attended one picnic because he claimed that "the physical exercise to keep up with Mr. Moody in a race was too much for me." An assistant at the picnics recalled that few at the picnics were his equal in racing, jumping, or other sports.

His practical jokes were also well known, and if a person could best Dwight in a joke, he was highly regarded, although this reversal seldom happened. Dwight especially enjoyed jokes with a cruel barb even to the end of his life. His son, Paul, recalled: "While the tenderest-hearted man in the world, he would enjoy laughing at something the victim did not consider so excruciatingly funny. When I was a teenager, I got into a swarm of bees and was being stung numerous times. Worse than the stings of the bees was the sight of my father actually rolling on the ground with laughter, but at a safe distance."

By December 26, 1863, Emma wrote to Dwight's brother Sam that the new Sunday school building was almost completed. She said they hoped to be in the building within a few weeks; she affirmed the tremendous need for the new building and mentioned a roster of several prominent clergymen from different cities who would come to preach.

The new building, the very first to be owned by the Mission School, was built on Illinois Street between La Salle and Wells Streets at a cost of twenty-four thousand dollars. Underwritten by several wealthy patrons and with lesser amounts donated from parents and scholars, the building was completely paid for when it opened in the early months of 1864.

People commented on the building's odd shape, calling it a queer-looking brick building with some semblance to a church. Someone else noticed that "houses crowd it in on either side so as to scarcely leave room for it to stand upon. It looks almost as if pains had been taken to make it as plain as possible so that no one, however poor, might be driven away by any outward display."

A huge gilded sign appeared on the right side of the entrance: EVER WELCOME TO THIS HOUSE OF GOD ARE STRANGERS AND THE POOR. A smaller sign read: THE SEATS ARE FREE. On the inside, various scripture texts were posted in strategic places on the walls. The wall behind the platform, for example, had GOD IS LOVE affixed to it.

Asking a small boy why he walked three miles every week to Illinois Street when there was a school near his home, Farwell was surprised to hear: "They love a fellow over here."

When Dwight's school met in the North Market Hall, Dwight always urged the new converts to find city churches to join. But some of the poorer people tended to feel out of place in the more beautiful church buildings. And now that the mission had its very own building, many of these individuals wished to see the mission become an independent church.

The gathering of a new church was neither unusual nor difficult under Congregational custom. But Dwight hesitated. His mission was not Congregationalist, but united, its one formal link being to the YMCA. He frequently repeated, "If I thought I had one drop of sectarian blood in my constitution, I would open a vein and let it out."

The pressure from the converts mounted toward Dwight to form a church. Otherwise, they said, they would be sheep scattered and unfed.

Finally, Dwight gave in. A church was formed, and the official Manual of Illinois Street Church, printed in 1867, reads: "All were agreed that the church must be independent of all denominational connection, since those already gathered in the work represented nearly every evangelical denomination. It was therefore voted that the church be an Independent Church." Dwight and two friends drew up a simple doctrinal statement and articles of organization based on Congregationalist custom. At Emma's request, a baptistery along with a baptismal font were installed to accommodate both adult and infant baptism.

At first, Dwight invited students from nearby Chicago Theological Seminary, a Congregationalist seminary, to fill the pulpit. One Sunday, when the designated student failed to show up, Dwight himself had to preach. About this same time, Dwight wondered if he should be ordained as a Congregationalist minister. The Chicago Seminary wanted to ordain him, especially since the Illinois Street Mission had become an independent church. Dwight asked his friend G. S. F. Savage what he thought about his being ordained. His friend replied, "Don't. If you are ordained you will be on the level with the rest of us. Now you are a preaching layman and that gives you an advantage. You are on the right road; keep to it." With that advice, Dwight declined ordination.

Dwight remained a lay pastor at the Illinois Street Independent Church until 1866, when a young seminary graduate was ordained to be minister. Dwight retained the title of superintendent—and effective control.

Still trying to conform to the ecclesiastical image of the day, Dwight's sermons tended to be clerical, his tone strident, and his themes evocative of fire and brimstone. So pronounced were his depictions of divine judgment, Emma said she cringed when listening to them.

When ministering only to children, Dwight had not had to face man's degradation as much as he did later. Dealing with people of all ages, he saw human nature at its worst and reacted in the fashion typical of mission preachers of his day. He unabashedly confessed: "I preached that God hated sinners; that He was standing behind sinners with a double-edged sword ready to cut their heads off."

Dwight seemed to be two different people. From the pulpit he pounded and preached the wrath of God in the tradition of the old camp meetings. But in his basic personality at home, he remained genial, buoyant, bubbling with love and merriment.

The birth of the Moodys' first child, Emma Reynolds, on October 24, 1864, contributed much to the joy and happiness in the Moody household. Dwight expressed his delight upon realizing that both her little fingers were as crooked as his own. Writing to his mother, he gushed: "They all say she looks like me but I must say I cannot see any resemblance."

However, Emma had no difficulty in seeing it. In some distress she confided to a friend regarding little Emma when she was two: "She is so full of mischief. You would certainly think she was a second edition of D. L. Moody in his childhood." Despite her mischievous streak, Emma soon became the darling of her parents' hearts.

NINE

As Dwight tried to settle back into some sort of routine following the war's end, he became more involved with the work of the YMCA. At the noon prayer meetings, Dwight was always on hand to greet everyone who entered. His enthusiasm and friendliness and genuine sincerity never failed to touch people.

Prayer requests would come in from all over the city and would be read by the day's leader. Often upon hearing a request, Dwight would weep like a child in empathy. In him lay always something of the impressionable child, never far from tears, never far from laughter. His boundless energy was known and appreciated all over the city of Chicago, and in 1866, when a prominent businessman turned down the presidency of the Chicago YMCA, he nominated Dwight Moody. Of course, Dwight had his detractors, too. Some said he was "too radical." Nevertheless, Dwight received the presidency at that time.

Too radical or not, Dwight was soon "on the warpath securing subscriptions"— as they described the energy with which he badgered the worthy and wealthy of the city. He reveled in turning the dollars of the rich into an institution that should, in a favorite phrase, "do good."

Becoming known for his bold faith, Dwight often experienced astounding answers to prayer. One day he rushed into the study of a Chicago minister with a sealed envelope. "Open that!" he cried. "Open it! There is a check for two thousand dollars in there."

"Are you sure? Have you seen it?"

"No. But I asked the Lord for it, and I know it's there! I came all the way across Chicago that you might prove my faith in prayer."

As the minister tore open the envelope, he discovered there was a two thousand-dollar check inside, payable to the order of D. L. Moody and signed by Cyrus H. McCormick.

Dwight shard his story with the minister. He had gone to the millionaire, stating, "Mr. McCormick, the mission school is in dreadful straits!"

"Why, you are striking me rather hard as of late. I gave you something not long ago."

"I want a thousand."

"A thousand! Why, surely you don't mean that, after all I've given you of late?" In any event, Mr. McCormick agreed to make a donation. He went upstairs to write out a check.

"Just then," Dwight continued, "I thought to myself what a fool I was not to ask for two thousand! And I fell on my knees there in the parlor, and asked for two thousand. Mr. McCormick came downstairs with this sealed envelope. I thanked him and rushed over to you. Isn't my faith confirmed?"

The old minister was so curious as to what happened that he went to Mr. McCormick. "Can you recall the inducements or influences acting on your mind leading you to make the check for twice the amount asked for?"

Mr. McCormick thought for a moment, then replied: "Well, as I remember, I went upstairs to my desk and took out my checkbook. I wrote in 'D. L. Moody,' and then I began to think of the noble work he is doing in our city, and what a splendid fellow he is. Finally I concluded to make the check for the amount I did."

Although Cyrus McCormick thought well of Dwight, Chicago's respectful estimate of him had dissolved since the war. "He was often most brutally ridiculed and buffeted and persecuted," recalled an acquaintance. "His language, his looks, his methods of work were made objects of ridicule and burlesque, and the most cruel remarks were passed from mouth to mouth about him."

Dwight had made a vow to God not to pass a day without speaking to someone about Christ. His stock question to everyone became, "Are you a Christian?" He shouted this question from the platform, he whispered it in the narrow passageway, he asked it of his dinner table companions. Wherever he happened to be, Dwight was sure to confront everyone nearby with this question.

Dwight's close friends winced with him from the ridicule, and Farwell even suggested that he was doing more harm than good when he shouted at people at every turn. Dwight replied calmly, "You are not my boss. God is my boss."

These were the years when Dwight's nickname became Crazy Moody. He drove himself mercilessly. He admitted later, "I was an older man before thirty than I have been since." Despite his frenzied, sometimes obnoxious ways to win others to Christ, Dwight's humility redeemed him. He always showed a willingness to listen, to learn, to experiment, and he possessed a basic common sense, which helped him immeasurably. His burning desire as far back as he could remember was "that every soul be saved."

Although Dwight was willing to continue working in Chicago, his wife's health changed his mind.

TEN

Occasionally in his rare quiet moments, Dwight had thought about visiting England. He felt his spiritual and mental needs keenly. But he moved much too fast in Chicago to address them.

Much as he desired to travel to England, Dwight would never have gone had Emma's doctor not suggested it for her asthma. Mrs. Revell gladly kept baby Emma, and Dwight and Emma set sail for England on February 24, 1867, shortly after Dwight's thirtieth birthday.

Emma loved the sea voyage, but poor Dwight suffered from seasickness the entire trip! Shortly after their arrival, Dwight, still recovering, said, "One trip across the water is enough for me;" then he added, "I do not expect to visit this country again." The couple's first impressions of England left something to be desired. It either snowed or rained most of their first week. Dwight disliked the British formality. Although a born Londoner, Emma agreed completely with her husband. She considered London as sooty as Pittsburgh; the Bank of England timeworn; and St. Paul's Cathedral a very grand building but more appropriate for any other kind of performance than for a church service!

Making their way the following Sunday to the Metropolitan Tabernacle, Spurgeon's church, Dwight marveled at the huge congregation of at least five thousand. He remarked to Emma later, "When Spurgeon walked to the platform, my eyes just feasted upon him, and my heart's desire for years has at last been accomplished!" It seemed to Dwight like a dream come true, to be listening to Spurgeon after all the time he had admired him. Silently Dwight prayed, "Oh, Lord, help me to preach and minister like Charles Spurgeon! I pray for grace and to be filled with the Holy Spirit to minister to Your people."

In London Dwight met George Williams, founder of the YMCA, and received an invitation to the annual breakfast of the original YMCA in Aldersgate Street; Dwight encouraged the association to start a daily noon prayer meeting similar to the one in Chicago. The meeting flourished, continuing without interruption until World War I.

As time passed and spring came on, the Moodys were invited to various social gatherings, and their perception of England began to change. Emma told Dwight, "[I] liked the English better than when I first came. I do not think them as reserved as I expected them, but do not think them as free and open as Americans."

Dwight enjoyed the sensation of being appreciated. In Chicago, he recalled, Episcopalians would pass by on the other side of the street or call him names. But in England, the Church of England clergy and laymen he met were kind to him. Evangelicals, both Anglican and nonconformist, took to him.

Of course, Dwight appeared somewhat of a novelty to the British. His expansive geniality, his sincerity and drive caused a religious newspaper to declare, "How deeply and quickly Dwight L. Moody has won the affections of a multitude of Christian brethren." Dwight relished the new attention, and his estimation of the British climbed because they received him so openly.

Some of the interesting people Dwight met in England had lasting impact on him. One of them was a wholesale butcher in West London, Henry Varley. Varley, close to Dwight's age, belonged to the Plymouth Brethren group. His preaching, however, was remarkable; he preached with such force that several hundred people would gather to hear him.

Dwight, curious about Varley's power, visited him to discover his secret of success. Varley believed in much prayer, so he prayed at home. Then, as they took a small carriage over the rough stone streets of London, he said, "Now, brother, let us have prayer for the meeting," and he knelt on the swaying carriage floor, among the wisps of straw.

Dwight had never tried praying aloud in a carriage as it swayed back and forth and rumbled along over the cobblestone streets. In fact, it wasn't exactly a formidable or convenient place to pray! But following the evening service, he watched spellbound as seventy butchers with tears streaming down their faces gathered around Varley, truly a man of God. Dwight knew that prayer was Varley's secret.

At Varley's invitation, Dwight received several opportunities to preach, which he gladly fulfilled. At the close of a service he preached in Dublin, he heard someone speak at his shoulder level: "Ah'm Arry Moorhouse. Ah'll coom and preach for you in Chicago."

Dwight turned around. Just in front of him stood a beardless, insignificant-looking, small man. He appeared to be about seventeen years old. Slightly annoyed, yet attempting to hide his disdain, Dwight smiled a benevolent smile.

Harry Moorhouse's name had been mentioned to Dwight, and he knew a few things about him. God had retrieved Harry from the gutter and from picking pockets. Although Harry was known as the Boy Preacher, Dwight found it hard to believe this mere stripling of a lad could preach and soon forgot all about him.

Not long after the encounter with Moorhouse, Dwight and Emma returned to Chicago and were thankful to be home. Much to their surprise and delight, a home had been built for them on State Street and given to them as a gift. Their friend John Farwell had asked other friends of the Moodys to help purchase and furnish the house. Two portraits of Dwight and Emma had also been placed prominently in the new house. G. P. A. Healy, the most famous American portrait painter of the day, had painted Dwight's portrait without fee.

The opening of the new YMCA hall on Madison Street provided the Moodys with further excitement. Designed by W. W. Boyington, an outstanding architect in the area, the hall had been erected in the center of Chicago's business district. The first building in the world to be built by a YMCA, the hall rose five stories, had a marble façade, the largest auditorium in Chicago, five shops to lease at street level, a library, a reading room, lecture rooms, a gymnasium, a dormitory for forty-two people, and extra office space rented by the fire, police, and health departments.

Officials of the YMCA had intended to name the new hall Moody Hall, but Dwight demurred and insisted it be called Farwell Hall in honor of John Farwell. Everyone knew, however, that the new YMCA represented Dwight's crowning achievement in Chicago. They realized, too, that Dwight was one of their leading citizens, albeit a somewhat abused one.

A description of him appeared in a local religious newspaper in November 1867: "Mr. Moody is rather below the medium height, and inclined to fleshiness, not corpulence. He goes to the platform with a quick, nervous step that means business; and behind his round, ruddy and good-humored but earnest face is a busy brain." The newspaper account attached some further accolades to Dwight: "When Moody speaks, everybody listens, even those who don't like him. His remarks are short, pithy and practical, and his exhortations impressive and sometimes touching even to tears. He is aggressive and his remarks always have a martial ring." Just when Dwight thought his situation in Chicago couldn't get much better, he received an unexpected irritant in the form of a letter from Harry Moorhouse. The young man had arrived in New York and wanted to come to Chicago and preach for Dwight. Politely, Dwight dropped him a note saying, "If you come West, call on me." Dwight soon dismissed Moorhouse from his mind.

Twenty-seven-year-old Harry Moorhouse had served time in jail before his twenty-first birthday. After getting out, he came upon a backstreet mission and heard an ex-prizefighter and coal miner preach on the prodigal son. He became a respectable auctioneer, married a childhood friend, then moved to a tiny cottage on the outskirts of Manchester to give his whole time to preaching.

A whimsical, gentle, and self-effacing creature, Moorhouse possessed a burning sense of mission. A strong sense of humor and an ability to prick the slightest bubble of pretension brought a wonderful balance to his life.

On January 7, even as Farwell Hall still glistened with new paint, fire broke out. No police, health, or fire department on the premises could save it from the strong winds that blew that day. A young boarder, David Borrell, had reached the doorway, carrying his trunk, when Dwight called, "Borrell, throw it away and help me. We want to have a prayer meeting in the Methodist church." The noonday meeting took place, and even before the rubble cooled, the YMCA secretary and committee began soliciting for funds to rebuild the prestigious hall.

A few weeks after the fire, Dwight heard from Moorhouse again, much to his annoyance. In his letter he told Dwight the date and time for his Chicago visit. Reading it with some impatience, Dwight thought, *The man can't preach!* Fortunately, from Dwight's perspective, he had to be in St. Louis for the Missouri Christian Convention the day of Moorhouse's arrival.

The day of Dwight's departure for St. Louis, he asked Emma to put Moorhouse up, then he told the deacons, "Try him and if he fails I will take him off your hands when I come back." Then he boarded the train for St. Louis.

Dwight had been in demand in the Northwest as a convention speaker. His ability to draw ministers and laypeople of differing denominations and viewpoints was considered valuable. The men in charge of these conventions knew Dwight to be a man who could stir sluggish saints, resolve differences, and bring about unity in the effort against unbelief, apostasy, and indifference. Materialism, too, was fast gaining ground across the nation, and multitudes were being caught up in its pursuit.

Meanwhile, back in Chicago, Harry Moorhouse put in his appearance. With much misgiving that Thursday night, the deacons let Moorhouse preach at a small meeting in the basement. Even though they struggled to understand him and his message was very different from any they had heard, they agreed to have him preach again the following night.

When Dwight returned on Saturday, he asked Emma about Moorhouse. Much to his amazement, she replied, "They liked him very much. He preaches a little different from you. He preaches that God loves sinners!"

Dwight figured if someone preached differently from him, the other person was out of step. He looked with dread toward the next day because he knew he wouldn't care for Moorhouse's preaching!

ELEVEN

On Sunday morning Dwight found himself in a somewhat expectant mood. Emma, with enthusiasm, reassured Dwight. "Mr. Moorhouse backs up everything he says with the Bible. I think you will agree with him when you hear him preach."

Hearing a strange sound at the service, Dwight realized the people were all carrying Bibles. He had never told them that laypeople should bring Bibles, and it seemed odd to see the people coming in with Bibles and to listen to the flutter of Bible pages as the scripture was announced.

Then the service began and Moorhouse declared his text: "John 3:16: 'God so loved the world, that he gave his only begotten Son, that whosoever believeth in him should not perish, but have everlasting life.'" Instead of dividing the text into three parts in ministerial fashion, Moorhouse went from Genesis to Revelation, proving that God loves the sinner. Dwight's teaching that God hates the sinner as well as the sin suddenly lay in shambles at his feet. Admitting to a friend later, Dwight said, "I never knew up to that time that God loved us so much. This heart of mine began to thaw out; I could not keep back the tears."

Dwight's young brother-in-law, Fleming Revell, observed Dwight that Sunday and "saw him just drinking in the message that Sunday morning, February 8, 1868." Again, Sunday night, Moorhouse used the same text and unfolded from Genesis to Revelation God's love for man. It was not so much a sermon as a Bible reading, consisting of a string of related texts or passages.

Gradually, as the truth of Moorhouse's messages broke in on Dwight, he found himself being transformed into an apostle of love. No more would he preach the wrenchingly bitter and fearful sermons about God's hatred for man. How could he have so misunderstood God's Word? From then on, he would do his best to remedy whatever ills he had committed in his sermons.

During the daytime, Moorhouse enjoyed the place of honored guest in the Moody household. His little ways and comic sayings and Lancashire accent enhanced his charm, but more than those, he taught Dwight how to read and study the Bible.

Dwight had always looked on the Bible as a textbook and as a weapon. To him it was the Word of God, but he regarded it as an armory of well-worn texts on which to peg talks and sermons or to throw at individuals. He was curiously ignorant of much that the Bible taught.

Gently, Harry Moorhouse told Dwight that he didn't know his Bible; he showed him how to treat it as an entity and to trace the unfolding themes of scripture. He helped him see that "it is God's Word, not our comment upon it, that saves souls." Above all, Moorhouse warned Dwight that he needed to take in more than he gave out. It wasn't long before Dwight rose very early in the morning while the rest of the household slept. He lit and trimmed the oil lamp in the study and pored for an hour or more over his big Bible, scribbling notes in the margin.

After Moorhouse left, Fleming Revell recorded in his diary, "D. L. Moody had great power before, but nothing like what he had after dear Harry Moorhouse came into our lives and changed the character of the teaching and preaching in the chapel."

The years 1870 and 1871 were ones of major change for Dwight. He had long realized the importance of song in gospel meetings. Although he himself was virtually tone deaf and definitely not a singer, he could be powerfully impressed by a hymn. He saw that singing created a mood of worship and response, especially among the semiliterate poor.

For a few years, Dwight had searched off and on for a song leader. Sometimes an older man, Philip Phillips, known as the Pilgrim Singer, sang at Dwight's meetings. Phillips, unfortunately, did not live in Chicago.

Then in the summer of 1869, Dwight met another song leader, Philip Paul Bliss. Bliss was a lovable, cheerful man with beautiful manners and could write hymns that children and semiliterate people learned easily. Through Philip Bliss, Dwight's sense of the power of singing in gospel work crystallized.

Bliss helped Dwight on Sunday evenings when in Chicago, but in July he was lured away to become choirmaster of the First Congregational Church. One outstanding gospel song that Bliss wrote while working with Dwight was "Hold the Fort: I Am Coming," based on the defense of Altoona during the Civil War's Atlanta Campaign. Sherman had signaled the message "Hold the Fort" in the presence of the fierce defense. But the message took on Christian connotations and became popular in America and Great Britain.

Later in July, Dwight attended the YMCA International Convention held in Indianapolis. One morning when leading an early prayer meeting, Dwight saw Ira David Sankey, a participant, arrive late and sit near the door. A fastidious, well-groomed man, Sankey had every hair of his handsome, muttonchop whiskers in place. A long-winded man droned on and on in prayer, and the others began to get restless. Sankey's neighbor, a Presbyterian minister, whispered, "The singing here has been abominable. I wish you would start up something when that man stops praying, if he ever does."

When the man quit, Sankey started "There Is a Fountain Filled with Blood." The congregation joined in, and the meeting continued forward.

Afterward, the minister introduced Sankey to Dwight. As was his custom, Dwight sized him up in a second.

"Where are you from? Are you married? What is your business?"

Sankey, taken aback, quickly responded, "New Castle, Pennsylvania. I am married, two children. In government service, revenue."

Dwight shot back, "You will have to give that up."

Sankey could scarcely believe his ears. "What for?" gasped Sankey.

"To come to Chicago to help me in my work."

Over Sankey's protest that he could not leave his business, Dwight insisted: "You must. I have been looking for you the last eight years."

Sankey conceded finally to pray with Dwight briefly in the vestry but had no thought of giving up his position. The following afternoon he received an urgent note requiring him to come to a street corner. As factory crowds left for home, Dwight told Sankey to get on a soapbox, a comedown of sorts for this handsome young man. Commanded to sing, Sankey proceeded, and a crowd gathered. As Dwight began to talk, more and more people came to hear him. Twenty-five minutes later, Dwight told the people they would continue in the Opera House rented by the YMCA International Convention. Sankey and his friends led the way singing "Shall We Gather at the River?"

Sankey left Indianapolis, completely unsettled about the matter of joining Moody. In a tumult, he prayed, recalling later: "I presume I prayed one way, and he prayed another." It took just six months for Dwight to pray Sankey out of business!

Consenting to a trial week with Dwight in 1871, Sankey resigned his job with the civil service. His wife agreed, despite never having lived so far from New Castle. So Sankey and Moody joined forces, but local buffs were not impressed. John Hitchcock called Sankey "a comparatively obscure man whose presence amongst us is not regarded in musical circles as a great acquisition to their forces." Time would prove him to be wrong.

The Moody whom Sankey joined was a man facing a dilemma. Dwight's energies remained undiminished and his zeal for men's souls unsurpassed, but he was uncertain about remaining in Chicago with the mission school, the church, and his other activities and commitments.

In the summer of 1868, because of his success in Chicago's slums, a national convention held at the Marble Church in New York City extended an invitation to Moody. Someone at the meeting observed that Dwight "claimed attention at once, and I believe you could have heard a pin drop all through that hour. It seemed to me that he just grew larger and larger. Mr. Moody was a revelation to us on 'how to reach the masses.'"

Then there was the political maneuvering. . .when certain individuals wanted Dwight to run for Congress, for governor, and even for president! Dwight's response to all these ideas remained, "I have got a higher service than that!"

But where did God want him to be? He enjoyed his home, and while he had considered being an itinerant evangelist, he couldn't bear the thought of being gone so much of the time. He thrived on quick trips to this city or that for evangelistic-type forays but always looked forward to coming back home. Once little William Revell Moody put in his appearance on March 25, 1869, Dwight had even more reason not to stray too far from home.

As usual, ceaseless activity filled Dwight's days. Activities such as the tract campaign at the YMCA, where the men carried over a million tracts to Chicago's inhabitants, gratified him. He also participated in endless fundraising to keep all the projects going and organized a Yokefellows group that would frequent saloons, boardinghouses, and street corners to bring people into Farwell Hall.

Eventually he was on ten or twelve committees, and the situation finally became critical. Dwight realized that his hands were full, and said, sadly, "If a man came to talk about his soul I would say: 'I haven't time: got a committee to attend.'"

Dwight knew his life had gotten much too complicated. His involvement in various activities used to satisfy him, but now he sensed an inner struggle. He knew God was calling him into a higher service, "to go out and preach the Gospel all over the land instead of staying in Chicago. [He] fought against it."

The tension building within Dwight spilled over into his preaching. The inner tension, the half-recognized rebellion against God's will, the tangled objectives, and the utter lack of integration combined to ensure that Dwight's speaking and preaching were no longer like St. Paul's, "in demonstration of the Spirit and of power."

TWELVE

Sarah Anne Cooke had recently emigrated from England. Just ten years older than Dwight, she seemed wise in the ways of God and attended numerous religious meetings with regularity. A Free Methodist, Mrs. Cooke, as a friend described her, "spoke only in the language of Zion, was full of good works, and buttonholed the unwary to exhort them to flee from the wrath to come."

Attending a camp meeting in June 1871, Mrs. Cooke said reverently, "A burden came on me for Mr. Moody, that the Lord would give him the baptism of the Holy Ghost and of fire." Soon she solicited her friend Mrs. Hawxhurst, who was a widow, to pray with her.

The two women seated themselves in the front row of Dwight's church, and while he preached, they prayed.

After the service they would say to him, "We have been praying for you."

Unnerved, Dwight responded, "Why don't you pray for the people?"

The ladies: "Because you need the power of the Spirit."

Disgusted, Dwight muttered through his beard, "I need the power?"

They paid him no attention but just continued praying and, as they had opportunity, speaking to him.

He resented them sitting in the front row, and it became increasingly difficult to preach. The women persisted. As they continued to pray, Dwight asked them to come to his home and talk with him.

While there, the ladies poured out their hearts in prayer, asking God to fill Dwight with the power of the Holy Spirit. Unexpectedly, a great hunger began to form in Dwight's soul. He said later, "I did not know what it was, and I began to cry out as I never did before. I really felt that I did not want to live if I could not have this power for service."

But the power would not come, perhaps because Dwight refused to heed the call "to go out all over the land."

Dwight's inner struggle refused to resolve—he would not place himself on the altar, would not yield to God in his determination to stay in Chicago. But still Dwight heard the still small voice whispering to his spirit: "Go out and preach the Gospel all over the land." Surely God couldn't be telling him to leave everything he had worked for!

Sunday evening, October 8, a capacity crowd filled Farwell Hall. Dwight's message went forth supercharged, and Sankey sang "Today the Savior Calls" like an angel. As Sankey reached the closing words of the third verse—"and death is night"—the loud noise of fire engines rushing past the hall drowned out his voice. Then, the deep, sonorous tones of the great city bell in the old courthouse steeple pealed forth their warning alarm.

Confusion reigned in the street as people rushed by, and Dwight decided to close the meeting at once because of the audience's restlessness and growing anxiety.

As Dwight and Sankey sprinted out the back door, they glimpsed an angry red smudge in the southwest part of the sky. Immediately, they separated, Sankey to help at the scene, and Dwight to cross the river for home to reassure Emma and the children. As he hurried along, the southwest wind rose almost to hurricane force, and the sky became bright with a fireworks display as sparks blew and house after house caught fire from the hungry flames. By midnight the ravenous flames had engulfed much of Chicago. Crashing buildings, wild neighing of terrified horses, and shouts of firefighters and refugees combined in an ominous cacophony. The Moody home, temporarily thought to be secure, was quickly roused to action when police knocked on their door. Dwight speedily gathered some Bibles and a few valuables and arranged for a neighbor who owned a horse and buggy to take the children to friends in a northern suburb.

The fire raged throughout the next day. Thousands of homeless poured out of the city in an endless stream, thieves looted, martial law was proclaimed, and buildings were blown up to make a fire break. For twenty-four hours Dwight and Emma had no idea whether their children had been trapped or saved, and Emma's hair started to turn gray. They hoped and prayed that Sankey had not been burned to death. By Wednesday the fire had burned out, but Chicago lay in ruins. Everything he had labored for lay in shambles, so Dwight began to build again. Much of his ability resided in the area of solicitation, so he contacted all those who could possibly help in rebuilding. Dwight traveled to New York to meet with several wealthy prospects.

The response to Dwight's efforts proved to be generous, but he could scarcely face the prospect of rebuilding. To be reduced almost to begging for funds disgusted him. Inwardly, he puzzled over his attitude. Didn't he believe in the work anymore? No. His heart cried out for the filling of the Holy Spirit. That desire overwhelmed him and ruled over all others.

As he walked the streets of New York, he reviewed the situation. Farwell Hall and Illinois Street were in ashes, the ten or dozen committees had scattered like dying embers, nor could he face the exhaustion of reorganization. Had God burned him out that he should go all over the country, perhaps the world? Dwight still said no. All the chains binding him to Chicago had snapped except one: his own will.

Dwight's inner turmoil continued unabated. He craved power! He began to march around New York streets at night, wrestling, panting for a Pentecost.

In broad daylight he walked down one of New York's busiest streets, while crowds jostled and pushed by and carriages and cabs jingled in the streets and newsboys shouted in his ears. The last chain snapped. Quietly, without a struggle, he surrendered.

Immediately an overpowering sense of God's presence flooded his soul. He felt as though Almighty God Himself had come to him. He needed to be alone in some private place. Quickly he hurried to the house of a nearby friend, disregarding an invitation to "come and have some food." Dwight told his friend softly, "I wish to be alone. Let me have a room where I can lock myself in."

His understanding host led him to a private room in the rear of the house. Dwight locked the door and sat on the sofa. The room seemed ablaze with God. He stretched out on the floor and lay bathing his soul in the Divine. Of this communion, this mountaintop experience, he wrote later, "I can only say that God revealed Himself to me, and I had such an experience of His love that I had to ask Him to stay His hand."

The former turmoil vanished, conquered by an overwhelming sense of God's peace. Dwight's resolute will and determination suddenly came under new management as God remolded him and left him as gentle and tender as a baby.

No more would he choose his path. It was up to God to do that. He would lead, He would supply; Dwight need thirst no more. The dead, dry days were gone. Thankfully, Dwight thought, *I was all the time tugging and carrying water. But now I have a river that carries me.*

Crazy Moody had become Moody, the man of God.

THIRTEEN

Returning to Chicago within a short time, Dwight had three thousand dollars to start building a pine tabernacle. Incredibly, the building opened on Christmas Eve as a center of relief and evangelism.

A young man who visited the tabernacle for the New Year's Eve Watch Night Service on December 31, 1871, recorded his impression: "Consider the desolation all about. The midnight, the midwinter stillness, the yawning cellars and gaunt walls one had to pass walking southward for 45 minutes before reaching buildings and inhabited houses again. Then below zero, a clear sky, a full moon overhead and absolute quiet." In the midst of the devastation, the young man came to the tabernacle, almost like a beacon to desperate souls. Filled almost to its 1,400-seat capacity, the tabernacle represented hope.

In January Dwight traveled to Brooklyn, New York, to hold a series of meetings in a new mission chapel. Afterward, a well-to-do layman, Morris K. Jessup, expressed his appreciation of Dwight: "The more I see of Moody the more I like him. I believe God is making him the instrument of a great work among the people." Jessup wanted Dwight to come to New York to live and work, but Dwight would have none of it.

That summer Dwight went by himself to the British Isles. He wanted, as he put it, "to study the English Christians" and to attend conventions and conferences, but primarily he desired to rest. Near Dublin a wealthy Plymouth Brother opened his mansion for a "Believers' Meeting," and here Dwight met "Butcher" Henry Varley again. Altogether, some twenty people met to spend a night in prayer. As Dwight left with Varley the next day, Varley let slip a remark that inspired Dwight: "The world has yet to see what God will do with a man fully consecrated to Him."

As Dwight pondered the phrase, he determined by the grace of God to be that man. Later, as he sat in Spurgeon's church, he realized for the first time that "it was not Spurgeon who was preaching: It was God. And if God could use Spurgeon, why could He not use [Moody]?"

Following this revelation, Dwight received an invitation to preach at Arundel Square near Pentonville Prison, in a lower-middle-class district of London. Visiting during the Sunday morning sermon, Dwight was irritated at the congregation's indifference. The people seemed to be lifeless and uninterested in anything the minister had to say. Dwight was tempted not to preach that night and wondered what message he could possibly bring in the evening service that would have meaning for them. But that evening, as Dwight brought the message, the entire atmosphere seemed charged with electricity, and the congregation listened attentively and in quietness. In closing, he urged any who wanted to have their "lives changed by the power of God through faith in Jesus Christ as a personal Savior," who wanted "to become Christians," to stand so he could pray for them. People stood all over the chapel.

Astonished, Dwight thought they had not understood and asked them to sit down. He stated again what becoming a Christian meant and then invited those who wished to do so to depart to an adjoining hall. He watched in amazement as scores of men, women, and older children made their way quietly to the connecting door. A schoolroom had been prepared as an inquiry room by setting out one or two dozen chairs. Many more chairs had to be added to seat the overflow crowd of people who expressed an interest in salvation.

Addressing the crowd, Dwight enlarged on repentance and faith, and again asked the people about becoming Christians. Once more, the whole room stood. In shock, Dwight told them to meet with their minister the following night.

The next morning, he left London, going to another part of England, but on Tuesday he received a telegram urging him to come back to the London church. More people had come to the minister's meeting on Monday night than had been in the room on Sunday!

Returning to London, Dwight spoke at the Arundel Square Church each night for two weeks. Some fifty-three years later, a Baptist minister, James Sprunt, recalled that the results were staggering: "Four hundred were taken into the membership of that church, and by the grace of God I was one of that number."

Following this experience, Dwight returned to Chicago, but with several doors left ajar for him to come back to preach in England. He also wanted to return with a singer for any future meetings.

A wide-open door soon appeared in the form of a letter from William Pennefather in England. Mr. Pennefather, an outstanding evangelical Anglican, had heard Dwight preach and "was strongly impressed with the conviction that Mr. Moody was one for whom God had prepared a great work." In his letter to Dwight he told him "of the wide door open for evangelistic effort in London and elsewhere" and promised to help in whatever ways he could to guarantee the success of the venture.

Oddly, Dwight made no response to the letter. In fact, he had received invitations of a sort from two other individuals in England as well, Henry Bewley and Cuthbert Bainbridge.

In Chicago, during the winter and spring of 1872–1873, Dwight made it plain that he would not remain with the mission and tabernacle. He had helped rebuild and reestablish the work and felt no more desire to stay.

His heart now lay across the sea. Speaking at a conference held in Chicago's Second Presbyterian Church in the spring of 1873, Dwight said he wanted to dream great things for God—"to get back to Great Britain and win ten thousand souls!"

In the meantime, a letter came from a young chemist in the city of York, George Bennett, founder-secretary of the local YMCA. He invited Dwight to speak at York. Dwight responded to the letter indirectly through Morgan and Scott, religious publishers in London. Dwight's response was quite vague, stating he had "thought of coming," and since Bennett seemed earnest about having him preach, he might begin his tour at York.

Even so, he continued to prepare for an evangelistic tour in England—one he thought was being organized for him. With so little actual preparation, Dwight booked steamship passage for himself, Emma, their two children, and for Sankey and his wife on June 7, 1873. Farwell brought a gift of five hundred dollars; Dwight kept just fifty dollars, believing all his expenses would be paid!

The families managed to get to New York on the fifty dollars, but then Dwight had to wire Farwell to send the rest of the money.

At least while in New York, Dwight had notified Harry Moorhouse of his plans, so the small Englishman met the Moodys and Sankeys in Liverpool. He came on board ship and told them that Pennefather and Bainbridge had both died recently, and Henry Bewley must have forgotten his commitment to Dwight.

The families were stranded three thousand miles from home. Dwight looked at Sankey and observed, "God seems to have closed the doors. We'll not open any ourselves. If He opens the door we'll go in. If He don't we'll return to America."

As the Moodys and Sankeys talked and prayed about what to do, Dwight fired off a telegram to George Bennett in York.

FOURTEEN

On June 18, 1873, while waiting in Liverpool for Bennett's reply, Dwight and his family were taken in by Richard Houghton, a shipowner interested in the YMCA. Harry Moorhouse hosted the Sankeys in Manchester. A reply came from Bennett on Friday morning asking Dwight to PLEASE FIX DATE WHEN YOU CAN COME TO YORK. Dwight's response was immediate: I WILL BE IN YORK TONIGHT TEN O'CLOCK STOP MAKE NO ARRANGEMENTS TILL I COME.

When Dwight descended from the train, he was met by a somewhat bewildered Bennett. That night over supper, the two men planned their strategy. Sankey arrived Saturday afternoon and found Dwight in a jovial mood. "I say, Sankey," Dwight related, "here we are, a couple of white elephants! Bennett is away all over the city now, to see if he can get us a place."

Bennett returned discouraged. Ministers were suspicious, saying things like: "Americans? Why do they want to come to York? What's the YMCA up to? Whoever heard of a mission in midsummer?" In spite of this, Bennett had been able to book the large and ugly Corn Exchange for Sunday afternoon. The Congregationalist deacons had grudgingly promised the morning pulpit at Salem Chapel because their new minister was away. Meanwhile, posters were being printed to advertise the meetings, and the news was being spread by word of mouth.

The Sunday morning message little affected the congregation made up of tradesmen and their families, a few footmen from the Deanery and Cannons' houses, some soldiers from the barracks, a smattering of washerwomen, and railway men from back streets beyond the station. In the afternoon an undaunted Dwight and somewhat less confident Sankey walked with Bennett to the Corn Exchange. Dwight stopped at the YMCA and filled his arms with Bibles. He urged Sankey to get some, too.

Roughly eight hundred people waited in the Corn Exchange, which was not quite filled to capacity. Dwight ran around distributing Bibles here and there with a slip in each, designating a scripture number and reference.

He told them to read the text when he called out their number. The novel but effective Bible lecture that resulted on "God is Love" piqued their interest; the *Yorkshire Gazette* even reported on it.

The evening chapel services seemed lukewarm to George Bennett, but the Spirit of God worked unseen in people's hearts. Many of them thought the songs Sankey led them in singing were strange—very different from the dirgelike hymns they thought proper for church services. When the charming

Sankey sat at the little harmonium organ, his solos, with every word distinct, lifted hearers to worlds unknown and brought to their remembrance buried Christian teaching about God's love.

Dwight's preaching also shocked and intrigued. His hearers noted that he did not seek to score by denigrating the regular ministry. He let them know that he "preferred preaching in chapels and strengthening existing causes" to beginning any new work. He emphasized repeatedly that religion is a friendship and quoted, " 'As many as received him, to them gave he power to become the sons of God.'" Then he would add: "Him, mark you! Not a dogma, not a creed, not a myth, but a Person." They noticed the blend of reverence and affection with which he would speak of "the Lord Jesus."

Dwight also started a noon prayer meeting in a small room at the YMCA in Feasegate. The meeting turned out to be preparation for a great harvest.

On the second Wednesday, July 2, the Spirit's movement broke through the surface. Dwight spoke at the Wesleyan chapel on "Redeemed with the precious blood of Christ." Bennett witnessed that "the Holy Spirit's power was mightily manifested," and many people expressed great concern for their soul's salvation. Caught up in the rapture of the moment, the elderly chapel superintendent could only weep for joy and astonishment.

Since that evening had been the last at the chapel, the meeting moved to a new Baptist chapel on Priory Street. The young minister, Frederick Brotherton Meyer, wondered what an evangelist would do that he could not do himself. Meyer possessed flawless doctrine and deliberate preaching, and he hesitated before opening his pulpit to Dwight.

Dwight's retelling of the "Dying Teacher" whom he accompanied back in Chicago failed to move the Reverend F. B. Meyer. But when Meyer casually asked the woman who taught the senior girls' class her opinion, she blurted out, "Oh, I told that story again and I believe every one of my girls has given her heart to God!"

Her response shook Meyer, and he began to watch intently night after night as the moderate-sized chapel, vestries, lobbies, and even the pulpit stairs were crowded with people. Each night he also watched reverently as the people crowded his minister's parlor, seeking the knowledge of salvation.

As an old man, F. B. Meyer remembered Moody's visit: "For me it was the birthday of new conceptions of ministry, new methods of work, new inspirations and hopes." After going into the ministry, Meyer admitted his lack of spiritual understanding: "I don't know anything about conversion, or about the gathering of sinners around Christ. I owe everything in my life to that parlor room where for the first time I found people brokenhearted about sin. I learned the psychology of the soul. I learned how to point men to God."

After a brief foray to Sunderland for a "campaign," as Dwight began to call his meetings, the evangelists were invited to Newcastle-upon-Tyne, twelve miles northwest of Sunderland. Despite mild opposition to the Americans, Dwight determined when he arrived on August 25 "to stick there until prejudice died."

The Newcastle campaign started among the well-churched middle classes and slowly spread upward and downward. Rich merchants, shipbuilders, and coal mine owners began to attend after the *Newcastle Chronicle* praised the "wonderful religious phenomenon."

The article especially acclaimed the meetings' "lack of sectarianism, the single-mindedness of Moody," and the fact that no offerings were taken.

One class that Dwight longed to reach, but that had not yet attended, were the "Geordies," the people of the slums. They had to work long hours underground, barely existed on scanty diets, and breathed coal dust day and night.

Dwight created an opportunity to reach this class when a baby cried at one of his meetings. Instead of censoring the mother and demanding the baby be taken out, he decided then and there to hold "Mothers' Meetings," which no one could attend without a baby. The lower-class women flocked to these meetings, and Dwight was gratified that he could now reach out to these poorer classes.

Increasing attendance also brought a demand for copies of the hymns that Sankey sang, especially of "Jesus of Nazareth Passeth By." Sankey had the only copies and wrote to the English publishers of Philip Phillips's collection, offering his own selection without charge if they would print it as a supplement. The publisher refused, and Dwight promised another publisher, Richard Cope Morgan of Morgan and Scott, to guarantee an edition of a sixteen-page pamphlet of Sankey's selection.

On September 16, *Sacred Songs and Solos* appeared in its first short form at sixpence a copy, or a penny for words only, to be used in alliance with Phillips's book, which was also on sale.

As Dwight planned where to go next and tentatively considered a nine-day opportunity in Darlington and some other small towns, a Scottish minister, the Reverend John Kelman, approached him after the evening meeting.

"Come to Edinburgh. I and my friends of the Free and Established Churches will form a committee. We will prepare the ground, and I believe that every presbytery will support you. Win Edinburgh, and you will win Scotland. Scotland needs you!"

Speechless, Dwight hardly knew how to respond. Could it be that Edinburgh, the Athens of the North, would really receive a man who had little formal education and still lapsed into poor grammar in unguarded moments? Then he thought about the able Presbyterian theologians, dry scholars of intense earnestness, grave, discriminating, rigid, who would be on the platform.

His rapid torrent of anecdote and informal Bible teaching might shock or irritate.

And what about Sankey? Most Scotsmen considered the singing of anything other than metrical versions of the psalms to be offensive. Unable to give an immediate answer, Dwight needed time to think, to pray about his decision. This was so momentous an opportunity—the first one to work in a capital city prepared by a representative committee. Edinburgh's leading men of religion, Kelman assured him, would stand behind him. If he accepted the offer, it would be at the risk of being made Britain's laughingstock. Never would he be able to show his face again in the British Isles.

The Moody and Sankey families arrived in Edinburgh at Waverly Station on November 22, 1873, on a stormy Saturday night. The Sankeys had been invited to stay with Horatius Bonar, the veteran hymn writer; the Moodys were to be guests of William Blaikie, a friend of David Livingstone.

The first meeting began the next evening on Princes Street. While the committee tried to estimate the attendance, Sankey could see the city's largest hall "densely packed to its utmost corners; even the lobbies, stairs, and entrance were crowded with people, while more than two thousand were turned away." All these people made Sankey nervous. He had heard the complaints about his "human" hymns and even more against his "kist o' whustles," as the Scots called the little harmonium organ that accompanied him.

The chairman's announcement at the outset that Mr. Moody, due to a sore throat, would not attend that evening brought gasps of disappointment.

Sankey stood up and invited the congregation to sing with him a familiar tune, the "Old Hundredth." When he sang "Jesus of Nazareth Passeth By," an intense silence pervaded the huge audience. Sankey felt reassured about the merit of "human" hymns to work in people's hearts. Following the address given by James Hood Wilson of the Barclay Free Church, Sankey concluded with "Hold the Fort," and to his delight, the congregation joined wholeheartedly in the chorus.

After spending the day spraying down his throat with medicine, Dwight rejoined Sankey the following night in Barclay Church. Dwight had his work cut out for him in the formidable Scottish religious climate.

Extreme Calvinism had long held sway in the majority of churches. In fact, Old Testament Law had been deemed superior to "the royal law of love," the "joy of the Lord" had been defeated by rules and regulations, and most people believed it blasphemy to claim the certainty of going to heaven. They would say that though Christ died for all, none know whether they are predestined to salvation.

Because of this extreme Calvinism, many of the lower classes never attended church at all; on the other hand, the educated classes were racked by doubt and unbelief, which had led to much division and suspicion among the churches of Scotland.

The Scots took to Dwight immediately and even excused and enjoyed his profuse diction, which stopped neither for colons nor commas. They tolerated his Yankee accent and forgave him for sometimes deliberately making them laugh in church. His audiences found themselves surprised by joy.

Growing more confident through his open acceptance, Dwight's assertiveness in the power of Christ to save continued to increase. A steady brightening, like some spring sunrise dispelling the chill November gray, filled people's hearts as men and women grasped the astonishing fact that God loves sinners.

Members of the audience listened enthralled as Dwight shared with them his convictions. One night he told them about a young man who thought himself too great a sinner to be saved. Dwight's response: "Why, they are the very men Christ came after! 'This man receiveth sinners, and eateth with them.' The only charge they could bring against Christ down here was that He was receiving bad men. They are the very kind of men He is willing to receive. All you have got to do is to prove that you are a sinner and I will prove that you have got a Savior." His hearers scarcely believed their ears. It sounded so simple. Scottish preaching for many years had emphasized cold, dry doctrine and told its adherents that they were the subject of God's wrath. The only way to obtain forgiveness was by believing in a complex theological puzzle.

For these strangers to appear suddenly and begin expounding a theology that God didn't "hate" them was a shock. Time was required for these new ideas to sink in. Moody and Sankey stressed God's goodness and forgiveness, a simple but welcome new idea.

When Dwight kept his messages down to less than an hour in length and interspersed them with silent prayer or a song from Sankey, the Scots thought the American duo even more novel. They expected a sermon to last at least an hour and a half.

Another novel aspect to the Scots was that Dwight made no attempt to play on their emotions through sensation or excitement; he also provoked "no articulate wailings, no prostrations, no sudden outbursts of rapture" found in other revivals, according to one observer.

Nevertheless, Dwight preached for decision. People had to choose Christ as their Savior. He would not acquiesce to suit Calvinistic hesitancy that feared, lest appeal for a definite step of faith overrode predestination—a word Dwight could barely pronounce!

He placed his emphasis "upon the doctrine that Christianity is not mere feeling, but a surrender of the whole nature to a personal, living Christ," said Mr. Blaikie. Inquiry room sessions after each meeting played a pivotal part in a person's decision for Christ.

Some people expressed suspicions about the inquiry, thinking it might be an emotion "forcing house," or a complete surrender to an unbalanced doctrine of free will. Some even feared that it was a dark imitation of the Roman Catholic confessional. These fears quieted as ministers had personal contact with the work and with the inquiries themselves.

The methods advocated in dealing with the inquirers were new, too. Dwight urged the "personal workers," as he called them, patience and "thorough dealing with each case, no hurrying from one to another. Wait patiently and ply them with God's word, and think, oh! think, what it is to win a soul for Christ, and don't grudge the time spent on one person."

By the middle of December, several weeks after the meetings began, Edinburgh had been stirred to its depths. The meetings were on everyone's mind. Many had been strengthened and helped, and unity began to appear in Scottish churches and even among the clergy.

An Edinburgh University professor, Professor Charteris, said, "If anyone had said that the sectarian divisions which are so visible not only in ecclesiastical concerns but in social life and in private friendships would disappear in the presence of two evangelists who came among us with no such ecclesiastical credentials, the idea would have seemed absolutely absurd." By January 1874, news of the revival in Edinburgh had spread all over Scotland. The leading Edinburgh ministers and laymen sent out an "Appeal for Prayer" to every minister of every denomination in Scotland. The ministers also collected a special fund to provide a weekly copy of "The Christian" to send to each minister throughout the British Isles. The publication carried special reports about the meetings.

Sudden fame had come to thirty-eight-year-old Dwight and his thirty-five-year-old song leader. Dwight knew he was merely the recipient of a higher power and remained humble, but Sankey probably enjoyed the new status. He stood more erect and had a new spring in his step.

FIFTEEN

Following a few weeks in Dundee, Dwight and Sankey and their families arrived in Glasgow. The people there had made full preparations for the campaign: They had readied massed choirs, covered the meetings with prayer in large prayer meetings, and distributed tickets for people to attend nightly meetings to avoid unsafe overcrowding.

Dwight and his family stayed with Andrew Bonar, who was a well-known Bible teacher. He came into Dwight's life at just the right time. Dwight had been giving out to the people night after night and was in danger of spiritual drought. Ecstatic over Bonar's biblical wisdom and insight, Dwight would call to a friend to "come and join us! We are having a dig in the Rock!" He remarked later that Bonar was one of the two men in Britain who helped him most in understanding the depths of the Bible.

The campaign opened at nine on Sunday morning, February 8, in the city hall with three thousand Sunday school teachers. After Bonar's opening prayer, Sankey began to sing "I Am So Glad That Jesus Loves Me," a tune written by Phillip Bliss. Although unknown to most of the audience, the song ministered to people's hearts.

So powerful was the meeting that morning that Dwight and Sankey were carried along on a revival tide. Week after week through the cheerless, cold winter and on into spring, the meetings continued in churches, the city hall, and last of all, in the Kibble Palace, an enormous glass exhibition building generally called the Crystal Palace. People came by every means possible: on foot, by horse-tram, by train, in carriages, and in cabs. They came from every walk of life to attend the meetings: from shipyards, mills, tenements, and the surrounding middle-class homes.

Dwight's amazing energy also impressed people. Dutifully, Sankey managed to keep up with him. A newspaper commented on their daily schedule: "The mind experiences a sense of fatigue in detailing their efforts. On weekdays, the huge hourly prayer meeting is held at noon; one to two o'clock, they converse with individuals; four to five o'clock, they have a Bible lecture, attended by some twelve or fifteen hundred; seven to eight-thirty, the evangelistic meeting takes place with the inquiry meeting afterward; and nine to ten o'clock, the young men hold a meeting." He reserved one day a week for relaxing, usually on Saturday.

"For the last three months I have had to refuse money all the time!" wrote Dwight to his Chicago friend Whittle on March 7, 1874. "At Edinburgh they wanted to raise me two or three thousand pounds but I would not let them. I told them I would not take it."

Not only did Dwight refuse personal money, but he also turned down collections for campaign funds. Letters had appeared in the papers, asserting the whole campaign to be a glorious hoax organized for gain by Barnum, the American showman. As Dwight explained to Farwell, "Of course I have a good many enemies over here who say I am a speculating Yankee." He would tell the campaign committee to raise funds privately, and very occasionally he accepted personal gifts for his own use, beyond hospitality and expenses.

But Dwight stayed adamant about preaching "for filthy lucre." He realized the temptations involved with money, and the Scottish people, despite their renown for thrift, wanted to shower him with finances. Much of what he received he sent on to help another evangelistic team in America, Whittle and Bliss. The money would help them abandon their business and devote themselves full time to ministry. Wealthy individuals, such as chemical manufacturer Campbell White, were lavish in extending money to Dwight, and many people thought he was amassing a small fortune. He reached the wealthier classes, but always his heart was turned over the poor. Many of them would not attend the meetings, so Dwight urged wealthy men to reach out to the poor after the campaign was over.

To Dwight's delight, the United Evangelical Committee reformed to become the Glasgow Evangelistic Association and began a long career in evangelism and philanthropy, spawning agencies such as Poor Children's Day Refuges, Temperance Work, Fresh Air Fortnights, the Cripple Girls' League, and the Glasgow Christian Institute. On Sunday mornings on Glasgow Green, young men brought in the homeless and derelicts for a free breakfast.

Of course there were about to be detractors, and Dwight's daily mail brought in hundreds of letters, many that were critical. They were everywhere! His host, Hood Wilson, said the library had become "a perfect sea of letters, which were not only an inch deep on the large round table in the middle of the room, but covered chairs and shelves in every corner."

One of the strongest criticisms came in the form of a pamphlet circulated by an influential Highland preacher, John Kennedy. In the pamphlet, entitled, "Hyperevangelism: 'Another Gospel' Though a Mighty Power." Kennedy charged that "the present movement ignores the sovereignty and power of God," that the emphasis on faith hindered the work of the Holy Spirit and denied "the utter spiritual impotence of souls 'dead in trespasses and sins.'"

Kennedy blasted the inquiry room, the singing of "human" hymns, the use of organ music ("unscriptural, and therefore all who have subscribed the Confession of Faith are under solemn vow against it"), and alleged that prayer meetings had been turned into "factories of sensation."

Such attacks from rigid High Calvinism could be expected. Dwight said he could not have pointed out more faults in his work himself! But he sensed criticism must be coming from other sources as well to account for the subtly poisoned atmosphere that was beginning to surround the campaign.

While Dwight pondered how to squelch the vicious attack from someone the simple Highlanders revered, he received a letter from a Chicago acquaintance. John Mackay, a lawyer and recent Scottish immigrant, had circulated a scathing letter denigrating Dwight.

Soon afterward, Farwell secured the signatures of thirty-five Chicago ministers to an endorsement of Moody's Christian character, and he cabled the document to Edinburgh. Farwell demanded a retraction, but the Scottish immigrant refused to do so. Then Farwell threatened him with the law, but Dwight would not pursue litigation.

In the final days of the Glasgow campaign, even the invective of Kennedy could not destroy what God had accomplished. On the last Sunday in May, the Great Western Road leading to the campaign site had been black for over three hours with an endless stream of humanity.

That day Dwight preached in the Botanical Gardens from the box of a carriage to a crowd estimated at twenty or thirty thousand.

Afterward, he readied himself to return to English soil.

SIXTEEN

Prior to leaving Scotland, and after a brief leisurely trip to Loch Ness and the Caledonian Canal, Dwight preached a few more times near Campbelltown where he and his family stayed with Peter and Jane Mackinnon.

The Mackinnons and Moodys found great compatibility. Dwight remarked that Peter, a partner with the British India Line, became like a father to him, more so than "any man that has crossed [his] path."

Treasuring Dwight's famous anecdotes, Jane made note of several when he stayed with them. Returning from a meeting on a windy night, Dwight remarked, "The gas made such noise, it roared and I had to roar, and it was a battle between us, but I think I won!" He also related how the custodian kept opening a door that Dwight shut because a draught interfered with the inquiry work, so he locked it and put the key in his pocket; how he would inspect a church for ventilation before speaking and had all his wits about him even for the smallest detail. She also realized his flexibility in the services: "He said he never knew, even a few minutes before, what he was going to do. I suppose he asks guidance at every step, and is sure he gets it."

Jane enjoyed both Moodys and thought them good company. She especially liked Dwight's combination of playfulness and seriousness. He also played croquet and helped the children catch crabs on the beach.

Emma, too, won a place in June Mackinnon's heart. She saw at once how valuable Emma was to Dwight: "The more I saw of her, the more convinced I was that a great deal of his usefulness was owing to her, not only in the work she did for him, relieving him of all correspondence, but also from her character." Jane became aware of Emma's independence of thought, her humility, and especially the calmness with which she met Dwight's impulsiveness.

The Moodys rejoined Sankey in Belfast, Ireland, where the crowds were similar to those of Edinburgh and Glasgow; then they traveled to Dublin, although Dwight had been warned against going there because of its Roman Catholic majority. As usual, Dwight called the warning foolishness and proceeded full-speed ahead.

For the first time, Dwight and Sankey had the full support of the Anglicans, including several bishops of the recently disestablished Church of Ireland. But Dwight stunned the Irish by refusing to attack Roman Catholics. His refusal opened the door for everyone of whatever religious persuasion to attend the meetings.

The campaign became the center of conversation, and even music halls were not exempt from having fun over the evangelists' names. At one music hall, a comic turned to another and said: "I am rather Moody tonight. How do you feel?"

"Sankeymonious!"

The gallery hissed. Someone started singing "Hold the Fort," and the whole audience began to join in while the comedians fled the stage.

Even the leading newspapers commented on the campaign, and the *Dublin Times* correspondent noted favorably that the campaign was "the most remarkable ever witnessed in Ireland; it had a character essentially different and seemed to possess elements of vitality wanting in others." In particular the correspondent was impressed with "the reverence and devotion of the services," and "not only the absence of any effort at self display but rather a sensitive avoidance of it."

As the campaign came to a close, ministers and laity from every part of Ireland joined together in a great "Christian Convention for Ireland." The meeting was held at the Exhibition Palace with thousands in attendance. The submerging of bitter sectarian feelings caused wonderment to many but became almost a trademark of Dwight's wherever he went. His touch could be felt in the committee's arrangement that clergymen from a distance were lodged with clerical families of denominations other than their own.

By November 1874, the Moody and Sankey families crossed the Irish Sea to Liverpool and on to Manchester, England. Harry Moorhouse waited to greet them. He welcomed them with open arms, rejoicing that "success has not made Dwight proud. He uses his ten talents, I use my one, and we both together praise the Lord for using us at all."

Dwight held campaigns in Manchester, Sheffield, and Birmingham in quick succession with good results in each place. A Church of England newspaper, the *Record*, reported, "There is a degree of religious feeling in the town which has not been equaled for years."

Thrilled over such an unusual opportunity, an Anglican clergyman wrote of the Birmingham campaign, "Such a chance of guiding souls comes only once in a lifetime."

One puzzled minister, Dr. Dale of Carr's Lane Congregational Church in Birmingham, had been expecting a revival for a few years. But he expressed bewilderment when it came through two American strangers.

Watching the attentive faces of the huge crowd at Bingley Hall, he saw "all sorts, young and old, rich and poor, keen tradesmen, manufacturers and merchants and young ladies who had just left school, rough boys who knew more about dogs and pigeons than about books, and cultivated women. . . . I could not understand it."

Dr. Dale told Dwight, "The work is most plainly of God, for I can see no relation between yourself and what you have done." Dwight chuckled in his inimitable way and told him, "I should be very sorry if it were otherwise."

D. L. MOODY

Probably much of Dwight's success lay in his simple preaching. As Dr. Dale noted, "He talks in a perfectly unconstrained and straightforward way, just as he would talk to half a dozen old friends at his fireside."

The English preachers, on the other hand, were given to an ornate style of preaching. Spurgeon, for example, piled metaphor upon metaphor, but Dwight simply chatted about what he saw in the Bible.

He made the Bible come alive in everyday language. Daniel in the lions' den looks at his watch to see if it is time to pray. Scoffers before the Flood "talk it over in the corner grocery store: 'Not much sign of old Noah's rainstorm yet!'"

Blind Bartimaeus, suddenly able to see, rushes into Jericho "and he says, 'I will go to see my wife and tell her about it'—a young convert always wants to talk to his friends about salvation."

Or it was Zacchaeus (or "Zakkus" as Dwight would say) sitting in the sycamore tree. So the sermon would shift from one scene to another of Christ meeting people in their need.

Somehow when Dwight preached, he would fade from his hearers' consciousness. Someone remarked about his ability: "Throughout his address you entirely forgot the man, so full was he of his message and so held were you by his earnestness, intensity, and forceful appeal. He had many illustrations drawn from his personal experiences, but never did self appear prominent. He was completely absorbed in the message and in getting it over to the mind, heart, and conscience of those listening."

In Liverpool at a men's meeting, several rationalistic thinkers were present who did not acknowledge Christ's death on the cross. But as Dwight prayed in the speakers' room before the service, Reverend F. B. Meyer found himself awed by Dwight's overpowering "burden of heart."

After Dwight preached that night, large numbers stayed for the after-meeting. Dwight came down from the platform, got up on a chair, "and launched out in a wonderful discourse. His invectives against sin, and his lashings of the conscience, were awful. He seemed to be wrestling with an unseen power. Beneath those burning words men's faces grew pale under a conviction of the broken law of God. Then he began with the wooings of the Gospel, in a strain of tender and heartbreaking entreaty; by the time he finished, the whole audience seemed completely broken. One man arose and said, 'Mr. Moody, I want to be a Christian.' It seemed but a moment when forty or fifty men were on their feet."

The England Dwight had come to had been primed on Christian doctrine, and most people knew something about Christ and about the Bible. However, Christianity had gained respectability in the Victorian age to the point where sins of the flesh had been concealed behind a veneer of the spirit. Dwight was able to pierce through the hypocritical veil many wore.

More importantly, real Christianity had been distorted by an ineffective gospel that preached a good person would go to heaven, a wicked one to hell. Little was known or taught of God's grace. Against this warped teaching, Dwight proclaimed eternal life as the gift of God to the undeserving. He did not deny eternal punishment for those who refused this gift, but he would say, "I believe the magnet that goes down to the bottom of the pit is the love of Jesus."

A popular example Dwight used to illustrate the difference between law and grace was the story of the prodigal son. "When the prodigal came home, grace met him and embraced him. Law said, Stone him!—grace said, Embrace him! Law said, Smite him!—grace said, Kiss him! Law went after him and bound him. Grace said, Loose him and let him go! Law tells me how crooked I am; grace comes and makes me straight."

Dwight's message emphasized that God wanted men more than they wanted Him. He proclaimed that salvation was not a grudged reward for a consistent climb into goodness but the new birth of a repentant sinner into the life of Christ. "Instant salvation," he called it over and over. His preaching, said Dr. Dale, "was in a manner that produced the sort of effect produced by Luther, and provoked similar criticism. He exulted in the free grace of God. His joy was contagious. Men leaped out of darkness into light, and lived a Christian life afterwards."

Not since the days of Wesley and Whitefield had people from so many social classes found joy in Christ. Some of the very poor people had been helped by General William Booth and the Salvation Army, but at last many of the middle and upper classes were also discovering salvation in Christ.

Dwight had preached in the provinces, but he knew that for the movement to become national, he must win London. The London committee, made up of the clergy, members of Parliament, and high-ranking officers, had done much preparation work for the Moody campaign. The committee members had inundated London with posters and notices of all kinds and had organized teams to visit the entire city. They had also secured the Agricultural Hall in Islington for at least a ten-week stretch. The home of the annual prize cattle show in north London's principal middle-class area, the Agricultural Hall had been freshly refurbished and fifteen thousand chairs installed.

On opening night the hall was in readiness with seats on the left for participants and distinguished guests, a railed pulpit area in the middle, and on the right seating room for a two-hundred-member choir. Red banners hung all around the hall proclaiming such texts as: REPENT YE AND BELIEVE THE GOSPEL, THE GIFT OF GOD IS ETERNAL LIFE, and YE MUST BE BORN AGAIN. When Dwight and Sankey stepped onto the platform at seven thirty and Dwight told the audience, "Let us rise and sing to the praise of God; let us praise Him for what He is going to do in London," a wave of expectancy swept over the tremendous crowd.

A *London Daily Telegraph* article spoke quite favorably of Dwight and the campaign, generally calling Dwight's stories "good American stories picked up in Chicago." The reporter commended the campaign's tone that pointed the way for men and women to become better, and for them to have "a better hope in this world and the next."

Dwight knew from the outset of the campaign, however, there would be opposition. He warned his committee: "We must expect opposition. If you think a great work is to be done here without opposition you will be greatly mistaken. There will be many bitter things said, and many lies started, and as someone has said, a lie will get half round the world before the truth gets its boots on!"

He spoke accurately; before long, articles in the *Morning Post* called his teaching "wild, baseless, and uncertain," adding that "Moody and Sankey will be a puff in the wind." In the *Morning Advertiser*, people read, "There must have been thousands in that crowd of uplifted faces who looked with horror and shame on the illiterate preacher making little better than a travesty of all they held sacred." The article played on the word "vulgar," calling Moody's accent vulgar and stating he was "a ranter of the most vulgar type."

There were other more penetrating criticisms that could not be easily dismissed: "Where the corpulent old expounder is known he is regarded as a selfish, sensual, hypocritical variegator of facts." And poor Sankey was accused of starting his career as a black "minstrel" until he found that evangelism paid better. The article also stressed all the money the two evangelists were making. They would return to America and "gaze upon their cosy homesteads purchased with good English gold" and claim that they had "spoiled the Egyptians."

Actually, Dwight and Sankey had refused to touch the considerable money from *Sacred Songs and Solos* and had worked out an arrangement with Hugh Matheson to give the royalties to worthy charities.

Despite libel and criticism, attendance at the Agricultural Hall rose to an estimated twenty thousand. More space was made for an overflow crowd. Even the Lord Chancellor of Disraeli's new Conservative Government, Mr. Cairns, attended the meetings frequently. And former Prime Minister Gladstone talked privately with Dwight, also sitting on the platform once or twice.

Although the crowds overflowed night after night at Agricultural Hall, Lord Shaftsbury, a recent ally of Dwight's, thought he should move to the Queen's Opera House where he could reach the upper classes of people. Dwight expressed reluctance, but finally acquiesced to at least have afternoon Bible readings in the Opera House.

The wonderful response to the afternoon Bible readings caused Dwight to turn over the Agricultural Hall meetings to an associate nine days early and begin evening meetings at the Opera House in the Haymarket. Then he announced two evening meetings: one at the Opera House, the other at Bow Common where he could reach another class of people.

A much poorer class of people lived near Bow Common, but Dwight yearned to reach them, too. With the sawdust floor, galvanized iron roof, and gaslight shining on the faces of the ragged, unkempt people at Bow Common, Dwight felt right at home—like he was back in Illinois Street, preaching to the people he loved best!

Each night Dwight would preach at 7:30 to roughly eight or nine thousand at Bow Common. Then at 8:30 he and Sankey jumped into a brougham, trotting as swiftly as traffic allowed up the Mile-End Road and through the city, under shored-up Temple Bar, and around Trafalgar Square to the Haymarket: They would traverse from the East End to the West End, from a world of slums and squalor to that of great mansions and the royal parks, from dock workers to duchesses.

Dwight's flexibility in preaching to two very different sorts of crowds impressed an attending aristocrat: "Nothing showed me the wonderful adaptability of Mr. Moody more than his coming from Bow Road, the poorest part of the East End, to the very antipodes of it all in character and surroundings, and yet at once hitting on the right note of dealing with the new conditions." Near the Opera House were St. James, Mayfair, Westminster, Belgravia, and the heart of fashionable London.

Opening the campaign at the Opera House turned out to be an excellent idea, for it ensured that even aristocratic people could attend. In fact, one of Dwight's staunch supporters turned out to be the duchess of Sutherland, who "insisted on going every day." The Sutherlands had entertained Dwight at Dunrobin Castle in the Highlands where the duchess was a countess in her own right as well as a chieftain. The duke, according to common knowledge, owned more acres than any man in Europe.

The duke expressed his thanks for Dwight's ministry in a letter where he told him, "God bless you. I shall never forget what I have heard from you. If you knew what a life mine is, in ways I was not able to tell you the other day, and what a terrible story mine has been, you would pray for me much." In a subsequent, more positive letter, the duke thanked Dwight "for all the joy and strength our dear Lord has given me through you, and I pray that your wonderful work may be more and more blessed."

In her enthusiasm for Dwight's meetings, the duchess would collect numerous friends and relatives at palatial Safford House and whisk them in her carriage along Pall Mall to the Haymarket. Some of them objected to it: "The mixture of religious fervor and the most intense toadyism of the duchess was horribly disgusting," said Lady Barker with considerable disdain.

After preaching to huge crowds gathered at Bow Common and the Opera House, and even schoolboys at Eton—although Dwight and Sankey nearly had eggs tossed at them there—they were ready to travel back to America to see their friends and loved ones again.

They had arrived in England on June 17, 1873, and were scheduled to leave on the SS *Spain* on August 4, 1875. The attendance at the meetings in London's centers alone totaled 2,330,000. Scotland, Ireland, and England would never be the same. Much of the evangelistic mission work started as a direct result of the Moody campaign and continued under the able hands of local laymen and ministers.

SEVENTEEN

Moody and Sankey had left New York in obscurity; they returned on August 14, 1875, international celebrities. Critics such as the *New York Times* still asserted they had been sent to England by showman P. T. Barnum. But an elderly London minister's remark indicated what lay ahead for the two in their own country: "America had heard with shock how they were run after. They owe their success partly to their cheek, partly to their music."

A bevy of reporters surrounded the Moody and Sankey families, wanting to know their plans. Characteristically, Dwight would say nothing of the future except, "I am going right up to Northfield, Massachusetts, to see my mother." His whirlwind campaigns had left little time for correspondence, and he was eager to hear about his family and news of home.

Reaching Northfield on August 16, Dwight, Emma, and the children found Dwight's brother George waiting for them in an old, dilapidated buggy drawn by a plodding farm horse. Samuel followed in a wagon with their baggage.

The Moody and Sankey entourage wound slowly over the narrow Connecticut River by the railroad toll bridge, up the hill into the avenue of majestic elms arrayed in summer splendor, and on to Betsey's little white house.

Seventy-year-old Betsey, demure in her dainty white widow's cap, stood in the doorway, waiting for her son. She had pride in Dwight. She had heard about the huge crowds that came to hear him in Scotland and Ireland and England, even dukes and duchesses and other fine lords and ladies. She didn't understand why they would come—she still did not approve of what Dwight preached.

As Dwight hugged his mother, she clung to him with a strength that surprised him. He realized at that moment how much his mother loved him. He wished he could stay nearby. She needed to have her family around her, not scattered across the country.

Somehow they all squeezed themselves into the small frame house that already contained Betsey and the unmarried brothers Edwin and Samuel. How happy Dwight was to be home with his family—especially with his brother Samuel. Samuel's personality endeared him to people, despite the fact that he was the town tax collector. His slight frame combined with chronic epilepsy made him seem vulnerable, and most of the townspeople reached out to him.

The days at Northfield refreshed Dwight. He and Samuel climbed the surrounding hills and drove in the buggy along old familiar lanes. He remembered all the pleasant scenes of his childhood: where he had picked berries, pastured cows, and gathered chestnuts.

D. L. MOODY

Dwight hoped to spend his days at Northfield, exercising his body and soul. He knew his body badly needed exercise; he had had so little time to exercise while he was overseas!

But his soul needed refreshing, too. Dwight yearned to spend hours just studying the Bible and meditating on what God said in His Word.

Although he had intended simply to rest during his stay at Northfield, his heart burned for his family, cousins, neighbors, and the whole community—all "cold Unitarians"—to be drawn to Christ. So grudgingly, the Orthodox, Trinitarian minister, T. J. Clark, agreed to an extra service in Second Parish Church on Sunday afternoon, September 5.

Everybody in the community came—even Betsey, whose pride in her famous son overrode her Unitarian convictions. Samuel came, too—perhaps as much out of curiosity as anything else. He chuckled over Dwight's "revivalist tendencies."

Before long, the church literally bulged; the underpinning was giving way! George Moody strode up the aisle as the people sang hymns prompted by Dwight. George whispered in Dwight's ear, and at the end of the verse, Dwight lifted his hand. In a casual tone but with a broad smile on his face, he announced: "The place is full. Many are still outside. I'll preach on the steps so all can hear. While we sing the next number all will go out, beginning at the rear."

The people sat around on the grass and in the dusty street, and a small boy wriggled up an apple tree. Only when some saw the old white building sagging dangerously did they understand Dwight's skill in emptying the church swiftly and averting sudden panic. The deacons shored the building up before the next meeting!

Sankey perched his little harmonium on the narrow covered platform designed for churchgoers to step off wagons without getting their feet wet and began singing "The Ninety and Nine." Dwight preached about Zacchaeus, and the Northfield townsfolk never forgot that unusual Sunday afternoon.

People from nearby communities swarmed into Northfield to glimpse the famous evangelists. Special trains arrived from Brattleboro, Vermont, and converged upon the Orthodox church. Betsey, too, and other family members, including Samuel, continued to come to the meetings.

There was opposition, especially from the town blacksmith. Dwight said the blacksmith "hated me, spoke most bitterly against me. The smithy was the rendezvous of all the strong opposition men."

So Dwight prayed and wrestled with God for his family, his loved ones, his townspeople. Above all, his heart nearly burst for his mother to know the Savior. Perhaps some song, some graphic Bible story would pierce her shield of moral confidence. But she gave no indication of any inner stirrings until one of the last evenings when Dwight invited those to rise in their places who wished to acknowledge Christ as the Son of God and trust in Him as Savior, "that we might pray for you." Betsey stood up. Dwight was so overcome that he could barely ask one of the others to lead in prayer.

On the last night, Samuel stood.

Samuel's conversion was solid. Like a river that had been dammed, a torrent of love began to pour through him. From then on, he took a leading part in religious meetings. He would go out and talk with weak brothers and help them to their feet. Like his older brother, Samuel would search for souls on both sides of the Connecticut River, in both sides of the valley. When Northfield formed a YMCA, they elected him president.

Following Dwight's preaching in Northfield, it became a center of "the greatest revival ever known in that part of the state," according to W. T. Holton. Prayer meetings were held in schoolhouses and private homes, and active workers, speakers, and singers alike would travel around spreading the gospel.

The acceptance and love Dwight received from his hometown and family and their new interest in his work caused him to realize that he needed to put down roots.

He had not really considered putting them down in Northfield. Then his mother's chickens kept crossing over to a neighbor's cornfield—much to the neighbor's annoyance. Dwight had to make things right with the neighbor, so he approached him.

Dwight stopped his buggy and told the neighbor, Elisha Alexander, "I want to buy a strip of that field."

Elisha responded, "No. I don't care to sell unless it's the whole place."

"How many acres?"

"Twelve."

"How much?" Dwight asked.

"Well, I'll take thirty-five hundred dollars for the whole place with house and barns."

"I'll take it!"

It just happened that some money had recently been sent to Dwight as a gift, so he was able to pay the entire amount. He was now a proud owner of a house in Northfield.

At the time, Dwight could scarcely know what lay ahead for him and his modest purchase. Just now, he needed to get back to business—but in New York, not Chicago.

EIGHTEEN

During their stay at Northfield, Dwight and Sankey made plans for their future campaigns. Dwight desired to reach America for Christ—but would America receive him and his message? "Water runs downhill and the highest hills are the great cities," said Dwight. "If we can stir them we shall stir the whole country."

Others also wondered if the evangelistic team would be effective in their own land. Many of the New York newspapers expressed skepticism, and the famous Brooklyn preacher DeWitt Talmage had wondered whether his weekly journal should support or discourage the meetings.

America needed a religious awakening. The wounds created by the Civil War a mere decade past had not totally healed. In the North, an obsession with money prevailed, while in the South, reconstruction had failed and people struggled in the midst of poor living conditions. Numerous immigrants had also altered the texture of the nation. And most Americans, whether newcomers or those with deep roots, looked to some technological utopia to cast aside old moralities.

Dwight chose Brooklyn as his jumping-off place, much to the chagrin of numerous pessimists. His detractors were bewildered when an overflow crowd of between twelve and twenty thousand people pressed into and around the rink on Clermont Avenue to hear him.

Streetcar companies had laid extra tracks to the building, and at the close of the service thousands had to walk to their homes because of the many extra passengers on the cars. Dwight wrote Farwell in Chicago, "Pray daily for me. I never needed the help of my friends as much as now."

Some of these detractors soon had to admit that Dwight had held some of the largest assemblies in America in rapt attention. Of course Dwight realized that some people came out of curiosity, but the Lord could still reach them. After a month's duration, when the Brooklyn meetings closed, Dwight's heart was heavy because of vast numbers of still unreached, unchurched people living there. Dwight and Sankey went from Brooklyn to Philadelphia in November 1875. Great preparation had taken place for the mission, and John Wanamaker, a good friend of Dwight's, had bought the old freight depot of the Pennsylvania Railroad, completely refitting it and offering it rent-free for the campaign.

One hundred eighty ministers of every denomination had signed the invitation for Dwight to come and worked diligently to make the campaign a success. Every Friday Dwight held special meetings for alcoholics. He also had women's meetings, but as in Scotland and England, his delight was in the young men's meetings.

Princeton University issued Dwight a "special request" to come for a day, which he gladly did. Dwight said later, "I have not seen anything in America that pleases me like what I have seen in Princeton. They have got a Holy Ghost revival there. The president of the college told me he had never seen anything like it in Princeton."

Working in Philadelphia, Dwight showed himself to be the same unaffected, integrated personality his friends in Britain had known. As usual, he was utterly absorbed in his work. One of his Chicago church officers came to the platform at the close of an evening service as the inquiry meeting began. "I touched Mr. Sankey on the shoulder, and he did the undignified thing of embracing me," he said. "After a little conversation with him I went to where Moody was, and touched him on the shoulder also, when he turned and quickly and earnestly said, 'Talk to that woman!'"

Even as a serious evangelist, Dwight retained his playful side. He and his family stayed at the Wanamaker mansion during the Philadelphia campaign, and when his work was over for the day or evening, he had the ability to relax in the moment. One of the Wanamaker children said of him: "The thing I remember most was Mr. Moody and father playing bears with us children. Such wild exciting times as we had. They would get down on all fours and chase us. We would shriek and scream and run. It was pandemonium!"

The end of January 1876 brought a close to the Philadelphia campaign. Dwight and Sankey traveled to New York to begin a long-awaited series of meetings. Dwight arrived just a day before the campaign was to open, but he had let the committee of laymen and ministers know exactly what should be done, and they had organized it with true New York business skill. The treasurer, J. Pierpont Morgan, was the same age as Dwight; and thirty-two-year-old Cornelius Vanderbilt, Jr. was one of the private guarantors who advanced money against expenses.

The committee had leased Barnum's Great Roman Hippodrome, which stood on Madison Avenue, the future site of Madison Square Garden. The Hippodrome provided a dividing line between the very wealthy and the very poor. Dwight's heart always went out to the poor, but he also saw the same spiritual needs in the very rich.

The campaign chairman, William E. Dodge, informed a friend: "We are fitting up two large halls opening into each other; one, holding about eight or nine thousand and the other about six thousand." They had allowed for inquiry rooms, and an up-to-date touch was an internal electric telegraph whereby orders could be sent to regulate lighting, heating, and ventilation.

A thousand-voice choir led a song service for a half hour before the little door opened behind the wide platform and Dwight Moody stepped onstage. An onlooker said that Dwight seemed "to cover the space between the door and the pulpit in one step! Mr. Moody was a meteor. He was at the little railing in front, his hand raised, our heads bowed in prayer and we all saying 'Amen' almost before we knew it. How lithe, springy, and buoyant he was. How full of life and spirit!"

New Yorkers responded enthusiastically to the meetings. The new chairman, Mr. Dodge, wrote an English friend: "Nothing has ever reached our great masses of non church-going people as these meetings have. Our ministers have been warmed and helped, cold Christians restored, and many careless persons brought to Christ. I do not think the work has been truer or larger in any place Mr. Moody has visited. He is staying with me and I find his cheery whole-souled humble consecration a great spur and help."

Dwight preached the same message as in England but adapted it to his American audience. Even though he knew his calling to be an evangelist to the masses, he relished dealing with individuals in the inquiry room. He had long outgrown the habit of tossing off scripture texts to an inquirer; instead, "his questionings speedily determined whether an inquirer was sincere and genuine, or hypocritical and evasive. With astonishing rapidity he could turn a man mentally and morally inside out, expose his fallacies, moral inconsistencies, perversions, willfulness and alienation from God." He desired that laypeople "learn the art of personally winning souls."

At the campaign's close, even the *New York Times* conceded that "the work accomplished this winter by Mr. Moody in this city for private and public morals will live. The drunken have become sober, the vicious virtuous, the worldly and self-seeking unselfish, the ignoble noble and the impure pure. A new hope has lifted up hundreds of human beings, a new consolation has come to the sorrowful, and a better principle has entered the sordid life of the day, through the labors of these plain men."

Emma and the children had already left for Augusta, Georgia, because the New York weather had been too hard on young Willie. Their friend D. W. Whittle was holding a mission there, and Dwight soon joined them. Although Dwight came to Augusta to rest, he soon involved himself in Whittle's work. Whittle fought a slight temptation to resent his intrusion. But he calmed himself as he thought, *I have considered that Moody is an almighty man of God, the Whitefield of this century, owned and honored of God, and if he has been led of God to come here and speak it is a very petty spirit that would think of self in connection with the work.*

Whittle's understanding of Dwight paid off. Dwight took him into his confidence as they walked along the banks of the Savannah River in the spring sunshine. "I don't know that I will ever go to England again," Dwight said. "I am entirely bankrupt as to sermons and material—I have used up everything. I am going to study and make new sermons but I think it will be three or four years before I shall go—if I ever go. You and Bliss had better wait until next year before going, and you must study all you can."

Dwight felt empty—and spiritually bankrupt, as he put it. At the pinnacle of his influence in the United States, he stood in danger of spiritual burnout.

Not requiring much sleep, Dwight would rise early to read his Bible and pray, and he had the unique ability to catnap anytime of the day or night. His original filing system consisted of using a large envelope for each sermon. Then he would put a scrawled sheet of headings and notes and stories clipped from papers or jotted on paper for illustrations. He would label each envelope with the place and date of each delivery. This method enabled Dwight's sermons to be fresh. He might preach on the same topic, but he would vary it each time.

He also worried about divisions, jealousies—everything that hindered the cause of Christ. His desire was that Christians, especially ministers of the gospel, would put aside their differences and work together.

At that time, Dwight's influence in the country was enormous. But Dwight's opinion of himself continued to be an honest, humble one. On one occasion, he told a reporter, "I am the most overestimated man in America." He thought of himself simply as "the mouthpiece and expression of a deep and mysterious wave of religious feeling now passing over the nation. The disasters and disappointments of the year, the reaction against the skepticism and selfish greed of the day have prepared the minds of the people for a profound religious transformation or impulse." Nevertheless, everyone in the country, whether in log cabins of the Appalachians, in frontier wagons in some remote Montana valley, or in the soot and grime of Detroit or Pittsburgh, knew and loved Dwight Moody and Ira Sankey.

Leaving Augusta, the Moodys and Whittles stopped in Atlanta, then went on to Chattanooga, where Dwight spoke at a large gathering. On the way, Whittle enjoyed pointing out various battlefields and fortifications as the "reversed" Sherman's March to the Sea.

The rest of May, Dwight preached all over the Midwest: Nashville, St. Louis, Kansas, Omaha, and even in Council Bluffs, Iowa.

At Des Moines, the ministers had decided to cancel all Sunday services and tell their congregations to attend Moody's meetings at the campaign headquarters. However, F. G. Ensign, Dwight's friend from the previous decade, warned them he would not approve.

When a determined group met Dwight on arrival, its members told him their plans for the meeting. "Mr. Moody, we have decided, our association has voted, that we will not have any services on Sunday. We want all our people to go to the rink at ten thirty."

"No, I can't do that," Dwight protested.

"But we have decided it," committee members declared.

"I can't do it! You will have to have your church services. You must have your church services, and then at two thirty, so as not to interfere with the services, we have the meeting in the rink."

Dwight admitted to a friend: "I have often to do a shabby thing. A committee takes a great deal of trouble about something, I see it will not suit, so I cut discussion short by saying I am going to do it another way. It is very mean of me, but it would take a tremendous time in committee and I have to do it."

Sometimes his brusqueness offended others. Whittle said that Dwight's reception of members of a campaign committee was based on his ability to turn a situation around and have them think his idea was theirs: "About fifteen persons of the committee have been grieved because Moody has ignored them and gone ahead with meetings as he pleased. He keeps quiet, drawing out in full all the complaints and injured feelings and then explains and rights everything, suggesting what he thinks best and drawing out the ministers to adopt it as from themselves."

As the Midwest evangelistic tour came to a close, Dwight had come to a crossroad in his life. Where would he put down permanent roots? Would he put them down in Chicago or in Northfield? He loved both places—and his family badly needed a place to settle down. Much depended on his making the right choice, but for the moment he was in a quandary as to which decision was best.

NINETEEN

Dwight loved the Chicago church. After all, he had poured himself into building it, soliciting funds for its maintenance, and then preaching in it for years. He referred to the church as his "first love." He shared with Farwell that seldom would "[I] get on my knees in private but I think and pray for the dear church in Chicago."

The new church building stood on the Chicago Avenue site he had secured before leaving for Europe. Although the church was still in debt, when he returned he made a few successful calls for funds and cleared the indebtedness. Thus on June 1, 1876, despite a pouring rain, the church was opened and Dwight preached. The church was formally dedicated on July 16.

Dwight thought it strange to be back in Chicago—it had changed so much in the three years he had been gone. The surroundings he had known and loved were altered beyond recognition by rebuilding, yet were still smoky from the fire. The stockyard stench traveled everywhere, blanketing much of Chicago with its own peculiar aroma. But the crowds of people and the multitudes of ragged, dirty children remained the same. Dwight longed to reach out to them again in Christ's love. He sensed, too, that not only had Chicago changed, but he had changed.

On the spur of the moment he decided to accept the Chicago campaign invitation first, then the one in Boston. He even allowed himself to get back somewhat into the solicitation of funds to erect a temporary tabernacle. Prior to starting in Chicago, Dwight and his family returned to Northfield for a couple of summer months. They could enjoy their very own home, which delighted the whole family. Emma had much to do in Northfield, for, as she wrote Jane Mackinnon in Scotland on September 11, "We are in our own home, and though in a most delightful spot with such beautiful scenery, it is a place where it is very difficult to get servants, and I have had to act in all sorts of capacities. We have had company every day since we came into our house, and it has been a pleasure to my husband and myself, but I found my husband's urgent letters took most of my spare time."

Reveling in being with Sam, Dwight drove around Northfield with him and listened to his wonderful plans for Northfield. His plans included the spiritual and temporal welfare of the community. And Dwight's excitement concerning all the possibilities for his hometown knew no bounds.

Before long, the family returned to Chicago, arriving there on September 30. This time the Moodys stayed with Emma's sister and her husband, the Holdens.

D. L. MOODY

Six thousand Sunday school teachers, five hundred singers, and a hundred ministers filled the tabernacle at eight o'clock on Sunday morning. Following hymns, prayer, scripture reading, and Sankey's solos, Dwight began to preach the sermon "Rolling Away the Stone."

Whittle thought his talk was "as earnest, plain, simple, and practical and as absent from all self-consciousness as if delivered to his own Sunday school teachers. You are interested and inspired, and think he has just begun when he stops as abruptly as he began, offers prayer, pronounces the benediction and the meeting is over."

It seemed this campaign would proceed like any other. The first Sunday afternoon service was packed out, and with each subsequent service, thousands were turned away. Forgetting the Crazy Moody of old, Chicago now raved over its own world-renowned evangelist.

The Chicago Omnibus Company arranged for extra buses, timing each bus so it could connect with the tram cars. A theology professor who witnessed the crowds expressed puzzlement over Dwight's campaign: "It is perfectly astounding to me that a man with so little training should have come to understand the public so well. He cannot read the Greek Testament; indeed he has difficulty with parts of it in the English version, but he excels as any man I have ever heard in making his hearers see the point of a text of scripture."

Friday, October 6, Whittle dined with Dwight and found him obsessed with the thought of God "trying him." Later that evening, Dwight had invited the officers of the Chicago Avenue Church to have tea with him at Brevoort House before the meeting. Whittle came in late, bringing a stack of Dwight's letters and one telegram being held for him at the YMCA. He handed the stack to Dwight, who began opening the telegram. "While sitting at the table he read it and gave a cry of pain, stood upon his feet, and said, 'Sam is dead.' And sat down with his head buried in his hands to cry," Whittle recalled. "In a few minutes he said, 'Whittle, you will have to take the meeting tonight. I cannot be with you longer,' and went out."

When Whittle reached the tabernacle later in the evening, he found Dwight talking with the ministers. He was going east to bury his brother, and the committee unanimously asked Whittle to take over the meetings.

As Dwight journeyed on the train and wept from sorrow, his thoughts revolved around his family. "Oh, how deep the sorrow! The dear boy was gone for ever." Samuel, for whom he had prayed twenty years, who at the last "took a stand for Christ, and went to work, zealous work," was gone. As the train rumbled through Indiana into Ohio, Dwight wept and wept again until heaven's voice "at last made itself heard to [his] heart: 'Thy brother shall rise again.'"

After that, Dwight related, "The cloud was lifted, and for about 500 miles on my way to my home that verse rang in my ears."

Samuel's death gave Dwight a desire to do all that Samuel had longed to do for Northfield. But Dwight was needed in Chicago. He loved both places. The Chicago campaign forged ahead from 1876 into 1877. For a Presbyterian minister who took part, it was a turning point: "That wonderful revival. That tremendous audience, and its voice in song like the voice of the ocean. The mighty faith and courage of the undertaking. Think what it required to prepare for an audience of ten thousand people, and what failure, in the presence of such vast preparation, would mean!"

As the campaign reached its closing weeks, Dwight still faced a dilemma: Where should he put down roots? Another question also nagged at his soul: Would he burn out in a few more years?

During the course of the campaign Dwight had faced a number of tragedies: the death of his brother, Sam, and a dangerous attack of scarlet fever for twelve-year-old Emma. Also, although she did not tell Dwight, his wife, Emma, was told by her doctor that her heart was diseased and in critical condition

Another blow to Dwight came with the sudden death of Philip Bliss, who Dwight said was like his hymns, "full of faith and cheer—in all the years I have known and worked with him I have never seen him cast down." These sorrows made Dwight, according to Whittle, "very kind and tender."

In spite of the tragedies, Dwight still had work to do. On January 28, 1877, a week before his fortieth birthday, the Boston campaign began. If Dwight failed in Boston, it would be the death knell to his influence in America.

A tabernacle had been specially built for the campaign, with over ninety churches participating. Though the building seated only six thousand, Dwight and Sankey considered it one of the most pleasant places in which they had ministered.

"Christianity," Dwight exclaimed the first night, "has been on the defensive long enough, specially here in New England. The time's come f'r us to open a war of aggression. Remember during the War of the Rebellion some of the generals kept their armies on the defensive until they got confiscated? I guess a good many Christians here in New England have just got into their cushioned pews and gone to sleep." Dwight got their attention with these opening remarks!

Then he urged a course of action. Christians needed to "wake up and move forward in solid columns." And they should not be defensive, but aggressive. "These drinking shops 'n' billiard halls 'n' gambling dens should be visited 'n' told of Christ 'n' heaven 'n' if they won't come to the tabernacle 'n' hear the gospel, let us go to their houses 'n' preach the gospel to them 'n' it won't be long before hundreds are reached."

Many of Boston's newspapers took a positive approach to the campaign, and the weekday papers, in particular, gave it much space. The *Globe* actually recovered from financial disaster by printing ample coverage of the campaign.

So successful was the Boston campaign, as far as Dwight and Sankey were concerned, that they ranked it alongside the Edinburgh campaign. As usual, at the close of the campaign, Dwight held a two-day Christian Convention. He also tried to gain entrance to Harvard but failed. He advocated temperance, holding a Temperance Conference, and brought Frances Willard as a leader of evangelism for women. She was well known for her stand on temperance, and Dwight wanted her to sit on the campaign platform; she refused, saying she would not sit with Unitarians.

For Dwight, however, the future seemed not to be reckoned by sinners saved or drunks redeemed. Throughout the campaign, he stayed with Henry Fowle Durant, the founder of Wellesley College for girls. When Durant talked about his ideas implemented in his college, Dwight listened carefully. Durant's vision for Wellesley seemed to echo Samuel's dreams for Northfield that he had shared with Dwight the summer before he died.

TWENTY

During Sam's last summer, the two brothers had taken the buggy to look at cattle near Warwick. Sam was a library patron, had founded a debating club, and was outspoken at town meetings on Northfield's lack of good education—especially for girls such as his twin sister. As leader of the local YMCA and a lay evangelist making amends for twenty years of antagonism toward Christianity, his hopes and dreams for Northfield now blended with Dwight's.

On their return trip past a mountain lane, the brothers found a crippled, frail man standing in front of his cabin door and stopped to chat with him. He had been reading the Greek New Testament to his young daughters as they braided straw hats to earn a living. A pile of well-worn books—by Thomas à Kempis, Madam Guyon, John Bunyan, and others—were stacked close to Horace Parmelee Sikes's position on the couch.

Dwight asked him, "Where have you taken your education? How did you get along?"

Sikes replied: "I went to Oberlin College for four years in the 1840s and attended Wilbraham College some. I taught for a while at a good school, but then became paralyzed and had to quit." Sikes lamented that his daughters, Jennie and Julia, could not hope to have a similar education. Smiling, he said, "We don't have much roast turkey or plum pudding, but we get along!"

Mrs. Sikes stepped in just then, wiping soapsuds from her hands. "We just have to take things right out of the hand of God."

One of the girls added happily, "But we have a real home!"

As Sam and Dwight drove home, they discussed the Sikes's plight. Mr. Sikes could teach his daughters Greek, but what future could they have with no education beyond that and the little district school in the hills? The Sikeses could not pay board for the girls to attend the public high school at Greenfield. The girls' future could only hold a life of married drudgery on the mountain farm or as factory hands.

Sam said, "I tell you, Dwight, we've got to have a girls' school in Northfield! Otherwise their lives will be wasted!"

Dwight responded with a nod. Deep in thought, they continued home in silence.

Now with Sam gone, his dream became a sacred trust for Dwight. He might never have done anything toward its fulfillment had he not been a guest of Henry Fowle Durant in Boston during the first part of 1877.

Durant, a prominent wealthy Boston lawyer, had retired from the law to devote himself to Christian causes after the death of his only son. Dwight considered him one of his old friends, saying, "[Durant] stood by me in days before I was much known. All through the Boston work he was with me every night, and did a great work."

Durant had opened Wellesley College on part of his estate in the northwestern section of Boston. He wanted Wellesley to be a first-class college where girls of moderate means might receive "opportunities for education equivalent to those offered at Harvard." Durant had also adopted the idea from Mount Holyoke Seminary that every girl should do a regular share of domestic service. He said he did not want "velvet girls" but "calico girls." The fees charged were 250 dollars a year, or half the cost, the other half being made up by the college. Durant also required every teacher to possess not only academic skill but what he termed "vital Christianity," and Bible training became part of the compulsory requirements.

Dwight's stay with Durant crystallized his determination to organize a preparatory seminary "for young women in the humbler walks of life who would never get a Christian education but for a school like this."

After finishing the Boston campaign in the spring of 1877, Dwight and Sankey had shorter missions in several New England cities. They were thankful the tide had not turned against them, and they conducted several successful campaigns in places like Hartford, Connecticut, where the *Hartford Religious Herald* had positive things to say: "The wave of sympathy with them has been so strong that it seems to have flowed out and covered everything. We have come to a time when, for a season at least, Religion has come to the front."

Dwight even received an invitation to preach at Yale University in New Haven, Connecticut; he preached to eleven hundred students for two weeks in a specially constructed building. The students were respectful and receptive to the message Dwight preached.

But the dream of a girls' school in Northfield did not disappear, and by the fall of 1878 Dwight was in Northfield, discussing the school project with H. N. F. Marshall of Boston. Just then, the owner of sixteen acres adjoining Dwight's home passed by.

Dwight called to him, "Would you sell your property?"

Within minutes the papers had been exchanged and signed. Soon more adjoining lots were bought, and before long a hundred acres were available for the school.

While planning for the school continued, another great event took place in the Moody family. April 11, 1879, brought the birth of Paul Dwight Moody. He was ten years younger than Dwight's son, Will, and thirteen and a half years younger than Emma. How Dwight rejoiced over this newest addition to his family! How good God was to him!

Four months later, on August 21, Dwight laid the cornerstone for the recitation hall, using not a proffered silver trowel, but his father's old working trowel, and Sankey sang "The Ninety and Nine." Durant gave the dedication address, emphasizing the need for such a school and its aims and ideals: "It will be a thorough school, it will be non-sectarian, and it will be Christian. Working together, the Christian home, the Christian Church, and this Christian school will turn out young women of the type greatly needed to do the Lord's work in the world." They placed in the cornerstone a Bible, national and local newspapers, two histories of Northfield, some Moody heirlooms, and a piece of the early eighteenth-century Parson Doolittle's gravestone—the good parson's grave was on the same site as the school.

Dwight decided that if Wellesley College could fix its annual fee at 250 dollars, his secondary school need require no more than 100 dollars, half the estimate for keeping and educating the students. He asked friends, acquaintances, and wealthy philanthropists for money for his project, stressing the school's threefold basis: the Bible as a vital part of the curriculum; every girl to take regular share in domestic duties whatever her home background, thus inculcating a right sense of proportion while keeping down the cost of running the school; and the low fee.

After Dwight appointed as principal a young Wellesley woman, Harriet Tuttle, the school commenced its first term despite the unfinished recitation hall. To meet the need for boarding pupils since the dormitory had not yet been built, Dwight adapted part of the coach house on his property, forming cubicles for up to twenty-five girls.

The Moodys left in the fall for the Midwest, and on November 3 the first pupils arrived during a record blizzard that laid snow sixteen inches deep. Jennie Sikes, the girl from the mountain, got the highest marks on the entrance examination.

The recitation hall remained unfinished for another month, and lessons were done in the Moodys' parlor. Finally in the spring of 1880, Dwight could see his school taking shape. The recitation hall had been finished and the foundation laid for the first dormitory, East Hall. A hundred girls were enrolled, and Dwight ran races with them and addressed them at school prayers. The dream took shape despite setbacks.

Dwight spoke of his dream at the formal dedication of East Hall during summer vacation. "My lack of education has always been a great disadvantage to me. I shall suffer from it as long as I live. I hope after all of us who are here today are dead and gone this school may live and be a blessing to the world, and that missionaries may go out from here and preach the gospel to the heathen, and it may be recognized as a power in bringing souls to Christ." He declared as the school motto a verse from Isaiah 27:3: "I the LORD do keep it;

I will water it every moment: lest any hurt it, I will keep it night and day."

Last of all, Dwight prayed for the school. "The words of that prayer," said a participant from Boston, "burned into our souls." Dwight thanked God for the urge to found the school, for the friends whose gifts had raised it. Then he prayed, "O Lord, we pray that no teachers may ever come within its walls except as they have been taught by the Holy Spirit; that no scholars may ever come here except as the Spirit of God shall touch their hearts. O God, we are Thine, this building is Thine! We give it over to Thee. Take it and keep it and bless it, with Thy keeping power!"

Ever since the girls' school had started, Dwight had felt prodded to start something for boys—either that or admit boys into the present school. Why, Dwight wondered, should he "add to his troubles"? But the demands increased. One day wealthy Hiram Camp, befriended by Dwight in his 1878 New Haven campaign, appeared in Northfield. Would Dwight help him make out his will?

"Why not be your own executor?" Dwight asked. "You've had all the work of acquiring your means; why not have the fun of seeing it do good?"

"But," protested Camp, "I wish to give to something specific; I want to see what I do."

"All right," said Dwight. "Here is the very thing: People have been after me. . .to start a school for boys on the same lines as Northfield, but I want someone else to do it. Now, Mr. Camp. There is something for you to do."

The elderly Mr. Camp scarcely thought he could launch such a project, but he urged Dwight to undertake it and offered twenty-five thousand dollars as a starter. What an awkward position this presented to Dwight! He felt he was already spread too thin. How would he finance yet another school? But he had been so convincing, he found himself with no other recourse than to start it himself!

With the money from Mr. Camp, Dwight looked for a suitable site, and finally found 275 acres five miles across the river from the girls' school (called the seminary). Mr. Camp suggested the name Mount Hermon for the boys' school based on Psalm 133:3: "For there the LORD commanded the blessing, even life for evermore." The first boys, from eight to twelve years old, arrived on May 4, 1881. Three years later, with increasing applications from older boys and increasing troubles with the younger ones, Dwight decided to accept no applicants under sixteen. Like the seminary, the Bible was central, costs were one hundred dollars a year, and "manual labor" was required of all.

Each student was graded on the performance of his "dirty work," this grade being considered just as important an indication of character and future success as classroom grades.

The daily schedule from six a.m. to ten p.m. left little time for loafing, and unlike the seminary, Mount Hermon kept in session through the summer months, making three terms of four months each, partly due to the fact that the livestock and gardens needed tending all year. Within four years, with accommodations for only eighty, Dwight was besieged yearly with three hundred applications. A more cosmopolitan student body would have been hard to find. At one time, there were students from nearly every state and from thirty-two nations!

At first the school was little more than a fair grammar school. However, in 1883, after two years at Mount Hermon, two brothers announced to Dwight they were leaving for home because their mother wanted them to prepare for college.

Dwight begged them to stay. He believed and preached that education could make one only a more clever rascal! He shared with a friend that "education does not save a man. An educated rascal is the worst rascal of all. I have over 1,100 students in my school, and I have often said that if I knew they were going to turn out bad I wouldn't educate them."

In keeping with his views, Dwight made a point of notifying all applicants and their parents that Mount Hermon was no refuge for delinquents. "The school is for young men of sound bodies, good minds, and high aims. Vicious or idle boys are not wanted. It is neither a reformatory for the depraved nor an asylum for the exposed," he said on one occasion.

Gradually, as he worked increasingly with colleges and college students, Dwight's ideas changed, and Northfield began to take on more academic distinction. As long as he lived, however, his primary concern for each student was a spiritual one. He said, "I want to help the students into lives that will count for the cause of Christ."

Toward this end as each school year began, before he left for his winter season of big-city campaigning, Dwight urged the student body to become "out-and-out believers in Christ." There was no undue pressure, but Dwight wished every student to be a "wholesome, happy Christian."

Many students who could not have otherwise afforded even the very low cost of the schools were granted tuition-free scholarships, provided they met the preliminary conditions. But Dwight remained a strict disciplinarian regarding the rules set down.

With his evangelistic work and other obligations, the problem of school financing was not easy. The students helped with their manual labor to keep costs down, but still their one hundred dollars was but half the cost of providing their education, and how Dwight got the rest of the funds did not matter particularly to the resourceful educator.

Dwight was short on protocol but long on effectiveness. One day he heard that Pittsburgh's William Thaw was giving away his money. He packed his bag and went to see him, only to find a long line of people ahead of him.

He learned the philanthropist was giving a maximum of three hundred dollars to each case. When it came Dwight's turn he introduced himself as "Mr. Moody, from Northfield."

"What, the great evangelist! Well, I'm delighted to see you here."

"Perhaps," suggested Dwight, "you won't be, when you learn what I'm here for. We are trying to give poor young men a Christian education, and we have to turn away hundreds of applicants each year. I'd like you to give us ten thousand dollars toward a building."

"But I'm not giving more than three hundred dollars to each case."

"But, this is a special case."

"Yes, I know, and I'll give five thousand dollars."

"Don't you believe in me and this work? Why not at once give the money? I can stand in line and beg three hundred dollars at a time, but I must be off and build this building."

Of course, Dwight got his money!

A great surprise happened at "Temptation Hill," so named by Dwight that some friend might be tempted to give money enough to erect a chapel. By 1897, Dwight's sixtieth birthday year, nobody had taken the hint, so F. B. Meyer and Henry Moore took matters into their own hands and raised enough money in England and America to put up a memorial chapel. Dwight, however, refused to consider it a memorial for him, and would not permit a note of this on the bronze tablet in the vestibule: THIS CHAPEL WAS ERECTED BY CONTRIBUTIONS OF CHRISTIAN FRIENDS IN GREAT BRITAIN AND THE UNITED STATES, FOR THE GLORY OF GOD AND TO BE A PERPETUAL WITNESS TO THEIR UNITY IN THE SERVICE OF CHRIST.

Two other things Dwight refused were to raise the tuition and to have either school endowed. By raising the tuition he felt he would defeat the very purpose for which he had ordained the schools, that of helping the underprivileged, and by endowing them, he felt they would wither.

When asked why he didn't operate his schools on faith in a fashion like George Muller of Bristol, England, Dwight replied, "I do. I always have and always will. As an evidence of it you will tell me of any Christian man who had money to whom I have not written or on whom I have not called, I will do so at once. I show my faith when I go to men and ask them to give to God's work."

Dwight's parting words to the public regarding his beloved schools were given in New York City at the Fifth Avenue Presbyterian Church just before leaving for the Kansas City campaign:

You may read in the papers that Moody is dead. It will not be so. God has given me the gift of life everlasting. Five and twenty years ago in my native village of Northfield I planted two Christian schools for the training of boys and maidens in Christian living and consecration as teachers and missionaries of Jesus Christ. I bequeath as my legacy those training schools for Jesus to the churches of America, and I only ask that visitors to the beautiful native village where my ashes slumber on consecrated Round Top when they go there shall not be pained with the sight of melancholy ruins wrought by cruel neglect, but rather shall be greeted by the spectacle of two great, glorious lighthouses of the Lord, beaming out over the land, over the continent, over the world.

TWENTY-ONE

Even while Dwight was occupied with building two schools in Northfield, he saw the need for a school in Chicago to train Christian laymen for the church. He had nothing against theological seminaries, stating, "They have their place." As he pointed out, "A young man doesn't know until he is twenty or twenty-three what he wants to do for a profession. But if he waits till then to decide to be a minister and goes to college or seminary, he will be fifty years old by the time he is ready to begin work."

Dwight was interested in helping college and seminary graduates, ministers and missionaries, and laymen who were interested in pursuing English Bible study and practical evangelism. With the latter group he wanted to reach "the three-fourths that do not go anywhere to church," thus getting "a lever under all the churches." He wanted men and women who were willing to "lay their lives alongside the laboring-class and the poor, and bring the gospel to bear upon their lives." He spoke from his own background working with Chicago's poor and needy.

Instrumental in the planning was Emeline Dryer, who resigned in 1873 as head of the faculty at Illinois State Normal School to go to work for Dwight in Chicago. By 1883, with Dwight again in England, her Bible classes were drawing more people than ever.

When Charles A. Blanchard, a teacher at nearby Wheaton College, asked her what her plans were, she told him of Dwight's calling her from public school work to organize just such a training school. She needed, she told Blanchard, five hundred dollars to enlarge the operations. Blanchard got involved at that time and raised the necessary money.

By the fall of 1883, Dryer had gotten Dr. William G. Moorhead of Xenia, Ohio, involved and was teaching fifty young men and women.

The previous summer, Dwight had stressed the need for city missionaries in Chicago: "I know the need of this. I walked the streets of Chicago day after day, feeling that I must preach, yet knowing that I was not fitted for the work and wanted to learn. Had there been some place where I could have been trained and allowed to study, while I was at work, I could have been more successful."

Preachers also needed more than textbook learning; they needed to be "trained in the school of human nature." As Dwight explained, "They need to rub up against the world and learn how to read men. They fail to get hold of men for this very reason."

When a New Yorker pressed Dwight to take five thousand dollars for just such a school, he felt he could not turn it down. Coming to Chicago a short time later, another five thousand dollars was given him to start the school in Chicago.

Dwight returned to the British Isles in 1883, and while he was gone, Miss Dryer met with several others each Saturday morning to pray for guidance and support. She prayed that Dwight would "come and plan something commensurate with the needs." By January 1885, Dwight agreed to come and begin such a work if others would raise the money. But people who could do the fundraising were busy with other ventures.

The following January, Dwight made a public appeal for funds. He told his audience that $100,000 had been raised for a building in Edinburgh, and challenged them to raise $250,000.

Every time Dwight tried to forget about the Bible Institute, he would be persuaded otherwise. Finally, he started a subscription paper. Several people sitting on the platform of his current campaign subscribed five thousand dollars apiece. Cyrus Hall McCormick offered fifty thousand dollars. Dwight suggested, "Better make it a hundred." And McCormick, tickled at Dwight's boldness, said, "That will require some consideration," but nevertheless came through with the $100,000.

The money seemed to pour in from everywhere for the institute. In the meantime, training took place at the Chicago Avenue Church to provide workers for the mass evangelism Dwight had encouraged in the city. He gave the first one hundred dollars toward a large gospel tent to be pitched in "Little Hell," to be manned by an evangelist and a corps of assistants. In the winter, the mission moved into churches, missions, theatres, and even barrooms where beer kegs became seats.

Through a series of brief "Bible Institutes," training was given these workers in the scriptures and in "practical methods of Christian work." By May 1889 over two hundred people were attending these institutes. Dwight wrote to Whittle on May 24, telling him, "I have never been so hopeful about anything I have undertaken." He said he felt he was trying to solve "the great problem of the century."

Back in Chicago, Dwight became aware of three large houses for sale next to the Chicago Avenue Church. He bought them on the spot for three future dormitories to house fifty women seeking admission to the institute. Immediately he began work on a three-story brick building for the ninety men who were attending as well. And on September 26, 1889, Dwight opened the institute officially, putting Rueben Torrey, a minister formerly from New Haven, Connecticut, in charge. Dwight had selected the other necessary officials at that time, so everything was in place for the institute to grow and flourish.

The daily schedule was full, the Mondays were kept for "Rest Day." In addition to "domestic" work, practical work assignments in the city were mandatory. Each week students were responsible for such tasks as organizing and carrying on cottage prayer meetings, working in a city mission or industrial school, holding children's meetings, or otherwise supplementing the work of the city churches. In typical Moody style, inquiry meetings became the rule after virtually every service.

By 1890 the men's building was finished and Dwight, surveying it, exclaimed, "There is my life work!" By fall he must have been more convinced than ever when 248 students enrolled. That year, in addition to their study, they conducted over three thousand meetings, paid ten thousand visits to homes of the poor, and went to more than one thousand saloons. By the end of the year Dwight rejoiced to see his first graduates being placed at home and abroad. Three went to India, eight to China, seven to Africa, two to South America, six to Turkey, and one each to Bulgaria, Persia, Burma, and Japan.

Forty-six of the graduates remained in the States, going into evangelistic work; thirty-one went into pastoral work; five into Sunday school missions; two into home missions; seven to YMCA work; two into YWCA work; and six into "singing evangelism." A number took posts in charitable institutions; twenty went out as teachers; and twenty-nine went on to further education. The instructors were always chosen carefully and had to view the Bible as literal. Dwight gave them much academic freedom but admonished them about their biblical views: "Let us take our stand here, that any man can teach upon our platforms with absolute freedom whatever he finds in the Bible, but no man shall be allowed to pick the Bible to pieces."

Dwight's students highly respected him, even revered him. When he visited Chicago, he stayed in the men's dorm and ate with them in the dining hall. Each Monday morning that Dwight was away, Torrey would write a letter to him, including a statistical report for the previous week. Dwight was eager for optimistic statistics, but was even more concerned about each individual student. He held high standards and expected each of them to do the same. He wrote Torrey: "If any of the men do not come up to the mark, you will not keep them. That I told them when I left. Keep me posted about them, and give them a good trial." For all his good humor, Dwight expected every person to do his best.

Dwight implemented the Northfield plan for fundraising at the institute. He wrote potential donors, asking for 150 dollars to support one student. He and his wife each took one student, and he went out looking for two hundred more donors.

At the end of a decade or so, Dwight's institution was more than a mere "whistling in the woods," as he himself termed it shortly before his death. More than three thousand students had enrolled, tuition free, in buildings by then worth a third of a million dollars. About a third of the alumni had gone into Christian service full time, while most of the rest filled valuable lay positions in churches across the country. The Moody Bible Institute, as it became at his death, was now, according to the public relations department, the "West Point of Christian Work."

In addition to getting the Northfield Schools and the Bible Institute underway, the 1880s proved to be fruitful years for Dwight. He continued to receive many invitations to revisit Scotland and England. Finally, in September 1881, the Moodys and the Sankeys set sail for the countries of their early success.

Once again crowds thronged to hear Dwight in Edinburgh, London, and even at Cambridge University. He campaigned in most of the same places he had on the earlier trip. He was less a sensation this time and more the beloved Yankee who discovered a welcome spelled out in enormous crowds, eager to hear once again the homely aphorisms, the pungent epigrams, the down-to-earth applications, and the resurrection of Bible characters in a language that was at once simple and pithy, straightforward and humorous. In some respects this second great mission was a continuation of the first; in some respects, it was a duplication.

Altogether, Dwight traveled to the British Isles seven times. The first three trips helped him to set his sights. The fourth established him as front-page news in secular and religious papers alike. The fifth, sixth, and seventh trips helped consolidate and extend the work of the fourth. When he returned to America in 1892, this time to stay, he left behind a grateful people.

TWENTY-TWO

S ome day," Dwight was fond of saying, "you will read in the papers that D.
L. Moody of East Northfield is dead. Don't believe a word of it! At that moment I shall be more alive than I am now!" He would then describe heaven with such conviction that fully a million people, by some estimates, forsook the paths of sin to follow Moody's Christ.

He died as he lived—winning souls—for his supreme aim had become the conversion of as many souls as one man, bent on complete consecration, could muster for the heavenly roll call. It was this passion that drove him on to pace his workers as a fox paces the pursuing hounds, that drove him on when others dropped in their tracks from exhaustion, that drove him on to Kansas City, Missouri, complete with a grueling itinerary. He had promised them he would begin a campaign on November 12, 1899.

Dwight cried out to God for precious souls: "If only it would please God to let me get hold of this city by a winter of meetings! I should like to do it before I die," he confided to a friend before leaving.

As he stepped from the train in Kansas City on Saturday, November 11, the old throbbing in his chest had begun again. But he retained the old vigor, the same cheerfulness. The first night he preached on "Whatsoever a man soweth, that shall he reap." The audience hung on his every word, and many responded at the close of the message.

Dwight did not sleep that night, and his doctor insisted he quit speaking. True to form, Dwight would not quit the evening services, but he did stop the afternoon sessions. However, by afternoon he was worse, and finally he had to tell the committee that he would have to give up the meetings: "It's the first time in forty years of preaching that I have had to give up my meetings."

His associates rented a special railroad car, "the Messenger of Peace," and put Dwight aboard for the trip to Northfield. The train engineer had been converted under Dwight's ministry fifteen years before and did his utmost in speeding up the train to catch its eastern connection.

In Northfield again, Dwight rallied for a few days, and his old optimism returned. He still had plenty of work to do, "If God will grant me more days."

On the evening of December 21, lying on his bed at Northfield, Dwight wrote in pencil in his usual bold hand, "To see His star is good, but to see His face is better."

As the next dawn broke, Friday, December 22, 1899, Dwight stirred from an hour's deep sleep that had ended in a fitful night of increasing weakness.

Suddenly his son Will heard in slow measured words: "Earth recedes, heaven opens before me!" Will hurried across to him.

"No, this is no dream, Will. It is beautiful. It is like a trance. If this is death, it is sweet. God is calling me and I must go. Don't call me back!"

Just then, Emma Moody entered the room, and Dwight told her, "Mama, you have been a good dear wife." He slipped into unconsciousness, murmuring, "No pain, no valley, it's bliss."

After an injection by the doctor, he regained momentary consciousness and said he would like to get out of bed and cross over to a chair. He rose, walked to his chair almost unaided, and sat a few moments, then asked to be helped back to bed.

Nothing need keep him. His work was finished, and the chariot of God had come for him. Dwight L. Moody breathed his last and then gazed upon the face of the One whose love had given his life meaning.

C. S. LEWIS

Sam Wellman

ONE

A new officer's coming, Lieutenant Lewis."

Worst luck! thought Lieutenant C. S. Lewis of the 3rd Somerset Light Infantry, who did not feel like a welcoming presence that day in France. The German artillery, which had been dropping in shells more than usual all day, made him feel hunkered down. Rumors of mustard gas from the north had driven him to clutch his gas mask, and now his fingers ached. Worse yet, the scuttlebutt that approximately fifteen German divisions were ready to assault Arras, which lay directly behind Lieutenant Lewis, gnawed on his nerves. Blast it all, as ghastly as the trenches were, he was not fit to lead men against the Germans in the open.

Sighing, he studied the entrance of the communications trench. Suddenly the grimy face of a sergeant and the bright face of a new officer appeared at the entrance above him. A barely audible gasp revealed the officer's sudden realization that he was on a precipice. "We've come to a new trench, and this one must be another ten feet deep," he chirped.

"At least ten feet deep, sir," replied his sergeant. "We have been walking in a communications trench. This is a real trench. We're at the front line, sir."

"My legs are rubber," confessed the new officer, whose falsetto betrayed his youth. "Why is the communications trench so zigzagged? Seems an awful waste."

Lieutenant Lewis spoke up. "In case of a direct hit from artillery or a fusillade from small arms, we don't want the projectiles going up and down the whole straight-line trench, killing every one of us, now do we?"

The new officer spotted Lieutenant Lewis and gulped. "Of course not, Lieutenant." He descended a ladder and thumped onto the boarded bottom of the trench. Jack Lewis saw no need to get friendly. When this new man died, it wouldn't be so hard for him to accept. How many of his new friends had been killed already? He had lost count. Besides, this time he really felt like he was going to get killed himself. He watched the new officer climb up on the fire step by a periscope.

"Hard to see through all the barbed wire," muttered the new officer, gawking through the periscope. "How far away are the krauts?"

Jack Lewis squirmed against the hard-packed sandbags at his back and waited for someone else to answer the new officer. He hated the word *kraut*, which was short for *sauerkraut*, a common German dish. He didn't like the word *jerry* to indicate Germans either. Words were special to Jack. Even up here where a man might die any second, he guarded his language and chose his words with precision. Must a man become a sloppy pig simply because he lived in mud?

When no one volunteered to answer the new officer's question, Jack finally spoke up. "The distance across no-man's-land to the German trench? Fifty yards or so."

"But then shouldn't I be able to see. . . ? I do see a field-gray uniform and a soup-pot helmet! A kraut is walking along a trench over there! Careless bloke. I daresay I could plug him right in the head."

"Good idea," drawled Jack dryly. "Poke your head up and take a pot-shot."

"Oh, I see. One of them might shoot at me first. I say then, better yet, why don't we lob a rifle grenade into their trench?"

Someone groaned, but Jack Lewis had to laugh. He had voiced the exact same words to Sergeant Ayres back on day one of his entry into this Great War; it had been his nineteenth birthday, November 29, 1917, four and a half months back. "Once you start that business," instructed Jack crisply, "you'll get it back in kind."

The new officer was startled. "But aren't we supposed to kill the krauts?"

"Oh, don't worry. Death is a common commodity in the trenches and even almost guaranteed in that no-man's-land between our trenches and their trenches. You see, every inch of that hellish ground is covered not only by our machine guns, but their machine guns, too. Death is almost a certainty."

"So it's a stalemate," concluded the new officer, amazed.

"Only until some wine-sipping, chain-smoking general back at HQ gets antsy over his hors d'oeuvres because no map tacks are being moved on his map," grumbled Jack Lewis sourly, "and decides one of his tacks, which happens to be one of our battalions, should charge the Germans."

"You don't say. . . ." The young officer quirked an eyebrow.

"Go warm yourself by one of the fires," intoned Jack, brother-like. "Pick yourself a nice wire bunk in some dugout. Eat some stew. Read a good book." Jack felt like adding, *Because any day now—if you don't croak on mustard gas first—a whole division of Germans is going to storm across that fifty yards, and nothing our puny battalion can do will stop them, because this is their very last chance to win this terrible war before the Americans build up an army of several million men.*

But Jack didn't feel mean enough. Truth was he himself was frightened numb, more scared than he had ever been. He watched the new officer squeeze past a traverse and disappear. Traverses were thick walls of sandbags perpendicular to the trench. They occurred about every ten yards and served the same tactical purpose as zigzagging. The enemy could not devastate an entire trench with an exploding shell or a fusillade of bullets.

No one had handled the war quite as Jack had. He knew how to keep the future in its place. As an Irish citizen, he hadn't been required to volunteer for the draft at all. Precisely what had motivated him to do that noble act, he no longer remembered. Perhaps he had reasoned if he was going to take advantage of Oxford University in England he could jolly well fight for England. Or perhaps he had done it so he could call himself a Welshman as his father did. Or perhaps he had done it because since 1914 his brother Warnie had been fighting for England somewhere in this quagmire, too. For whatever reason, he had volunteered for the draft, then, duty done, he simply ignored the war.

While others related in trembling voices that the British had lost two hundred thousand men in only the first year of the war, Jack read fantasies by his hero George MacDonald. While others chattered endlessly about this and that awful battle, Jack digested Plato. When he finally had gotten drafted, it was as if he woke up to say, "Oh yes, the war. I'm ready, I suppose." Only when, on his first day on the front, he had heard a bullet scream by somewhere had intense reality pulsed through him. He actually admired some things about the war. For the first time in his life, he enjoyed the company of real men. It felt very good. Proper gentlemen talked about everything but themselves. A real man talked about things. A real man didn't complain. Yes, Jack Lewis liked the company of real men very much. Their laughter was music to his ears.

"Lewis!" called the familiar voice of Laurence B. Johnson, another lieutenant in Jack's battalion. "Take a break, old chap. I've found a splendid hole in the wall not far from here." That was Johnson, always cheery.

"Lead the way then," ordered Jack.

After they entered a freshly dug hole lit by a candle and almost warm from the earth, Johnson said, "See, it's plenty large enough for a spirited chat. Big enough for three gentlemen, really. I say, isn't there a new officer hereabouts?"

"I sent him to get some stew," explained Jack with little interest. He threw aside his gas mask.

"Well, I'll round him up," Johnson stated purposefully.

And with that he darted out. Yes, that was Laurence B. Johnson. Generous. Hospitable. Yanked away from Oxford just as Jack had been. Johnson practiced virtues, even took them for granted. He actually believed in a supreme being of some sort. In spite of that, Jack liked him very much. He liked him so much he felt the urge to imitate him, this scholar who could discuss things as sharply as Jack's old tutor, Kirk, yet believed in the old-fashioned virtues of truthfulness and chastity. Jack resisted those things. There was no rational reason to desire such virtues and less reason to believe them. Yet why was he attracted to Johnson so much?

"We're back, Lewis," announced Johnson, interrupting Jack's thoughts.

The new officer followed Johnson inside. He was strangely subdued now, the reality of the front lines having drained all the "cheery-ho!" out of him. "Jack Lewis and I usually debate theism, Thorne," explained Johnson, who had learned the name of the new officer.

"The existence of God? Go ahead then," said Thorne. "I'll listen. I'm afraid the day has dulled my brain too much to contribute anything very sharp." He sounded very depressed. Suddenly the earth shook and the candle went out. "What was that?" asked Thorne in a high-pitched voice.

"Just our own cannons," elaborated Jack dryly as Johnson lit the candle again. Dirt trickled from the ceiling.

"I believe Lewis here was on slippery ground last time we talked about theism," Johnson inserted perkily.

Jack stiffened for a good fight. "Just because I admitted the mind seems more like spirit than flesh?"

"Certainly, old chap," Johnson grinned.

"All right," Jack conceded, shaking his head. "I admitted that I resent very much that material things like bullets and such can extend their dominion over the mind, which seems to me the only source possible for beauty. And I also admitted that beauty—which exists only in the mind—seems like some sort of spirit thing."

Johnson was smiling.

"You needn't derive such satisfaction," objected Jack. "That conclusion doesn't necessitate what you believe in."

But deep inside, Jack was in agony over this cosmic debate. A separate spirit world was one way to explain the "otherness" of certain things that had thrilled him so much his entire life—things like his brother Warnie's toy garden or the Northern myths. Weren't those thrills possibly due to the tiniest glimpse into that spirit world?

"You admitted far more than that last time," goaded Johnson.

"You mean my simple equation? Matter equals nature equals Satan?"

"Satan!" echoed Johnson. "You see how far you've come, old chap?"

"Satan is just an invention of the Jews or other ancient civilizations."

Johnson's face was sober. "I believe in your heart, Lewis, you are a dualist already."

"What! Believe in two supreme beings? One evil and one good? Like William Blake did? Hardly." Jack added a quiet *humph*.

Deep inside, though, he was thinking along those lines. All he would admit to himself so far, however, was that he possessed some tiny chip of some unthinking universal spirit. He just could not bring himself to believe in spiritual beings that might actively be poking people this way and prodding people that way. And yet he could freely admit that the appetites of his flesh seemed to be counter to his conscious desire for beauty. Yes, to himself he truly seemed some kind of Frankenstein's monster created by nature or Satan. Here he was, desiring beauty, all the while fighting off the same lusty desires nature gives a loathsome beetle!

"Lewis is of all things, first and last, a book lover," announced Johnson breezily, perhaps sensing Lewis was cornered, tired, and confused. "Show us your latest, old chap."

Jack reached inside his heavy trench coat and pulled out a precious volume. "I'm reading *Middlemarch* by George Eliot right now."

Thorne perked up. "I say, I've been meaning to read Eliot someday myself."

Suddenly an explosion clapped their ears like thunder and the dugout was plunged into darkness.

TWO

"Are we alive?" whispered Thorne.

Johnson relit the candle. Dirt rained softly down inside the dugout. Thorne squirmed, unsure how to react. Johnson blew out the match, expressionless. Jack sighed and slipped his precious *Middlemarch* back inside his trench coat.

"So much for civilization," Jack sighed as he picked up his gas mask. "We had better go out and see who we lost in this Valley of Humiliation."

Solemnly, the three young officers left the dugout and attended to their duties. Worst luck, Jack thought, that he had to go to war to find such congenial company, because the destruction of war itself was the ultimate degradation. The soggy wetness. The clammy ears and noses. The sweaty feet in awkward gum boots. The cave-ins. The constant stench of human waste. The flies and maggots. And most degrading of all, the near misses that weren't near misses for companions suddenly torn and bloody and maimed, crawling and grasping and moaning and whimpering to their last breath.

Grim thoughts made him remember Paddy Moore. Moore was from Clifton College, but he had come to Oxford for officer training. Jack had grown to like Moore. He also liked Moore's mother and eleven-year-old sister, Maureen, when they came down from Bristol to stay until Paddy shipped out. Mrs. Moore was bossy, generous, caring, gregarious, affectionate—an Irish lady completely devoid of English reserve. She took Jack under her wing right along with Paddy and Maureen. And she wore well. Jack's affection for her grew every day. So the promise he made to Paddy Moore when they shipped out in their separate battalions didn't seem like such an earthshaking one. After all, Jack knew that Paddy was the most certain of all the soldiers to get out of the bloody war alive. But now Paddy was missing. His rifle brigade had taken the full brunt of the German attack in March.

I promised to take care of his mother for life if anything happened to him! . . . Well, so what? I probably won't be alive myself in a day or two. He squeezed through the next traverse. There he saw that fragments from the shell that had just burst and forced the three officers out of their dugout had downed one of the enlisted men. The soldier was gasping and whimpering. He must have been lying on top of his wound, because he didn't look all that bad, yet he showed all the signs of a man dying. He was Irish like Jack, but from his pained words, Jack knew this man had his Christ at the end. Jack Lewis had nothing. The enlisted man had the assurance of heaven. Jack Lewis had nothing.

There had been a time when Jack's mother, Flora, was alive that he knew

God was as real as the sunshine. Father, Mother, brother Warnie, and Jack had attended church regularly. The Catholics called them "Ulster Protestants." Although they considered their church much freer of ritual than the Catholic Church, it was nevertheless a rigid church, never swerving one iota from the *Book of Common Prayer*. Only the short, uplifting sermon was not dictated.

A right happy little boy he had been back in Ireland to be sure. One day he stomped his foot at his given name, Clive, and informed one and all from that day forward he was "Jacksy." Even Father called him Jacksy for a while, then Jack. Older brother Warnie seemed stunned. He had considered not being called Warren quite a triumph. Once in a while, Jack caught his own reflection in the nursery window. He had a pensive oval face with a thatch of short brown hair.

Jack giggled. "Guess what, Warnie?"

"In a minute, Jack," mumbled Warnie. "Let me finish this paragraph."

"What are you writing?"

"*The Rajah's Land.*"

"You're writing a story about India?"

"Of course. One can't draw pictures all the time."

Jack had to think about that. It seemed that from the beginning of time he had drawn pictures, even maps, of Animal-Land, but he had never written a story. The stories about Animal-Land just collected in his head.

Suddenly he saw a carriage drawing up in front of their house.

"Look!" he cried. "It's Uncle William."

"Nooo," whined Warnie. "Why couldn't it be Uncle Joseph? Or even Uncle Richard."

They were doomed, regardless of which uncle it was. No story of leprechauns from their nursemaid Lizzie tonight. They would be lucky to get half of *Peter Rabbit*. When Father, whom they secretly called "Poodaytabird" because of the funny way he said *potato*, had company, he always "invited" the boys to listen to their manly conversation. And it was always the same subjects: business and politics, mostly politics.

It was always the same. The boys listened and tried to process the seeming contradictions in the conversations. Poodaytabird considered himself a Welshman, although his mother was a Gee from Liverpool in England. The boys lived in Ireland, but somehow their city of Belfast was like an English city, unless of course one considered himself Scotch like Uncle Augustus Hamilton and his sister Flora—who was the boys' mother. Yet Grandmother Hamilton was a Warren, a family that considered itself English. It was certainly complicated. Only their nursemaid Lizzie seemed really rooted in Ireland.

"It's 1904," declared Uncle William as if that explained something.

"Perhaps you're right," acknowledged Poodaytabird. "Jack is only six, and he has such a weak chest."

Jack had lost the thread of the conversation. Uncle William was trying to get Poodaytabird to do something, but Jack had not been paying attention. What did Jack's weak chest have to do with anything? And why did Warnie look worried? Later in the nursery he blurted to Warnie, "Why did they talk about my weak chest?"

"Because Poodaytabird is worried about you catching cold, Small-Piggy-Bottom."

"So what, Arch-Piggy-Bottom?" countered Jack.

"He wants us to move outside of Belfast where it's healthier—up toward the Holywood Hills where Uncle Joseph lives."

"What? . . . Move? . . . Change?"

That night Jack had his worst kind of nightmare. He dreamed of beetles. They were so horrid. They had gnashing jaws. And their legs were covered with barbs. And they moved so much faster than Jack. And they chased him and crawled over his face all night. Oh, how Jack hated insects!

"Come out to the garden, and let's dig for a pot of gold," Warnie proposed the next morning.

"I'm staying inside," Jack insisted. Where was one sure to find beetles? Digging in the garden, naturally.

Jack occupied himself with Animal-Land. His main heroes were King Bunny and Sir Peter Mouse and Sir Ben, a frog. Naturally his heroes triumphed over any insect. From a book by Elizabeth Nesbit, Jack had discovered how things happened deep in the past. And so, that was where he placed his Animal-Land—deep in the past.

"Look what I've made for you, Small-Piggy-Bottom!" called Warnie, surprising Jack in his thoughts.

"What is it?" Jack leaned toward Warnie's outstretched hand.

Warnie held out the lid to a can. On it was a layer of bright green moss. Tiny twigs were stuck upright and topped by bits of moss. Pebbles defined a path. "I brought the garden inside to you," explained Warnie.

Jack was amazed. It was very skillfully done. It was more than a garden. It was paradise in miniature. Suddenly a feeling overwhelmed him. Oh, how he wanted to possess the garden. But in a way he already possessed it. It was something else he wanted. If only he could make himself small and wander there in that green paradise. No, that wasn't it either. He had never felt such a feeling as he felt now. It was a feeling of great want, yet in itself, one of intense satisfaction.

Suddenly the feeling was gone. He was looking at a small moss-covered lid dotted with twigs and pebbles.

"Most clever, Warnie," he said, weak from the intensity of the experience.

"You seem to have little concern for what Uncle William and Poodayta-bird said about me last night," complained Warnie.

"I never heard your name mentioned." Jack defended himself in surprise.

"Of course not. It's not as straightforward as that, Small-Piggy-Bottom. You see, Uncle William bragged on and on how our cousins Norman and Willie have prospered in the English 'public' schools, which of course are really private schools."

"I heard him say that. So what?"

"Didn't you see the look in Poodaytabird's eyes?" Warnie prompted.

"No." Jack shook his head, bewildered.

"Well, I did, and I saw Arch-Piggy-Bottom on a ship to England!"

"No. Are you going to be sent to England?" shouted Jack. "And the rest of us are moving up into the Holywood Hills?"

The family called their new house in the Holywood Hills "Little Lea." It was three bay-windowed stories of brick, fish-scaled shingles, stucco, and dressed stone. The roof showed no fewer than five chimneys. Rooms were large and sunny. And it was poorly designed, which made it a fairyland for boys. There were isolated spaces and tunnels for no purpose whatever—except for boys to explore and inhabit. Books were stored everywhere. Poodaytabird never borrowed books; he bought them. It seemed every book he and Jack's mother wanted to read he bought. And they both dearly loved to read. Soon the boys were reading the books, too. There were no restrictions.

And another great event took place. The brothers united Jack's Animal-Land with Warnie's India into a kingdom called "Boxen," generating stories and pictures furiously.

In less than a month, however, Warnie was gone. It happened so suddenly after moving into Little Lea that it seemed as if Jack just looked up from his book one day and exclaimed, "Where is Warnie?"

"Off to Wynyard in Hertfordshire," replied Lizzie sourly.

"England?"

"Yes."

"Then I'm alone?"

Jack wasn't really alone in the house, for it teemed with life. There was ever-constant Lizzie as well as a housemaid, a governess, a cook, and a gardener who smelled of wine. Animals also added to the activity: Nero, a small friendly dog, various aloof cats, and even pet mice and canaries from time to time. But Jack felt alone when he squeezed into hidden recesses no one else knew about. Although his mother was home, she always seemed to be somewhere else in the house. When Poodaytabird was home, he usually read books and discussed politics in the parlor. One evening Jack made a discovery that changed his image of Poodaytabird forever. Jack had with great relief left his father and

Uncle Joseph in the parlor during what was a seemingly endless discussion of politics. Later, when Jack had to retrieve a book in the room next to the parlor, he heard the liveliest conversation. Several people were in the parlor now, mocking, cackling, snorting, mimicking, telling jokes, teasing, guffawing, and in general having an uproariously good time. Jack crept over to the door and peeked. It was as if he suddenly saw an elephant playing the piano. Several people were not in the parlor at all—only his father and Uncle Joseph. All the voices were coming from Poodaytabird, his walrus-mustached father!

From that moment on, no storyteller Jack ever heard could match his father for sheer enthusiasm and animation and mimicry.

Mother was a plump, bespectacled blond who managed the house and sat knitting or reading every evening. Her smooth, pleasant face was misleading. She was a worrier, Jack knew that. Father worried, too, muttering always about financial ruin, but somehow Jack knew the muttering was no more than a release for him. Mother genuinely worried. She often disappeared with a headache. She was there but not there.

When Jack began his studies at home in earnest, however, Mother became more visible. His governess, Annie Harper, taught him every subject except French and Latin. These were taught by his mother, who demonstrated real mastery. She also knew mathematics, Jack was told, and he asked why she did not teach him that. Her soft smile told him beyond any doubt that he would not understand such a high level of mathematics as she knew. So Jack saw another elephant playing the piano, because his mother was a greater mystery than his father. He was very proud of her after that.

The neighborhood was not without relatives to visit, but Jack usually waited for Warnie's vacations to make the rounds of their cousins with him. So, with Warnie gone most of the time, Jack began to write Boxen stories. This was not an escape where he was part of the story himself. He had read enough books by now to know he was creating the story. The story stood alone—outside him, brimming with complicated plots and political intrigue. Not for nothing had Jack listened to Poodaytabird and his uncles talk of the real world. On two more occasions he experienced the rush of longing he had felt when gazing at Warnie's toy garden. Once when reading *Squirrel Nutkin*, he felt an overpowering longing. If only he could satisfy that hunger, yet he could not. Again he realized that the feeling of great want, in itself, was the satisfaction. Another time he was reading Longfellow—his reading varied wildly from *Peter Rabbit* to Milton's *Paradise Lost*. Jack liked Longfellow's poem *Saga of King Olaf* but was stunned when he ran across an unrhymed translation of an earlier poem that was little more than a footnote:

I heard a voice that cried,
"Balder the beautiful

Is dead, is dead!"
And through the misty air
Passed like the mournful cry
Of sunward sailing cranes.[1]

Suddenly a feeling of vast, cold northern skies overwhelmed Jack. He became sick with longing for what could only be described as something frigid and spacious and severe. Oh, how he wanted to possess what he came to think of as "Northernness." Had he once again glimpsed something beyond this world?

He came to regard these glimpses into otherness as joy and reveled in them. Nine-year-old Jack's contentment at Little Lea seemed like it could last forever, but his world turned black indeed in 1908.

Mother Flora had no appetite and complained of fatigue and headaches. She was only forty-six. Doctors found the problem: She was bleeding from cancer in her stomach. Loss of blood made her tired and nauseated. As soon as possible, they performed an operation on her in the home, as was the custom for the well-to-do, but that caused another problem.

Grandfather Lewis had already been living with them for a year. Although his smoking and spitting disgusted Jack, he was nice enough, supposedly quite an important man once, a shipbuilder.

"Grandfather Lewis is senile now," rationalized Jack's father, Albert. "He makes too much noise, and he doesn't keep himself clean. He can't live in a home where someone is recuperating from major surgery."

Thus Albert justified moving Grandfather Lewis into a nursing home. Grandfather did not understand. While Flora was recovering from her surgery, a broken Grandfather Lewis died at age seventy-six. By May, Mother was back on her feet long enough to take Jack to the seashore. She had overseen that summer excursion for years, yet it seemed the first time Jack was really aware of her presence. By June, pain drove her back into bed. Warnie was summoned home in July, strangely subdued, even with Jack. The outlook for Mother was grim. On August 23, Albert's birthday, she died.

"God gave us as good a woman, wife, and mother as a family ever had," Albert told the boys.

Uncle Joseph died ten days later. Grandfather, Mother, favorite uncle. All dead. How could life get worse for the Lewises?

THREE

This time Warnie did not leave for school in England alone. Although Mother had been in the grave only days, Jack went with him. One moment Jack was running around in shorts and casual shoes, and the next moment Lizzie was dressing him in dark woolen clothes, pants that buttoned at the knees, a stiff collar, and a bowler hat. His clothes might have been made of metal for all the comfort they gave. The clothing was hot and prickly.

"They won't seem so warm in England," commented Warnie grimly.

London was not that far south, but it may as well have been on another planet. Wynyard was in the village of Watford on the lower slopes of the Chiltern Hills, remote from inviting beechwood forests to the north. Jack hated everything about Watford. The ground was sickly yellow and flinty hard. The weather was colder than any he had ever experienced. And those were the least of his complaints.

Headmaster "Oldie" was a tyrant, a smelly, thick-lipped giant. He caned the fifteen or so boys who attended classes and railed at his own teachers, even though they were ordained deacons. The lessons were so bad the boys knew they were bad. Geometry was one of the very few subjects that seemed inspired, but Jack had no interest in math anymore.

"Why didn't you tell Poodaytabird how terrible this place is?" Jack asked Warnie.

"Have you ever tried to inform Poodaytabird about anything?" Warnie challenged.

"He listens, but he doesn't quite hear what you say, does he?" Jack nodded understandingly.

"And suppose he wrote Oldie a letter of complaint?"

"I see." Jack shuddered with the realization.

So the brothers endured the school month after month. Protected by Warnie, Jack easily slipped into the company of the other boys. Oldie's tyranny united them all. Besides learning how to cope with the complete loss of privacy, Jack discovered God again. He was appalled at first by the formal high Church of England atmosphere during services at Wynyard, but the sermons captured him. They were designed not to uplift, but to instruct. What Jack had already known in his head came to life in his heart.

He realized he really did believe in God. God was important in his life. And the fear of God was important. Lack of that fear led one straight to hell. This Jack began to appreciate all too well. Many a night he gazed out the curtainless windows of the dormitory at the moon and stars, boys snoring all around him.

God was infinitely larger than the moon and stars and all of space!

"To know God is to fear him," he acknowledged in fear and trembling. Knowing God didn't seem very pleasant.

After a year Warnie moved on to Malvern, a school for older boys many miles away, closer to Bristol than London. As the second year started at Wynyard, Jack was one of only five students! After another year at Wynyard, even Albert had to admit Wynyard was doing Jack, now eleven, more harm than good. By July of 1910, Jack was home at Little Lea, certain that he would never return to Wynyard.

For six months, Jack remained at Little Lea, halfheartedly attending a nearby school while Albert made arrangements for him to be taken in at Cherbourg Preparatory School, next to Warnie's Malvern School. In January, Jack was off to England again with Warnie.

Warnie's face quickly donned the smuggest look Jack had ever seen. Now fifteen, Warnie studied his manicured nails. "This time, Jack, I believe at twelve you're old enough to enjoy England."

And Jack did enjoy England. Now when he and Warnie sailed the Irish Channel from Belfast to Liverpool, they didn't breathlessly catch the first train south. No, they found a pleasant cafe and puffed cigarettes and read books for several hours. Then they leisurely returned to Malvern, preferably on the slowest train in England.

Now that the teachers were competent and Jack was challenged, school pleased him. In spite of his intense dislike for competitive sports, he got along with the other twenty or so boys. He even liked the surroundings, the soft green hills to the west and the low blue plain of the Severn River to the east.

The matron who looked after the boys made his days at Cherbourg even more pleasant. She was very kind, very popular, and she loved to discuss religion. But hers was not the cut-and-dried Christianity of the Church of England. She had moved beyond that. She discussed theosophy and spiritualism. She told the boys of a spirit world—not necessarily Christian—waiting beyond the material world. The challenge, she purported, was to communicate with that world. Jack's strong imagination was fertile soil for the words of his matron, and he trusted her. He began to long for that hidden world about which his matron talked.

During that time, Jack was also reading the classics in Latin and Greek. All these pagan writers discussed religion. Jack realized that ideas about religion were very old and assumed many forms. Was not one about as right as the other? Even more damning was the thought that religion had simply grown out of a fear of death. Might it be no more than a story to ease one's fears?

Jack discerned that many of his teachers embraced the ideas he was encountering in the classics and noticed that most of his fellow students were following the teachers, moving beyond mere disinterest to a complete shedding of their religion. They perceived religion as a very tiresome duty and the fear of God as a most unpleasant attitude. Eventually, Jack realized not only did he no longer fear God, he did not believe in God at all. Spirits might be beyond the material world, but not the demanding God of the Bible. He felt free.

Despite not experiencing—and actually forgetting—his otherness for several years, Jack found it again. Then, by pure accident, one day he saw in a magazine the words *Siegfried and the Twilight of the Gods*. Suddenly a feeling of vast, cold northern skies overwhelmed him again. He became sick with longing for something cold and spacious and severe: his old Northernness. Again, the unfulfilled desire became satisfaction in itself and seemed a glimpse into another world.

Jack learned that *Siegfried and the Twilight of the Gods* was an opera composed by the German Richard Wagner and forthwith changed his opinion that operas were simply overweight men and women screaming unintelligibly in German and Italian. Soon he was playing Wagner's operas on a phonograph, immersed in *Rhinegold* and then the Ring Trilogy itself. The music added yet another dimension to Jack's fondness for Northernness. The yearnings of his heart, however, were focused on those occasional glimpses into unutterable joy.

The late summer of 1913 brought great changes again to the Lewis brothers. "I've decided to join Field Marshall Kitchener," Warnie told Jack, wearing an expression he had now cultivated from mere smugness into absolute British superiority.

Kitchener was a great military hero, subduing the heathens in Sudan and keeping order in Warnie's beloved India. So Warnie had decided to make the army a career. There was only one way to launch a successful career in the army: One had to graduate from Sandhurst, England's great military academy. First things first, however; one had to pass a very difficult entrance examination to gain the privilege of attending Sandhurst.

"I'll prepare myself most diligently," Warnie boasted.

"What nonsense! Old Kirk will prepare you for the exam right proper," Albert announced, referring to his own tutor, W. T. Kirkpatrick, who lived in Great Bookham, south of London.

Jack's great change came when he moved on to Malvern School. How he had anticipated it! During frequent visits at Malvern School, he, along with the other Cherbourg boys, had been entranced at listening to the older boys. They represented the next necessary step to world power and glory. Warnie, an enthusiastic competitor at sports, had stood out there, so Jack had been treated with respect on his visits.

But now Warnie was gone. From Jack's first day, Malvern was misery and torment. Jack had no quality of his own that the older boys respected. He was not only no good at sports, he was a coward who avoided them. Neither was he particularly good-looking; in fact, he looked either hangdog or downright insolent. Furthermore, his personality was a pitiful sham; he was only a mimic. His chance to eventually become a "Blood," a member of the ruling class of students, was nonexistent. Beyond the verbal abuse were floggings. Jack himself was flogged for missing an event because a Blood had lied to him. And then there was the fact that younger boys were in constant servitude to the Bloods.

The humiliation was eased for Jack by the school library and one teacher. Younger boys were safe from Bloods only in the library. So Jack found both a refuge and an opportunity to indulge his voracious reading habits there. Who knows how many hundreds of books he had read by the age of fifteen? And he knew, if no one else did, that he retained what he read: word for word.

The teacher who inspired him was nicknamed Smewgy. Smewgy taught classics and English. He could read poetry with the subtlety of a Shakespearean actor. And more, he knew his subjects. He was neither familiar nor unfriendly. He quipped no cheap humor, only pungent comments.

The return home for winter vacation break yielded no relief for Jack. Little Lea became its own battleground. Jack's descriptions of Malvern's horrors and his pleas for Albert to remove him roused Warnie to defend his alma mater. For the first time, the brothers were really hostile to each other. Aside from the fraternal strife, Albert was haranguing Warnie.

"Old Kirk has written me that you are almost hopeless as a pupil, Warren."

"Perhaps I know a bit more than the old boy realizes," retorted Warnie defiantly.

"What nonsense!" ranted Albert.

Normally Jack could not have been whipped into visiting a neighbor, Arthur Greeves, who was Warnie's age, but now Arthur was sick and Jack was glad for any excuse to get out of Little Lea for a while. Arthur had tried to make friends in the past, but the brothers would allow no one inside their circle. Now as Jack stood by Arthur's bedside just enjoying being away from Little Lea, he spotted on the nightstand a book he had just read himself. *Myths of the Norseman* was the epitome of Northernness!

Soon they were sharing exact experiences of longing and indescribable stabs of joy. Their mutual love of Northernness seemed too good to be true. Arthur even loved books as much as Jack. Not just their substance, but their binding, their print, their page margins, their paper weight, their totality! Jack had found a soul mate. Jack and Arthur planned to write each other. Sharing their Northernness and love of books would make Malvern tolerable for Jack.

Almost miraculously, the strife among the Lewises that had ushered in the new year of 1914 was virtually forgotten by the end of January. Besides being buoyed by shared joys with his newfound friend, Arthur, Jack was elated by Albert's promise that he would not only take him out of Malvern but would send him to W. T. Kirkpatrick to be privately tutored.

Perhaps the most incredible development was Warnie's superior performance on the Sandhurst entrance exam. Albert was openly jubilant. "Warnie, you've placed twenty-first out of over two hundred candidates. You've confounded me and Old Kirk. You're being accepted as one of twenty-five 'prize cadets'!"

Jack survived the few remaining months of Malvern by indulging his Northernness. Inspired by Norse mythology, he wrote a play in classical Greek poetry that he titled *Loki Bound*. Jack, more and more sure his first calling was poetry, began to collect his lyrical poems in a volume he called *Metrical Meditations of a Cod*. In August of 1914, when the Great War broke out in Europe, Warnie's honored status at Sandhurst turned into what seemed to Albert a death sentence. Warnie was going to be rushed through training and sent to France to fight the Germans.

Jack left for Great Bookham, the village in Surrey, south of London, where he would live with his tutor, W. T. Kirkpatrick. Warnie had told Jack that Surrey was developed and populated, but from the train Jack saw only raw creeks and woods thick enough to be called a forest.

W. T. Kirkpatrick, white-haired and mustached, met him at the station. The older man was very tall and so thin that even his face seemed exposed muscles. His grip confirmed his wiry nature. He was every inch Old Kirk.

As they walked from the station, Jack said breezily, "I was surprised at the scenery. Surrey is wilder than I expected."

"What do you mean by 'wild'? And what basis do you have for your expectations? Maps? Perhaps some publications on the flora and fauna of Surrey?"

Jack stared at Kirkpatrick. The man was serious. "No, sir, I have no maps or publications. I was merely making conversation," replied Jack dubiously.

"Why would you do that?" demanded W. T. Kirkpatrick. "Tell me, what are your reasons?"

Jack fended off question after question all the way to Kirkpatrick's house. His anger cooled as he realized the incessant questions were not intended to be harassment or judgment or conversation or joking. The process was simply Kirkpatrick's way of knowing, as well as of making Jack realize he had used "wild" with no real definition in mind. Jack became very fond of W. T. Kirkpatrick, soon thinking of him as Kirk.

Kirk, as unique as Smewgy, was Jack's second great teacher. Whereas Smewgy's strength was in grammar and rhetoric, Kirk's strength was in dialectics, or discovering the truth through questioning dialogue. Jack guarded every statement now. He could have withdrawn, but he did not. Kirk was too sincere and too kind for Jack to respond in such a manner. Jack, an atheist now himself, was not bothered at all to find out Kirk was an atheist. Kirk was the only kind of atheist who mattered. He had reasoned it out, looking at every side of the cosmic issue.

Oddly, Kirk honored the Lord's Day and started Jack on Homer the next day. He simply read a few opening lines out of the *Iliad* and left Jack on his own. Jack floundered at first but quickly began to crave such independence. After a few days, he felt he was in paradise. He ate breakfast, prepared by kind Mrs. Kirkpatrick, at eight o'clock, then was at his desk at nine fifteen, studying or writing until one o'clock with a small tea break at eleven. After lunch he took a bracing walk. At four o'clock he returned for afternoon tea, then studied at his desk until seven. After dinner was time for discussions with Kirk or light reading or writing letters. At eleven o'clock he was in bed. Bed was delicious. The volume of work he was doing was astonishing. He had never been happier.

When Warnie got a leave from the Great War in France in early 1915, he stopped by Surrey to join Jack on a trip home to Little Lea. Albert looked at both sons differently now. Warnie was a grown man of almost twenty, a combat veteran. And Albert looked at sixteen-year-old Jack differently. Was it pride? Or was it disappointment?

"Did Kirk give you a report on me?" Jack asked him.

"So he did," revealed Albert. "Says you have mature and original literary judgment. Says you know first-rate work unerringly and can discern why it is first-rate."

So just as Albert and Warnie had focused on Sandhurst for a military career, now Albert and Jack began to consider the great choice any serious English scholar had to make: Oxford University or Cambridge University. Because Jack disliked science and mathematics, Cambridge, considered more in league with hard-boiled science than Oxford, was eliminated. From then on, Kirk was to prepare Jack with the eventual goal of passing the entrance exams at Oxford.

By no means did Jack abandon Arthur or his love of books. To Arthur he poured out his happiness over finding George MacDonald. Another author to add to their circle! Not since *The Well at the World's End* by William Morris had Jack enjoyed a book so much. He was sure once Arthur followed the hero Anodos of MacDonald's *Phantastes* along the little stream to the fairy wood like he had, Arthur would agree MacDonald was superb.

Life was wonderful for Jack. Every waking hour was filled with reading and writing, but finally came the time for accounting. In December he took the entrance examination at Oxford. Although the great, spired university was deep in the grip of winter and half shut down by the war, the exam was administered for several days in the Hall of Oriel College. The Hall, with its hammer-beam roof, was so cold Jack never removed his overcoat or his left glove.

Afterward he told Kirk, "There were no questions on the Latin and Greek authors I know best. I probably did fine on a question about Samuel Johnson, but I must admit I was stymied by a question on an esoteric poem by the German author Goethe."

"Is that so?" queried Kirk, pale as a ghost.

When Jack arrived at Little Lea on winter break, he found that Kirk had written Albert that he was beside himself with worry because Jack had probably failed. Albert was very depressed. Not even Jack's reminders of how pessimistic Kirk had been about Warnie's chances with the Sandhurst exam could cheer Albert up. The house seemed like a great empty barn now with only Albert, a housekeeper, and an aloof new dog, Tim. Albert waited with dread for the letter from Oxford. On December 13, it came.

Jack opened the letter, then looked at Albert with his best deadpan face. "It seems I've received a scholarship to University College at Oxford University."

Inside, Jack was rapturous. Although Percy Shelley had studied at "Univ" until they had thrown him out for being an atheist, they were more tolerant now to atheistic poets—like Jack. In April 1917, Jack began his studies at Oxford in spite of failing an additional test, called "Responsions," because of his inept mathematics. England was in no mood to quibble. Jack could take the test again—after the war. One month later he began officer training.

Since his mother had died in 1908, Jack's life had been peak and valley. The misery of Wynyard. The joy of Cherbourg. The misery of Malvern. The joy of studying with Kirk. And now this ultimate misery, this abomination: war.

"Lieutenant Lewis?"

"Yes, sir!" Jack snapped to attention. To see the major in the front trench was rare.

The major took him aside. "Bit of news, Lewis. Jerries have broken through our front lines to the north. Good old Somerset has to hit them from the side. Round up your men. Say good-bye to the trenches."

The bell tolled for him at last. Death.

FOUR

The Somerset Light Infantry wormed its way back several miles through the communication trenches. Jack learned the German Sixth Army had overrun the Portuguese troops to the north. The only good news was that there was no mustard gas. The Germans weren't about to saturate an area with gas that they expected to occupy themselves in a few hours. If there was a sudden onset of cold weather, the garlicky-smelling mustard gas could linger for days. No, the Germans had simply crushed the Portuguese with artillery, trench mortars, hand grenades, machine guns, and tanks.

The Somerset, weighed down with supplies, waited for dusk before leaving the rear trenches. Walking across open ground, the men felt strangely naked. For weeks in the trenches, Jack had learned to ignore the brilliant flares called Very lights. Now he was acutely aware of them again. They lit up the sky many miles to the north where the Germans were busy killing.

As dawn neared they found some rear trenches and slept. At dusk they ate and marched again. In the distance, artillery shells screamed. Presumably, the shells were flying east as well as west. Occasionally Jack heard the *knock-knock-knock* of machine-gun fire. Minutes before dawn he smelled smoke.

Jack learned that the barges in the La Bassee Canal had been set afire on the orders of some jittery British general to prevent the Germans from using them. The Germans, however, had not gotten that far. If war weren't so hideous, thought Jack, it might be amusing at times. Incredibly, the bridge across the canal had been left standing.

Dawn revealed hedges all over the countryside. The Somerset began scraping shallow holes as close as possible to the hedges. The holes would be just deep enough to keep the men's noses below shrapnel from exploding shells. The men began to grumble as they chopped through hedge roots, then discovered the ground was sticky clay only six inches below loamy soil. So they dug farther down into the muck, then covered the mess with topsoil so the clay would not stick to their clothing and gear. In full light, Jack looked around at the landscape. Cottages, gardens, and hedges. Even trees. This part of France wasn't like no-man's-land.

They arose that evening to eat tins of pork and beans and bully beef. Hardtack and plum jam did not compensate for the huge containers of hot stew they had downed in the trenches. Some soldiers of the Somerset were now assigned positions and stayed as the rest moved on to the north. Jack's battalion had the northernmost position.

Out of his battalion, Jack's platoon was nearly the last to be stationed to the north. He was on a rise called Mount Berenchon, near the village of Lillers. He and his platoon were a good twenty or so miles from where they had left the front lines.

At dawn on April 15, 1918, Jack could see the war right in front of him. Planes flimsy as dragonflies, scouting armies, and occasionally dropping bombs. Tanks belching smoke. Shell bursts spraying dirt. He was grateful that his platoon was well behind the fighting. No trench mortars this far back. How he hated that Roman candle *poof!* of the mortars! Then the shell dropped right into a man's funk hole. And the grenades, the potato mashers. They made no sound at all until they exploded. If one hit a man, he never heard anything. It was too late. His life ended on a heartbeat.

"The krauts are a hundred deep," estimated Sergeant Ayres, who now stood up.

Jack stood up, too. Yes, Ayres was right. The German forces stretched to the horizon. Several divisions must have massed against the First British Army between Bethune and Armentieres. The Germans were getting closer, too. Jack could actually watch them. The gallant men of Somerset were going to be annihilated.

"What was that?" someone screamed.

Jack's mind was spinning. Was he lying on his back? He wasn't sure. He couldn't see anything. He had been hit, probably. He didn't seem to be breathing, but he could hear voices. He had to be alive. No, he wasn't breathing. He was alive but dying. His thoughts were dying embers. He felt nothing. No regret. No sorrow. Nothing. It was over.

Or was he dreaming? The sounds of war still popped and cracked. His knees and palms hurt from sharp stones. Somehow he was on his hands and knees. His left arm hurt. Chest, too. He began crawling. Perhaps he was not dead. He was alive. But was he dying? Was he one of those poor crushed men who crawl about for a while like a smashed roach? Was this the last grim joke of a godless universe? He got to crawl like a stepped-on insect for a while, then die. Sharp pain stabbed him as he collapsed.

What seemed ages later, Jack heard muted voices, but he felt nothing. Saw nothing. So something was beyond death after all. Something dark and muted and slightly insane. It was the "dreary miasma" of the pagan hell, the Sheol of the Jews. The soul wandered in a stupor for eternity. Was this the edict of a merciless God?

"It's dressed, doctor," announced a woman's voice.

Was Jack alive? He tried to open his eyes. Yes, he saw light!

"Can you hear me, Lieutenant?" prodded the woman's voice. "You got a blighty."

A blighty! Jack's mind grappled with the information. A bad wound but not a fatal one. Bad enough to get a man sent to the hospital for a while. Maybe bad enough to get him sent back to England! Jack felt his heart thumping with joy.

"You're at Liverpool Merchants Mobile Hospital in Etaples, Lieutenant," supplied the voice.

Etaples. That was on the coast of France. How long had he been unconscious? Sometime later, when his sight returned, he floated in a sea of white. Fans were above on a high ceiling. Beds stretched as far as he could see. And in the beds were bandage-wrapped men. "What day is it?" Jack asked the nurse who finally appeared. When he had asked the men around him, he had gotten no answer. Apparently they were unconscious.

"April 16, Lieutenant."

"Just one day?"

She looked at his chart. "Yes, sir. You were wounded yesterday."

"What about the others? Sergeant Ayres and Laurence Johnson and. . ."

"I don't know, sir. I only see the soldiers who are brought here. I never know anything about the battlefield. I'm very sorry."

"You're very lucky," Jack corrected, nodding.

The next day Jack wrote a letter to his father. Writing was difficult both because he was sore and heavily bandaged and because of its recipient. Every word had to be weighed with careful consideration. If Jack minimized his wounds, Poodaytabird might be frantic because they were not bad enough to get him sent home. If he exaggerated the wounds, however, Poodaytabird might be frantic with worry. Now that Jack thought about it, he became rather angry. He had wired his father to visit him in Bristol before he was shipped out to France, and his father had not understood his wire at all. Either that or his father was still angry because Jack had spent most of his last leave with Paddy Moore in Bristol. Actually, Jack didn't know much about his wounds, only that his left arm was bandaged against his side and his left hand hurt. Finally deciding that no matter what he wrote, his father would make a thorough mess of it, he wrote that he had a flesh wound in his left arm.

That day Jack finally saw a doctor. "Do I have a blighty or not?" he asked bluntly.

"Yes, Lieutenant. You do indeed. You have shrapnel in your hand. That is minor. You have a tiny bit behind the knee in your left leg. That is minor. You have a chunk or two that went in under your left armpit. They are somewhere in your chest. They are not minor."

Not until a soldier came in who was wounded the day after Jack was did Jack find out how terribly the battalion had been mauled by the Germans. The shell that had hit Jack had been a fluke, maybe from their own artillery. Sergeant Ayres was dead, perhaps hit by the same shell that had felled Jack.

Laurence Johnson was dead, too. After Jack heard that, he closed his mind and stopped listening. Once again he had lost those who had meant the most to him. He couldn't bring himself to ask about Thorne.

He wrote letters to the living to take his mind off the dead. He read Anthony Trollope and Sir Walter Scott. He wrote poetry about Oxford, the war, and "spirit."

Jack rather shocked himself by what he had written. Jack's tiny chip of some unthinking universal spirit had grown! He argued with himself until he beat down his feeling of a supreme thinking being.

Progress in Jack's first days was very slow. Just being able to sleep on his right side after sleeping on his back for a month seemed a great triumph.

Near the end of May, the hospital was shelled. Jack, in bed and bandaged as tight as a repulsive pupa in a cocoon, was more terrified now than he had been in the trenches. Oh, would the grim ironies ever end?

Days later Jack was transported across the English Channel to England. On the ship Jack thrilled to the salt air and chopping sea. Later, from the window of the train, England was a feast. After the drab, cratered no-man's-land and the blanched hospital, England glowed a bright jolly green he had never seen before. Streams sparkled like blue diamonds. Hedges glinted silver. Distant fields of buttercups shimmered as plains of pure gold.

His hospital in London was a real palace: Endsleigh Palace in Endsleigh Gardens. The rooms were private and the beds large. Jack, now sitting up and feeling very fortunate, was exchanging letters with Arthur and admitting that the thrills he had felt from otherness were indeed contacts with some spirit world. Far from being the spirit realm of some great benevolent creator of the material world, however, the spirit world he imagined was the sworn enemy of the material world.

Jack asked Arthur to return a manuscript with some of Jack's early poems. He was planning to assemble a book of his poems and submit it for publication. He had been writing poetry all along. It seemed his calling. What wasn't on paper was in his head. His theme was that nature was wholly diabolical. If God existed at all, He was outside the cosmos and even disapproved of it. The obvious conclusion was that nature was a creation of a very powerful devil. Men had to struggle against the devil, unaided by an indifferent God. The slaughter of war only strengthened Jack's convictions. He wasn't going to try to publish some monotonous manuscript all in one kind of meter either. His theme would be offered in an interesting variety of meters.

The London bookshops accelerated Jack's recovery. By mid-June he was walking short distances. How else could he get to the books? He bought and read as many books as he could afford. He also visited Kirk one Sunday in Great Bookham, surprising the old man in his garden among the cabbages.

Although Kirk greeted him warmly, Jack was very pleased he received no special treatment.

But time began to wear Jack down. He wasn't quite as hale and hearty as he pretended. He wished he could see Warnie or Arthur or even his father. He had been on the mend for over two months and in London nearly one month now, but still his father had not visited him. Jack was surprised at how much that hurt. Toward the end of one letter to his father he poured out his pain:

> *I know that you will come and see me. . . . I was never before so eager to cling to every bit of our old home life and to see you. I know I have often been far from what I should be in my relation to you and have undervalued (your) affection and generosity. . . . But, please God, I shall do better in the future. Come and see me, I am homesick, that is the long and short of it.[1]*

Still Albert did not come!

A letter from Arthur hinted that Albert was drinking heavily. Perhaps he was. Two sons in France in a war that was killing men by the millions could do that to a man who lived alone and brooded, and Albert was phobic anyway about things not in his routine. He had never been able to stay with Flora and the boys in the summers at the seashore. Within minutes he would be pulling out his pocket watch, nerves a-jangle, looking like he was on the verge of hysteria.

One person who did seem to care enough about Jack to visit him without fail in London was Paddy Moore's mother. Paddy was dead. All five of the boys who had visited Mrs. Moore in the Oxford officer training days were dead—except Jack.

Jack, finally ready for the next step in rehabilitation, was scheduled to be moved to a convalescent home. After requesting one in Ireland and being told they were few in number and already crowded, he asked for one where he knew he would have at least one faithful friend. Thus, in July he was convalescing in Bristol, the city where Mrs. Moore lived.

The "convalescent home" was a thirteenth-century castle, much altered over hundreds of years. Wooded surroundings offered solitary walks interrupted occasionally by a bolting deer. Thankfully, Jack enjoyed the walks very much now, for, much to his disappointment, the library in the castle was kept locked. Other convalescing soldiers gave Jack ample evidence, however, for that restriction. The men seemed ignorant idlers, playing billiards and killing time. Jack found a small writing room where he could escape the whistling and chatter to read and write. He still corresponded with his father, inviting him to visit. Albert still remained friendly and caring in his letters but would not visit. Jack withdrew more and more from him. Jack's only constant visitor was Mrs. Moore.

One day Jack was more pleased than ever with her visit. "Why, it's *The Princess and the Goblin* by George MacDonald! One of his Curdie books."

"Maureen reads many fairy tales."

"Oh, this is of most excellent taste! It will lead the child into poetry and fantasy, not the cheap, twaddling novels of so many modern readers."

Jack found this Curdie story a delight. It was the best kind of fantasy, a story pulled along by the thrill of an adventure, yet bursting with profound meanings. In one part, the sleeping boy Curdie dreams he is waking up, but waking up is only a dream. To Jack this meant a person on a spiritual journey could imagine he had transformed himself, yet be merely indulging in the pleasure of the idea of changing and not changing at all. The real work remained to be done.

"The significance of that is terrifying," he admitted to himself, yet he craved the writings of MacDonald. To think that Mrs. Moore should bring him such pleasure. How his spirits would collapse without her!

Mrs. Janie Moore appeared too young to be the mother of Paddy. A solidly built blond with smooth milky skin, her strong jaw was softened by lively eyes and bubbling energy. Her kindness was overwhelming yet not suffocating. When Jack let the war and his father's inexplicable neglect poison his thoughts, she was the perfect antidote. To think Jack had promised Paddy to look after his mother; in fact, she looked after Jack.

FIVE

Jack was proud of Mrs. Janie Moore. She had weathered a very trying life yet never surrendered her generosity and good cheer. Her father, the Reverend William Askins, was a very hard man. Her sister, Edie, and her brother, Rob, both of whom lived in Bristol, too, confirmed that. Janie had helped raise the children until her own marriage. She was a prize: industrious, reliable, beautiful. She had married "well." Mr. Courtenay Moore was not only an engineer, but also a gentleman related to Lord Drogheda, a peerage from King Charles the Second. Yet Courtenay Moore was a brute. After Maureen was born, Mrs. Moore summoned the courage to take the two children and leave her husband. Of course, divorce in Ireland was impossible.

Mrs. Moore's greatest quality was hospitality. Jack, who tried to exclude uninteresting people from his circle, knew somehow Mrs. Moore was much more correct to include one and all. She was his mentor in all social things, including religion. In spite of being the daughter of a clergyman, she was very practical about religion. Yes, religion was desirable—how else could society keep some men from behaving like beasts?—but it should not be allowed to interfere with modern thinking.

Jack continued to compile his poetry. He now had the book organized into three parts: "The Prison House," "Hesitation," and "Escape." He was pragmatic, stating ahead of time that he would send it to all the large publishers. Mrs. Moore cheered him on. Even if all the publishers rejected his proposal, he would at least have gained some professional critiques of his poems and have them nicely typewritten and preserved. As August 1918 approached, no publisher had accepted his book proposal, now titled *Spirits in Prison: A Cycle of Lyrical Poems,* but he had a larger problem.

"August is the month I'm rumored to return to France, Mother," he confided to Mrs. Moore.

"But your shortness of breath from the shrapnel. . . Surely they can't send you back just yet."

"You don't know as I do how illogical the army is," he protested.

Yet when Mrs. Moore next came to visit him, Jack cried, "You were right all along!"

The doctors had pronounced him not ready to return to the fighting yet. Now he had only his *Spirits in Prison* to fret over. He had written Arthur that he was inserting new pieces and deleting old ones, so much so that he had finally begun to doubt his judgment. Perhaps he had tinkered with it too much. And then to his amazement the manuscript was accepted by William Heinemann in

London. So alienated was Jack from his father, that only now—and for the first time—did he write him about the book of poetry. Homebound Albert answered enthusiastically, helpfully pointing out that *Spirits in Prison* was a title already in use. Jack duly decided to change the title to *Spirits in Bondage*. When Albert quoted scripture and invoked Christ's blessing, however, Jack was repulsed. The constant invitations to his father to come and visit had humiliated Jack. No excuse he could think of was sufficient for a delay of four months. As a result, his requests for Albert to visit, heartfelt in May, turned sarcastic by September.

Jack, citing the army as his reason for using a pen name, had his book published under the name "Clive Hamilton" to honor the memory of his mother. When he went back to his regiment and the day to return was getting closer, he did not want to be known as "that starry-eyed poet" by every ignorant lout that hated the finer things. In October, he was posted to a depot at Eastbourne in Sussex. Nightmares of war blighted his sleep again.

Eastbourne was on the coast directly across the channel from France. "It doesn't take a genius to figure out where I will be moved next," he fretted to Mrs. Moore.

Although he had no enthusiasm to write his father, he wrote nonetheless, telling himself it was one way to keep a diary—his father saved everything in that barn of a house. Boldly he wrote his father that Mrs. Moore and her daughter Maureen were there to comfort him. What cad could possibly think anything was uncouth in such an arrangement? Would a lady do anything improper in the company of her daughter? Mrs. Moore wrote his father, too, explaining the vows Jack and Paddy had exchanged before leaving for France. Jack was now her son, too.

About nine o'clock in the evening of November 10, 1918, every siren in Eastbourne screamed. Searchlights swept the sky. Officers ran into the parade ground and shot off Very guns, piercing the night sky with fiery flares.

"The war is over!" chorused hundreds of voices.

That Christmas the three Lewis men were together again at Little Lea. Each one seemed shocked at the sight of the other two. Warnie was shiny-faced from gin and going plump; Albert was pasty-faced and still erect at fifty-six, though it seemed only an effort to support his protruding stomach; and twenty-year-old Jack was told in blunt, worried tones that he was baggy-eyed and pencil thin. Lapsing into morose silences, Jack knew now Little Lea was behind him. Warnie, too, was remote. He would return to France and await orders.

By January 13, 1919, Jack was back in Univ College in the golden-spired haven of Oxford University, but this time he was not alone. Mrs. Moore rented a house for Maureen and herself at 28 Warneford Road. The owner,

Miss Featherstone, remained living in one small room. The old lady walked to morning prayers no matter how foul the weather and insisted on serving Mrs. Moore tea when she returned. A Christian actually trying to live the gospel always deeply impressed Jack, but he assured himself it was only because he despised hypocrisy.

Jack quickly got in the routine of studying all morning, bicycling the two miles from Oxford to take lunch with Mrs. Moore, and then staying until late in the evening. At Mrs. Moore's insistence, most of his time there was spent studying. Then he returned to his rooms at Univ. As he lay in bed, he heard chimes striking midnight and felt blessed. He would live and die for Oxford: the ubiquitous yellow-gray stone, the cozy bookshops, the great vaulted halls, the unparalleled libraries, the poplars, the sleepy rivers. It seemed as safe and pure as Switzerland.

Postwar college life, however, was different. When he had departed for officer training, less than ten undergraduates had been in his college. Now Univ consisted of twenty-eight students and was steadily building up to full strength. Only a few older alumni had survived the war to pass on Univ traditions to the newcomers. As a result of a coal shortage, only one lecture room, the library, and the Junior Common Room were cozy warm. Sometime in the future the undergraduates would once again be served breakfast and lunch in their rooms, but for now they were served all meals in the Hall.

Jack was relieved to learn of one unexpected benefit of the war: The requirement to pass Responsions was waived for all veterans. Now he would never have to retake it. Other hurdles loomed, however, his next one being Honor Mods. He would be examined on Greek and Latin literature in his particular specialty: classics. If he passed, his degree would be graded "First," "Second," or "Third." With the rigorous preparation of Kirk behind him, Jack thought he could pass it right away.

"Any future as a scholar requires a 'First,'" advised his tutor, Arthur Poynton, "and I don't believe you could get a 'First' just yet."

Poynton was a Fellow of about fifty, distinguished in the classics, so Jack gladly took his advice. What was the hurry? Deferment and knowing he was enhancing already more than adequate knowledge certainly made studying less stressful. Beyond Honor Mods, he would be studying ancient history and philosophy in the classics for the second academic hurdle, "Greats." There, too, he determined to achieve a First.

His goal was nothing less than getting a fellowship and becoming an Oxford don.

As was the Oxford tradition, Jack met with Poynton only once a week for an hour. There he discussed what he had read. Actual attendance at the college was not heavy either. During the entire year the student had to be in residence only during three eight-week terms: the fall term, Michaelmas; the winter term, Lent; and the spring term, Easter. Jack was gratified to realize, however, that the serious students usually studied there during the so-called vacations, too. Good. He would now have no reason to return to Little Lea and be with his father. Correspondence with him, which Jack did not mind, would be sufficient; he would add to his "diary" and also fulfill the sense of duty he felt because he received support from his father.

In March of 1919, *Spirits in Bondage* was published by Heinemann. Reviews by newspapers were complimentary. The most important review in Jack's mind was the literary supplement of the *London Times*, known in his intellectual circles as the "TLS." It deemed his poetry "graceful and polished." His father's and Warnie's opinions of the book were remarkable in their breadth. Warnie liked the book, but he feared Jack was foolish to blatantly embrace atheism. To get ahead in England, a man had to believe in God and the king. On the other hand, father Albert had faint praise for the book but did not believe Jack was an atheist at all. Jack was some kind of dualist. Sales of the book were anemic, but how many books of poetry sell well? At least the book gave Jack some recognition at Oxford. Some jokingly called him the "famous Lewis." To many others, he was the "mysterious Lewis." Who else bicycled off every day, disappearing for hours? Jack had to admit his passion for compartmentalizing his interests. Only Arthur and Mrs. Moore were familiar with Jack's other worlds.

One of those rare occasions transpired in June of 1919 when Arthur visited Oxford. Since Arthur already knew much about Mrs. Moore, Jack took him straight to her, and she treated him like a son, too.

Jack remembered old letters to Arthur that had hinted that more than a mother-son relationship had developed between Mrs. Moore and himself. Observing Arthur, he realized he wouldn't have to explain that fabrication; Arthur was figuring it out. Now that Jack thought about the intimation, he realized the lie probably had made Arthur react the wrong way with his father, thus considerably contributing to the worsening relationship with his father.

In spite of Jack's involved domestic life, he certainly did not neglect Oxford. He accepted an invitation to join a literary club called the "Martlets." They invited only a dozen or so undergraduates. The Martlets introduced Jack to the kind of lofty world Oxford could be. They were talking about visiting John Masefield or William Butler Yeats! Masefield's strong, narrative poetry was very popular. Talk of his becoming England's poet laureate buzzed. Jack, on the other hand, much preferred Yeats. He adored Yeats's lyrical poetry based on pagan Celtic mythology.

Shortly, Jack met Leo Baker, Owen Barfield, and Cecil Harwood. All three men had started at Wadham College the fall term of 1919. Their razor-sharp dialectics, as well as their decency and honesty, reminded Jack of Laurence Johnson. Kirk would have approved of them. Jack felt he was bettering himself just being in the company of such gentlemen. Not that they were in any way sissified. The feisty, chisel-jawed, wild-haired Barfield and Jack were at loggerheads immediately, and they were well matched.

Nonetheless, Barfield became Jack's second great friend; Arthur was the first. Arthur, however, was Jack's alter ego, agreeing with Jack in almost everything. He deviated from Jack at first only in liking very much everything—even the homely. Eventually, Jack had come to Arthur's viewpoint, reading novels that he never would have read otherwise, and enjoying the countryside he once would have dismissed with a glance. Barfield, by contrast, was Jack's negative image. If Jack said white, Barfield said black. If Jack said black, Barfield said white. Like Arthur, Barfield shared all of Jack's chief interests, but his conclusions were invariably and unmitigatedly opposite of Jack's. Amazingly, instead of repulsing each other, they eagerly anticipated their next argument!

To Jack, acceptable companions had to defend their opinions not only with logic, but also with feeling. Yet brilliant, passionate dialectics was not enough; any who displayed flippancy or cynicism were disqualified. Those who advanced only anecdotes or mere disjointed facts were held in lowest regard. Few people met his stringent standards.

Oxford provided a delightful place for debates between Jack and the handful who met his standards. In the winter they gathered around fireplaces. In all weather they took long walks on tree-lined paths and longer walks into the surrounding hills and vales. Walks were a way of life with Oxford gentlemen, either in solitude or in camaraderie. And for a man like Jack, who despised sports, his walks kept him fit. In warm weather, the coterie canoed or swam in the Cherwell River. Along the river's most secluded area, Parson's Pleasure, they sunbathed and swam.

Jack was no longer willing to return to Little Lea unless Warnie was present to provide some cushion against Albert's prying. Albert remained suspicious of Jack's alliance with Mrs. Moore and obsessed by what it might mean. Jack resented his father more and more. Gentlemen simply did not pry into the private affairs of other men. Any attempt by another undergraduate to pry, subtly or otherwise, could so effectively turn Jack from a congenial companion into a shockingly angry antagonist that the trespasser never repeated the offense.

Pasley's remark about Lewis being an intimidating "brain" carried only half the truth. The other half was the overwhelming force of Jack's liberated intellect. The reticent student had clearly evolved into a formidable one. He was definitely the product of Kirk. The most casual remark was taken as a summons to debate.

Ironically, his forceful intellect had been emancipated by the company of

Mrs. Moore, who made him feel older and more sociable, and the company of men like Barfield, who made him feel like he was a good man, too—as good as any. Now he was completely at ease with other undergraduates, free to unleash the relentless dialectics he had learned from Kirk.

Opponents who could withstand Jack's onslaught for a while were mentally graded by him as As, Bs, and Cs. (Owen Barfield was at the top of a handful of As.) Jack had no sympathy, however, for the poor souls who could not defend their assertions. These, he secretly dismissed as dolts.

By April 1920, Jack had taken a First in his Honor Mods, confirming his high standing among undergraduates. Only a very few received Firsts. He moved on to prepare for Greats, an effort that entailed mastering Greek and Latin histories as well as philosophy.

He also moved in another direction. A student was allowed to live off campus after two terms. Many nights now he would not return to his rooms at Univ at all, choosing rather to stay in his own small bedroom in the house of Mrs. Moore at 28 Warneford Road. This arrangement was not a secret from his closest friends, for Barfield, Baker, and Harwood frequented the home for tea or late evening discussions. Mrs. Moore tactfully avoided the company, as was the custom of women when men smoked pipes and chatted around a fireplace. Jack made no attempt to deceive his friends or to explain his relationship with her. Some winter evenings he would rise during a conversation and merely say, "I must fill Mother's hot water bottles." He was sure they had come to understand that Mrs. Moore was the closest thing he had to a mother and that he was the closest thing she had to a son.

SIX

Jack received a terse telegram from his father. GOOD HEAVENS, OLD KIRK DIED.

Smewgy had died during the influenza epidemic of 1918. Now Jack's second great mentor had died. In his head, Jack knew that Kirk would be the first to warn him not to be sentimental, but in his heart, Jack knew his intellectual weapons had been honed razor-sharp by the taskmaster Kirk. Who had made it possible for Jack to enter Oxford? Kirk. Who had taught Jack how to be unrelenting in his clarity of thought? Kirk. Who had taught him to be rigidly honest in his thought? Kirk. And what fine memories he cherished of the old man: his dry humor, his imperturbable good temper, his fiery energy! Few men measured up to Kirk.

"How he loved virtue," Jack fondly remembered, "and he was a man who did not accept God."

Paradoxically, many of Jack's friends embraced Christianity or, at the very least, theism, albeit Barfield and Harwood now embraced the anthroposophy of Rudolph Steiner, the Austrian scientist and philosopher. Steiner focused on the human being, not God. Man's spiritual capacity had been quelled by devotion to materialism, but the spiritual world was accessible to the properly developed intellect. To Jack, Steiner seemed no more than a Gnostic, an ancient sect of vain mystics. "Anthroposophy is somewhere between self-worship and irrational mumbo-jumbo," he needled Barfield.

Later that spring of 1921, Jack's composition on "Optimism" won the vice chancellor's prize for best English essay. In June, Oxford held its graduation ceremony called "Encaenia," which was attended by all the grandees. Participants wore not only full evening dress but caps and gowns of scarlet and blue and silver. The highlight of Encaenia this year was bestowing an honorary degree on the great French leader Clemenceau. As part of the ceremony, student prizewinners were to read two minutes of their winning essays. Jack's ego withered as he observed other prizewinners speak.

Arthur Poynton, Jack's tutor, was delighted at Jack's success, since it was partly his, too. Jack was surprised, though, by the reaction of his fellow undergraduates. Men he considered louts—defined by him as ignorant brutes who had too much money, excelled at sports, and unwittingly blocked passageways with their beefy bodies—congratulated him. There it was again. That civility that some possessed. Jack would never have congratulated them on a sports accomplishment. Abruptly Jack considered, *Perhaps I am the lout!*

One day in his Oxford rooms Jack was shocked by his mail. Albert, Uncle

Augustus Hamilton, and his wife, Aunt Annie, would rent a car in Wales and tour England.

Since Jack kept his room at Mrs. Moore's, he had to make a choice now either to reveal the truth or concoct an elaborate lie. A small lie wouldn't suffice. With a sinking heart, Jack admitted that his father wouldn't be the only one disappointed in him. Aunt Annie was his favorite aunt, the aunt who had always been the comforter at Little Lea after his mother had died. She was the one who had packed his clothes for school and given him that soft, sweet-smelling hug good-bye. She had been the closest thing he'd had for a mother until Mrs. Moore had come along. How disappointed Aunt Annie would be! No explanation about Mrs. Moore would satisfy her. A substitute for her dear sister-in-law Flora? Indeed!

So Jack chose to lie. He wrote his father, saying he had been moved out of the college and was sharing an apartment with Rodney Pasley. He suggested his father and uncle and aunt make the quickest stop possible in Oxford because Rodney was studying day and night for exams. A much better and more relaxing option would be for him to leave Oxford with them and accompany them on part of the tour, he suggested. Albert agreed.

What was it that made Jack so duplicitous? Once again it seemed to be his compartmentalization. It was the remnants of childhood, the annoyance with a domineering, snoopy father. To judge from Jack's acid comments to Warnie, Albert was the most incompetent and comical of figures. In Jack's unguarded moments, though, he recognized that Albert was yet very forceful and articulate, the sire of the very forceful and articulate Jack himself. Furthermore, as the purseholder, he still dominated part of Jack's life.

Even at twenty-two, Jack felt no guilt for his deceit.

After Albert's visit, which Jack believed would be his last for many years to come, Jack became domestic, cooking, cleaning, shoveling snow, and performing all the duties of an older son. Not only was he like a son to Mrs. Moore, but he was like an older brother to Maureen, helping her with school projects in woodworking and art. She was very bright and, at times, remarkably mature and tactful, but most of the time she was an exasperating adolescent. Jack was becoming hospitable, too. As much as he owed his intellect to Smewgy and Kirk, he owed his burgeoning gift of hospitality to Mrs. Moore. The threesome began entertaining more. Mrs. Moore's physician brother, John Askins, who lived nearby in Iffley, often visited. Gradually their circle of friends widened. Finally he had his Oxford friends coming to dinner. On these occasions, the ebullient Mrs. Moore shone, as perfect a hostess as her rice pudding. Although she voiced her opinions when she was alone with Jack, she remained silent or politely agreeable during his conversations with his friends. Jack was certain his friends now understood his affection for her and figured that the presence of teenaged Maureen, astonishingly gracious and articulate, confirmed the innocence of his relationship with the Moores.

In June 1922, Jack took his Greats in Greek and Latin histories as well as philosophy. The tests lasted six days. The candidate had to write two three-hour papers each day. The topics included Roman history, Greek and Latin translations, philosophy, Plato, Aristotle, logic, general ancient history, Greek and Latin prose works, morals, and politics. Much emphasis was placed on skill in translating. Few could excel Jack at that. Years before, Kirk had told Albert that Jack was the most gifted translator he had ever known. Jack achieved Firsts again.

Many positions were now beckoning Jack. He had offers from Cornell University in America and from Reading University in England. He wanted only Oxford. Oh, he had an offer from Wadham College at Oxford, but it would require him to eventually become its law tutor. So Jack would accept none of these offers. His heart was set on a fellowship at Oxford in the classics or philosophy because a fellowship guaranteed a lifetime of fruitful work. Surely to one with his succession of Firsts, a fellowship was inevitable. Once a Fellow, he would become one of the staff, a don. But no fellowship materialized!

Poynton commiserated with Jack. "A student these days, no matter how brilliant, rarely walks right from Greats into a fellowship. Something will open up eventually. Be patient. In the meantime, take another Great. A First in English would make you very employable."

Jack was stunned. More studies? That meant he would have to ask his father for more money. And so he did:

> *If, on all this, you feel that the scheme is rather a tall order and that my education has already taken long enough, you must frankly tell me so...[on the other hand] if you think that the chance thus offered can, and ought to be taken, I shall be grateful.*[1]

Albert finally answered Jack's request for more money by suggesting other options, primarily law and business. Jack flatly averred that an academic career was his only option. Hadn't Kirk said the same thing? Since Albert revered Kirk, he eventually agreed to continue supporting Jack. He would not permit Jack to stoop to second best, even in academics. If Jack wanted Oxford, so be it.

So Jack began his career in English. He would now study the same great works he had always read for pleasure: Chaucer, Shakespeare, Spenser, and dozens more. His first project was to learn Old English in order to master *Beowulf* and smaller gems like the haunting *Dream of the Rood*. Next, for the enchanting medieval legends, he would study Middle English under C. T. Onions.

The Great in English was very demanding. His tutor was Frank Wilson, a plump man of about thirty, at Exeter College. He rather doubted that Jack could get through the Great for English in nine months as he desired, but he did not know how readily Jack picked up languages. For Kirk, he had mastered Italian in seven weeks. In no time at all, he had become adept in Old English and now was zipping through English literature, which was no less than the history of England. In general, Jack felt his old friends, Barfield and Harwood, could have thrashed the students at Exeter, but for one exception: a very forceful, brilliant classmate in a discussion class led by the scholar George Gordon. The student was Nevill Coghill.

While Coghill was not the dialectician Jack and his other friends were, he had a very powerful, artistic mind and was inclined toward the theater. *Wonder of wonders*, mused Jack, *Coghill is a Christian, too! Why are all the most brilliant students believers? Except me. . .*

Meanwhile Barfield hung around Oxford, picking up jobs editing for small magazines, in an effort to stave off the practice of law. Other friends of Jack, however, were deserting Oxford. For instance, Harwood, deep into Steiner's anthroposophy, was setting up a school. Rodney Pasley had become headmaster at a public school. Leo Baker had taken a fling at acting in the local theater groups in Oxford, then traded Oxford's limited opportunities for the actor's Mecca: London.

In August Warnie visited Jack. "I patiently await release from my 'imprisonment' in the army," he said. "I acknowledge Wordsworth my master, wanting only 'tranquillity to all things' and 'peaceful days for their own sakes, as mortal life's chief good.'"

Although Warnie now seemed peculiarly eccentric and reclusive to Jack, Warnie was not the one who had changed. Jack had changed, thanks to Mrs. Moore. As if to remind Jack how unsociable he had once been, Warnie refused to stay with them and instead chose a hotel. He also declined an invitation to tea. Then Warnie abruptly changed his mind and agreed to stay at the house.

In the days that followed, he socialized pleasantly with the Moores and several young ladies who were frequently there, including Smudge, and joined their excursions enthusiastically. Jack expected Warnie to collapse during the two weeks of rowing, walking, bicycling, and tennis playing, but he held his own. Though much heavier than before, he was more fit than he looked. Jack was very pleased with the way things worked out. To Warnie's great surprise—but not to Jack's—Mrs. Moore insisted that after Warnie left the army he had to live with them!

Domestic life continued to flourish, especially after Jack and the Moores moved into a respectable brick home in Headington, a village east of Oxford. This house earned the name Hillsboro. As if Jack didn't have enough turmoil in Oxford, Aunt Lily, his mother's older sister, came to live in a cottage in Forest Hill. Now widowed, she was somewhat overwhelming like Mrs. Moore, but in a bizarre way. In just three days, she had instigated several run-ins and had written a fiery letter to the local newspaper. Her greatest passion was for animals.

Aunt Lily was a bubbling volcano of facts, speculation, and pure blather. She liked Jack very much because, as she said, she rarely found her intellectual equal. She and Albert were not on speaking terms. As she referred to him as "ignorant Allie," Jack quietly relished her hostility toward his exasperating father.

By 1923, Jack was trying to become a completely rational man. He allowed himself to be drawn to psychology and determined to put aside the romantic myths that had attracted him so much when he was younger. As he pondered the fact that he and his talented friends, despite having amassed Firsts, were not finding positions, he suffered spells of dread. He also began doubting his own poetry. Owen Barfield had apprised him bluntly that he wrote too much and revised too little. Barfield saw clearly that Jack, capable of writing the very finest sort, wrote much that was not fine at all. "Slow down," counseled Barfield. "Revise." In his heart Jack knew Barfield, the finest mind he knew, was right; he was right about nearly everything. Yet heedlessly, Jack raced ahead with his poetry.

"*Dymer* will put an end once and for all to my shabby desire for some otherness," he reassured himself.

Dymer, his long narrative poem, would make clear that fantasizing made men weak. Men retreated within themselves. His hero in the poem was a dreamer who realized in the end that his dreams had caused chaos, and that his redemption lay only in fighting a monster that would surely kill him. Jack wrote four cantos of the poem. Free verse was the fashion, but his gadfly, Barfield, had convinced him that sometimes ancient things are superior to modern things and to think otherwise was mindless modern prejudice. So Jack wrote poetry the way he wished to read it himself. He rhymed and scanned and constructed complex stanzas.

A real-life example of the danger of fantasizing, or probing the edges of the spirit world, hit Jack right at home. The victim was none other than John "Doc" Askins, Mrs. Moore's physician brother. Doc had dabbled in theosophy, spiritualism, yoga, and every aspect of the occult. He had once seemed to Jack a living testimony that such endeavors were safe. In early 1923, however, Doc began acting peculiar and talking about death.

"If one really thought about what awaits us, he couldn't last one hour in this world," Doc agonized ominously. Jack was nonplussed. To him, Doc was "the most unoffending, gentle, and unselfish man imaginable."

Each day Doc worsened. Then suddenly he was so bad, screaming and moaning about hell, that he was moved into their Hillsboro house. Doc's wife Mary needed help with his "fits." Doc had to be watched constantly and physically restrained during his wild seizures. Since Mrs. Moore's other brother Rob, in Bristol, was also a physician, he arrived and arranged for Doc, who was a veteran, to be taken into a pension hospital. They were informed they would have to wait ten days for approval!

"Please, don't send me to hell ahead of time!" Doc would scream as they tried to subdue him. "Don't shorten my time here on earth!"

The next days were unremitting torment as Doc seemed to improve, then slip again, each time becoming more hopeless. He became so much more threatening, and his resistance was so much more violent that sleep for the others was nerve-racking.

SEVEN

The inhabitants of Hillsboro house felt like they had not slept for weeks by the time the taxi finally came to transport Doc to the hospital. He screamed, he fought, he spit, he collapsed and became rigid. But at last he was gone. He had stayed at the house fourteen days. Three weeks later he died. That such a peaceful, mild-mannered man could be so transformed into a kicking, screaming maniac and slide into hell, either self-made or real, frightened Jack into holding tight his shaky rationalism.

From childhood Jack had suffered from nightmares. Gnashing, clawing beetles had been succeeded by merciless maniacs at public school. Then for years he had relived real horrors of war. Now in his dreams he seemed to be fighting Satan and his minions. But how could a rationalist believe in the devil? Just where did these nightmares come from? Jack wailed within himself. Was there no relief from the bogies of life even in bed? Where was peace? He became quite depressed. Often he daydreamed and his thoughts were morbid.

How could anyone study successfully while such turmoil writhed inside? Yet, later in 1923, Jack triumphed with a First in his Great in English. Of all the candidates in all thirty-five colleges at Oxford, only he of Univ and Nevill Coghill of Exeter College got Firsts. Jack was confident now that he would obtain some position at Oxford. But days of expectation became weeks. Then weeks became months. Jack graded papers and tutored to earn a bit of money. Money had never been so short for him and the Moores. He tried to borrow money from Warnie but learned that in nearly ten years of military service, Warnie had saved not a penny. In fact, Warnie had wrangled a stipend from Albert!

Jack gave up smoking. The Hillsboro household gave up its maid, her household duties assumed by Jack more than anyone else. Gregarious Mrs. Moore could not help having guests as she always did, though. And what was a home without dogs and cats—five in all? Jack shrugged. He wasn't starving. Once while walking he heard himself called "Heavy Lewis." Thus, he learned his nickname among his detractors. It was certainly true. He was now as plump as Warnie had appeared to him the year before.

His misery was deepened, of all things, by a visit from Arthur. Someone had convinced Arthur to be his natural self and satisfy his desires.

Further discussions revealed that Arthur now believed in heaven but not hell. Jack was appalled at Arthur's blasé and simple-minded beliefs. How had he overlooked them before? Arthur's faults had never been more objectionable, his manners more incorrigible. After Arthur returned to Ireland, Jack could scarcely bring himself to write him anymore, partly because of Arthur's disgusting new personality and partly because he fed Jack's love for otherness. Jack was determined, since Doc's death, to purge his love for otherness.

One year after Jack finished his Great in English, he was waiting eagerly for a fellowship in philosophy at Trinity College. Meanwhile Univ offered Jack a year's position as tutor in philosophy. He would replace a fellow on sabbatical to America. What choice did Jack have? He was hanging on to Oxford by a mere thread. He wrote his father that he would give fourteen lectures next term, a total of fourteen hours, and joked that he could exhaust his total knowledge of philosophy in only five hours. His assigned subject was "The Moral Good." He had never worked harder to prepare. He pored over Hobbes, Hume, and one of his favorites, Henri Bergson. Somehow Bergson reinforced his new outlook. One must not nitpick futilely over the very idea of existing but deal realistically with the material world.

He was now a don—at least temporarily, and was required to live at Univ during the week. Thus, he stayed at Mrs. Moore's only on the weekends now. Breakfast at Oxford was served in his rooms. Besides his lectures, he gave tutorials in the morning, took lunch at Mrs. Moore's, did odd jobs around Hillsboro house, then returned to Oxford for more tutorials and dinner. Once again he dined in the great Hall, but now he dined among the dons sitting at the dais on one end. He wore a gown, something that was second nature to him after six years.

All year he applied for every opening at Oxford in both philosophy and English. One opening was at Magdalen College. He debated about applying for such a choice position because many men his senior were applying, even his old English tutor, Wilson. Eventually, Jack halfheartedly applied anyway. Soon he found out Wilson had not applied. That had been a rumor. Jack rushed to Wilson to ask him for a recommendation. Wilson apologized. Because he had heard Jack had given up English for philosophy, Wilson had glowingly recommended Nevill Coghill of Exeter, Jack's main rival in English. Jack was certain he had no chance now. Coghill was truly Jack's equal, and now he even had a recommendation from Jack's own tutor!

Then he received great news. Coghill had received a fellowship from his old college, Exeter, and had withdrawn his application for Magdalen. Wilson enthusiastically recommended Jack. Was there still a chance? When Jack was invited to a dinner in May with the other candidates, however, he botched the invitation. Jack appeared in white tie and long tails; all the others wore black ties and dinner jackets. Somehow he survived the blunder, then surprisingly learned that he was one of two candidates remaining. In a week of very gloomy weather, he became doubtful again when he saw the other candidate, who couldn't conceal his absolute conviction that he had won. Jack's hope fell further when he was summoned by the president of Magdalen College in a curt note, then kept waiting outside his office for half an hour. The future did not look promising.

But when he exited the president's office, he muttered through a relieved smile, "Thank goodness, he's just a brusque man by nature." Jack had received a five-year appointment as fellow in English at Magdalen College.

Immediately he wrote his father. A future of financial independence seemed to free Jack of his bitterness toward Albert. For years he had corresponded with duplicity. Now he truly felt grateful.

Free at last, he felt guilt. Even though his father had held the purse strings, Jack had justified his resentment because his father snooped and pried. Now Jack realized his resentment had been much more. He resented Albert's bluster and Albert's insight. He resented Albert's neurotic homeboundness. He resented the way Albert raised his eyebrows. Every one of Albert's mannerisms exasperated him. But why? He heartily enjoyed Aunt Lily's eccentricities, and they were far more outrageous than any Albert displayed!

When Jack returned to Little Lea in September, his visit with Albert was relaxed, even without Warnie and Arthur as buffers. Warnie wasn't there, and the new-and-improved Arthur was of little interest to Jack now. (Even the old Arthur, because he fed Jack's fantasy too much, would have been off-limits.) When Jack returned to England, he felt pleasure at being able to decline Albert's offer to pay his passage.

At Oxford Jack lived in his rooms at Magdalen College full-time during the term. His only regular visits to Mrs. Moore were for lunch. His rooms—on the second floor of the three-story New Building—were splendid, even though "new" meant new in 1733! Because Magdalen was built outside the city walls to the east, it was the most spacious and the most unfettered of all Oxford colleges. Jack's three white-paneled rooms on the east end of the second floor seemed the most unfettered of all. He wrote his father:

> My external surroundings are beautiful beyond expectation and beyond hope. . . . My big sitting room looks north, and from it I see nothing, not even a gable or spire, to remind me that I am in town. I look down on a stretch of level grass which passes into a grove of immemorial forest trees, at present colored autumn red. Over this stray the deer. . . . Some mornings when I look out there will be half a dozen chewing the cud just underneath me. . .or one little stag. . . standing still and sending through the fog that queer little bark. . .a sound. . .I hear. . .day and night.[2]

His smaller sitting room and his bedroom looked south across the broad lawn to a great Cloister Quadrangle and the ancient Magdalen Tower. This was paradise, and he had even forgotten to mention the River Cherwell that bordered Magdalen on the east and stretched north before his eyes, too. In spite of being required to furnish bed, carpets, tables, chairs, sofa, fire irons, coal box, and drapes—which consumed about one-fifth his annual salary—he was certain his years of struggle were over.

So daily he tutored and lectured English and ate and talked with new colleagues. Only a few, like C. T. Onions, who had taught Jack Middle English, were acquaintances from the past. Onions, about fifty now, was also one of five outstanding colleagues Jack admired at Magdalen, the others being C. C. J. Webb, F .E. Brightman, P. V. M. Benecke, and J. A. Smith. Any one of them would say, "Oh yes, you'll find what you want in such and such," to any question Jack asked.

Chief among the five were Benecke and Smith. Paul Benecke, fifty-seven, very tall and angular, taught classics. Handsome to a fault, he was also righteous, and both were reasons for many men to dislike him. He was a teetotaler, he fasted, and he never missed a church service in chapel. Although he spoke often on any subject out of conscience, he rambled in a nervous, unhappy voice and was, consequently, ineffective as a debater. Despite that, Jack found himself drawn to Benecke and his overt Christianity and sat with him often at meals.

Under his gown, Benecke dressed poorly. His only extravagance was his collection of miniature pigs: stuffed, ceramic, wood, glass, ivory. His holiness showed through best when he talked of animals. "The melancholy in a dog's eyes is from its pity for men," he informed Jack one day.

J. A. Smith, even taller, older, and more sober-looking than Benecke, taught philosophy and was an authority on Aristotle. As a moralist, he often made pronouncements, but as a philosopher, he was very slippery, not arguing directly. He had also become, through the years, a philologist, one who cherishes the history and meaning of words. He was an entertaining raconteur like Jack's father, Albert. And to top it all off, J. A. knew Norse mythology. Jack rarely missed a chance to talk to him, aware of the paradox: Traits irritating in his father were endearing in others.

Jack did not like some of the other dons at all. Although Thomas Weldon was also a veteran of the trenches, Jack only talked reluctantly to the younger don. He was a philosopher and very close to Jack in his beliefs, yet Jack found him thoroughly disagreeable. He was cynical, scorning all creeds. But one night he shocked Jack.

Referring to the *Golden Bough*, he urged, "Forget Fraser's dying God!" He hesitated. Nothing he had said so far had surprised Jack at all. "I've been reading the New Testament," continued Weldon, sounding apologetic. "It almost looks like it really happened."

"What!" exclaimed Jack. "You can't believe that."

Oh, but I've thought it all through. More than once. I've been in war. Men don't willingly sacrifice themselves for a hoax. His followers did that only because they had seen him risen. There's other evidence as well. Worst luck!"

Jack was stunned. Christianity was only a myth—and a sorry one at that. But what if it wasn't? He had read G. K. Chesterton's *Everlasting Man* and found his argument fascinating. Either Christ was who He said He was—the Son of God—or He was an absolute lunatic. And Christ didn't sound like a lunatic—not even to the most cynical man alive!

Uncomfortable, Jack shrugged off the temptation. He had purged himself of otherness and dreams and myths. He operated in the real world now. He was unpleasantly reminded of *Dymer*, his work that showed the folly of dreaming. How many days, weeks, months had he labored on it? Yet it was stalled, its lack of fruition haunting Jack like a dying friend. With Barfield too remote now for advice, Jack turned to Nevill Coghill at an English faculty meeting in February 1926. Almost apologetically, Jack asked him to look at *Dymer*.

To Jack's astonishment, Coghill raved about it, proclaiming Jack to be another Masefield. Jack could not keep quiet. "Aren't you bothered by the theme: 'Too much dreaming destroys a man'?"

"Not at all. Besides, it is only one of several themes." Coghill paused tactfully. "In another of your themes, you redeem the man through his dying in a final battle against his own offspring."

"That has nothing to do with Christianity, if that's what you are thinking," Jack interrupted. "Redemption through death is a common theme in myths." But Jack was no longer so certain. Barfield had liked *Dymer*, too; his only complaint had been Jack's lack of polish.

Then, most incredible of all, Coghill located a publisher for Jack! On April 1, J. M. Dent and Sons accepted *Dymer*. What a relief for Jack to have his creation off and running. Now he could focus on other business.

On May 11, Jack attended a meeting of English dons to discuss the English curriculum. The meeting, at first hopelessly disjointed to Jack, finally evolved into a struggle between those who wanted to emphasize languages and those who wanted to emphasize literature. One pale, slender don in his mid-thirties cornered Jack after the meeting. "Language is the thing," he insisted. "English is not the study of history but the study of languages. From day one."

"I suppose you would have everyone learning Icelandic?" growled Jack, who favored the emphasis on literature.

"Certainly," rejoined the don.

"Good heavens!" Jack glared, exasperated, at Exeter's don of Old English:

J. R. R. Tolkien. That he was bright, Jack had to admit, but he needed to be taken down a peg or two. On learning more about Tolkien, however, Jack no longer wondered how the man was almost 100 percent wrong. Tolkien was another Christian and apparently practiced his faith. Jack cautioned himself to carefully protect his hard-earned realistic view of life. On the side, he was currently reading about the philanthropist Hannah More. Though she had started out a solid humanist, she fell into the snare of Samuel Johnson, and probably John Wesley as well. Eventually, the poor woman ended up firmly in the quicksand of Christianity. Yes, he would have to be very careful.

In July, he found himself reading Morris's *The Well at the World's End* again. "There it is!" He wagged his head. "I triggered the old 'joy,' that brief, very satisfying glimpse into something beyond."

Why had he done that? He guarded against that. It wasn't consonant with his newfound rationalism, or humanism, or whatever he wanted to call it. The truth was that his intellectual state was a thorough muddle. He had passed through a smorgasbord of ideas and glutted on all sorts of them, ideas that seemed now to disagree with him. He had tasted scraps of Barfield's anthroposophy, bits of the new psychoanalysis, great chunks of Kirk's rationalism, Yeat's fairy world, and Arthur's Northernness. "Now even my rationalism is shaky." He shook his addled head. "Good riddance to Barfield and his ilk!"

Owen Barfield had planted the seed, the terrible notion that—aside from supernatural influence—there is no satisfactory explanation of knowledge for man. Knowledge depends on the validity of reason. "The new naturalists with their explanation of the natural universe as a totally accidental, random thing have shot themselves in the brain," Barfield had insisted. This random process could not validate reason. Why would anyone believe random electrical processes in the brain could yield reason and knowledge? Yet nearly all men admit reason and knowledge are real.

"So what is the source of that reason?" Jack grilled himself. "Once again I've come back to spirit." He gritted his teeth. "Barfield!"

Jack's great love, literature, chafed him, too. Why did he revel so in George MacDonald? MacDonald wasn't even a first-rate writer. Like Fielding, he somehow mounted such a forceful story—in MacDonald's case, something akin to a myth—that it overcame the bad writing. And then there were the top-drawer writers like Chesterton and Samuel Johnson and Spenser and Milton and Bunyan. Their writings were deep and rich, imminently truthful about everyday life. They were towers of reason and sanity. Yet they were Christians! And why was he so deeply moved by *Dream of the Rood*? And Dante, Langland, John Donne, and George Herbert? These men, too, were Christians.

And what of the greatest humanists, most of whom were atheists? George

Bernard Shaw, H. G. Wells, John Stuart Mill, Gibbon, and Voltaire? Why did their works seem so thin and cheap, so devoid of real meaning for everyday life?

And what of his friends? Weren't his very best, brightest friends all Christians, or at least theists? Barfield. Harwood. Coghill. Good old Laurence Johnson. Even good—but spoiled, childish—Arthur.

And which Magdalen faculty members did he eagerly seek out at meals? Paul Benecke and J. A. Smith—the Christians, of course.

Dymer was published in September 1926. Jack again employed his pseudonym, Clive Hamilton. Reviews were good; sales were not. *Such is the lot of some poets,* reasoned Jack. Wasn't understanding the scope of literature his charge? Some poets were discovered and championed hundreds of years later, William Blake and John Donne, for instance. Jack ached inside, not sure he wanted to claim *Dymer* in the first place. It seemed more to belong to a confused cynic like Weldon than himself.

Another narrative poem Jack was creating only added to his confusion. Should he continue working on it or not? His time was so limited. He had started it in Bristol in 1918. By 1920 it had evolved into a poem he called "Wild Hunt." By 1924 it had haunted him enough that he had revised it yet again. It was now called "King of Drum."

"Why don't you come to the Kolbitars, Jack?" asked C. T. Onions one day late in 1926.

"The name sounds suspiciously Norse," Jack hazarded.

"It's Icelandic for 'coal-biters.' It means those who sit so close to the fire they can almost bite the coals. Tolkien organized it."

"Tolkien." Jack humphed, then shook his head.

"We're reading the Icelandic sagas in the original," Onions recounted. "George Gordon is there. Nevill Coghill. Myself."

"Coghill? You?"

As Onions explained how they tackled the sagas, the process of learning seemed absolutely Kirkian. Jack had certainly thrived in that procedure. But Icelandic?

Onions, observing Jack's hesitation, chuckled. "The Norse legends are much more exciting than the original Greek legends."

"How so?" challenged Jack.

"Their gods are heroes. Their gods die."

"Then why does no one other than a few stuffy professors know the Norse legends?" posed Jack just to be difficult. He knew the answer. Besides, the pale little Tolkien was behind it.

"The Norse never had a Homer. Their stories are poor poetry."

"I'll think about it," Jack conceded.

He already knew German and Old English and would probably pick up Icelandic fast. Oh, to read the Norse mythologies in the original. What Northernness! It was tempting. But would it endanger his rationalism? No, surely not. This would not be an indulgence for joy; this would be academic. Nonetheless, he was sick inside as he remembered the confused, miserable state of his rationalism.

EIGHT

But soon Jack was keenly anticipating participation with the Kolbitars. On January 28, Jack borrowed J. A. Smith's *Icelandic Reader*. Soon Jack was hammering his way through the first chapters of *Younger Edda*. The first glimpses of the very words for "god" and "giant" in Icelandic ignited the old thrill and threw him back fifteen years into vast northern skies and Wagnerian music. The memory was deliciously poignant. Jack could hardly believe after all these years that he was going to read his early loves in their original language. "It's a good thing this is purely academic," he reassured himself.

That spring of 1927, Jack joined in a walking tour through the Wiltshire and Berkshire Downs with Owen Barfield, Cecil Harwood, and "Wof" Field. They wore twenty-pound packs and walked briskly. The goal every day was to end up at an inn for a delightful dinner. Nothing fancy. Quite the opposite. Just good boiled beef and bitter ale from wooden casks. To be first rank, the inn had to have wooden tables, tops waxed. In cold weather a wood fire was preferred. All the while they ambled, they breathed the outdoors. And of course they joked and argued. Jack was in his element: He was opposed by three anthroposophists!

Walking tours became annual spring events for Jack and his friends. In 1928, the same group walked through the Cotswolds, west of Oxford. Friendships were such joy.

The privileged life Jack had so ardently courted expanded his world, but it also came with unwelcome duties. Many of the students he tutored seemed impossibly backward. He had no Christian charity, so he felt no guilt calling them "fools" and "lumps" and worse in his diary.

At times, however, the faculty irritated Jack as much as the students. The scrap between languages and literature in the English curriculum persisted. Although he was changing his mind about J. R. R. Tolkien and actually beginning to like him, that only deepened his concern. Tolkien was very competent. As such, he might succeed in getting languages to be a major portion of the English curriculum.

Eclipsing all the aggravations was the announcement that the president of Magdalen would retire in November 1928. Hogarth, every don's choice as successor, suddenly died. Intending to push his own agenda, Weldon, the cynical philosopher, put forward Chelmsford. Others put forward Paul Benecke, the classicist Jack admired so much in spite of his being a Christian. The campaign became ugly.

Jack wrote Barfield:

*This college is a cesspool, a stinking puddle, inhabited by things. . .
in men's shapes climbing over one another and biting one another in the
back, ignorant of all things except their own subjects and often even of
those; caring nothing less for learning; cunning, desperately ambitious,
false friends, nodders in corners, tippers of the wink; setters of traps and
solicitors of confidence; (a pox) upon them—excepting always the aged
who have lived down to us from a purer epoch.[1]*

Jack could not bring himself to acknowledge that "purer epoch" as Christian, but he knew the young dons were the ones who had turned the campaign ugly. When forty-seven-year-old George Gordon was ultimately elected, Jack was pleased with the choice. The thought that all the good men were old and would pass on one way or another lingered and haunted him. Jack had no desire to be left solely among rationalists.

Why does the ancient world seem civilized and the modern world barbaric? Jack's own internal war never abated. Above all, he was old Kirk's dialectician. The truth was he no longer believed in materialism and rationalism. They simply did not explain the human experience. Man's possession of logic required a cosmic logic, yet he still could not bring himself to call that logic "God."

While he did not read for that purpose, much of his reading illuminated his new suspicion of a supernatural influence. More and more of the great thinkers were reinforcing the supernatural. *Hippolytus* by Euripides annihilated his last remnants of rationalism. Suppressing emotion and spirit was folly. Jack craved again that other-worldliness that thrilled him with joy. Samuel Alexander's *Space, Time, and Deity* convinced him that his joy was not something he could contemplate. Rather, it was a mental track left by the passage of joy. Jack had been wrong about desiring just the brief glimpse itself. The "passage of joy" was a tiny moment of clearest consciousness when Jack ached for reunion with the utter reality, the Absolute.

Night after night, alone in his rooms at Magdalen, he resisted the identity, the reality of the Absolute. Then in the spring of 1929, he was riding a bus in Oxford. Suddenly without words or images, he felt at bay. Next he felt encumbered. Choice loomed momentous, yet cold and infinite: He could shed or not shed. An image formed in his mind. He was a snowman, impenetrable. Then he was melting. Drip, drip. Trickle, trickle. At last, his self dissipated. He believed. The Absolute was Spirit. Spirit was God. Jack Lewis was a theist.

In August, Jack unsealed an alarming letter from Uncle Richard, who lived in Scotland but was vacationing in Belfast. Albert, felled by excruciating stomach pains, was in the hospital getting X-rays. No one had to tell Jack what that could mean! Would stomach cancer claim his father as it already had his mother? Jack left for Little Lea at once.

In Belfast the doctor calmed Jack. "The obstruction in his bowel is not cancer."

Jack stayed with his father in Little Lea. The horrors surrounding the death of Mrs. Moore's brother, Doc, besieged Jack, yet were another variety. Albert was in agony, but he was sane. Worse for Jack, however, every room seemed choked with the bogies of childhood—the awful rows with his father, the dreaded returns to school, the heartbreak of a dying mother. In September, Albert was taken to the hospital again.

The doctor was contrite. "It is cancer. We'll have to operate."

"Recovering" in the hospital, Albert died at 68. To Warnie, who was in China, Jack wrote on October 27:

> *I always before condemned as sentimentalists or hypocrites the people whose view of the dead was so different from the view they held of the same people living. Now (I find) out that it is a natural process. . . . A dozen times while I was making the funeral arrangements I found myself mentally jotting down some episode or other to tell him. . . . As time goes on, the thing that emerges is that. . .he was a terrific personality. . . . Remember (the quote): "(Samuel) Johnson is dead. Let us go on to the next. There is none.". . . How (Father) filled a room. . .(although) physically he was not a big man. . . . Our whole world is either direct or indirect testimony. . . . The way we enjoyed going to Little Lea, and the way we hated it, and the way we enjoyed hating it. . . . And now you could do anything on earth you cared to in the study at midday on a Sunday, and it is beastly.* [2]

That Jack and Warnie would discuss selling Little Lea whenever Warnie could return from China seemed unbelievable. But what choice did they have? Jack was committed to Oxford. Warnie had a solid fifteen years invested in the army. Retirement for either of them in Ireland was years away. The only benefit about the whole sad affair was Jack's reconciliation with Arthur. When he returned to Oxford, the letters began flowing back and forth again. He and Mrs. Moore even stayed as guests at Bernagh, Arthur's home, in December.

By Christmastime 1929, Jack was meeting regularly with Tolkien, whom he now affectionately called "Tollers." Usually they met Monday mornings in Jack's rooms at Magdalen. Incredibly, Tolkien had won Jack over so completely that Jack now supported Tolkien's change in curriculum. Old English and Middle English were expanded at the expense of Victorian literature. Now the study of English literature stopped at Keats's death in 1821.

"You may study more recent writers if you wish," Lewis would tell his pupils plainly, "but I doubt if I can spare the time to discuss them with you."

While Jack enjoyed Tolkien's friendship, he was not a first-rate dialectician like Barfield. Tolkien was too passionate; he lost his temper, which was fatal. Obviously, Jack's stringent standards for companions had mellowed. Or perhaps they had been false. Jack had never held Arthur to those standards, and Tolkien was like Arthur, with the added ingredient of genius.

Tollers related to Jack that not only was he, too, a product of Norse mythology and the modern mythmakers, George MacDonald and William Morris, but also that he was writing a myth for England. As Jack began to realize the scope of Tolkien's *Silmarillion*, however, he was astonished. Tolkien had created an enormous ancient world: Middle-earth. It was not alien, but the precursor of our own. Deep in antiquity, it swarmed with elves and dwarves and evil orcs. The elves fashioned three great jewels, the "Silmarilli." The jewels were stolen by the evil Morgoth. Many wars followed as the elves fought to recover them. Tolkien had even invented two languages for the elves: Quenya and Sindarin. They were languages with many hundreds of words, all meticulously fashioned from root words.

"But where is your Christ?" Jack teased gently.

"The 'One' is the Trinity in my story. The 'Valar,' the guardians of my world, are angelic beings. Only once in the story do they surrender their power to the 'One.' The Trinity, or 'One,' reigns over this ancient world but is never seen. You see, the story is remote and strange, but it's not a lie."

Jack's own world continued to expand and change. Over his own writing, he agonized long and hard, considering prose as an option. Although at one time he had purposed within himself that he would do anything to get published and have a huge literary success, he did not feel that way at all now. And he was not being false. He credited it to his newfound faith in God.

In April of 1930, Warnie returned from China. Together the brothers started sifting through everything in Little Lea. Memories threatened to suffocate them. They set aside all they wanted to keep in one room. Childhood toys they buried in the backyard. The rest of the belongings were designated to be thrown away, given away, or auctioned. Warnie volunteered to request a transfer to England so that he could arrange thousands of letters and documents Albert had left behind. Knowing already that Mrs. Moore wanted Warnie to live with them, Jack invited Warnie again.

"You'll be leaving the army in a few years," reasoned Jack. "Tell me, what better place is there to stay than with us? We can take the money from Little Lea and buy a house in Oxford."

Warnie agreed.

Back in Oxford, Jack and Mrs. Moore set out to find a house. Of course it had to be east of Oxford so Jack would not have to worm his way through the town's entire conglomeration of autos and bicycles and pedestrians to reach

Magdalen. In July, they checked a house three miles east of Oxford on the flats below the north flank of Shotover Hill.

"Goodness!" exclaimed Jack as they were driven down a road barely more than two worn ruts. Then the car turned onto a trail even more primitive. "Are you sure you want to continue?"

"Think of the privacy," she instructed, but doubt softened her voice. "We've come this far; let's see it."

Soon they entered the property, facing the back of the house. The house, of red brick with a clay-tiled roof over a dormered second floor, appeared larger than the one they lived in. They left the car and entered the house through the back door. The main floor had two sitting rooms and two bedrooms besides a kitchen, a pantry, and a maid's room. The second floor had three bedrooms. Electricity was provided by a gasoline generator. All hot water had to be heated on the kitchen stove.

"We must have this house," whispered Mrs. Moore to Jack.

"Perhaps we should look at other houses," grumbled Jack as they stepped outside the front door. Then he blinked. The grounds in front of the house took his breath away.

"The grounds go all the way onto Shotover Hill, up to that belt of fir trees," pointed the man who had brought them. "Eight acres."

"No!" doubted Jack. "All the way onto Shotover Hill?" It was too good to be true. Besides the lower wooded slope of Shotover Hill, the grounds included a good-sized lawn, a tennis court, a greenhouse, a work shed, the two enormous brick kilns, and a very large pond from an old clay pit.

"We must have it," Jack whispered now to Mrs. Moore.

The next day they brought Warnie. He, too, blinked in disbelief. "I can't imagine such a house and grounds being available near Oxford for three times what they are asking." He began calculating what it would cost to add two more rooms so that each brother might have his own private study.

They purchased the house. All legal work was processed by none other than Owen Barfield, who had been forced to relegate literature to a hobby. Mrs. Moore put up half the money and became the official owner. The Lewis brothers put up the other half. Mrs. Moore's will left the house to the brothers for their lifetime. After that, the house would become Maureen's.

By October, all but Warnie had moved into the redbrick house, though Jack still lived in Magdalen much of the time. From then on their house was called the "Kilns." That same month he started to "fly the flag" for God and began to attend service in chapel every morning.

At dinner one night, Mrs. Moore suggested widening the road into the Kilns. "But won't that require cutting down all those lovely silver birch trees?" objected Warnie, who was on a short leave from the army.

He looked to Jack for support, but Jack said nothing. Later, Warnie, much upset, brought up the subject privately with Jack. How could he let Mrs. Moore remove all those lovely trees?

Jack smiled. "You must resist the temptation to react to domestic proposals by Mrs. Moore or Maureen. Nine out of ten are never mentioned a second time."

In January, the two brothers took their own walking tour together, trekking over fifty miles along the Wye Valley. Warnie still had to learn from Jack who had learned from Arthur that one had to enjoy every outing, no matter how cold or foggy or rainy. Before long, Warnie became a congenial companion.

On their return to the Kilns, the brothers planted forty-three trees: chestnuts, ashes, oaks, and firs. Over the next few months, Jack was surprised to learn Warnie was coming to God, too, most reluctantly, almost apologetically—just as he had. In Jack's mind, Warnie's idea of good was much less than his own. Warnie believed the old chestnut that it merely meant that one didn't harm other people. Warnie could attain his idea of good; Jack could not possibly achieve his ill-defined holiness. In May of 1931, Warnie openly embraced Christ, really stunning Jack. After all their years together, Jack never expected that. One Saturday, explained Warnie, he suddenly became aware life could not be an accident and began saying his prayers. He had no more explanation than that.

Quite often they discussed Jack's dilemma over Christ. "What holds me back," Jack expounded, "is that I cannot conceive of the immediacy of Christ. Except as an example, how can the life and death of someone who lived two thousand years ago help me here and now? I know enough about Christianity to know Christ's example is not the heart of Christianity. You must believe the blood of the Lamb atones now."

Jack further discussed his dilemma with Tolkien. One such meeting took place September 19, 1931. This meeting was not their customary one during the week; it was on Saturday. It was not in the morning; it was at night. It was not in Jack's room; it was on Addison's walk among the deer and elms. Jack and Tolkien were joined by Hugo Dyson, a professor of English at Reading University, whose specialty was the late seventeenth century. Jack considered him "a fastidious book man" yet "burly, both in mind and body, with the stamp of the war on him."

Dyson was not only a Christian, but also a tireless, irrepressible needler. "You're an Old Testament Jew, Lewis."

"Perhaps, but Orthodox Jews don't crave immortality," Jack came back defensively. "Such a desire corrupts belief because it demands belief."

"Christianity is not desirable for that reason," countered Tolkien, "or for any reason of convenience. Christianity is true, a historical fact."

"If I can't understand the meaning of the crucifixion or of the resurrection or of redemption, how can I believe in Christ?" Jack expostulated.

"You love myth, don't you?" pressed Tolkien, already knowing the answer.

"Of course. Balder thrills me as much now as ever."

"So you like the element of a god dying and coming to life again?"

"Yes," Jack granted, "but I'm not sure why."

"Indeed. Nor am I," answered Tolkien. "Why do you make such demands for clarity on Christianity? Just accept the fact that Christianity is a myth that really happened."

"But myths are lies," argued Jack, "worthless, even though they are breathed through silver and magnificent."

"No," Tolkien contended. "The myths that you consider lies are the myths of men, though they contain fragments of truth. The myth that is wholly true—the birth, death, and resurrection of Christ—is God's myth."

"Maybe I am demanding too much of the mystery," Jack conceded lamely, "but isn't belief ultimately from the grace of God?"

The following week, Jack rode in the sidecar of Warnie's motorcycle as the two brothers set out from Oxford for the wonderful new Whipsnade Zoo. It was only a trip of thirty-plus miles, but to Jack the trip spanned two thousand years. Later he could not formulate any reason or process that could explain what took place. It was as if Jack, lying long in bed, suddenly was aware he was awake, because when he climbed out of that sidecar, he believed in Christ.

"God's grace," concluded a humbled Jack.

NINE

Jack seemed really settled now. He was a Christian, and he had a wonderful, secluded home at the Kilns. Every aspect of his life seemed better than he had ever imagined it could be. Now thirty-three, he decided that if he ever was going to be a poet of any consequence, it was high time to pursue it. And what better subject than his own conversion? He began such a story in verse, but it sputtered. Poetry seemed very difficult for him now.

Perhaps prose was his calling. He was already well under way on what he hoped would be a major academic work on the medieval tradition, the development of the romantic epic and no less than the evolution of the concept of love. Like Tolkien, he adored the Middle Ages. Jack was more and more defensive of the past. Current novels were pitiful to Jack. Even when the writing was brilliant, he deemed it wasted. On one occasion he wrote Arthur that he was reading Virginia Woolf's *Orlando* and praised her power to convey the feel of landscapes and moods, then expressed frustration with the total absence of substance on which she used her power. Above all, he loathed her cynicism, regardless that she was the darling of the modern intellectuals.

And so Jack willingly embraced the Middle Ages as he grappled with his work on the medieval tradition and the development of the romantic epic. The Middle Ages were the height of Christendom, the height of chivalry, really the height of love. Jack thought long and hard how to know the glorious fruits of the Middle Ages. First, one had to know the soil that spawned the Middle Ages. A solid knowledge of the Bible was so significant that without it, the task was hopeless. Almost as important in the fertile soil were the classic Latin and Greek works, especially Plato and Aristotle. To reap the bounty of the Middle Ages was to understand allegory and how it worked in the hands of masters. Certainly one could not ignore the English authors Chaucer, Langland, and Spenser. Two specific works of the age were paramount: the French classic, *Romance of the Rose*, and Dante's allegory, *The Divine Comedy*. In Jack's mind, *The Divine Comedy* was the greatest single achievement by one man in literature. It was the culmination of the wisdom of the Middle Ages.

Jack knew his work on medieval tradition would take several years, but as he grappled with the concept of allegory, the idea for a book about his conversion solidified. Allegory was not popular with moderns. Even Tolkien bristled at the suggestion that his *Silmarillion* was allegory. Jack was convinced, however, that in the hands of a master an allegory could reveal truth that could not be revealed as well by any other method. Well-contrived allegory approached myth in power and had to be understood with the imagination instead of intellect. As Jack pondered the most effective context of his conversion as an allegory, he naturally associated it—since both were quests for salvation—with John Bunyan's great seventeenth-century allegory, *Pilgrim's Progress*. Sporadically Jack would think on it, allowing the idea to ferment for a while. Although the thought that he again had picked a literary form unpopular with moderns flitted through his mind, it didn't bother him.

Meanwhile Warnie had been reassigned to China, stationed again in Shanghai. Perhaps he wouldn't get out of the army so soon after all. Jack's life, to the contrary, continued in full flourish. He embarked on his usual walking tour in 1932 with his friends. The outing was not so contentious now that Jack was a Christian, but they still found plenty about which to needle each other. As far as the outdoors was concerned, Jack perceived it all as colors and smells and sounds and moods. Only occasionally did he know the name of a plant or a rock. Nor did he care, for to him the name conveyed next to nothing. A scientific name was nothing but two Latin words, forever pitifully enslaved.

But 1932 became unusually burdensome for Jack. By the end of July, he noted that because of sickness, tutoring, lecturing, and academic writing, he had not enjoyed one morning with a book for eighteen weeks! Certainly he had not written any account of his spiritual conversion. "This has been the driest spell of my adult life," he lamented. He could hardly wait for the August vacation he had planned with Arthur.

Upon reaching Arthur's home, "Bernagh," in Ireland, he attacked the writing of his conversion in a frenzy. "Pen! Ink!" he bellowed as he launched the allegory of his quest for salvation. Jack's pilgrim John, taught to fear the Landlord of his native country Puritania, visualizes an island, Joy, and sets off to find it. After many false destinations, John finds his way back to Puritania, the symbol of his mother church, and salvation. Because the hero finds salvation by retracing his steps to Puritania, Jack titled the book *Pilgrim's Regress*. By the time he departed Ireland, it was finished.

The feat of writing such a work in two weeks stunned Jack as much as anyone. Prose gushed forth from him, and revisions were minor. Nonetheless, writing prose was not mere words. It was a creation, a mass of ideas. Suddenly, it was clear to Jack that he had a gift for writing prose. Writing verse was torture in comparison. And who could say one form was better than another? In fact, he detested modern poetry, not only because of its free verse, but because it embraced atheism and Marxism.

J. M. Dent, who had published *Dymer*, liked Jack's prose well enough to accept *Pilgrim's Regress* and schedule it to be released in the summer of 1933. Because the Japanese attacked China in 1932 and the situation was rapidly deteriorating, Warnie applied for retirement from the army and left China. By Christmas of 1932, he was back in England—a civilian, and resident of the

Kilns. Because the two-room "wing" had recently been completed, the two brothers had their own studies.

That winter dumped the worst snowstorm in thirty years on Oxford—the snow drifted into eye-level dunes. Although Jack lay in bed with a cold, he truly relished the "ordinary" sickness. After trying to keep apace with an unrelenting and tiring schedule, nothing afforded more delight than a concrete reason to stay in bed. Of course, he was never too indisposed to read, especially *Phantastes*, which was practically his devotional.

At Oxford, the Kolbitars had read all the Icelandic sagas and the group had evaporated, but Tolkien and Jack were too close now not to meet and share their writings. Together they joined an undergraduate writing club hosted by Edward Tangye Lean called the Inklings. When Lean graduated in June of 1933 and the Inklings, as an undergraduate club, died, Jack adopted the name for the meetings he was already holding for his colleagues once a week in his rooms at Magdalen. No records or minutes were kept. The sole purpose of the meetings was to provide a forum for the Inklings to read their writings to one another. Because Jack was a firm believer in William Blake's maxim "Opposition is true friendship," the criticism was friendly but severe. The new group was powerful: Owen Barfield, Nevill Coghill, Hugo Dyson, and, of course, Lewis and Tolkien. All A's.

Meanwhile the Kilns had taken on a more permanent look. The staff consisted of a maid and a rough handyman from the countryside, Fred Paxford. He was the gardener, the grocery shopper, and the chauffeur, for although Jack had paid for the car, only Paxford and Maureen drove it. Paxford knew how to pinch a penny. He was as focused as a surgeon as he took inventory of the larder, then purchased the tiniest amount of groceries that would suffice. He was loyal and honest and exasperatingly opinionated. Inwardly he was an optimist, but outwardly he was a pessimist.

Fred Paxford irritated no one but Warnie with his homespun pessimism. Warnie, retired after eighteen years of the army, quickly decided he would not even attempt to manage the Kilns while Jack toiled in Oxford. Mrs. Moore and Fred Paxford were already doing that in tandem. Instead, Warnie gradually transferred all his papers and most of his books to Jack's small sitting room in Magdalen. Each morning he would arrive to catalog the "Lewis Papers." Quietly fixing tea, he even became a regular among the Inklings, though he only occasionally commented. Warnie had mastered the art of being polite and unobtrusive.

Maureen, now twenty-five and boarding at a music school in Monmouth, was at the Kilns less and less. Sunday evenings Warnie played his Beethoven records for Jack and Mrs. Moore. Jack preferred to hear complete symphonies rather than excerpts as he once had. Of course, he had strong opinions.

The movement he liked best was the Seventh Symphony's third, although the finale ruined the Seventh as a whole for him. The Fifth was the best symphony overall, he acknowledged, reluctantly siding with nearly everyone else in the world, but he went against the grain in completely disliking the Third Symphony—Eroica. Perhaps it was because Beethoven had dedicated it to Napoleon.

"Quite frankly," he expressed to Warnie, "Napoleon reminds me of Adolph Hitler." Hitler was a demonic German who claimed by persecuting Jews he was doing the will of God. His claims were stupid but not amusing. Now the chancellor of Germany, he was freshly granted dictatorial powers. He spoke of rearming Germany, and all opposition was consigned to concentration camps. All over Germany, Italy, Austria, Japan, and Russia—the very countries that might form an alliance around the devilish Hitler—voices of moderation were being assassinated. War loomed on the horizon. Oxford no longer felt as safe as Switzerland.

On May 21, 1936, Clarendon Press of the Oxford University Press published Jack's *Allegory of Love*, his scholarly work subtitled "A Study in Medieval Tradition." One of his own stated objectives was to trace the twelve-hundred-year history of Christian allegory from its birth in the Latin Prudentius to the medieval masterpiece *Faerie Queene* by Spenser in the late 1500s. A second objective was to trace through time the romantic conception of love. On June 6, the literary supplement of the *London Times*, Jack's TLS, stated in a very detailed 2,000-word review:

> [The book is]. . .scholarly, fascinating, and original. . . . Mr. Lewis is both interested and skilled in the history of human psychology. He is obviously qualified to write literary history of the best kind; for his book is an example of it.

One month later in America the *New York Times* reviewed *Allegory of Love*:

> At first glance one might not imagine that there was anything more than an antiquarian interest in a subject such as the allegorical love poetry of the Middle Ages. . . . But C. S. Lewis shows that it is as impossible to extricate ourselves from our literary progenitors as from our physical forebearers, and that such a form as the medieval allegory of love was not only born of the thought and customs of a particular era of history, but bequeathed an important legacy to the future and finds its reflection in some of the outstanding works of our own literature.

The *Spectator* indirectly admitted the difficulty of what Jack achieved:

> *The book is learned, witty and sensible, and makes one ashamed*
> *of not having read its material; in the first flush of admiration for the*
> Romance of the Rose, *I tried to read the Chaucerian version. . . . But*
> *it is. . .far better to read Mr. Lewis and his admirable quotations. . .and*
> *frankly admit that there are great pleasures not our own.*

Jack's life was altered. As far as being popular with the general public, he was an unknown, but he was now certainly more than a mere intimidating presence known on the sprawling campus of Oxford. He was now becoming known to English scholars all over the world. Although he shunned such accolades, many newspapers and magazines were acknowledging him as the expert on medieval literature.

One of his new admirers was Charles Williams, an editor with Oxford University Press in London. The coincidence was remarkable because Nevill Coghill had just persuaded Jack to read Williams's novel, *The Place of the Lion*, a very sophisticated and deeply religious thriller. The heroine, who studies angels and demons in academic smugness, is lured into the supernatural world. The book illuminated humility for Jack as never before.

In 1936, upon Arthur's urging, Jack read *Voyage to Arcturus* by David Lindsay. The book, published sixteen years before, was a haunting spiritual journey, much like George MacDonald's *Lilith* or *Phantastes,* except that it was more diabolical than holy. Jack was stunned. Lindsay had shown him that what George MacDonald had done—even what Charles Williams had done—could be done in space fiction. To prick even more Jack's desire to write such a fantasy was a remark by an undergraduate, praising the future opportunity for man to colonize the planets. Jack found that thought revolting, knowing the kind of men who would lead such an effort.

He accosted Tolkien. "You create your myth—that tiny splinter of Christianity, the great Truth—in the distant past, influenced by the Icelandic sagas. Perhaps I can create my myth in the future."

Influenced by what? Believing the Middle Ages the epitome of Christendom and decency, Jack would use the "Medieval Model" for his mythmaking in the future. For Jack the "Model" was the very comforting amalgamation of Christianity, Platonism, Aristotelianism, Stoicism, and least of all, paganisms other than Latin and Greek. Of course, Christianity would always overrule the other elements in the event of conflict. This amalgamation of elements had influenced some of the greatest writers in the world: Augustine, Dante, and Spenser. Because it had held its appeal long after the medieval age, it had affected even Shakespeare, Donne, and Milton.

The Model indicated that although the universe is infinite, everything is not relative. Up is up, and down is down. The earth is the center of this universe of Ptolemy but nonetheless a sphere. At the center of earth is hell. Therefore, in the Medieval Model, earth not only represents the center of the universe and all existence, but the lowest of all existence!

Surrounding earth are nine concentric "celestial spheres," sometimes called "wheels." Moving within the spheres are the moon, the sun, and various planets. They all have attributes. The moon is dangerous; the sun is beneficial. Venus represents love and beauty. Mars represents belligerence. Giant Jupiter, the best planet, symbolizes serenity, magnanimity, and cheerfulness. Saturn, the worst, embodies aging, sickness, disease, and treachery. The eighth sphere carries the stars with their various constellations signifying different things. The Primum Mobile, or First Cause, of the ninth sphere carries no bodies but imparts the movement that pushes the bodies on all the inner spheres. Beyond that is the "Tenth Heaven, absolute reality and empyrean." It has no movement, no duration, but is eternal and infinite. Each sphere produces a perfect tone. "The harmonics are called the 'music of the spheres,'" Jack explained to Warnie.

The Medieval Model honored the Trinity. God is not the Jewish God, immediate, passionate, and terrifying. God is remote. His immensity is explained by Dante; it is the paradox of increasing space as one enters inner circles. God is a point, yet more immense than anything! The immediate God of the Trinity is Christ. All-pervasive among Christians is the Holy Spirit. Created spirits are well-detailed by Medievalists. Each of three hierarchies consists of three species. The hierarchy uppermost and facing God consists of seraphim, cherubim, and thrones. The next, still facing God, has dominions, powers, and virtues. The lowest hierarchy are messengers: principalities (or princes), archangels, and angels. "And angels are greater than men," commented Jack. "The Model puts us in our place."

Several levels of created material essences also exist in the Medieval Model. Lowest is all nonliving matter. Next is living matter without senses: plants. Another is living, with the five senses, but without power to reason: animals. Then highest among all created material beings is man. Mankind can reason. Reason governs the five wits: common sense, memory, imagination, fantasy, and instinct. The wits are supposed to control animal appetites or passion. Thus moral conflict is a conflict between reason and passion. On the one hand, mankind is given dominion over all living things. On the other hand, mankind is under the dominion of God, but accepts the rule of monarchs.

"But as any Medievalist knows," Jack told Warnie with great relish, "yet another kind of material being with senses and the power of reason lives on earth and in the air. The *longaevi*."

The *longaevi*, though not immortal, live long lives. They are not under mankind's dominion. Capable of being good or evil, the assemblage includes pans, elves, giants, goblins, fairies, nymphs, dwarfs, and other *longaevi* who avoid men. In Jack's mind, for mankind has not always agreed on whether *longaevi* are to be feared or enjoyed, they softened the classic severity of the grand design, despite their slight rebellion.

He set his perspective to verse for Tolkien's ancient myth:

> *There was a time before the ancient sun*
> *And swinging wheels of heaven had learned to run*
> *More certainly than dreams; for dreams themselves*
> *Had bodies then and filled the world with elves.*
> *The starveling lusts whose walk is now confined*
> *To darkness and the cellarage of the mind,*
> *And shudderings and despairs and shapes of sin*
> *Then walked at large and were not cooped within.*
> *Though cast a shadow; brutes could speak: and men*
> *Get children on a star. For spirit then*
> *Threaded a fluid world and dreamed it new*
> *Each moment. Nothing was false or new.*[1]

Of course, Jack did not believe the Model literally. The Model was but an image for mythmaking.

TEN

Images that preceded all of Jack's fiction constantly bubbled in his mind. Sometimes he felt no urge to put them into some form, and sometimes he did. This time he most certainly did, as the effervescence nagged him, disturbing his work, his meals, his sleep. He knew Earth had to be the hellish planet. He finally determined to use the scientifically known arrangement of the solar system but follow his own image of space, inspired by the Medieval Model. Planets are not merely islands with possible life in the void of space. Space itself is alive, tingling. The planets are holes in God's living heaven.

In Jack's space fiction, Maleldil is the Christlike one of the Trinity. Maleldil is spirit but also being and immanent. Maleldil's father is the remote God, who is terrifying. This awesome God is not vague because he is indefinite, but vague because man can't describe such concreteness. God is light, landscape, beauty.

Each planet is ruled by an angelic being called "oyarsa." Oyarsas are roughly equivalent to principalities (or princes). They are not infinitely wise, but are angels far superior to men. Under them are eldils. All these spiritual beings move about freely in the Field of Arbol (the living space) and speak Old Solar. Lesser beings—not spirit but material—have their own languages. To celebrate, the spiritual beings all participate in the Great Dance—the harmony of the spheres.

The earth is unique. Its oyarsa—the Bent One—rebels. His evil is moral evil. Because God permits natural evil, as in animals, but not moral evil, earth becomes isolated, the Silent Planet. Old Solar is completely lost. The Bent One has already attacked the moon and Mars—the latter the location of Jack's novel. The outer surface of Mars is a dead wasteland, but on a deeper level live three kinds of material beings.

And so Jack wrote his space adventure called *Out of the Silent Planet*. An evil scientist, Weston, wants to "conquer" space. He kidnaps the hero Ransom and takes him to Malacandra (Mars) because he thinks the rulers there want a sacrifice. Instead, Ransom escapes and makes friends with the three kinds of material beings that live on Mars. The inhabitants are universally obedient and uncorrupted because they have no free will. Finally Weston is subdued by the oyarsa and sent back to earth with Ransom.

Publishers, unimpressed with *Out of the Silent Planet*, doubted that it would be commercial. Influenced by hard science fiction with its gadgets, they scoffed at Jack's metaphysics. With Tolkien's help, however, Jack finally secured a publisher, Bodley Head. In general, the book was warmly reviewed after it was released in 1938. Reviewers recognized that the writing and sophisticated metaphysics were vastly superior to most space fiction. In Jack's fiction, the underlying Christianity was far more apparent than in Tolkien's.

By early 1939, Jack confided in Owen Barfield that he was almost totally convinced he had no future in poetry. He didn't have to mention how freely his prose works flowed. At that time, Oxford University Press had just published a book written jointly by Jack and E. M. W. Tillyard, a literary critic at Cambridge University. They had taken opposing views of a subject that was one of Jack's pet peeves. Jack argued very strongly that to critique an artist's work by studying his life was not valid. If the artist was truly objective about his work, his own personality could not be discerned in the work. Jack believed that with all his heart. Many writers did. Moreover, the new criticism seemed a form of titillation, a sleazy peek into an artist's private life. To Jack, who liked to compartmentalize his life and cherished privacy, the whole approach was offensive.

Also in 1939, Oxford University Press published a collection of Jack's essays called *Rehabilitations*. He regarded their only common theme to be "a certain belief about life and books." One of the nine essays was a defense of ancient English poetry that used alliteration—the repetition of consonants—as the primary poetic device. W. H. Auden and Tolkien were fond of alliteration, too. Jack used his own poem "Planets"—choked with medieval meaning—to illustrate. A portion on Jupiter read:

> *Of wrath ended*
> *And woes mended, of winter passed*
> *And guilt forgiven, and good fortune*
> *Jove is master; and jocund revel,*
> *Laughter of ladies. The lion-hearted,*
> *The myriad-minded, men like the gods,*
> *Helps and heroes, helms of nations*
> *Just and gentle, are Jove's children,*
> *Work his wonders. On his wide forehead*
> *Calm and kingly, no care darkens*
> *Nor wrath wrinkles; but righteous power*
> *And leisure and largess their loose splendors*
> *Have wrapped around him—a rich mantle*
> *of ease and empire.*[1]

Reviewers began to voice their awe at Jack's ability to illuminate any subject. That same year of 1939, Jack was approached by Ashley Sampson, whose Geoffrey Bles Publishing ran a series of books called "Christian Challenge."

Would Jack write a 40,000-word book on "the problem of pain"? His treatise would be the essential defense, or apology, to the atheist's favorite proposition: "If God were good, He would want his creatures to be happy. If God were all-powerful, He would see that they were. But they are not all happy. Therefore, He lacks goodness or power or both!" Implied in the question was that God didn't exist at all.

How familiar to Jack were all the stock arguments against God! Who had used them more relentlessly than he had before 1929? And hadn't he been battered down over thousands of hours by the likes of Barfield and Harwood and Tolkien? So he accepted the assignment. This challenge would add one more aspect of writing to his growing repertoire: his defense of Christianity, or "apologetics," written not for the scholar but for the layperson.

As a Christian, Jack was only about ten years old. How could he be so certain about Christianity? How did he have such ready answers not only to all the old chestnuts but to difficult impromptu questions? He was certain because he felt as G. K. Chesterton had felt. Christianity is true and real and historical. Thus, no matter from what angle you approach it, it is reality.

In August of 1939, Warnie reported to Jack, "Russia has signed a 'peace' pact with Germany and backed off to watch. The countries to the east, between Germany and Russia, are ripe for the German harvest. Unfortunately, one of them is Poland. We Brits are obligated to defend Poland. War for us is inevitable, Jack."

Life changed for everyone in England. The very next month, Warnie—as an army reservist—was called to duty in Yorkshire. Jack enlisted in the Home Guard and volunteered to be a religious lecturer to airmen and officers in the Royal Air Force. Because it seemed London would be bombed by the Germans, most children were evacuated. The rest of England took them in. The Kilns was no exception. Mrs. Moore welcomed several schoolgirls. Then, as everyone expected, Germany invaded Poland, and England and France declared war on Germany. By October, Warnie was sent with British troops to France.

Jack was invited to give a sermon to the faculty and undergraduates at Oxford's historic Church of St. Mary the Virgin. He felt humbled as he climbed the same spiraling stairway to the same pulpit that had featured John Wesley and other great spiritual leaders. Personal emotions, however, provided no excuse to shirk responsibility. Jack's mission was no less than to explain to the undergraduates why they must pursue their education with all diligence, even though the war was very likely to drag them away, even though they might never return. "Fear must not deter us from doing our very best for the glory of God," he insisted.

Jack, who had suffered the trenches of a war, spoke with the advantage of firsthand experience, but he quickly discovered that lecturing airmen around England was far different than speaking to fellow scholars in a hard-fought, well-known vernacular. Understandably, these laymen had their own vernacular, and it was no less valid than that of the scholars, but Jack had to adjust to the fact that many terms understood among scholars to mean a specific thing meant something else to the laymen. To the laymen, "church" meant a sacred building, not a body of followers in Christ. "Charity" meant alms for the poor, not Christian love. "Dogma" was some unproved assertion presented in an arrogant manner. "Crucifixion" did not convey an execution preceded by agonizing torture; its familiarity had made it a painless, sanitized ritual. "Primitive Christianity" was not at all to the laymen the wonderful, pure Christianity practiced by the apostles. No, it meant something backward, crude, and unfinished!

"Defining every term is self-defeating," Jack discussed with Tolkien. "Nothing can be done unless we move completely away from this language of the scholars and the clergy. Apologetics has to be driven by the simplest words in the English language." Jack was intrigued by the fact that, two hundred years before, John Wesley had ventured away from Oxford to evangelize with those identical conclusions about language.

While Jack's teaching load was wilting as undergraduates went to war, his mind was teeming with ideas for books. Besides *The Problem of Pain,* he had a sequel to *Out of the Silent Planet* and a satire about devils in mind. The war in Europe was a disaster. Germany had run the British army, including Warnie, right off the continent. By August of 1940, Warnie was put in the army reserve and allowed to return to Oxford.

That same month Maureen married Leonard Blake, the musical director at Worksop College in the county of Nottingham many miles north of Oxford.

Now both brothers served in the Home Guard, lugging a rifle around the dark streets of Oxford one night every week or so. Both also attended the meetings of the Inklings on Thursday nights. Charles Williams, now working in Oxford because the Oxford University Press had closed his London office, had joined the Inklings. Jack had never met anyone with a physical presence like Williams: He exuded holiness. Not only Jack felt that way. W. H. Auden and T. S. Eliot, men not easily impressed, were dumbfounded by the same feeling about Williams. Auden began touting Williams as the mentor of his later verse. On the other hand, Eliot began claiming Williams as his protégé.

Jack and Charles Williams became great friends, without regard to the fact that they were not uncritical of each other's work. Jack thought Williams was undisciplined, and that once in a while this fault exploded into poor taste. Conjuring up a romance between Mary Magdalene and John the Baptist, as Williams did in one work, grated on Jack like chalk screeching on a blackboard, yet he admired Williams's incredible imagination, the most fertile Jack had ever been around. Williams erupted with original ideas. He was electric. Like Jack, he could astonish even other scholars by quoting long passages from memory.

Williams urged Jack to take more chances with his writing, yet, on the other hand, he continually expressed awe both of Jack's mastery of the classics and of his unparalleled ability to assess literature. Williams had met those who had attempted lofty conversations, but none had possessed the vigor and joy the Inklings, especially Jack, displayed.

In October of that same year, Geoffrey Bles published Jack's *The Problem of Pain*. Scholars ignored it, but since its plain, everyday language was aimed at the layperson anyway, from that standpoint it was an immediate success. The book had to be reprinted twice that year, and sales did not slack off the following year.

"Its sole purpose is to explain suffering," maintained Jack. "Most pain in men is inflicted by other men, perhaps even Satan. Yet," Jack yielded, "some pain must be attributed to God. Why would God make men suffer? The hard answer is that in no ways other than pain and death can God make man surrender his self to God. 'Happy' people ignore God; 'unhappy' people seek God and desire the peace and security of his Kingdom." Thus Jack explained why an all-powerful, loving God permits pain. Jack even dealt with pain in animals, a fact many moderns find more intolerable than pain in humans.

The book dealt with far more than "the problem of pain." In it, Jack described the fall of man and his elemental wickedness, which moderns prefer not to acknowledge whatsoever. He explained heaven and hell. He addressed the phenomenon of the "numinous" and discussed the awe, even dread, we feel for the supernatural. He extolled the nature of God and His love for us. He emphasized the love God expects from us. He examined all the doctrines modern man finds so difficult to accept. All these were the doctrines that the liberal clergy, unable to explain, were abandoning.

In May of 1941, Jack began writing weekly installments of satire for the *Guardian*, a weekly newspaper of the Church of England. Each segment was a letter from the retired devil, Screwtape, to his young pupil, Wormwood, who was tempting his first human. The first letter to Wormwood detailed how to undermine the victim's faith in prayer. Each subsequent letter took up another way to tempt and trip and snare, and each was devilishly witty. Eventually Jack wrote thirty-one letters, enough to compile a book.

Already Jack was evangelizing on another front. The director of religious broadcasting for the British Broadcasting Corporation (BBC) was so impressed by the lucidity of *The Problem of Pain* that he asked Jack to speak on BBC radio. Jack detested the radio, yet agreed because thousands might hear him. He knew exactly what he wanted to say. The New Testament assumed men understood God's natural law and knew when they were wicked. All ancient men, even pagans, knew right and wrong; modern men were ignorant. They had to be instructed in God's natural law before they were ready for the fruits of Christianity. Jack produced a series of four talks billed as "Right and Wrong."

He spoke at a deliberate, slow, conversational pace of about 150 words per minute. Listening to the recordings, he was surprised how the slow delivery had heightened his Oxfordian accent. The radio consultants, however, pronounced his baritone voice as superb for radio: It was articulate, lucid, and resonant. His talks were so well received, he was later informed, that he was talking not to thousands but hundreds of thousands!

The Royal Air Force now solicited him to specifically instruct airmen in basic Christianity. Any reluctance he might have felt about surrendering more of his time dissipated when he visited the air base in Norfolk. The crews were flying into Europe on night bombing raids.

"The airmen have a tour of duty that lasts thirty missions," stated the chaplain.

"They must be very relieved when their tour is completed," sympathized Jack.

"On the average," the chaplain paused, "a man lasts only thirteen missions." Jack was stunned. "Then they are most likely doomed!"

"Yes." The chaplain's voice had gone flat.

"No one needs Christ more than these men do."

When Jack was urged also to continue his broadcasts, he began another series of radio talks in the same vein called "What Christians Believe." He had less and less time now for his former activities. To make matters more difficult, he and Warnie had to sell their car. Gasoline was too hard to obtain. Once again, the brothers rode a double-decker bus to and from Oxford. Still, in Jack's spare moments, he managed to write. As his radio talks made him more well known around England, he began receiving hundreds of letters. He answered every one.

The Screwtape Letters was published in February of 1942. Jack had resolved his guilt over profiting from religious writing. The money from any of his religious works was donated to charity. He dedicated *The Screwtape Letters* to Tolkien. Previous books had been dedicated to Hugo Dyson, the Inklings, and Warnie. No friend needed to be concerned about being left out at the rate Jack was publishing his prose.

ELEVEN

Jack was very interested in how TLS, the literary supplement of the February 28, 1942, *London Times*, would review *The Screwtape Letters*. He read:

> *On the whole the book is brilliantly successful. A reviewer's task is not to be a prophet, and time alone can show whether it is or is not an enduring piece of satirical writing. . . . It is much more to the point that in so readable a fashion Mr. Lewis has contrived to say much that a distracted world greatly requires to hear.*

So TLS was hinting the book might be enduring. Only time would tell. *The Manchester Guardian* was not so cautious:

> *In a book of any length, satire easily topples over into farce and any levity in the treatment of such a subject would be fatal. Mr. Lewis never fails. The book is sparkling yet truly reverent, in fact a perfect joy, and should become a classic.*

A classic! Jack had to brush off such praise. It was dangerous. Praise in other reviews, however, was unstinting as well. The first printing of *The Screwtape Letters* sold out before publication because of its following in the *Guardian*. The book soon merited a life of its own. It was reprinted eight times in the first year! C. S. Lewis was now truly a national figure.

In 1942, Jack was asked by his old tutor Wilson to contribute to the *Oxford History of the English Language*. Jack's specific assignment would be the sixteenth century. Not to be only the highlights of giants like Spenser and Shakespeare but a complete survey of writers good and bad, it would be an immense undertaking. Before long Jack was referring to the ever-looming, ever time-consuming work as "Oh Hell!" the pronunciation of the acronym for the *Oxford History of the English Language*, O. H. E. L. Yet he knew "Oh Hell!" as the legacy of a scholar would be as important as his *Allegory of Love*.

Jack also satisfied his desire for thoughtful scholarship that year by writing *Preface to Paradise Lost* for Oxford University Press. He dedicated it to Charles Williams. "Preface," however, was a gross understatement. The commentary lasted for eighteen chapters and filled 139 pages. Half of the "preface" defined what an epic was supposed to be. The other half described the medieval Christianity that had shaped Milton's morality and recounted how Milton had differed from it.

Reviews in England and America were generally complimentary. After all, the *Preface* was a great help to those tackling Milton. Nevertheless, some academics fumed over the work. How dare Jack lecture them on morality and Christianity? His evangelizing was permissable for common people, but it was presumptuous when it affected professors!

Sometimes people sought Jack out at the favorite public haunts of the Inklings. Once, at the Eagle and Child pub—known affectionately as the Bird and Baby—he was confronted by Roy Campbell, a fiery poet who was also a brawler. Although Jack had lampooned Campbell's poetry, Campbell had come not to fight but to enjoy the give-and-take. He had fought in the Spanish Civil War against the Communists. Both Tolkien and Jack despised Communism.

Only rarely did Jack's swashbuckling style carry over into his tutorials. In fact, his demeanor was intentionally low-key and unemotional. Very conscious that some pupils were only seventeen or eighteen, he usually extended quiet civility to his pupils, just as Smewgy had done for him. Scarcely ever did he bully them or even raise his voice.

As a rule, Jack met with each student for one hour a week. During the first meeting, he specified the background the pupil would need to master English literature from Old English to 1821. "The great English writers assume a sound biblical and classical background," he would advise a pupil. "Be certain to read the historical books of the Old Testament, Psalms, and the Gospels, particularly the book of Luke. If you read the Vulgate version, you can brush up on your Latin, too." Though sorely tempted, Jack purposely never evangelized a pupil.

"But, Mr. Lewis, when do we read Shakespeare?"

"Oh, you will," he would assure, "but to understand Shakespeare best we must master the Bible and the classics. Don't bother with Greek. Read Virgil, Boethius, Ovid, and Cicero."

"Quite a load, sir." The student would sigh.

"Yes. To be sure," Jack would agree before continuing. "You also need to know how to scan hexameters." Inevitably, the pupil's face would pale. Analyzing the meter of classic poetry by quantity rather than stress numbed students with fear. "Now to the English writers," Jack would breeze, observing the student perking up. "Chaucer, Shakespeare, and Milton are imperative. Know them. At other various times, you're sure to encounter Malory, Spenser, Donne, Browne, Dryden, Pope, Swift, Johnson, and Wordsworth. Any questions?"

During the term, having studied and written an essay before each week's meeting, the pupil would take a chair in Jack's large sitting room and unwind during two or three minutes of polite conversation with him. Then the pupil would begin the lesson by reading his essay. Usually the essay was read in about fifteen minutes. Reading beyond half an hour was considered bad form;

it left little time for discussion.

Jack had several favorite comments at the conclusion of the reading. "There may be something in what you say" meant the essay was bad. "There is something in what you say" indicated the essay was barely acceptable, as did "Too much straw and not enough bricks." If the essay was good, he would allow, "There is a good deal in what you say." "Much of that was very well said" recognized an outstanding essay.

Next, Jack, who had taken notes, would direct, "Now we shall discuss these points in your essay: verbal structure, rhythm, and clarity. Also, to remind you that I'm no great fan of clichés and figures of speech, we shall discuss precision."

The main points of communicating having been discussed, Jack and his pupil would finally examine the material under study. Occasionally Jack would astonish his pupil by quoting verse after verse of *Paradise Lost*. Even more amazing was his gift of instant entry into the classic. If a pupil would quote one line, Jack would instantly quote subsequent lines. His memory was photographic.

Though remaining frank in his opinions, through the years his Christianity compelled him more and more to soften criticism with a joke or praise. "That's really quite imaginative. Perhaps we can discuss some mistakes to improve your future work."

At the end of each term, Jack reserved a private room at Magdalen and gave a dinner party for his pupils. For this event, he entertained in the raucous way he did with his closest friends, in the way his father had done with his friends. To Jack, the celebration was almost a rite of passage for the pupil, so he conducted it like a medieval rite, bringing forth not bawdy songs, but what he called "bawdry" songs, clever songs of coarse humor and irreverence.

"In the Middle Ages," he reminded his pupils, "this type of a festive gathering of men brought forth devotions and tragedies as well as bawdry songs—all in an oral tradition, of course—authors now long unknown."

Meanwhile, Jack's works outside of Oxford continued to flourish. In July of 1942, Geoffrey Bles published Jack's two series of radio talks, "Right and Wrong" and "What Christians Believe," as the book *Broadcast Talks*. Jack was so well known now that no other title was necessary. A new, third series of talks, called "Christian Behavior," encouraged Christians to pursue holy lives and was scheduled to be published as the book *Christian Behavior* in 1943.

Broadcast Talks presented to the layman, in the most comprehensible English, Jack's arguments for that basic Christianity recognized by Protestants and Catholics alike. There is an underlying law of morality, he insisted, that all mankind intuitively knows is the right way to behave. This suggests a "mind" rules the universe. Yet mankind constantly misbehaves anyway. Therein lies a great paradox: If the "mind" is not good, mankind is lost; if the "mind" is good, mankind is in dire trouble for misbehaving!

In his treatise, Jack then reviewed the great religions. He propounded that only those religions that believe in a creator outside the universe deal with the problem of a loving God permitting evil and suffering: Judaism, Islam, and Christianity. And why do Christians believe Christ is also God? Because Christ is a historical fact; because He claimed to be God; because He died and is alive again—hundreds of witnesses saw Him both before and after the resurrection.

Initial belief is but one step. The next step is to live as a Christian. All mankind recognizes the goodness of the four cardinal virtues: prudence or common sense; temperance or self-control; justice or fairness; and fortitude or courage. The Christian has three more virtues: hope, that continual looking forward to God's eternal world; faith, to ward off the black moments of disbelief or suffering; and charity, the greatest virtue of all, loving as God loves.

A Christian who tries to treat everyone kindly finds himself liking more and more people, even people he could not have imagined himself liking initially, but Christian charity must be practiced even when the Christian doesn't "feel" loving. When the Christian "feels" no real love of God, he acts as one acts who does love God. Jack insisted that when this is done, love will come. Thus he concluded *Broadcast Talks*.

In 1943, Jack received from J. B. Phillips the clergyman's own translation of Paul's letter to the Colossians. Phillips was proposing no less than translating all the letters of Paul into modern English! Jack read a passage that had always troubled him, even though he was a superb translator of Greek himself.

"I see the meaning clearly now!" he exclaimed. "It's like seeing a familiar picture after it's been cleaned."

Jack was genuinely pleased with Phillips's translation of Colossians. Jack did not object to a qualified scholar translating the Greek of the New Testament into the common language of the modern Englishman. Oh yes, he loved the poetry of the King James Version, but hadn't it become a luxury of the scholarly? How many modern Englishmen knew the subtleties of seventeenth-century English? And hadn't Jack advanced his apologetics the same way, moving away from troublesome jargon to the simplest modern language possible?

Meanwhile, the success of *The Screwtape Letters* still reverberated. By 1943 the American press had picked up on it. The *New York Times* commented:

> *"The devil," said Thomas More, "cannot endure being mocked," and which, if correct, means that somewhere in the inferno there must be considerable annoyance.*

The *Saturday Review of Literature* was even more impressed:

> *Whatever you may think of the theses of Mr. Lewis, presented as they are in a bizarre and slandicular manner, the fact remains that there is a spectacular and satisfactory nova in the bleak sky of satire.*

The Screwtape Letters not only sold well itself in America but created demand for Jack's previous works: *The Problem of Pain, Out of the Silent Planet*, and *Broadcast Talks* (printed in America as *Case for Christianity*.) Even *Pilgrim's Regress* was reprinted and sold well in America because all of these reissued books received good reviews in American magazines and newspapers.

Publishers were now slavering after the sequel to *Out of the Silent Planet*. Jack knew exactly what he wanted to write—he just had to find the time in which to do it. His second space fiction would again involve the "good" man Ransom and the "evil" scientist Weston, but this time on Venus, or "Perelandra," as he called it. The time of the story would be before the Fall, and the vast watery world of Perelandra would be in complete harmony. There would be an Adam and an Eve, under different names, of course. Weston would represent the devil, trying to tempt "Eve" to disobey.

Jack had no deluded image of Adam and Eve as primitive, hairy simpletons. No, his image, already expressed in *The Problem of Pain* and his *Preface to Paradise Lost*, was quite the opposite. All great thinkers since Saint Augustine deemed humans before the Fall to be vastly superior to humans who followed—they were supremely in tune with nature, themselves, and God. They exercised their will over all the animals. They could will their bodies to do anything. They talked to God face-to-face.

"If such a man or woman were to appear among us," insisted Jack, "the holiest one among us would immediately be on his knees."

The astonishing rate at which Jack was publishing would never have been possible under a normal workload at Oxford, but most of the students were still off fighting a war. Having never been busier, he wondered how he would cope with the workload after the war. Because of the staggering volume of letters, they worked out a routine by which Warnie could help Jack answer each one. Jack would read a letter and jot a thoughtful answer on it. Warnie, who had taught himself to type while organizing the "Lewis Papers," would then type the response for Jack's signature. Eventually, Warnie knew exactly how Jack would answer the more routine letters, and he began to answer them for Jack. Jack had only to sign at the bottom. Because Jack's response would not have been different, neither brother considered the method dishonest at all. Through this cooperation, Jack began noticing that Warnie was indeed a very gifted writer.

Warnie spent much more time at the Kilns now than Jack, who seemed committed at every moment. Jack's socializing at the Kilns had almost stopped. His get-togethers with the Inklings and the Socratic Club—even his frequent pub visits to the Bird and Baby—seemed a natural extension of his life's work rather than socializing. The Kilns grew more and more remote. Jack knew failing health was making Mrs. Moore, now 70, very cantankerous, but Warnie, irritated by her, hinted that she was becoming irrational. For years already, Warnie had silently but obviously sympathized with Maureen in squabbles with her mother. Besides that, Mrs. Moore's generosity and kindness presumed on those in the household. She was not the one who walked Troodles and Mr. Papworth and Bruce and all the other dogs she took in. Nor was the busy Paxford. No, the dogs were cared for by Jack and Warnie. And now that Jack was rarely present, their keeper was barely willing Warnie.

In 1943, Oxford University Press published Jack's *Abolition of Man*. The book, though based on a series of lectures, was aimed at the general public, and it missed the mark. It had none of the warmth and strength of his other works. It was too detached, too scholarly. Jack was convinced it was a very important work: It did no less than point out how and why our modern society was going haywire. Maniacs like Hitler and Stalin, however, should have made the point obvious.

The book also failed to reach the intellectuals. The new philosophers at Oxford, adherents of logical positivism, a new approach that was tearing down all absolute morality, nitpicked every definition that defended absolutes. Could it be proved mathematically? If not, it was meaningless. So beauty and ugliness were only relative at best, and right and wrong meant nothing at all.

Jack would have to make the point of *Abolition of Man* in another way. Already his mind was cranking. The dread destroyers of order and decency would be the villains of his next space fiction, the conclusion of his trilogy.

TWELVE

In 1943, the second book of Jack's space trilogy was published. *Perelandra* was a smashing success with most reviewers, English and American, religious and secular.

Personally Jack felt it was his best fiction yet, but resentment was stirring among those who embraced the glory of science and humanism, and even atheism, because Jack was becoming too successful. Some reviews were sprinkled with such unfavorable comments as, "For the reviewer, *Perelandra* . . . was a place of nightmare horror," "Mr. Lewis loads the dice heavily," "metaphysical abracadabra," and "nonsense."

Also in 1943, Geoffrey Bles published *Christian Behavior*, the next installment of Jack's radio broadcasts. No longer were his religious books reviewed only by *Catholic World, Christian Century*, and other religious periodicals, although these certainly praised *Christian Behavior*. Now his religious exposition was noted by the secular press, especially in America. The *New York Times* praised the book and said of Jack:

His mind is very clear; his style exhibits the costly simplicity that is achieved only after much learning and thinking and pruning away of non-essentials.

In 1944, Geoffrey Bles published *Beyond Personality: The Christian Idea of God*, a compilation of more of Jack's radio talks, and his most ambitious effort at theology yet. Many advised Lewis not to do it because he explored the very nature of God; he asserted man is alive and part of the "bios" but not part of "zoe," or the spiritual life that exists in God; he advocated that the whole purpose of our existence is to be taken into the life of God.

Jack further explained the Christian concept of the Trinity: three Gods in One. God is the spiritual being we are trying to reach and reflect. Christ is the only real source of our knowledge of God. The Holy Spirit is the part of God within us. Because God is not in time, He can attend personally to each individual. When we become Christlike, we are drawn into God.

Beyond Personality was also evaluated by an array of reviewers. Religious publications were ecstatic with his success. *Catholic World* acclaimed, "Gifted Mr. Lewis. . .(has an) almost unique ability to make abstractions intelligible and interesting." *Churchman* applauded: "Once again this brilliant author. . . endeavors to explain the orthodox Christian faith in the simplest terms."

Jack now devoted much of his time to writing two books scheduled for publication in 1945, his third space fiction and another fiction unlike any he had done: *The Great Divorce.* ("Divorce" referred to the chasm between heaven and hell.) Jack's book would be a loose rewrite of Dante's trip in *The Divine Comedy* through modern eyes. For instance, Jack's guide, instead of Virgil, is his own mentor, George MacDonald, and a busload of egotistical sinners are shown heaven, where they struggle with all their might to preserve their damnable identities.

After *The Great Divorce* was published, it was praised by the *New York Times*, the *New Yorker*, the *Library Journal*, and the *Weekly Book Review.* Other reviews were lukewarm, like the review in TLS. A few, like the one in *Kirkus*, expressed disappointment. A very few, like the one in the *Spectator*, were antagonistic. As TLS pointed out: "Those who find themselves in agreement with the arguments put up by the Ghosts for not being saved will be unlikely to finish this book!"

All the Inklings but Tolkien seemed to approve Jack's clever device for fiction in *The Great Divorce.* "Dante is spiteful and malicious," asserted Tolkien. "He's all about petty people in petty situations." Thus he condemned one of Jack's heroes and indirectly Jack's fiction, too.

Jack's third space fiction, *That Hideous Strength*, particularly caused a rift between himself and Tolkien. Tolkien was writing a book all the Inklings called *The New Hobbit*, regardless that its official title was to be *The Lord of the Rings.* Tolkien's style had changed in this new work. The narrative was faster paced and more compelling. The message of the myth was enormous. Jack, convinced that *The Lord of the Rings* could potentially be a major work of the century if Tolkien could sustain it, encouraged Tolkien more than anyone else. Curiously, however, Tolkien had to be prodded and prodded. Sometimes he would put down *The New Hobbit* and not work on it for months and months. Jack was the catalyst that kept the effort going.

Yet when Jack read to the Inklings his third space fiction, *That Hideous Strength*, Tolkien openly despised it. "Too many themes are jumbled together," he carped. Moreover, Tolkien thought Jack was pandering to Charles Williams by introducing King Arthur themes, and he made no effort to conceal his opinion.

The first two fictions, especially *Perelandra*, were pared to the bone, lean and magnificent. In this book, Jack had been very much inspired by Williams. He had indulged his imagination; he had indulged friends. In this book, he had alluded to both Tolkien and Barfield; he had created one character who was clearly his old tutor Kirkpatrick; and he had metamorphosed Ransom into an image of Charles Williams!

Many reviewers agreed the book was disappointing and criticized Jack for weaknesses that were usually his strengths. *Catholic World* suggested "drastic pruning" could have made it "timely and rousing." *Churchman* found the characters and motives "sometimes incomprehensible." *The Saturday Review of Literature* complained "the redemption of one intellectual opportunist" seemed poor reward for reading such a tome.

So the reviews confirmed that truth had been in Tolkien's carping, but his jealousy over Charles Williams was difficult to ignore. That Jack enjoyed the company of Williams more than anyone he had met—other than Owen Barfield—was true. Jack still reckoned Barfield the greatest intellect he had ever known, but Charles Williams was a close second. Despite Tolkien's jealousy, Jack promoted Williams all the more. Jack hoped that, with his backing, Charles Williams could acquire a post at Oxford as professor of poetry, his lack of a college degree notwithstanding. Preliminarily, Jack helped Williams revise what many thought was his best supernatural thriller, *All Hallows' Eve.* Jack also used his influence with Geoffrey Bles to procure Williams a contract for a book on forgiveness in their Christian Challenge series.

Mere days after World War II ended in May of 1945, Jack received his greatest blow since his father had died in 1929. Charles Williams, only fifty-eight, died in what Jack had presumed was minor surgery. Jack sensed his presence, as if Williams were in a state of bliss yet somehow able to look upon the living. Jack felt pain and loss, but no resentment—Christ had changed that. How could a Christian resent a friend going on to paradise?

Because Jack felt a great debt to Williams for expanding his imagination, he had solicited essays from friends that were to be a farewell gift to Williams as he left for London. Now the essays by Jack, Tolkien, Dorothy Sayers, Owen Barfield, and other contributors would be a memorial. Jack could not bring himself to change the title: *Essays Presented to Charles Williams.*

In the book he depicted Williams, the man:

> *In appearance he was tall, slim, and straight as a boy, though gray-haired. His face we thought ugly. . .but the moment he spoke it became. . .like the face of an angel. . . . No man whom I have known was at the same time less affected and more flamboyant in his manners: and also more playful.*[1]

Jack had certainly been victimized by his playfulness. Once Williams had engineered a lunch meeting between Jack and his longtime nemesis, T. S. Eliot. As the two enemies carried on an interminable icy conversation, Williams enjoyed the occasion enormously. Jack had harbored no grudge. Perhaps the meeting might have been a success. Was it Williams's fault? Or the fault of two proud antagonists?

The essays themselves were not tribute enough for Jack. In a tribute he entitled *Arthurian Torso*, he gathered several unpublished chapters that Williams had written on the King Arthur legends, then added his own unstinting praise on Williams's poetry called the Taliessin cycle. Jack asserted that in certain of these poems Williams had produced word music unsurpassed by any other poet of the twentieth century. Both tributes were eventually published by Williams's own publisher, Oxford University Press.

Jack compiled an anthology of excerpts from MacDonald's writings that illuminated Christianity, then wrote a preface of about four thousand words. Not fawning and uncritical, he acknowledged that MacDonald was not a writer of the first rank, but that he had so successfully created myth that it overcame writing too often florid and verbose. Without reservation Jack could recommend his fantasies: *Phantastes, Lilith,* and the two "Curdie" books. Jack knew others, such as J. R. R. Tolkien, W. H. Auden, and G. K. Chesterton, shared his high opinion of MacDonald's mythmaking. The anthology was published in 1946.

Jack continued to explain the truths of Christianity, addressing any stumbling block that caused people to turn away from finding Christ. What was mentioned as a stumbling block more often than the miracles in the Bible? How often had Jack heard people mutter, "If only it weren't for the miracles. . ."

Thus, in his book *Miracles*, virtually completed in 1945 but not published until 1947, Jack's goal was no less than to convince skeptics the miracles were not unusual at all—for God. It was a very bold book, finished only through inspiration gained from Charles Williams. In it, Jack argued powerfully that not supernaturalism but naturalism was self-contradictory. His book was no less than a proof of the supernatural.

Religious publications like *Christian Century* openly praised *Miracles*, but reviews in secular publications were cautious. Praising the book seemed too much like substantiating supernaturalism. Most reviewers, therefore, recommended the book yet tried not to endorse the ideas. *Miracles* cemented with the public his reputation as a popular apologist for Christianity. He was featured on the cover of the American magazine *Time*. Inside, a lengthy article teemed with inaccuracies and rumors about his private life. The reporter had assumed that any questions unable to be answered by Jack's friends indicated Jack was secretive. The magazine raised the possibility that Jack was a hypocrite who simply wrote for money. Jack did not bother to refute the charge by revealing that profits from his religious books went to charity.

Nevertheless, Jack, the literary critic, was pleased with some of the writing in *Time*. The article acknowledged his debt to George MacDonald and Charles Williams. And descriptions of himself were amusing:

The lecturer [Jack], a. . .thickset man with a ruddy face and a big voice, was coming to the end of his talk. Gathering up his notes and books, he tucked his horn-rimmed spectacles into the pocket of his tweed jacket and picked up his mortarboard. Still talking—to the accompaniment of occasional appreciative laughs and squeals—he leaned over to return the watch he had borrowed from a student in the front row. As he ended his final sentence, he stepped off the platform. The maneuver gained him a head start on the rush of students down the center aisle. Once in the street, he strode rapidly—his black gown billowing behind his gray flannel trousers.

True enough. The article was also faithful to mention his extraordinary teaching load during the postwar years. It included some nice quotes on the absurdities of pantheism and the wish for sexual pleasure in heaven. The reporter confirmed Jack's belief that many of the faculty were jealous of his success, some to the point of promoting the lie that he wrote to make lots of money. Some complained instead about his bluntness. It was true; he was blunt.

The article, no matter how lengthy, failed to cover even a tenth of Jack's responsibilities. In spite of Jack's deliberate effort to keep his pupils at a distance emotionally, some came to him with problems.

The *Time* article quoted the Oxford undergraduate magazine, *Cherwell*, in which Jack had warned:

> *Christianity is now "on the map" among the younger [students]. . .*
> *the days of simple "unfaith" are as dead as those of "simple faith. . .[yet] we must remember that widespread and lively interest in the subject is precisely what we call a fashion. . . . Whatever in our present success mere fashion has given us, mere fashion will presently withdraw. The real conversions will remain, but nothing else will. . .we must cherish no picture of the present intellectual movement simply growing and spreading and finally reclaiming millions by sweet reasonableness.*

Jack knew all too well that to many, Christianity was initially appealing but finally, as they learned more of it, repulsive. Christianity was hard. It demanded total surrender and exposed the great gulf between nature and the supernatural.

THIRTEEN

On February 2, 1948, when the secretary of the Socratic Club announced, "Our topic today is 'Miracles: A Reply to Mr. C. S. Lewis,'" one of the new philosophers, Elizabeth Anscombe, rose and attempted to destroy his argument. Jack found himself, as usual, refuting the opposition. He was aggressive, bullying in his defense. And the evening became one of his worst memories!

Elizabeth Anscombe was no shrinking violet. Large and beefy like Jack, she wore pants and even smoked cigars! Worse than that, though, she was brilliant enough to hopelessly entangle Jack in definitions. As a logical positivist, she had to be persuaded with mathematics, Jack's anathema. So she also made him appear to be waffling. Later, although his loyal followers insisted he had won the debate, he was very depressed.

"Lord, how will one ever communicate right and wrong, much less the glory of Christ, with the modern philosophers and their unfortunate disciples?" pleaded Jack.

Some started a rumor that Jack was so depressed by Anscombe's thrashing that he refused to write any further apologetics. This was utter nonsense, because Jack had told the *Time* reporter six months before the confrontation with Anscombe that he was planning no more apologetics in the near future. For the present, he had written what he wanted to write and was moving back into fiction in some form.

"I won't refute every malicious rumor," determined Jack. "Surely intelligent people can decipher the truth." And he prayed that they would. Christ was now his anchor.

Jack was pleased to see J. B. Phillips's translation of the letters of Paul finally in print. He had certainly done his part in nudging it to fruition. After many rejections, his own publisher, Geoffrey Bles, had agreed to publish it on his recommendation. Jack had suggested the title, *Letters to Young Churches,* and written the preface, pointing out that the 1600s traditionalists had also objected to the new version being authorized by King James! He made another point, too: The King James Version is *not* a translation of the New Testament in its original Greek; the King James Version is a translation of a Latin translation of the original Greek. "As beautiful as the King James Version is, who could object to a more direct approach by a modern scholar?" Jack queried.

Possibly on the basis of Jack's appeal and the prominent display of his name on the dust jacket, *Letters to Young Churches* sold very well right from the beginning and by its own merit soon gained a life of its own. It steadily gained popularity until it appeared it would actually become a best seller.

Despite the popular press lauding Jack as the great champion for Christianity, life seemed sour to him in 1948. He turned fifty. The teaching load was enormous. He couldn't change the fact that Williams was dead. Tolkien was peevish and disagreeable. And the people of Oxford he saw every day were more and more hostile. In their cultured opinion, wearing Christianity on one's sleeve, like he was doing, was rather unfashionable. Day-to-day life at Magdalen was more and more stressful, and the sad truth was that the Kilns offered no relief. In fact, Jack went there with a sense of dread. Rationing of food had everyone on edge. Now even potatoes, which they relied on as their main "filler," were rationed. What quarrel would greet Jack at the Kilns? With whom was Mrs. Moore fighting now? The cook? A new maid, perhaps?

Was Warnie of help? Yes, when he was not drinking heavily. Once or twice a year now, he binged, usually disappearing to visit friends who also drank or Ireland to drink anywhere. Jack expected a call for him to come to Warnie's aid at any time. During Warnie's binges, his drinking accelerated until he was in a deathlike stupor. Then Jack would find some hospital or rest home to take him in until he recovered. Yet, even in this turmoil, the hope offered by Christ sustained Jack, and his work continued.

Many years before—perhaps when he had been only sixteen—he had seen a vision of a faun carrying an umbrella and a parcel through a snowy wood. As the war began and the schoolgirls from London arrived in 1939, he actually transcribed some of the story about the faun, his main characters none other than four children who had left London because of the war: Ann, Martin, Rose, and Peter. They stayed with a very old professor.

Six years later, in 1945, Jack perused the manuscript of a children's story by Roger Green, a former pupil. Some of its elements remained vividly with Jack. In 1948 he resumed his own story, and, with Green's permission—Green had never published his narrative—Jack incorporated some of Green's ideas. The children became Susan, Lucy, Edmund, and Peter Pevensie. Soon Jack had created the fantasy world of Narnia, which the children visited by walking through a magic wardrobe in the professor's house. Jack had been dreaming about lions, and the story crystallized when he introduced Christ in the form of a magnificent lion named Aslan. By Christmas of 1948, the story was finished.

Jack's publisher, Geoffrey Bles, was not enthusiastic about the story. Now dubbed *The Lion, the Witch, and the Wardrobe,* it combined Christianity, Santa Claus, talking animals, fauns, witches, and real people. On the other hand, Jack did have a name that sold books, so Bles would risk the project. Perhaps, Bles suggested, Jack could write a subsequent episode; a series might allow them to recover their investment. So Jack forged ahead with the sequel, *Prince*

Caspian. For the first time in a long time, Geoffrey Bles would not go ahead straightaway with one of Jack's books.

Life at Oxford seemed diminished for Jack, too. He no longer enjoyed the Socratic Club, though serving as president since its inception. He was tired of fending off the logical positivism of atheists and agnostics.

Besides his discontent with the Socratic Club, Jack was disgusted about being denied a professorship, even after many years. Tolkien had been a full professor since 1945. Essentially, Jack was exhausted. Full professors did not have to tutor, but he, without the professorship, was still tutoring after twenty-five years!

The years immediately after the war had been particularly difficult. Many soldiers had returned to resume their studies. Tutoring had never been a greater burden, requiring morning, afternoon, and evening sessions, but Jack, never one to slight his duties, had simply refused to cheat a pupil out of what was rightly his.

Demands on Jack's energies intensified as Warnie's drinking reached new levels. Already completely exhausted, Jack became depressed. Nonetheless, he persistently strove to finish his enormous volume of the *Oxford History of English Literature*. One night in June of 1949 at the Kilns, Jack began to hallucinate. Thankfully, Mrs. Moore, not healthy herself, had the presence of mind to call the ambulance. Thus, when Warnie returned, Jack was in the hospital receiving shot after shot of penicillin.

Jack realized he could no longer hide Warnie's drinking. No longer would he speak of Warnie suffering from "insomnia" or "nerves." Warnie was an alcoholic.

For once, Jack even sought advice outside his usual close circle. "Only the alcoholic stops drinking," counseled those wise in the ways of drinkers. Jack was disheartened, aware that Warnie still deluded himself about drinking, purporting that he could still drink, he just needed to exert more willpower. Deep inside, Jack knew only one hope for Warnie. So he prayed.

Life at Oxford continued to ebb. The Inklings never met again. The end had been coming. Jack had not read any of his work to the group since Tolkien had savaged *The Lion, the Witch, and the Wardrobe*. As well, because Hugo Dyson had repeatedly ridiculed *The Lord of the Rings*, Tolkien had not presented any of his work since 1947!

Meanwhile, Warnie, in his sober moments, labored as Jack's secretary. "Well, here's another feminine admirer from America," he teased Jack in 1950, waving a letter.

Jack reached for it somewhat reluctantly. "Not another celebrity worshipper, I hope." Moments later, however, he was chuckling. "She writes very well. Just the kind of humor I like, too. What's her name? Joy Gresham." He sat down and immediately composed the brilliant reply it demanded.

Over the next months, Jack exchanged letters with Joy Gresham. Having steady correspondents who considered him their spiritual mentor because of his books was not at all unusual for Jack. He had several such "pen-friends." Joy was a writer with two small boys and a husband who resented her writing. In no way did she express any self-pity, but Jack, because of his own difficulties, could tell her life was not smooth. As Joy continually posed conundrums that corroded her newly acquired Christianity, Jack felt obligated to destroy them one by one.

In April 1950, Mrs. Moore, now seventy-seven, frightened Jack. She was obviously senile and kept falling out of bed. To ensure that she was properly cared for, Jack took her to Restholme. Now beyond reach mentally, when she wasn't cursing the nursing home, she was inventing tragic news.

Although life at the Kilns was less stressful now—when Warnie was not drinking—the rest of Jack's life still seemed sour. A few friends met very informally every Tuesday night at the Bird and Baby, but the assemblage was no substitute for the Inklings. The very atmosphere at Oxford felt hostile. Tolkien's peevishness intensified because he was unable to find a publisher for *The Lord of the Rings*. The apparent ease with which Jack wrote and was published seemed to irritate him.

Jack wished for his previous lack of trouble in getting published. Geoffrey Bles refused to publish *The Lion, the Witch, and the Wardrobe* until he had in hand Jack's third book, *The Voyage of the Dawn Treader*. When the first book was finally published in the fall of 1950, it received favorable but cautious reviews. Reviewers admitted Jack's writing was superb as usual but asserted that modern children, who want to know how to cope with real-life problems, dislike moralistic fairy stories. Critics deemed Jack's characters too old-fashioned, too simple, too straightforward, and, some, altogether too scary! All in all, the book was not thought likely to appeal to modern children.

By late 1950, Jack admitted to himself that Mrs. Moore had put him under great stress for several years. Without her presence, the Kilns was now a peaceful home. Nonetheless, he faithfully prayed for her and asked friends to pray for her, too. He also visited her nearly every afternoon. Sometimes she raved angrily; sometimes she babbled like a child. He assured himself she would not have been one bit happier at the Kilns. Gradually, his health improved as he enjoyed more walks and even began swimming again at Parson's Pleasure.

In January of 1951, Mrs. Moore died from influenza at the age of seventy-eight and was buried in the churchyard of Holy Trinity Church in nearby Headington Quarry. Jack suffered greatly; he was very attached to her. Guilt of his own pettiness and stinginess haunted him, too, because he had begun to resent the crushing expense of Restholme. Little by little, he realized that he worried about finances just like his father had. He also noticed something else. He preferred a rigid church service just like his father had. Jack understood now that the predictability of form, unlike the distraction of something novel, allowed him to focus more intensely on prayer.

Although Warnie had been too drunk to attend Mrs. Moore's funeral, Jack knew from experience he was not beginning one of his customary binges. Eagerly Jack rushed off to Ireland to visit Arthur. After only a few days, he felt happier than he had in many years, much prayer having helped him accept that feeling without guilt. Then sales of *The Lion, the Witch, and the Wardrobe* skyrocketed. The Narnia story seemed to be exactly what the children wanted.

By the time Jack's second Narnia book was published before Christmas in 1951 and was selling as well as the first, Tolkien was still searching for a publisher for *The Lord of the Rings*. Meanwhile Jack slightly revised *Broadcast Talks*, *Christian Behavior*, and *Beyond Personality* and combined them into one book: *Mere Christianity*. It was an immediate best seller in 1952.

When Jack's third Narnia book was being prepared for publication in 1952, Tolkien yet remained without a publisher for *The Lord of the Rings*. Jack had almost finished writing the entire Narnia series, seven in all, the biblical number of perfection. Though the books had not been written in chronological order—for instance, the creation of Narnia was told in the sixth book: *The Magician's Nephew*—he had covered Narnia from its creation to the last battle. Jack knew that far from being a hodgepodge of elements, the Narnia series paralleled the truths of Christianity.

One morning in September, Jack informed Warnie, "Joy Gresham is visiting here in Oxford today."

"Your pen-friend from America!" exclaimed Warnie.

"Come and meet her," Jack urged. "She has invited us both to lunch at the Eastgate Hotel."

In the company of Warnie, Jack felt safe enough. If she was a nuisance, like one woman who had claimed to be his wife, he would make it a short lunch indeed. He felt a very haggard fifty-four. Joy Gresham, a bubbly, witty thirty-seven, made him feel like Methuselah. She was springtime, with large Bette Davis eyes behind horn-rimmed glasses, and full-figured. In some ways she reminded him of Charles Williams, homely until she began talking. Then, to Jack, she transcended her plain features and became angelic.

Her conversation was lively and as irreverent as Hugo Dyson's, and though she flattered Jack in an obvious way, he liked it. Jack admired her for having risen so far above her terrible personal problems. She was spunky, rebellious, full of good-natured exchanges. Jack had never met a woman so like his best friends. She was nearly a perfect companion. Of course he did not mean romantically; he simply meant that her wit and vivacity and shocking frankness made her enjoyable. Even Warnie liked her.

Because Jack and Warnie liked her bubbly company so much, Jack invited Joy to stay with them at the Kilns during the holidays. After some deliberation, he and Warnie decided they should behave just as they always did: walking, reading, and visiting pubs. A serious writer with several books already published, Joy fit right in, and Jack critiqued the manuscript of her book *Smoke on the Mountain*, her interpretation of the Ten Commandments.

During Joy's visit at the Kilns, she received a letter from her husband, William Gresham, asking for a divorce. Gresham often drank and had a violent temper. By now, Jack knew that he was a writer, too, with one very successful book, *Nightmare Alley*. His letter shocked even Joy. He planned to marry her cousin Renee, who would soon get her own divorce, and take in Renee's two children. Gresham informed Joy she was to live nearby with their two boys so he would be able to share raising them.

After she left, Jack grumbled, "Joy is going back to face the most selfish man in America. I wonder if we'll ever see her again."

FOURTEEN

Both brothers were very relieved when Joy returned to England in February of 1953. Any suggestion that Jack had anything to do with her divorce was squelched when she took up residence in London. She enrolled her boys in a prep school there and lived off royalties from her books and alimony. Jack didn't see her again until Christmas of 1953.

"So these are the boys," he greeted, looking at David, nine, and Douglas, eight.

They were thin, large-eyed boys with furry hair and animal energy. At first they were quiet, but they soon grew restless. Jack decided, since he was quite the walker, he would see that they were kept busy.

For four days Jack met the challenge, only allowing himself to collapse after Joy and the boys left for London. He had given them a manuscript of *The Horse and His Boy*, his fifth Narnia story, and promised them he would dedicate it to them. He always claimed to be uncomfortable around children, but his only fault was trying too hard to entertain them. He was a child himself in many ways.

After that introduction to the boys, Jack and Joy began seeing each other both in London and Oxford. Many of Jack's colleagues in Oxford were very cool to her, apparently resenting her brashness. Even Tolkien was cool. Since that was his way most of the time, Jack did not hold it against him any more than he did his ruthless honesty, but it stung nonetheless. When Tolkien's first volume of *The Lord of the Rings—The Fellowship of the Rings*—was finally published in 1954, Jack wrote a review and a dust-jacket blurb of highest praise.

Reviews of *The Fellowship of the Rings* were universally good. The only negative parts of the reviews were vicious attacks on Jack's comments! Sales were strong, and almost immediately it was obvious that Tolkien had accomplished a major commercial success, too. Although he had lived in Jack's shadow as a published writer for years, now Tolkien was on the rise.

That same year Jack's "Oh Hell!" was finally published. It was the third volume of *Oxford History of English Literature*, titled *English Literature in the Sixteenth Century Excluding Drama*. The very first chapter of the 696-page opus was a shocker. In it, he asserted no less than that the Renaissance as understood never existed in England; that the great flowering of literature in England that had reached its apex in Shakespeare was a separate phenomenon! From there, Jack proceeded to defend the Puritans and damn the humanists. Next he surveyed all the writers of the sixteenth century, good and bad. This first chapter alone was bound to make Jack a lightning rod among scholars.

Reviews praised it as they had *The Allegory of Love*. Academic circles, however, were not as pleased with the book. They attacked it. How dare he promote Christianity and condemn humanism in what was supposed to be a scholarly work?

Meanwhile Jack was writing *Surprised by Joy*, the account of his conversion. He related it from his earliest memories of childhood, especially his glimpses of joy, to his final conversion to Christianity on the road to Whipsnade Zoo in 1931. He portrayed Warnie, Mother, Poodaytabird, the public schools, Smewgy, Arthur, Kirk, Sergeant Ayers, Laurence Johnson, Barfield, Coghill, Benecke, and many others. Sometimes the very individuals who moved the plot remained unnamed. He excepted no one but Mrs. Moore, knowing already that to include her would only detract from his story because many refused to believe the mother-son relationship they had shared. He plumbed the depths of Oxford for all his old memories as if purging them because, deep in his heart, he had given up on Oxford.

A movement in the English Department in 1954 to restore Victorian literature to the curriculum had been the last straw. Years before, Jack had fought alongside Tolkien, at his behest, to successfully remove it. Now to his utter amazement, when Tolkien was in the influential position of full professor, he was waffling. Yes, Tolkien allowed, he might be in favor of restoring Victorian literature. Jack led a mighty resistance against the restoration and it was defeated, but his disgust with Oxford was complete.

When the English faculty at Cambridge University learned of Jack's unhappiness, they created the chair of Medieval and Renaissance studies specifically for him. Jack had a problem, however. He couldn't afford to purchase another house because the Kilns, which would legally pass on to Maureen, could not be sold. He and Warnie had to keep the Kilns. On the other hand, he couldn't leave Warnie at the Kilns for weeks at a time. Warnie's last binge in August had landed him in a nursing home again. Warnie's book on seventeenth-century France, *The Splendid Century*, had been published in 1953 with pleasant reviews, and he was now writing another book. But the binges continued.

Cambridge tactfully bent the rules for Jack. During term Jack would be allowed to return to Oxford for weekends. Though he dreaded the change from Oxford, Jack gave his inaugural lecture at Cambridge in November 1954. The hall was packed. Jack described himself as an Old Western man and expanded on his Medieval Model that reigned to the time of Milton. The audience roared its appreciation. Delighting in the hospitable atmosphere for Christianity, he realized his change had been wise.

At Cambridge, Jack lived as an ascetic. In each sitting room, he placed only bookcases, a table, and hardback chairs. He refused the loan of sofas and easy chairs to purposely lead an austere life.

He traveled back and forth between Oxford and Cambridge on the slowest train available. The train he dubbed the "crawler" traversed the seventy miles in a very leisurely three hours. Habitually far too early at the station for his departure, he would pace the platform. Then he would select a window seat near the front of the car, alternately gazing at scenery and reading a book.

Occasionally, toting his "pack—an old khaki rucksack containing rain gear, a lunch of sandwiches, and perhaps cheese—he would ride the train to visit a friend. That the visit would be structured around walks was understood. He and his companion would alternate carrying the pack as they walked. Every half hour or so they would rest. As in the past, arriving at an inn at an appointed hour was very important. Although Jack was much less aggressive in conversations now, one thing had not changed: He still focused conversations entirely outside himself. Topics discussed were literary or ethical conundrums. He thwarted all attempts to pry into his life. When someone became too personal, his face would ice over, his eyes become distant. Nor did he pry himself. Understandably, he repelled gossip immediately, but he also excluded even routine chitchat about his family and friends. The only exceptions were conversations between Jack and Owen Barfield, or Tolkien, or Arthur, or occasionally Warnie.

In 1955, Joy and her sons moved to Headington, only one mile from the Kilns. From that time on, Jack saw her every day that he was back in Oxford. Her younger boy, Doug, remained sunny, but her older boy, David, unable to accept his mother's decision to leave America, had become hostile. To rebel, he insisted on being Jewish although Judaism had never been practiced by either of his parents.

Then a new problem loomed. Joy learned her work permit might not be extended. Jack couldn't bear to think of her going back to America and coming under the influence of her violent, immoral ex-husband. There was a solution, a way she could stay in England: He could marry her. Jack agonized over the idea.

One day, with a friend from Oxford, Jack discussed poet Ruth Pitter. Ruth's poetry humbled Jack. After he had read her poetry, which to Jack soared to the heights of Mozart, his own seemed as harsh as a brass band. Then Jack added, "Ruth would be a perfect wife for me."

"It isn't too late," encouraged the friend, stunned by such a personal revelation from Jack.

"Oh, but it is too late." Jack's candor was surprising even himself, but this friend was unfailingly discreet, and Jack had to have a sounding board. He laid out Joy's whole problem. Then his solution. "We wouldn't live as man and wife," he clarified. "The marriage would just be a formality."

"Not true at all," objected his friend hotly, who seemed to discern that

Jack was altogether unsure of the solution. "If anything were to happen to Joy, you would be legally responsible for the two boys."

"Nevertheless, if they refuse to extend her permit, I can't let her go back to America."

In 1955, *Surprised by Joy* was published. Reviews were mixed. Some thought the train of thought unconvincing. Some did not believe reason could lead someone to the gospel. Some thought only a few individuals with Jack's intellect and classical background could follow such an intellectual path.

Some were merely curious. Why was Jack not naming some names? What was he hiding? Where was the dirt? Even friends joked it should instead be titled, *Suppressed by Jack*. Even so, Jack was satisfied that he had explained his conversion precisely the way he remembered it. And the book sold very well.

Joy latched on to one of Jack's old ideas and undertook to persuade him to brave a bold direction. Since his undergraduate days, Jack had toyed with and abandoned the myth of Cupid and Psyche. "Why not resurrect it?" she prodded. "Aren't the Narnia stories the perfection of an idea you once abandoned? And look how well they turned out!" As Jack contemplated that the seventh and last of the series would be published in the fall of 1956, he agreed to seriously consider the myth again.

In Roman mythology, the story begins with Venus, goddess of love, jealous of the mortal princess Psyche's beauty. Venus orders her son, the god Cupid, to make Psyche fall in love with the ugliest man in the world. Instead, Cupid falls in love with Psyche and carries her off to a remote palace where he visits her only by night, unseen and unrecognized by her. He forbids her ever to look at his face, but one night Psyche looks upon him while he sleeps. For disobeying him, Cupid abandons her. Psyche wanders the world in search of him. After many trials, she is reunited with Cupid and is even made immortal by Jupiter, the king of the gods.

With Joy's help, Jack created a new character, Orual, the ugly half-sister of Psyche. The story unravels through her eyes. Orual is the one who persuades Psyche to look at Cupid, thereby causing her to wander the earth. Then using an artifice of the supernatural that Charles Williams used, Jack has Orual suffer for Psyche. When Psyche and Cupid are reunited, Orual discovers that her sacrifice has redeemed her and that she is now beautiful, too. Jack realized worriedly that he had created a plot far more complex than any in the space trilogy. The motives of the ministering angels were formidable to decipher.

By April 1956, Joy had learned her work permit would not be extended. On April 23, 1956, therefore, Jack and Joy were married in a civil ceremony. Jack insisted it was only a technicality, a necessary requirement so that his good friend could remain safe in England. He told almost no one except Warnie and the discreet friend. Joy remained living in her house in Headington, and they continued the very best of friends. Then Joy, at only forty-one, began to suffer aches and pains in her left hip.

"The quacks say it's fibrositis, a weird form of rheumatism," Joy explained to Jack.

Jack's story of Cupid and Psyche, *Till We Have Faces*, came out in the fall of 1956. Critics overwhelmingly admired it. Jack had explored all the meanings of love in a very complex myth. Also, the meaning of the story was not apparent until the very end. Jack's public, on the other hand, was baffled. The story was so difficult to follow, and they had not the patience to pursue it to the end. They did not read C. S. Lewis to be mystified. And where was the Christianity? What were they to think? The book sold poorly. In Jack's mind, though, *Till We Have Faces* and *Perelandra* were his two best fictions—and who was a better judge of fiction?

Some of the old Inklings told him in brutal frankness that it was his only truly original work. In all his other works he had imitated a mentor: Bunyan, Chesterton, MacDonald, Williams. *Till We Have Faces* was the true Jack: deeply classical and quite complex, far too complicated for any ordinary reader to comprehend.

To Warnie, Jack expressed disappointment. "I suppressed explicit Christianity, and I didn't mix themes. This should be the one book Tolkien really likes, but I hear nothing from him."

In October, Joy fell at her house in Headington and was helpless until found by a neighbor. To Jack's horror, X-rays of Joy revealed the earlier diagnosis of fibrositis was completely wrong.

FIFTEEN

Under the cold fluorescent lights of the Wingfield-Morris Hospital, where Joy was now a patient, Jack broke the news to the two boys when they recessed for Christmas vacation. "It's cancer," he told the boys quietly. They looked like he had slapped their faces. Douglas started crying. "Don't give up hope," Jack encouraged. "She has a chance to recover. They're going to operate to remove the cancer."

"Cut out cancer so bad it has eaten through a bone already?" challenged David.

Later, with Warnie, Jack was explicit. "They're transferring her to Churchill Hospital—our local cancer ward. There they'll remove a tumor in her breast as well as the cancerous bone and her ovaries. She has a moderate chance of lingering for a few years, but more likely, she will die in a few months."

"You haven't mentioned her chance for a full recovery," Warnie hoped.

"Less than 1 percent," Jack unintentionally whispered.

Joy looked it. Her skin was greenish yellow. Dark circles around her large dark eyes made them huge wells of suffering. Yet who bolstered Jack and the boys? Joy—the dying, owl-eyed victim. Instead of wallowing in self-pity or smoldering in anger at her fate, she attempted to lift the spirits of everyone around her, cracking jokes and pricking every little balloon of pity.

"What pluck," admired Warnie several weeks later. "Surely she is recovering."

"No," said Jack. "The cancer is only stabilized for a while. Eventually she will have to convalesce at home."

"She can't go back to the house in Headington," insisted Warnie. "We must have her at the Kilns."

"I was hoping to hear you say that. There's another matter to take care of." Jack hesitated.

"We'll care for the boys. . . ." Warnie's voice trailed off.

"Yes. I meant something more immediate though. We must publish the marriage in the newspaper so no one will question her right to be at the Kilns."

So, the marriage was revealed in the newspaper, but the fact that Jack had kept it secret for several months did nothing to help his relationship with old Oxford friends like Tolkien. Jack, not one to expect others to explain their personal lives, felt no obligation to explain his own. He was interested in issues and morality.

Warnie, thinking to escape trauma by sinking back into the bottle, was soon lost in an alcoholic haze again. Through Christmas of 1956, Jack, with

369

no domestic help, tried to manage the Kilns, Joy's two sons, four geese, ten chickens, a cat and a dog, and a very sick Warnie in bed.

Over the next several months, Jack admitted to himself that he truly loved Joy. Not only was she enduring the severest trial a person can suffer, she was triumphing. Not in physical recovery, but in spirit. He realized God meant her to be his real wife. One day in March he confided to Warnie, "The doctors advise me to take her out of the hospital. Nothing is working now, and the expense is crushing."

"It sounds like a death sentence," Warnie sighed.

Jack barely nodded before announcing, "I'm going to marry Joy."

One of Jack's former pupils, the Reverend Peter Bide, married Jack and Joy in her hospital room March 21, 1957. The following week, a full-time nurse was hired, and Joy was installed at the Kilns on the first floor.

In April, Jack wrote Arthur that Joy was fading fast. It was only a matter of time. Her mental state was not helped by her ex-husband, who wrote to assert his claim on the boys once she died.

For some time already, Jack had been intrigued by a certain phenomenon: a miracle whereby one person actually takes on another's suffering. Charles Williams had insisted it was true. Jack himself had used it in *Till We Have Faces*. Even Tolkien half believed it, once hearing a very convincing story of such substitution from his own dentist. So Jack began to pray for such a thing. One day when Joy's legs ached so intolerably she could no longer hide it and she cried in agony, Jack went off to pray more fervently than ever for God to transfer Joy's pain to him.

Immediately his legs were seized by discomfort. Then, within only a few short minutes, his legs pulsated with excruciating pain. He kept from screaming only by gritting his teeth. Hours later the pain finally faded. Drained, he hobbled into Joy's room. She smiled. She had not looked so well in a long time.

Finding out if Joy actually felt better was hard. She always said she felt better—even as a twitch in her face betrayed a sudden stab of pain. Jack constantly badgered himself, wondering if the severe pain he was enduring meant nothing. "Oh, how the devil would enjoy such a trick!" he muttered, exasperated.

Nevertheless, he continued praying, and his prayers seemed answered, because he was becoming very ill. He ached all over all the time as if he had the flu and occasionally experienced real torment.

One beautiful day Joy's face was clouded in gloom. "You're in pain," he sympathized.

"Not at all," she insisted. "I feel no pain at all. You must believe me. But on such a day as this, I want very much to live, and I know it's hopeless."

"A dungeon is never harder to bear than when the door is open and the sunshine and bird song float in," he philosophized. "Nevertheless, Christians always have hope."

Jack continued to suffer mightily himself.

"Enough is enough," decreed Jack's old friend and physician, Robert Havard. "Let's get you off to the hospital."

Tests at the hospital revealed Jack was losing calcium. His osteoporosis was remarkable. Baffled, he pondered his condition. *Have I so convinced myself to suffer for Joy that I am losing my bones, too? For what purpose?*

Then the miracle was confirmed. Tests on Joy revealed that her bones were regenerating!

"Praise the Lord!" exulted Jack.

By September, Joy, who in April had needed to be lifted onto a bedpan, was walking. Since Jack's osteoporosis was being treated, he was improving, too. Incredibly, they seemed to have a future together.

"Well, dearest, now we can have some relaxed days together," promised a cheery Jack.

"Not on your life," Joy contradicted.

Jack's brow furrowed. "Whatever do you mean?"

"I mean the house, dear." The Kilns had suffered greatly from the war and the rationing after the war. Because coal had been in short supply, the house had never been kept warm enough. The resultant moisture had bubbled and flaked off the wallpaper. Mrs. Moore had been too ill to do anything about it; Jack and Warnie had chosen to ignore it as unimportant. Much more inconvenient was never having a hot bath. And sleeping in a room so cold that the water in the washbasin froze during the night!

Joy made her point in an unusually tactful manner. "The light switches sting my fingers like wasps. The floors are rotting under these thirty-year-old carpets. The roof leaks. We are in danger of plaster falling on our heads."

"That bad?" queried Jack, looking up. "I say, there is rather a bad water spot up there. I never noticed."

"With your permission. . ." Joy tilted her head to one side.

"Certainly, dear, if you're willing to spearhead the thing. Yes"—Jack suddenly was convinced—"it's just the thing!"

For weeks the Kilns swarmed with electricians, plumbers, carpenters, painters, and decorators. A central heating system was installed. The kitchen, no longer archaic, boasted a modern gas stove. The transformation was incredible. Even Jack noticed it.

Hedges were trimmed, flowers were planted, trellises were repaired for climbing roses, and Joy discovered their worst eyesore. Their pond and woods had become a gathering place for adolescents at night, and the boys and girls were not smelling flowers and reading poetry to each other. They were drinking alcohol, stealing wood, and worse. After many warnings were scorned, a couple of shotgun blasts high over the heads of the trespassers discouraged them from returning. Once again Jack and Warnie possessed all of their acreage. Now David and Douglas could roam the grounds without being threatened or stumbling into sin.

Jack, quickly assured that he need not travel to America, was invited by Christian radio in America to record a series of talks for Americans. Given his choice of topics, he selected the four loves: *eros, philia, storge,* and, the only virtuous form, *agape.* He immediately began writing his scripts. His relationship with Joy had crystallized his thoughts on love. As he had freely shared in a letter to a friend, his love for Joy had begun with *agape,* or Christian charity. Then it had grown to include *philia,* the undemanding love between friends. Later, eros, physical love, had developed. *Agape* seemed to have incarnated for Jack.

"It's virtually the same theism that I held for two years on my path to Christ," he described to Joy.

Joy's cancer was in complete remission. By July of 1958, both Joy and Jack were so healthy again—even taking one-mile walks—that Jack decided she must see Ireland. Because a sea voyage was too risky—a fall by either one of them would be disastrous, for the first time in his life, Jack traveled by plane.

After a terrifying takeoff that seemed to him like the launch of a rocket ship, he relaxed. The glorious cloudscape mesmerized him. Once in Ireland, Arthur chauffeured them about in his car. For two weeks Jack delighted in Joy's discovering the blue mountains and yellow shores of Ireland.

Warnie still disappeared on binges. More and more he ended up in Ireland because Lourdes Hospital in Drogheda showed inexhaustible patience with his drinking. Around Oxford's convalescent centers, he had become a pariah. Yet his productivity while sober was astonishing. He typed all Jack's correspondence, besides having written three full-fledged and well-reviewed books on French history.

Another reason behind Warnie's Irish destination was Joy's presence at the Kilns. She wielded a very sharp tongue, but, more important, Warnie did not like to disappoint her. He knew she had suffered more than enough under one drunk.

That fall of 1958, Jack's book, *Reflections on the Psalms,* was enthusiastically received by the public. A religious book in hardcover selling eleven-thousand copies before release was remarkable. Although the critics were less enthusiastic than the public, one of the most complimentary reviews came from Jack's favorite, the TLS.

Other critics emphasized its lack of scholarship, apparently oblivious to Jack's explanation in the introduction that it was from a layman's point of view. "As a literary critic myself," he told Joy, "it pains me to endure careless reviews."

His radio talks on the four loves inspired him to expand on the subject for a book. Everything seemed back to normal, even better than normal. Had he or Joy ever relished life so much as now? They completed a second trip to Ireland in the summer of 1959. Then they planned a trip for 1960 that Joy had always craved: the isles of Greece. Agreeing to this trip was quite a concession by Jack. He loathed foreign travel—even to a favorite place in literature.

Joy was ebullient when she went for routine X-rays in October of 1959. For the first time she did not dread the results. She was certain that she was well.

SIXTEEN

The cancer was back!

The first escape had been a miracle. Could they escape again? And could Jack's faith remain intact? To sympathetic friends, Jack tried to be as cheerful as Joy. "Yes," Jack assured those who questioned, "no matter what happens, we are indeed grateful to God for the miracle that allowed us two active years together." But deep inside he was fighting his own ugly black cancer: doubt.

He spent as much time with Joy as he could and determined that as long as she was alive he would make her happy. Making her happy meant that, sick or not, she wanted to go to Greece. So, there in April of 1960, Joy tried very hard to see the ancient glories. She actually climbed up the Acropolis, strolled with Jack through the streets of the village of Lindos, and reached the Lion Gate at Mycenae.

One particular day, April 6, seemed perfection to Jack—one of the supreme days of his life. They left Athens in a car with a guide to cross Mount Cithaeron and descend through pine woods and olive groves to the Bay of Corinth. At Aegosthena, with the azure bay of Homer and Plato glistening in front of them, they whiled away the hours, sipping retsina and eating Mediterranean delicacies.

By the end of the trip, however, Joy was drinking heavily to smother her pain. Within days of their return to Oxford, she underwent surgery to remove cancer from her breast. She seemed to rebound, once again returning to the Kilns, but recovery was only temporary. By the middle of June, she began failing very rapidly and returned to the hospital. By sheer willpower, she seemed to recover again, returning to the Kilns with enough pluck to play Scrabble. On the morning of July 13, however, she screamed in agony.

Back in the hospital that afternoon, heavily drugged yet lucid, Joy advised Jack, "Don't buy me a fancy coffin. Fancy coffins are all rot." During the late evening, she assured Jack that he had made her very happy. Then she told a chaplain she was at peace with God. Minutes later, she died. To Jack, who had seen many violent deaths, her dying seemed very natural.

Joy wished to be cremated, her dust scattered. There would be no memorial other than a plaque at the Oxford Crematorium. The day of her funeral was bright and sunny. The complete absence of Jack's friends was chilling. Later he wrote his friends brave letters that said, "We enjoyed the fruits of a miracle. I'm not sure it would. . .[be] right to ask for another." Regardless, the reality of his dismal, confused circumstances grew.

Jack started a journal to record his turmoil. At first he praised his beloved:

> *Her mind was lithe and quick and muscular as a leopard. Passion, tenderness, and pain were equally unable to disarm it. It scented its first whiff of cant or slush; then sprang, and knocked you over before you knew what was happening. . . . I soon learned not to talk rot to her.*[1]

Thoughts turned to his own lack of drive:

> *Except at my job where the machine seems to run on much as usual—I loathe the slightest effort. . . . Even shaving. . . . It's easy to see why the lonely become untidy.*[2]

The self-confident apologist became acutely self-conscious:

> *I cannot talk to the children about her. The moment I try, there appears on their faces. . .the most fatal of all non-conductors, embarrassment. . . . I felt just the same after my own mother's death when my father mentioned her. . . . It's the way boys are. . . . It isn't only the boys either. An odd by-product of my loss is that I'm aware of embarrassment to everyone I meet. I see people, as they approach me, trying to make up their minds whether they'll "say something about it" or not. I hate it if they do, and if they don't. . . . Perhaps the bereaved ought to be isolated in special settlements like lepers.*[3]

And finally the confusion and embarrassment sought the ultimate cause:

> *Oh God, God, why did you take such trouble to force this creature out of its shell if it is now doomed to crawl back—to be sucked back—into it?*[4]

His torment changed to anger:

> *Meanwhile where is God?. . . When you are happy, so happy that you have no sense of needing Him. . .you will be—or so it feels—welcomed with open arms. But go to Him when your need is desperate, when all other help is in vain, and what do you find? A door slammed in your face, and a sound of bolting and double bolting on the inside. After that, silence.*[5]

He argued with himself, the apologist of old:

> *Not that I am (I think) in much danger of ceasing to believe in God. The real danger is of coming to believe such dreadful things about Him.... "So this is what God's really like. Deceive yourself no longer."*[6]

His thoughts became uglier:

> *Sooner or later I must face the question in plain language. What reason have we, except our own desperate wishes, to believe that God is... "good"? Doesn't all prima facie evidence suggest exactly the opposite?... [What if Christ] were mistaken?... ["Why hast Thou forsaken me?"]... may have a perfectly clear meaning.*[7]

He wallowed in introspection—the one thing he had avoided for years:

> *It's not true that I'm always thinking of [Joy]. Work and conversation make that impossible. But...there is spread over everything a vague sense...of wrongness.... What's...wrong? Then I remember.... We were even told, "Blessed are they that mourn," and I accepted it.... Of course, it is different when the thing happens to oneself, not to others....*
>
> *If I had really cared, as I thought I did, about the sorrows of the world, I should not have been so overwhelmed when my own sorrow came...if my house was a house of cards, the sooner it was knocked down the better...[if a "restoration of faith"]...happens I shan't know if it is [another house of cards]...until the next blow comes.*[8]

Then he would scold himself for being so self-absorbed. What was his suffering compared to Joy's?

> *What is grief compared to physical pain?.... Physical pain can be absolutely continuous...like the steady barrage on a trench in World War I, hours of it with no let-up for a moment.*[9]

Slowly he justified suffering, even if one cannot understand it at the time:

> *Suppose...[God is like a]...surgeon whose intentions are wholly good.... The kinder he is...the more inexorably he will go on cutting... . If he yields to [our cries to stop]...all the pain up to that point would have been useless. But is it credible that such extremities of torture should be necessary for us? Well, take your choice.... If they are unnecessary,*

then there is no God or a bad one.[10]

Finally Jack saw a ray of sunlight:

> *Something quite unexpected happened. . .this morning. . .my heart was lighter than it had been for many weeks. . .and when, so far, I mourned* [Joy] *the least, I remembered her the best. . . . It was as if the lifting of the sorrow removed a barrier.*[11]

And Jack began to see his intense mourning denied the love he should be giving God:

> [Joy]. . .*and all the dead are. . .*[remote]. . .*like God. In that respect loving her has become, in its measure, like loving Him. . .there's no practical problem before me at all. I know the two great commandments, and I'd better get on with them. . . . While she was alive I could, in practice, put her before God.*[12]

And, regaining his first priority, God, after many weeks, he felt the presence of his wife for the first time:

> *Last night's experience. . .was quite incredibly unemotional. Just the impression of her mind momentarily facing my own. . . .Not at all like a rapturous reunion of lovers. . .*[but]. . .*intimacy that had not passed through the senses or the emotions. . .*[yet]. . . *complete—sharply bracing. . .* [If that is the love of the world beyond] *how many preconceptions I must scrap!* [The world beyond is not emotional but]. . .*solid. Utterly reliable. Firm. There is no nonsense.*[13]

At last Jack could now think what had been unthinkable. He would not call Joy back even if he had the power to do so:

> *How wicked it would be, if we could, to call the dead back! She said. . . "I am at peace with God."*[14]

Eventually, he sent his journal to the publisher Faber and Faber. How could he deny others who might be grieving a history of his own grief and recovery? It could help them cope. All the same, he decided to use a pen name: N. W. Clerk. He had good reasons. First of all, he did not want to undermine the air of certainty in his other books about God. Second, he felt obligated to answer all serious letters. And third, he could not bear the thought of answering the hundreds of letters that would pour in.

He had to get on with his life. His weight had dropped from 200 pounds to 170 pounds. He was responsible for the two boys. William Gresham had come to England shortly after Joy had died, but surprisingly he had made no demands. He had wanted only to console the boys. They had seemed just as embarrassed by his consoling as Jack's.

Meanwhile, in intervals of escape from his grief, Jack had finished two books for 1961: *An Experiment in Criticism* and *Studies in Words*. *An Experiment in Criticism* attacked the growing tendency among even serious scholars to form opinions not after having read the original works but after consulting mere critiques of original works. He had to defend good reading itself.

For obvious reasons, the book was coolly received by critics. On the other hand, critics liked *Studies in Words*. The TLS called it "weighty." The general public had adored *Four Loves*. Too anti-Freudian for intellectuals, it had received a very mixed reception in late 1960 by critics who seemed to think Jack had just pulled his four loves out of the air. How could one understand love without modern psychoanalysis, they wondered. Now, though, the public showed no interest whatsoever in either of his latest books.

Jack faced a more immediate problem, however. His own health was failing.

SEVENTEEN

Y our prostate is enlarged, Jack," reported his physician, Robert Havard. "You need surgery.

The surgeon had other ideas, though, because Jack was not strong enough to risk surgery. Toxemia from infected kidneys instigated an irregular heartbeat. The cure was antibiotics and a special low-protein diet. He was advised to sleep upright in a chair. Worst of all, he was told not to return to Cambridge for the fall term.

Nevertheless, he attacked his writing. Would he ever be so sick he could not write? He wanted to unite all his lectures on medieval and renaissance literature between two covers and title it *The Discarded Image.* He also wanted to write a book on prayer. Thus, late in 1962, he began writing *Letters to Malcolm.* His health began to improve.

That fall he had to tell the two boys very disturbing news from America. Their father had developed cancer of the tongue. Rather than endure what would be a horribly prolonged and painful death, he had committed suicide. So Jack was the boys' last hope. Thank God, he could provide for their education. He already had it all set up with Owen Barfield.

By the spring of 1963, friends commented that Jack looked his old self. His health was so improved that Warnie left for Ireland. Jack planned a trip there himself in July with seventeen-year-old Douglas helping him out.

One day in June, however, he was rushed to the hospital for dialysis. The next thing he knew he was talking to friends sometime later. The gist of their conversation was that he had been in a coma. But hadn't he been talking to Charles Williams's wife? Why was she hiding an important unpublished manuscript under her mattress? Hadn't he just talked to Mrs. Moore? Finally it dawned on him that he had been hallucinating. From the drugs? Or perhaps he was only partially out of his coma?

Then he remembered Warnie was in Ireland, drying out at Lourdes from his latest binge. Letters to Warnie informing him Jack was ill went unanswered. Jack was angry, thinking how Warnie collapsed in every crisis. A young American, Walter Hooper, was eager to help Jack. Because Jack was mainly concerned about the Kilns, he asked Hooper to move in. Then Jack took a giant step—backward. He resigned his position at Cambridge. Why deny opportunity to someone else? He could remember well enough waiting desperately for a position to open up. He was no hypocrite. Hooper and Douglas retrieved Jack's belongings from Cambridge.

By September, Jack was back in the Kilns, reading all his favorites: Homer,

Plato, Virgil, Dante, George Herbert, and more. He was feeling better. When Hooper had to return to America, Jack especially wished Warnie would come home from Ireland. Finally Warnie returned. Never had Jack been so glad to see his pear-shaped, apple-cheeked brother, face dark and shiny with a barroom tan. Perhaps this delay by Warnie was best after all. Perhaps Warnie would now be able to resist drinking for a good long time while Jack really needed him.

The two brothers became close again, and talk turned to Boxen and Wynyard and Malvern—the good and bad, the beautiful and ugly. With Warnie there, Jack's old bogies didn't matter.

Tolkien visited. "We're like old trees losing our leaves one by one, Jack," he illustrated. Then he became the old Tolkien—brutally honest. "Seeing you like this, Jack, is an ax blow near my roots."

Jack was very sleepy now, almost all the time. Only on rare occasions, as when talking with old friends like Tolkien, could he stay awake for quite a long time. Usually he read his glorious books at the Kilns and drowsed. Was there anything more delicious this side of heaven? Perhaps facing a blank sheet of paper, pen in hand, was just as delicious, but he no longer burned with the fire to write. His Christian duty was done. It was time to be judged.

He allowed himself a very rare retrospective: Fourteen novel-sized pieces of prose fiction, wasn't it? A number of short stories, and how many lyrical to long narrative poems? His works of imagination totaled a million words probably. His apologetics ran toward a million words, too, he supposed. Then there was his academic work, another million words more or less. Including how many essays? More than a hundred? And introductions to other works? Hard to remember. And who was to say the ten thousand or twenty thousand letters he had written with a clear head and a mission were not a legacy?

On November 22, 1963, he was just one week short of his sixty-fifth birthday. Not that it mattered much to him. Not where he was going. Time was a thing peculiar to the material world. Jack was now more tired than ever. It seemed he had been sleeping all day. Warnie woke him up in his easy chair after lunch and advised him politely to go lie on his bed for a nap. At four o'clock, Warnie brought him tea. Fair enough. How often had he brought Warnie tea? Or picked him up off the floor? Warnie talked cheerily about his latest book on French history. Jack felt proud of Warnie. Yes, he was flawed, the poor wretch—like all of us—but he did grand things in his sober moments. He had helped Jack enormously, never complaining overmuch—for a brother. Jack thought of all those years with Mrs. Moore's haranguing, remembering that Warnie scarcely complained although Jack knew he had been fuming inside. Having a brother like that was nice. Jack had heard that the sisters in Droghela surmised that Warnie was much more devout than he let on. That was important. Warnie was saved. So was Jack. There just wasn't much left for Jack to do.

"Rest up, Small-Piggy-Bottom," teased Warnie as he left the room.

Golden light flooded the room. It was five thirty, time for Jack to enter that precious otherness for which he had always longed.

NOTES

Barbour Publishing, Inc., expresses their appreciation to all those who generously gave permission to reprint copyrighted material. Diligent effort has been made to identify, locate, contact, and secure permission to use copyrighted material. If any permissions or acknowledgments have been inadvertently omitted or if such permissions were not received by the time of publication, the publisher would sincerely appreciate receiving complete information so that correct credit can be given in future editions.

C. S. Lewis

CHAPTER 2
1. Excerpts from "Tegner's Drapa" taken from *The Poetical Works of Longfellow* by Henry Longfellow (Houghton Mifflin, 1975).

CHAPTER 4
1. Excerpts from *Letters of C. S. Lewis* by C. S. Lewis, copyright 1966 by W. H. Lewis and the Executors of C. S. Lewis and renewed 1994 by C. S. Lewis Pte., Ltd. Reprinted by permission of Harcourt Brace & Company.

CHAPTER 6
1. Excerpts from *Letters of C. S. Lewis* by C. S. Lewis, copyright 1966 by W. H. Lewis and the Executors of C. S. Lewis and renewed 1994 by C. S. Lewis Pte., Ltd. Reprinted by permission of Harcourt Brace & Company.

CHAPTER 7
1. Excerpts from *Letters of C. S. Lewis* by C. S. Lewis, copyright 1966 by W. H. Lewis and the Executors of C. S. Lewis and renewed 1994 by C. S. Lewis Pte., Ltd. Reprinted by permission of Harcourt Brace & Company.

CHAPTER 8

1. Excerpts from *Clive Staples Lewis: A Dramatic Life* by William Griffin (Harper & Row, 1986).

2. Excerpts from *Letters of C. S. Lewis* by C. S. Lewis, copyright 1966 by W. H. Lewis and the Executors of C. S. Lewis and renewed 1994 by C. S. Lewis Pte., Ltd. Reprinted by permission of Harcourt Brace & Company.

CHAPTER 9

1. Excerpts from "Poema Historiale" by Humphrey Carpenter. Taken from *The Inklings* (Houghton Mifflin Company, 1979). Reprinted by permission of Houghton Mifflin Company. Canadian permission to reprint granted by HarperCollins Ltd.

CHAPTER 10

1. Excerpts from "Planets" taken from *C. S. Lewis: Poems* by C. S. Lewis, copyright 1964 by the Executors of the Estate of C. S. Lewis Pte., Ltd., and Walter Hooper. Reprinted by permission of Harcourt Brace & Company.

CHAPTER 12

1. Excerpts from *Essays Presented to Charles Williams* (Oxford University Press, 1947). Reprinted by permission of Oxford University Press.

CHAPTER 16

1. Excerpts from *A Grief Observed* by C. S. Lewis. Copyright 1961 by N. W. Clerk. Reprinted by permission of HarperCollins Publishers Inc. Canadian permission to reprint granted by Faber and Faber Ltd.

2. Ibid.

3. Ibid.

4. Ibid.

5. Ibid.

6. Ibid.

7. Ibid.

8. Ibid.

9. Ibid.
10. Ibid.
11. Ibid.
12. Ibid.
13. Ibid.
14. Ibid.